D1433077

A COMPENDIUM OF THEOLOGY

Comprising the Essential Doctrinal Points of both Dogmatic and Moral Theology, together with the more Important Notions of Canon Law, Liturgy, Pastoral and Mystical Theology, and Christian Philosophy

BY

The Very Reverend J. BERTHIER

Founder of the Missionaries of the Holy Family

AUTHORIZED TRANSLATION FROM THE FIFTH FRENCH EDITION

By

The Rev. SIDNEY A. RAEMERS, M.A., Ph.D.

of the

Department of Philosophy, University of Notre Dame

VOLUME II

B. HERDER BOOK CO.,

15 & 17 SOUTH BROADWAY, ST. LOUIS, MO.,

AND

33 QUEEN SQUARE, LONDON, W. C.

1932

NIHIL OBSTAT

Sti. Ludovici, die 24. Maii, 1932,

Joannes Rothensteiner,

Censor Librorum

IMPRIMATUR

Sti. Ludovici, die 25. Maii, 1932,

✠ Joannes J. Glennon,

Archiepiscopus

Vail-Ballou Press, Inc., Binghamton and New York

To

JOHN MORTIMER MONAHAN

Prominent Catholic Layman

CONTENTS

PART II

(Continued)

v

THE SACRAMENTS

750. God dispenses His grace in diverse ways. At one time, He infuses it into the soul interiorly, without resorting to external means; at another, He has recourse to external means. These latter are the Sacraments, of which we must now treat.

The Sacraments are sensible signs, established by God to signify or produce grace.

751. Were there any Sacraments in the state of innocence? Some theologians answer this question in the affirmative, most others, in the negative. The latter view would seem to be correct, because in the state of innocence the Sacraments were not essential for the sanctification of man. The Sacraments, says St. Thomas, are remedies for the injuries caused by sin, and remedies are necessary only for the sick.

752. Were there any Sacraments before circumcision? This question is also controverted. All writers, however, agree that, after the fall of Adam, faith in Christ was always an indispensable requisite for salvation. Adults were justified through this faith, and children, through the faith of their parents. This rule applies even to those Gentiles who had kept faith in Christ. Moreover, the more common and more probable opinion has it that there existed an external means of incorporating such Gentiles into the body of the Jewish people, and that for them, as well as for young Jewish girls, this means was other than circumcision, which was reserved for the male children of the race of Abraham.

753. Was circumcision a Sacrament? This question is also controverted. It is *certain*, however, that Sacraments

existed under the Mosaic law, for the Council of Trent (Sess. 7, can. 2) distinguishes between the Sacraments of the New and those of the Old Law. Moreover, fallen man has need of Sacraments, as St. Thomas proves by many reasons. It is in the nature of man, he says, that he be instructed in the things of the soul by means of the things of the body. By his fall he has developed an inclination for material things; it is only fitting, therefore, that he should humble himself, and seek the remedy in the very source of the evil. Lastly, faithful observance of these rites will help him guard against superstitious practices. (*S. Theol.*, 3a, q. 61, art. 1.)

754. Which were the Sacraments of the Old Law? Here again we find divergent opinions. The greater number of theologians teach that circumcision prefigured Baptism; the Pascal lamb and the loaves of proposition, the Holy Eucharist; the purification rites, the Sacrament of Penance; and the consecration of priests, the Sacrament of Orders. According to common opinion, however, the Sacraments of the Old Law did not give grace by themselves, *ex opere operato,* but by faith, *ex opere operantis.* This does not mean that the effect of these Sacraments was dependent in children upon the faith of the ministers or the recipients, but rather upon the faith of the people of God in the Redeemer to come; and circumcision produced its effect *ex opere operato* in virtue of this faith, because it was the *conditio sine qua non* of the grace consequent upon faith. The Sacraments of the New Law produce grace by a power inherent in them or *ex opere operato.*

755. The Sacraments of the New Law may, therefore, be defined as sensible signs instituted by God to signify and produce grace. "If any one saith, that these Sacraments of the New Law do not differ from the Sacraments of the Old Law, save that the ceremonies and the outward rites are different; let him be anathema." (C. of Trent, Sess. 7, can. 2.)

756. The Sacraments of the New Law are seven in number. This is *of faith*, against Protestants who reject all the Sacraments, with the possible exception of Baptism and the Holy Eucharist. It is the explicit teaching of Holy Scripture, as we shall have occasion to show when treating of the Sacraments individually. Moreover, five things are essential for the existence and maintenance of the life of the body: generation, growth, nourishment, cure, and convalescence; and the life of the soul is perfected by Baptism, Confirmation, the Holy Eucharist, Penance, and Extreme Unction. Finally, the Church as a society must be governed and propagated, and these two things are accomplished through Holy Orders and Matrimony.

"If any one saith, that the Sacraments of the New Law were not all instituted by Jesus Christ, our Lord; or, that they are more or less than seven, to wit, Baptism, Confirmation, the Eucharist, Penance, Extreme Unction, Orders, and Matrimony; or even that any one of these seven is not truly and properly a Sacrament; let him be anathema." (C. of Trent, Sess. 7, can. 1.)

757. The same Council adds: "If any one saith, that these seven Sacraments are in such wise equal to each other, as that one is not in any way more worthy than another; let him be anathema." And finally: "If any one saith, that the Sacraments of the New Law are not necessary unto salvation, but superfluous . . . though all are not indeed necessary for every individual; let him be anathema."

We shall treat, first, of the Sacraments in general; and, secondly, of each one in particular. And, in order to avoid repetition, we shall append immediately to our dogmatic treatment of the subject any questions of Moral Theology or Canon Law pertaining to it.

FIRST SECTION

THE SACRAMENTS IN GENERAL

758. Three things must be studied in every Sacrament: (1) the Sacrament in itself; (2) the minister; and (3) the subject.

CHAPTER I

THE SACRAMENT IN ITSELF

759. A Sacrament is: (1) A sensible sign, (2) instituted by Jesus Christ, (3) to signify and produce grace.

Art. I. The Sensible Sign.

760. The Catechism of the Council of Trent quotes St. Augustine as saying that "No society of men, professing a true or a false religion, can, as it were, be incorporated, unless united and held together by some federal bond of sensible signs." The Catechism then continues: "The Sacraments of the New Law accomplish this by distinguishing the Christian from the infidel, and connecting the faithful by a sort of sacred bond. The sensible thing, although constituting but one sign, is of a twofold nature. . . . By the words 'sensible thing' the Fathers understand not only the matter or element, such as water in Baptism, chrism in Confirmation, and oil in Extreme Unction, all of which fall under the eye; but also the words which constitute the form, and which are addressed to the ear. Both are clearly pointed out by the Apostle, when he says: 'Christ loved the Church, and de-

4

livered Himself up for it, that he might sanctify it, cleansing it by the laver of water in the word of life.' . . . 'The word,' writes St. Augustine, 'is joined to the element, and it becomes a Sacrament.' Water, for instance, has the quality of cooling as well as cleansing, and may be symbolic of either. In Baptism, therefore, unless the words were added, it would not be certain, but only conjectural, which signification was intended." (McHugh and Callan's tr., p. 150 f.)

To deny, then, that the Sacraments are made up of matter and form would be tantamount to heresy.

761. Such being the nature of all the Sacraments, each of them has a threefold significance, reminding us of something past, which is the Passion of Our Lord; indicating something present, which is our own sanctification; and foretelling something future, which is eternal life, merited for us by the Passion and constituted by it as the goal to which our sanctification should be referred. (*Ibid.*, p. 147.)

We must treat therefore: (1) of the matter, (2) of the form, (3) of the union of the two, and (4) of the changes which may occur in each.

762. *The Matter*. The matter is the sensible thing which must be determined by the form in order to constitute the Sacrament. This is the definition of remote matter. Proximate matter is nothing more than the application made of remote matter. In Baptism, *e. g.*, water is the remote matter, and the actual application of this water to the head of the child is the proximate matter.

In the administration of the Sacraments, the minister is obliged under pain of mortal sin to make use of matter which is morally certain and not doubtful. To act otherwise would be to show irreverence for the Sacraments and jeopardize the effects which they are intended to produce in the soul. However, in the Sacrament of Penance it suffices that the penitent be properly disposed, and give the confessor no reason to suspect the contrary. When the dispositions of either subject or minister do not affect the validity of the Sacrament, it suffices that he probably has the dispositions for lawful administration.

763. One would not be permitted to make use of doubtful matter or form in the administration of the Sacraments when certain matter or form is available. The contrary opinion has been condemned by the Church. Whenever possible, therefore, the safest opinion must be followed, and if this is impossible, as in the case of imminent danger or death, one may, nay, must, use the more probable matter with condition. If more probable matter is not available, merely probable matter must be used, because the Sacraments have been instituted for the sake of men.

One is never allowed, however, to make use of doubtful matter or form in the administration of the Sacrament of Orders or in the confection of the Holy Eucharist, the purpose of such legislation being to remove the possibility of even material idolatry. It is probable, on the other hand, that one may use doubtful matter or form when constrained to do so under threat of capital punishment, provided the threat is not instigated by contempt for religion. Finally, there are cases where absolute certainty is not required. Thus, one may baptize a child when its parents assert that it has never been baptized. (For the Sacrament of Penance, see no. 811.)

764. *The Form.* By form we understand the words which determine the matter to produce the effect of the Sacrament and to signify it with unmistakable clearness. Signs may replace words only in the Sacrament of Matrimony, thus making provision for the valid marriage of deaf-mutes. Protestants contend that the form of the Sacraments amounts at most to an exhortation intended to arouse the faith of those

who heard the words. Against them the Council of Trent has decreed that the form is verily *consecratory*, and that as soon as the word is added to the element, the Sacrament is administered and all its effects are rendered present. The Baptism of infants and deaf-mutes is valid even though they do not hear the exhortation spoken of by Protestants (see no. 899), but the words of the form would be invalid were they addressed to the subject in the shape of an exhortation, promise or question.

765. *The Union of Matter and Form.* The same minister must apply both matter and form to the same subject, otherwise his words would not express the truth. If several ministers were to confer the same Sacrament at the same time, all pronouncing the same form in applying it to the same matter, or each one positing matter with the corresponding form in Sacraments which admit of several matters, the Sacrament would be valid, but outside of urgent cases of necessity, the action of the ministers would be gravely illicit. An exception is made to this rule in behalf of young priests, who may, nay, must, celebrate their first Mass together with the bishop.

The matter and form must be so united that the matter is applied when the form is begun, and before it is completed. If the matter is applied immediately before or after the words are pronounced, the Sacrament is valid according to the common opinion of theologians, but invalid according to that of some. And since the safest course must always be followed in the administration of the Sacraments, great caution must be used to observe the above-quoted rule. In the consecration of the Holy Eucharist in particular, the word *this,* which begins the form, demands the physical presence of the matter at the moment the word is pronounced. On the other hand, the matter and form in the Sacraments of Penance and Matrimony admit of a certain lapse of time between them without impairing their validity, because Penance is administered in the form of a judgment, and Matrimony follows the rules of contracts.

766. *Changes which may occur in the Matter and Form.* We must distinguish between a *substantial* change, in which a matter and form would be used other than those prescribed by Jesus Christ; a *doubtful* change, called by this name because we are not positive that the change is substantial, and rendering the Sacrament probably invalid, and outside of cases of necessity gravely illicit; and an *accidental* change, which would introduce slight variations into the matter and form without detracting from the essentials of the Sacrament.

A substantial change would occur were we to mix with the matter prescribed a foreign substance in larger or equal quantity. Such a change would render the Sacrament not only gravely illicit, but also invalid.

An accidental change does not render the Sacrament invalid, but, according to whether the change is slight or grave, renders it gravely or slightly illicit.

Subtract nothing from the form, add nothing to it, change nothing in it. Do not transpose the words, pronounce them clearly, and do not pause between them. A pause of the length of one Our Father between the words comprising the form probably renders the Sacrament invalid. If in a distracted moment the celebrant should say over the bread: "This is the chalice," he should not be content, according to the safest opinion, to substitute the word "my body" for the words "the chalice," and continue from there on, but he should repeat the whole formula from the words "Who, the day before He suffered," etc. Ordinarily, the Sacrament is not rendered invalid by the insertion of a few words foreign to the form, although any one indulging in such a habit would be guilty of irreverence, if not of serious sin.

According to some theologians, the form is rendered invalid by a short pause between the syllables of the same word, especially if a foreign word is inserted between them.

767. If a substantial or doubtful change occurs in the administration of a Sacrament which can be received but once, the Sacrament must be re-administered *conditionally*, even though the reasons causing one to doubt are doubtful themselves or slightly probable. The observance of this rule is of the utmost importance in the administration of Baptism and Holy Orders.

The same rule must be observed, and for the same reasons, in regard to a person dying in the state of sin, to whom absolution has been doubtfully administered. If the doubt arose from the fact that the person was given absolution when deprived of his senses and the Sacrament of Extreme Unction was administered immediately afterwards, although in a way that would cause the minister to entertain doubts concerning its validity, Extreme Unction should also be repeated. Outside the cases of danger of death, a prudent doubt must be present before a Sacrament which can be received but once, may be re-administered. When a prudent doubt is present, the Sacrament *may* be re-administered whenever such a course of action is to the advantage of the subject; the Sacrament *must* be re-administered whenever it is essential to the recipient, as in the case of Penance for a person dying in the state of sin. In all these cases of doubt, the Sacrament must be re-administered *conditionally*. The condition is affixed to the form in order to safeguard the Sacrament from possible profanation by preventing it from being administered the second time if it were administered validly the first. (See no. 1213.) The Church has ruled that this condition should be expressed in the administration of Baptism and Extreme Unction; she has made no such law for the other Sacraments, although, according to St. Alphonsus, it would be safer to express it every time. (*Retract.*, q. 17; see also nos. 791 and 792.)

768. Observe that there are Sacraments which do not admit of the condition "if thou art disposed" being appended to the form, even mentally. With this condition present, the Sacrament would not be administered validly, if the subject did not possess the required conditions. And so a person in whom these conditions were lacking, and to whom Baptism, Confirmation, Orders, and Extreme Unction were thus administered conditionally, would not really receive the Sacraments, and would not be able to enjoy their effects at a later date by making acts of attrition or contrition. The greatest care should be taken to arouse within the subject the proper dispositions, but once this has been done, the Sacrament should be administered absolutely.

To re-administer a Sacrament in the case of a vain doubt would be to commit a serious fault, from which scrupulous persons would be excused only because of their erroneous consciences. It would not be a serious sin to repeat one or two words of the form.

Art. II. Divine Institution.

769. God alone can attach to a sensible sign the power to produce grace, and hence it is *of faith,* according to the Council of Trent, that Jesus Christ instituted all the Sacraments. (See no. 756.) However, it is the teaching of some theologians that the Council has not defined that He instituted all the Sacraments immediately, and, therefore, one would not be a heretic, but merely guilty of rashness, if he asserted, as did some theologians before the Council of Trent, that Christ instituted some of the Sacraments through His Apostles. All Catholic divines agree that Jesus Christ

instituted the effect of each Sacrament, that He determined, at least in a general way, the matter and form of each, and that He specifically determined the matter and form of Baptism and the Holy Eucharist.

770. Some theologians are of the opinion that Christ specifically determined the matter and form of all the other Sacraments, and this would seem to be the mind of the Council of Trent, which says: "The Council declares that this power has ever been in the Church, that, in the dispensation of the Sacraments, their substance being untouched, it may ordain, or change, what things soever it may judge most expedient, for the profit of those who receive them." (Sess. 21, ch. 2.) Whence it follows that the Church cannot make any changes in the substance of the Sacraments.

Other theologians hold that Christ specifically determined the matter and form of Baptism and the Eucharist, and generically those of the other Sacraments, leaving the rest to the discretion of the Church. If latitude of action of this kind were not conceded to the Church, it would be difficult, as Hurter well remarks, to explain the many variations which exist at the present time in the matter and form of some of the Sacraments and also those which have existed at different times in the Latin and Greek churches respectively.

771. Did Jesus Christ institute the Sacraments as God? Some theologians answer this question in the affirmative, others teach that He instituted them as man, in virtue of a power of excellence possessed by Him alone, but which, according to St. Thomas, He could have communicated to others had He wished. (See no. 598.) The teaching of the Angelic Doctor is that Jesus Christ instituted the Sacraments as God, in so far as God is the principal agent of the Sacraments and their efficient cause, but that He instituted them as man, in so far as Christ is their meritorious and instrumental cause. And yet, while we must grant that He is the

instrumental cause of the Sacraments as man, He is their principal cause in reference to the men who now administer them. (*S. Theol.*, 3a, q. 61, art. 3.)

772. Whence we must conclude: (1) That the sacramentals, of which we shall speak in no. 817, are not Sacraments, since they owe their institution to the Church; and (2) that other rites which Christ performed *transiently* and not *permanently,* such as the washing of the Apostles' feet, were not Sacraments either.

Art. III. Production of Grace or Effects of the Sacraments.

We must treat first, of the production of grace, and secondly, of other effects of the Sacraments distinct from grace, and in particular of the sacramental character.

773. *The Production of Grace.* The Sacraments produce grace by their own power, *ex opere operato,* in subjects who place no obstacle in the way of grace. This is *of faith,* against Protestants who claim that the Sacraments are only the external signs of justice communicated in faith, or the means of arousing within us the faith which justifies. "The grace of God which is in thee, by the imposition of my hands." (2 Tim. 1, 6.) "If any one saith, that by the said Sacraments of the New Law grace is not conferred through the act performed; let him be anathema." (C. of Trent, Sess. 7, can. 8.)

It is also *of faith* that, as far as God is concerned, the Sacraments always produce grace in all men. (*Ibid.*, can. 7.)

774. *The manner in which the Sacraments produce grace.* God alone is the principal author and cause of grace, and yet the Sacraments are not empty signs of grace produced in the soul, nor a mere *conditio sine qua non* of its production. All Catholic writers agree that the Sacraments are secondary instrumental causes of grace. The principal instrumental cause is the sacred humanity of Jesus Christ, who, as man,

is an instrument in the hands of the deity, whereas the Sacraments are a separate instrument within His hand. I am the efficient cause of an object which I move, my hand may be the principal instrumental cause, and the stick which I hold, the secondary instrumental cause. But an instrument can act either physically, like a sword which pierces an object, or morally, like the cackle of a hen gathering her chicks. Some theologians more probably assert that the Sacraments produce grace physically, others that they produce it morally, in the sense that they incline God to produce it when they are administered.

Cardinal Billot denies that the Sacraments produce grace physically, since Sacraments are material things and grace is spiritual; or that they produce grace morally, since God cannot be moved by something extrinsic to Himself. Moreover, if God were moved by the Sacraments to produce grace, the Sacraments would not be efficient causes of grace. He holds that the Sacraments produce grace, in as much as they *ex opere operato* create a disposition in the soul which authors call "sacrament and thing" (see no. 781), and that the instrumental power which they derive from their divine institution, is not physical, but intentional. This power would be somewhat similar to that of the preconization of new bishops in consistory, which is an intentional instrument conferring upon them episcopal powers and authority.

775. *The grace produced.* It is *certain* that the Sacraments produce sanctifying grace. The Council of Trent says: "Through these most holy Sacraments of the Church, all true justice either begins, or, being begun, is increased, or, being lost, is repaired." (Sess. 7.) There are some Sacraments, therefore, which produce *first* grace, or the state of grace in sinners. These Sacraments are Baptism and Penance. They also most certainly produce at times *second* grace, *i. e.*, an increase of grace, in those who are already justified by a

perfect act of contrition. But since the primary purpose of their institution is to produce not second, but first grace, they have been named *Sacraments of the dead*. The other Sacraments presuppose the presence of grace in those about to receive them, and are intended to communicate second grace. For this reason they have been called *Sacraments of the living*.

776. Do the Sacraments of the living produce first grace by their own power, *ex opere operato,* in persons who receive them with attrition, and who are ignorant of the fact that they are in a state of mortal sin? Some writers reply in the negative; others, more probably, in the affirmative. And even the majority of those who reply in the negative claim that the recipients of such Sacraments are justified by the perfect contrition which the Sacraments incite within them.

According to Lehmkuhl and Bucceroni, it is *certain* that Extreme Unction produces first grace in one who receives it with only interior attrition, even though it is *in se* and primarily a Sacrament of the living. Indeed our faith teaches us that Penance is the essential means of salvation for the sinner, a statement that would be meaningless if it were the primary purpose of Extreme Unction to remit mortal sin. Persons about to receive the Sacrament should, therefore, prepare themselves by perfect contrition or by attrition plus absolution, and in practice always by absolution, since the precept of confessing one's sins is binding especially in danger of death.

Nevertheless, Extreme Unction is secondarily and by divine institution a Sacrament of the dead, according to the words of St. James: "And if he is in sins, they shall be forgiven him." These words of the Apostle constitute a positive proof that the remission of sins is not the primary purpose of Extreme Unction, and that this Sacrament is only secondarily a Sacrament of the dead.

777. Besides sanctifying grace, the Sacraments produce a grace which is proper to each, and which is called *sacramental*. This grace is habitual grace in so far as it is given by this or that Sacrament, and in so far as it imparts special supernatural help or at least the right to receive this help from time to time, to attain the end intended by the Sacrament. It is theologically *certain* that each one of the Sacraments produces its own specific sacramental grace, otherwise one Sacrament would suffice, and the Sacraments would differ from one another only by reason of the external rites accompanying their administration. The sacramental grace of Baptism is to regenerate and purify the soul; that of Confirmation, to strengthen one in the faith; that of the Holy Eucharist, to nourish the spiritual life; that of Extreme Unction, to communicate the strength necessary to overcome the final assaults of the devil; that of Holy Orders, to furnish the candidate with the necessary help to carry out his functions in a worthy manner; and that of Matrimony, to assist husband and wife in their duties and obligations towards one another and towards their children.

778. Is the amount of grace conferred by the Sacraments equal in all cases? Some writers hold that, since the Council of Trent acknowledges the Sacraments to be unequal in dignity, the grace conferred by them must also be unequal; others claim that the grace conferred by them is equal. According to the common opinion, the same Sacrament administered to subjects equally well disposed produces the same effects, provided no obstacle is placed in the way, but the same Sacrament administered to subjects differently disposed produces different effects.

779. Does the grace conferred by validly administered Sacraments, but withheld because of some obstacle (*obex*), revive when this obstacle is removed? This question has been the object of much controversy. In practice we may say that

the effects of Penance and the Holy Eucharist never revive, but those of the other five Sacraments do.

780. What must be done to remove such an obstacle? According to several writers, the disposition necessary to receive a Sacrament worthily suffices to repair the damage done. If this be so, attrition probably suffices in the case of the Sacraments of the dead. According to other writers, this same disposition suffices also in the case of the Sacraments of the living, when the latter have been unwittingly received with improper dispositions, provided that no mortal sin has been committed in the mean time. If a mortal sin *has* been committed, perfect contrition becomes imperative, or else attrition plus sacramental confession. If the Sacraments were received knowingly with improper dispositions, perfect contrition is again essential, or else attrition plus sacramental confession. And even in this latter case, it is not credible that a person who knowingly has made bad confessions and sacrilegious communions should be able to revive the grace which the Sacraments he has so profaned were destined to confer. It would seem that God would be showing enough mercy if He remained content to forgive the sinner his sacrileges. (See no. 1397.)

781. *The other effects of the Sacraments and in particular the Sacramental Character.* Besides sanctifying grace and sacramental grace, which the Scholastics call *res sacramenti* or *the thing;* preferring to reserve the word *Sacrament* for the sensible sign, the Sacraments produce another effect which authors have termed *the thing and the Sacrament together* (*res et sacramentum simul*). This effect is distinct from grace, since it precedes, causes, and signifies grace.

Grace cannot be called a Sacrament, since, not being sensible, it cannot signify. Furthermore, the Sacrament does not render grace sensible, since it frequently happens that the Sacrament is validly administered without producing grace because of improper dispositions in the subject. For this reason grace has been termed *the thing and not the Sacrament*. The Sacrament or the external rite, validly administered, is not the thing signified, since it is the sign of the thing itself and consequently *the Sacrament and not the thing*. Finally, the *thing and the Sacrament* is an effect produced by the external sign every time the Sacrament is validly administered, even though grace is not conferred. It follows upon the external rite, as the effect follows upon its cause; it precedes grace, if not in time, at least in nature, and it effects in the soul, *ex opere operato,* a disposition which, if no obstacle is placed in the way, must infuse grace in the soul. We must, however, guard against confusing this disposition with attrition or with the other dispositions *ex opere operantis*. This effect is produced every time the Sacrament is validly administered, no matter what the dispositions of the subject. It is signified by the external rite and, united with this rite, signifies the last effect of the Sacrament, or grace. Finally, it is this effect which causes the Sacrament to revive, once the obstacle which prevented the advent of grace has been removed.

Just as natural causes, the effects of which have been prevented by some obstacle, produce these effects as soon as the obstacle has been removed, when these causes have created in the subject in whom the effects are to be produced a disposition rendering him capable of receiving them, so the Sacraments, when validly administered, produce their effects when the obstacle to their efficacy has been set aside. The Sacraments are efficient causes, and causes of this kind cannot operate before they are in existence nor after they have ceased to be. When, therefore, a Sacrament has been validly administered to a subject not rightly disposed, it is imperative that the grace never revive, or that, if it does revive, it create in the soul an immediate, persisting effect which in turn is dependent upon grace for its own ability to revive. (Billot.) In Baptism, Confirmation, and Holy Orders the *res simul et sacramentum* is the character of which we are about to speak. (Franzelin, *De Sacramentis*, 3rd ed., p. 176.)

It is an article *of faith*, defined against Wiclif and Martin Luther, that these three Sacraments imprint a character in the soul of those who receive them with the right disposition. "If any one saith, that, in the three Sacraments, Baptism, to wit, Confirmation, and Order, there is not imprinted in the soul a character, that is, a certain spiritual and indelible sign, on account of which they cannot be repeated; let him be anathema." (C. of Trent, Sess. 7, can. 9.)

782. The *sacramental character* is not, therefore, a purely external mark or name, but a real sign or seal imprinted in the soul. It is *of faith*, that this sign is indelible in this life, and it is the common opinion of theologians that it is indelible also in the next. The sacramental character is a permanent accident of the soul, but, according to some writers, it adorns the very substance of the soul, somewhat like beauty adorns the body. The subject of this character, according to St. Thomas, is the intelligence, which is the seat of faith, and to some degree it is a participation in the priesthood of Jesus Christ. (*S. Theol.*, 3a, q. 63, art. 3.) It is a sort of spiritual power by which the soul is rendered capable of receiving or administering the other Sacraments. The character of Baptism stamps the true sheep of Jesus Christ; that of Confirmation singles out the soldiers of the Lord; and that of Holy Orders indicates the chosen ones of God.

783. In the Holy Eucharist, the *res simul et sacramentum* is the body of Jesus Christ rendered present under the appearances of bread and wine; in Matrimony, it is the indissoluble bond. Concerning the *res simul et sacramentum* of these two Sacraments there is no controversy; the same is not, however, true of Penance and Extreme Unction. Cardi-

nal Billot is of the opinion that in Penance it is the right granted to the penitent through absolution in virtue of which he obtains the remission of his sins; and in Extreme Unction, it is the consignment of the sick person into the hands of God, in virtue of which he has the right to some relief from his suffering, provided no obstacle is placed in the way of the Sacrament.

784. What is the effect of a vow to receive a Sacrament on the part of a person who is unable to receive it? Certainly the Sacrament does not imprint any character, nor does it produce any grace *ex opere operato*. And yet, if such a vow be coupled with perfect contrition, it produces sanctifying grace and may even induce into the soul graces of a nature similar to those produced by the Sacrament.

CHAPTER II

THE MINISTER OF THE SACRAMENTS

785. The perpetual tradition of the Fathers teaches that the office of ministers is as indispensable for the administration of the Sacraments as the matter and form. Manifestly, the existence of a form would be of no avail were there no minister to pronounce it. We must believe with a certain and constant faith that the Sacraments are dispensed interiorly by God through the medium of Jesus Christ. It is He who baptizes. "If Judas baptizes," says St. Augustine, "it is Jesus Christ who baptizes." Therefore, Jesus Christ is the principal minister of the Sacraments, and all other ministers are instruments in His hand. It is for this reason that the Sacraments would produce their effects even though they were administered by unworthy ministers. Hence a *secondary* minister is one who applies the form to the matter of a Sacrament in the name of Jesus Christ. St. Thomas teaches

that, by a special delegation from God, the angels and the blessed in Heaven might dispense the Sacraments, and if they did so, we would have to believe that the Sacraments were validly administered; the case would be different were the ministers the spirits of untruth. (*S. Theol.*, 3a, q. 64, art. 7.) However, the ordinary course followed by Providence is that the Sacraments be administered in the Church, not by men. A priest risen from the dead could certainly be a minister of the Sacraments if his body were still mortal; if it were glorified, some theologians opine that he could be a minister, others that he could not. "If any one saith, that all Christians have power to administer the word, and all the Sacraments; let him be anathema." (C. of Trent, Sess. 7, can. 10.)

The secondary minister of the Sacraments may be ordinary or extraordinary. The ordinary minister is he who administers the Sacraments according to the regular custom established by Jesus Christ and the Church. The extraordinary minister is he who administers them outside of the regularly established order, or by special delegation, or in a case of necessity.

786. As a general rule the same person may not be the minister and the subject of the same Sacrament at one and the same time. No one can validly administer to himself Baptism, Confirmation, Penance, Extreme Unction or Holy Orders. The very wording of the forms of these Sacraments suggests that they must be administered to a person other than oneself. Matrimony is the only exception to the above rule. It is a contract raised to the dignity of a Sacrament, and, therefore, each one of the contracting parties is at the same time both minister and subject. A priest can administer communion to himself, but to administer communion is not to produce the Sacrament.

In nos. 917, 2434 ff. and 3680, we shall treat of the obliga-

tion of administering the Sacraments; here we limit ourselves to a discussion of the conditions for validity and
liceity.

Art. I. Conditions of Validity.

787. *Faith is not a requisite.* This is *of faith* for the Sacrament of Baptism, defined against the Donatists and against
all heretics who advocate re-baptism; it *borders upon faith*
for the other Sacraments. The Church has always regarded
as valid the Baptism administered by heretics and even infidels, and we may believe the same in regard to the other
Sacraments, with the sole exception of Penance, the valid
administration of which depends also upon jurisdiction.

788. *Holiness of life is not required.* This is also *of faith*,
defined against Wiclif and Martin Luther. "Neither he that
planteth is anything, nor he that watereth; but God that
giveth the increase." (1 Cor. 3, 7.) The tree grows no matter
by whom it is planted.

Furthermore, Jesus Christ is the principal minister of
the Sacraments; all other ministers are instruments in His
hands. It makes little difference, therefore, whether this
instrument be living, like the arm of a human body, or dead,
like the axe which the arm wields; it is always efficacious.
"If any one saith, that a minister, being in mortal sin—if
so be that he observe all the essentials which belong to the
effecting or conferring of the Sacrament—neither effects,
nor confers the Sacrament; let him be anathema." (C. of
Trent, Sess. 7, can. 12.)

789. Besides the power necessary to administer the Sacraments, power which in the case of Penance must be coupled
with the necessary jurisdiction, the minister must also have
the intention of doing what the Church does. This is also
of faith. "If any one saith, that, in ministers, when they effect
and confer the Sacraments, there is not required the intention

at least of doing what the Church does; let him be anathema."
(C. of Trent, Sess. 7, can. 11.) The administration of a Sacrament is a human act, and as such must be accompanied
by an intention.

790. *What must this intention be?* There are different
kinds of intentions. *Actual* intention is the intention one has
at the time when the action is performed; this intention is
the best. *Virtual* intention is that which persists as a consequence of a previous volition. *Habitual* intention is one
which actually existed at one time and has never been retracted, but of which there is at present no positive trace.
Interpretative intention is that which we do not have in
reality, but which others assume we would have if we reflected ever so little on our act.

791. It is *certain* that interpretative and habitual intentions would not suffice in a minister, that actual intention is
not necessary, and that virtual intention suffices. This is the
opinion of all theologians. St. Alphonsus observes that a
minister who performs the acts necessary for the administration of a Sacrament in a routine way would be acting imprudently if he doubted his intention, unless he had positively excluded the same.

It is *certain* also that the intention must be determined in
such a way and for such a subject, otherwise the words of
the form would have no particular application. An army
chaplain could not absolve five out of ten soldiers who, before
engaging in battle, publicly confessed to him some sin, before
determining whom he intended to absolve. On the other
hand, if the minister were mistaken in regard to the sex of
the subject, the validity of the Sacrament would not be im-
paired, except in the case of Matrimony.

792. It is certain that a *conditional* intention, to be realized
some time in the future, invalidates all the Sacraments ex-

cept Matrimony, which is validated only after the intention has been fulfilled.

If, on the other hand, such an intention bears on something past or present, it does not invalidate the Sacrament. Nevertheless, a minister would be guilty of venial and sometimes of grave sin if he thus administered the Sacraments conditionally without serious reason. (See nos. 767, 768 and St. Alph., l. 6, 28.)

An intention formed under grave fear suffices for all the Sacraments except Matrimony. (*Ibid.*, 1, 6, 19.) Two contradictory intentions entertained at the same time are mutually exclusive, and render the Sacrament invalid, unless one of the two is predominant in the mind. If two such intentions are successive, the second is adjudged to prevail, unless, of course, it had been expressly excluded by the first. And if the first excluded the second, the second is adjudged to prevail, unless it too had been expressly retracted. These same rules are to be observed also in regard to the application of the fruits of the Holy Sacrifice.

793. *What must be the object of this intention?* Protestants maintain that the intention to jest in applying the form to the matter in the Sacraments would be sufficient for their validity. Against them the Church has ruled that the intention must be to do what the Church does. For this reason all Catholics hold as *certain* that, for validity, the minister must in all seriousness posit, at least exteriorly, the act which is posited by the Church of Christ.

It is not necessary that the minister have the intention to do what the Catholic Church does, since the Church regards the Baptism of heretics as valid, nor to perform a sacred rite, except such an intention be knowingly excluded, since the Church regards the Baptism of infidels as being also valid and they do not believe in this sacred rite. If by some

mistake the minister should preclude the intention of performing a sacred rite, thinking that the act he was positing
was not sacred, but having in mind the predominant thought
of sincerely doing what Christians do, the Sacrament would
be valid.

794. *Does the mere external intention suffice, or, to put
it differently, would the minister be conferring a Sacrament
validly if to all outward appearances he performed the rite
in all seriousness, but inwardly withheld his intention or
purposely mocked at the Sacrament?* Catharinus claims that
it would, but his opinion cannot be maintained. Benedict
XIV decreed that a Sacrament administered under such conditions should be repeated, or recourse be had to the Holy See.

The opinion of Catharinus was dealt another severe blow
by the condemnation, by Alexander VIII, of the proposition
that "Baptism is valid if conferred by a minister who observes the whole external rite and form of the Sacrament,
but says in his heart: 'I do not intend to do what the Church
does.'" A gratuitous contract is binding only if consented
to interiorly by the person entering into it. On the other
hand, let us again observe with St. Alphonsus that a priest
who performs all the acts necessary for the validity of the
Sacrament, has no reason to doubt the sufficiency of his intention, unless he excluded the right intention by positive act.

795. *Is it a condition for validity that the minister must
hear himself pronouncing the words of the form?* The answer to this question is given in no. 899. We might observe
here that the form is a sensible sign and, as such, must determine the matter in a sensible manner. Who can say without
a doubt that improperly pronounced words, or words so
jumbled together that their meaning would not be apparent
even to him who pronounced them, certainly produce the
Sacrament?

According to a decision of the Sacred Pentitentiary, given on the 12th of September, 1908, the minister need not and may not repeat the words of the form which he has pronounced loud enough to hear them himself, even though, in consequence of some noise, he did not actually hear them.

Art. II. Conditions of Liceity.

796. These conditions are: (1) The minister of the Sacrament must be a worthy and duly qualified person; (2) he must administer the Sacraments worthily and according to the prescribed rite; and (3) he must administer them only to worthy subjects.

797. *The minister must be worthy and duly authorized.* The minister must be appointed by the Church, either in a general way, as every man is for Baptism in case of necessity, and as each contracting party is for his own part in Matrimony, or in a special way, as is the case for the other Sacraments. The Catholic Church possesses, by divine institution, supreme authority in the matter of the administration of the Sacraments, consequently he who dispenses them without authorization from her is guilty of sacrilege. Moreover, no Sacrament can be administered licitly in a particular church without at least the presumed consent of the pastor. Outside the church any priest may hear the confessions of the sick, provided he has proper jurisdiction.

798. *The minister must be in the state of grace.* Holy things must be handled in a holy fashion. All priests, therefore, whose office it is to administer the Sacraments, should constantly maintain themselves in the state of grace, and there is a grave obligation binding any priest who has fallen into mortal sin to go to confession before saying Mass. A priest who celebrates the Holy Sacrifice in the state of mortal sin offends grievously, according to St. Alphonsus, (1) by consecrating; (2) by administering the Sacrament unworth-

ily; (3) by administering it to an unworthy person; and (4) by receiving it unworthily.

799. We cannot lay too much stress on the importance of confession for one who is in the state of mortal sin, and upon whom it devolves to administer a Sacrament other than the Holy Eucharist. However, confession is not absolutely indispensable if one has perfect contrition. Perfect contrition suffices, but it is also necessary without confession, unless one is so pressed for time that he is unable to elicit even this act. The more probable and more common opinion of theologians holds against De Lugo and others that the priest or deacon who distributes holy Communion in the state of mortal sin, commits a grievous sin. It is more probable, however, that such a minister is guilty of only one mortal sin, even if he distributes several communions at one time. More probably also, a confessor in the state of mortal sin offends grievously as many times as he absolves penitents, although there are some writers who maintain that he is guilty of only one sin if he absolves several persons without interruption. By parity of reasoning the same holds true of the minister who baptizes or confirms. Finally, the more probable opinion has it that it is not a grievous offense to hear a confession in the state of mortal sin, if one does not give absolution.

800. *Does a person sin grievously who administers in the state of sin a Sacrament for which he was not ordained, or a Sacrament for which he was ordained, but which he is administering without solemnity?* To illustrate: Does a midwife in the state of sin offend grievously by administering Baptism to a child at the point of death? Or does a priest not engaged in the ministry offend grievously by baptizing the same child privately? Some answer this question in the affirmative, others, more probably, in the negative. However, a priest who is engaged in the ministry always sins grievously

in these cases, unless he is so pressed for time that he cannot make an act of contrition.

801. Do clerics offend grievously when they perform the functions of their respective Orders in a state of mortal sin? Some writers reply in the affirmative, including within their rule even clerics in minor Orders; others probably reply in the negative. It is not certain, therefore, that such clerics sin grievously even when they touch the Holy Eucharist, by transporting it, or by giving benediction; but if they are not actually guilty of sacrilege, their conduct closely verges upon it.

802. *The minister must administer the Sacraments worthily.* By stating that he must administer the Sacraments worthily, we mean, with the required religious respect and attention. Any serious act requires attention, and, therefore, he who is voluntarily distracted while administering the Sacraments, sins at least venially. According to a more probable opinion, a voluntary distraction in the confection of the Holy Eucharist would constitute a mortal sin. And, even though there are writers who are less severe in regard to this Sacrament, it is hard to see how a priest who would entertain voluntary distractions during an important part of the canon, could be excused from mortal sin. Manifestly, distractions which would tend to impair the validity of the form would be of a far more serious nature.

803. *The Sacraments must be administered according to the prescribed rite.* From the words of the Council of Trent (cited in no. 770), we have seen that the Church has the power to regulate the ritual of the Sacraments. "If any one saith, that the received and approved rites of the Catholic Church, wont to be used in the solemn administration of the Sacraments, may be contemned, or without sin be omitted at pleasure by the ministers, or be changed by every pastor of the churches into other new ones; let him be anathema."

(Sess. 7, can. 13.) Unless a special privilege authorizes the use of rites other than those approved, the ones to be employed are those contained in the *Roman Ritual* and the *Roman Missal*. Throughout the Latin Church the use of the *Ceremonial of the Bishops* is also obligatory.

It would be a serious offense to contemn a ritual the very antiquity of which makes it an object of reverence and veneration for the faithful, and the very purpose of which is to inspire them with a greater respect for the Sacraments.

To omit these ceremonies, except in case of necessity, would constitute a grave or slight sin according to the nature and extent of the omission. It would be a grievous sin to institute a change merely for the sake of variety or novelty. On the other hand, one could continue with parts of the ceremonial not affecting validity which one had omitted unwittingly.

In the administration of the Sacraments, the priest should wear a surplice, but not a rochet. Over the surplice, he should wear a stole of the color prescribed by the Ritual. The stole should never be worn as a mark of distinction or dignity; its use should be reserved for the Sacraments, the sacramentals, the functions where it is prescribed by the Ritual, and, where the custom exists, for preaching. The common opinion of theologians is that in cases of necessity Baptism, Penance, Confirmation, Extreme Unction, and even the Holy Viaticum, may be administered without the use of any sacred vestments.

The very form of the Sacraments suggests that they be administered separately to each individual subject. In cases of necessity, however, one would be permitted to baptize or absolve several subjects together. It would probably not be a serious fault to administer them in this manner, even outside of cases of necessity, provided the validity of the Sacraments was in no wise imperiled. Finally, several ministers may validly administer one and the same Sacrament at the same time, under the conditions stated in no. 840. (See nos. 765, 1400, and 1442.)

804. *The Sacraments must be given only to the worthy.* "Give not that which is holy to dogs." (Matt. 7, 6.) There is a grave obligation binding upon every priest to refuse the Sacraments to all who are unworthy, unless he has a serious reason for acting otherwise. Always remember: *Sacramenta propter homines.*

Meekness and prudence should, however, be exercised in refusing the Sacraments. Defamation of character is punishable by law; then too, the door should always be left open to the reconciliation of the sinner with God.

805. The following rules should be observed. A *public* sinner, whether he be such *by law,* having been condemned by the sentence of a judge, or *in fact,* being known to all as a man of evil ways, must be refused all the Sacraments except Penance and Extreme Unction. In the case of Penance, absolution must be withheld, if he does not exhibit the required dispositions; in the case of Extreme Unction, he must be unconscious. The other Sacraments must be refused if he presents himself as a subject, either privately or publicly, unless he has manifested his repentance and sincere purpose of amendment before witnesses. Communion may, therefore, be administered to a public sinner who has made confession of his faults before several persons, unless he is known publicly to be in a permanent occasion of sin. At the hour of death, a priest should be as merciful as possible. However, even in this case, all strict requirements should be exacted by the priest, and even lesser ones, if by leaving the dying person in good faith on minor points, there be danger of creating a public scandal. A priest may assist at the marriage of a public sinner to avoid disaster, for the priest is not the minister of, but merely a witness to, the

matrimonial contract. If a sinner is publicly known as such in one locality, but not in another, he may not be refused the Sacraments in the latter, unless the priest knows that he is soon to be exposed in that locality also.

806. A *notorious* sinner, according to some theologians, should be treated like a public sinner; according to others he may not be refused the Sacraments. In practice, the latter opinion should be followed.

807. If a *secret* or *occult* sinner presents himself as a subject in the sole presence of the minister, or in the presence of little children, he must be refused the Sacraments, unless he has previously given signs of repentance. If the same sinner petitions for the Sacraments before witnesses, he may not be refused the Sacraments, with the exception of Holy Orders. Even a secret sinner must be barred from Holy Orders. No sinner should be refused the Sacraments if his sins or impediments are known to the priest only through confession. In this case, it is not even permitted to administer a slight admonition. (See no. 1571.) If the crime is doubtful, and the repentance also, the Sacraments should not be withheld, in virtue of the principle: *"Favores sunt ampliandi."* If the crime is certain and the repentance only probable, some say that the Sacraments should be withheld, others, that they should be administered. It would certainly be prudent to defer the administering of communion.

According to can. 2197, a sin is *public* if it has actually been divulged, or if circumstances are such that it easily can and must become public; it is *notorious* by notoriety *of the law* after the sentence of a competent judge from which there is no appeal, or after a confession made in court in the presence of the judge; and finally, it is *notorious* by notoriety *of fact*, if the offense is publicly known and cannot be kept secret or excused.

808. Could the Sacraments be administered to an un-

worthy person *if failure to do so entailed death?* Certainly
not if the threat to kill was advanced in contempt of religion or gave scandal to the faithful. Outside of this case,
some answer the question in the affirmative; others, with
St. Alphonsus, more probably in the negative.

May one administer the same Sacrament to several persons at the same time? This is possible only in the cases of
Baptism and Penance, and when necessity requires, is both
valid and licit.

809. Is one ever allowed to feign the administration of a
Sacrament in order not to give offense by refusal? By feign-
ing the administration of a Sacrament we mean using the
matter and the form, or merely the form, according to the
Ritual, without the intention of conferring the Sacrament.
Such a practice is never licit, for Innocent XI has solemnly
condemned the proposition that "urgent fear furnishes a just
cause for simulating the administration of the Sacraments."
One is never permitted, therefore, to pronounce the words of
the form without having the intention of doing what the
Church does, or to celebrate Mass without consecrating, or
to administer communion to the faithful with an unconsecrated host.

To dissimulate the administration of a Sacrament by leading the faithful to believe, without using either the matter
or the form, that it has been administered, when as a matter
of fact it has not, is lawful under certain circumstances.
Thus, a priest may recite a few prayers over a penitent, instead of giving him absolution when he judges him to be
lacking in the proper dispositions. Some authors, whom St.
Alphonsus does not condemn, hold that in such cases a
priest may even say over the penitent: *"Ego te* NON *absolvo."* A priest may also enter into agreement with a person
who is obliged to appear at the communion rail, in order to
escape ignominy, to pronounce over him the usual words

"Corpus Domini nostri Jesu Christi," without placing the host on his tongue. Finally, according to common opinion, two persons may simulate marriage when threatened with death, because without interior consent there is neither matter nor form of the Sacrament.

CHAPTER III

THE SUBJECT OF THE SACRAMENTS

810. The only fit subject for the reception of the Sacraments is man in the wayfaring state. "Every high priest taken from among men, is ordained for men." (Hebr. 5, 1.) Sensible signs cannot be applied to souls separated from their bodies. Every man in the wayfaring state is a fit subject for Baptism, even infants. Men who have not received Baptism are not fit subjects for the other Sacraments, although Baptism does not render one a fit subject for the reception of all the Sacraments. Persons who have not the use of reason are not fit subjects for the reception of Penance and Matrimony; persons in good health are not fit subjects for Extreme Unction; women are not fit subjects for Holy Orders; and clerics in Major Orders or religious with solemn vows are not fit subjects for Matrimony. With these preliminaries in mind, we are now ready to discuss the requisites on the part of the subject, first, for the valid, and secondly, for the licit reception of the Sacraments.

811. *Requisites of Valid Reception.* Faith is a necessary requisite only for the reception of the Sacrament of Penance. The Baptism and ordination of heretics have always been considered valid.

The state of grace is not required. This is *certain.* In the Sacrament of Penance, however, the prescribed dispositions of the penitent are indispensable, since they constitute the matter of the Sacrament. (See no. 1041.) And yet, although we must be certain that we possess the dispositions requisite for the validity of this Sacrament, a high probability that we possess these dispositions is to be regarded as the equivalent of sufficient certainty.

Attention is not required. This, too, is *certain*.

812. In adults, the intention is absolutely necessary. This is *certain*. No one can be sanctified without his consent. And if a person were ordained against his will, or if he were indifferent, the ordination would be invalid.

What sort of intention is necessary? *Actual* intention is not necessary. *Virtual* intention suffices for all the Sacraments, but is necessary for Penance and Matrimony. *Habitual* intention suffices for one who enters into the marriage contract by proxy, and it is required for Baptism and Orders. According to common opinion, it suffices for all the Sacraments except Penance and Matrimony. The other five Sacraments would, therefore, be validly administered to an insane person, if he had asked to receive them before losing his mind. A priest would even be permitted to give such a person conditional absolution, and should give it if he were threatened with permanent insanity or in danger of death. Outside of these two cases it would be illicit to absolve him or administer the other Sacraments to him, although more probably the act would be valid. Whoever has had the intention once during his lifetime of receiving the Sacraments, is presumed to persist in this intention at the hour of death or in danger of perpetual insanity. However, it would not be right to conclude from this that such a person had the intention of receiving these Sacraments under all conditions, as, for instance, while he was asleep. And so, if Baptism or any other Sacrament were administered to him while he was in this state, the Sacrament should be re-administered conditionally later. (Lehmkuhl, 48.)

Implicit intention suffices in a dying person who has lost the use of his senses. It would be permissible to administer to such a person Confirmation, the Holy Eucharist, Extreme Unction, and the Sacrament of Penance conditionally.

Implicit intention, such as is found in attrition, probably suffices for Baptism in the case of an infidel deprived of the use of reason. But if, after regaining consciousness, he should assert that he never had the intention of receiving the Sacrament, it may be administered conditionally.

For children and persons who have always been deprived of the use of reason the Church supplies the intention. Through no act of theirs they sinned in the first Adam, and through no act of theirs they are reinstated in the second Adam. It is *an article of faith,* defined by the Council of Trent, that their Baptism is valid. (Sess. 7, can. 13.) It is certain that Confirmation, the Holy Eucharist, and Holy Orders may be administered to them validly. The ancient practise of giving communion to little children was based on this reason, and it certainly produced grace in their souls.

813. *Requisites of Liceity.* The Sacraments must be received worthily. For the Sacraments of the dead, faith, hope, and attrition, but not charity, are required; for the Sacraments of the living, the state of grace. A person receiving the Sacraments of the living in the state of mortal sin, would be guilty of a serious fault. There are, of course, exceptions even to this rule. Such a person would not be guilty of a serious fault if he consumed the sacred species in an attempt to save them from profanation, and neither would another be guilty of serious sin if he recalled at the sacred table, at a time when he could not withdraw without disgrace to himself, a grievous sin for which he had no time to excite himself to contrition. In Sacraments other than the Eucharist, the state of grace acquired through perfect contrition suffices without confession, although the latter should be

strongly recommended. Any person desirous of approaching the sacred table should have recourse to confession in the case of mortal sin, no matter what his contrition may be, unless confession be impossible and the obligation to receive grave and urgent. (See no. 762.)

814. *The Sacraments must be received from those who are worthy of administering them.* The natural law forbids us to receive the Sacraments from an unworthy minister without a grave reason. To receive the Sacraments from an unworthy minister, means to co-operate in his sin. An obligation arising from precept would be a sufficient reason for requesting them, as also the alternative of remaining for one hour in the state of mortal sin. No priest is to be adjudged unworthy unless he has proved himself such, and when a priest has sinned, it is to be presumed that he has done penance, unless he is still in the occasion of sin, or has said Mass, etc., without going to confession.

815. The laws of the Church forbid the faithful to receive the Sacraments at the hands of an excommunicated, interdicted, or suspended minister, if he is *vitandus* or has been sentenced by a judge. In danger of death, the faithful are permitted to ask such a minister for sacramental absolution, and if there are no other priests available, also for the other Sacraments and the sacramentals.

For any good reason the faithful may ask ministers who are under censure for the Sacraments and the sacramentals, and the censured priest who is asked to administer the Sacraments, may do so without inquiring for the reason why he was requested. (*C. J. C.*, can. 2261.)

Heretics, schismatics, and, *a fortiori,* notorious apostates are on a level with those who have been sentenced by a judge in the matter of the administration of the Sacraments. (Can. 2372.)

One may not request the Sacraments from such ministers

except when there is danger of death. Furthermore, if the circumstances were such that one's action could be easily interpreted as tantamount to the surrender of the faith, or adhesion to heresy or schism, he would not even be permitted to request Baptism or Penance in danger of death. The only possible course of action in a case of this kind would be to try to excite in oneself perfect contrition.

816. Would one be permitted to pay a minister who would not be willing to administer the Sacraments free of charge? Yes, in extreme or grave necessity.

We may bring this treatise to a close with the words of the Catechism of the Council of Trent: "In communicating the Sacraments to the faithful, the pastor will keep in view, principally, two things: the one, to impress on the minds of the faithful a deep sense of the honor, respect and veneration due to these divine and celestial gifts; the other, to urge on all the necessity of having recourse, piously and religiously, to those sacred institutions established by the God of infinite mercy. . . . For as we are ushered into spiritual life by means of the Sacraments, so, by the same means we are nurtured and preserved, and grow to spiritual growth."

Fortunate indeed are those pastors who remain faithful to this admonition, and who, by dint of hard work and all the holy expedients of charity, succeed in training those under their charge in the love and respect for these sacred rites, and in inculcating in them the habit of receiving them frequently. They are training future saints. The lesson of experience is that the total abandonment of, or merely casual recourse to, the Sacraments is the source of all evil.

THE SACRAMENTALS

817. The sacramentals are ceremonies or external acts of religion instituted by the Church for the honor of God and the sanctification of souls. (See no. 771.) The principal

sacramentals are comprised within the following Latin verse: *"Orans, tinctus, edens, confessus, dans, benedictus."* The Lord's Prayer, or a prayer prescribed by the Church or recited in a consecrated church, holy water, blessed bread, the *Confiteor* recited at Mass or in the Office, almsgiving prescribed by the Church, the blessings given by bishops, abbots, and priests in the course of their ecclesiastical functions, the distribution of ashes, *Agnus Dei*, exorcisms, all these are sacramentals.

818. The purpose of the sacramentals is to remit venial sin, excite us to piety, obtain for us temporal goods such as health and prosperity, and put to flight the evil spirits through prayers, the efficacy of which does not depend upon the minister. The effect of exorcisms upon the evil spirits is infallible, even though those possessed of the devil are not always delivered thereby. It is more probable that the sacramentals do not remit venial sin *ex opere operato*, but only by the pious movements which they arouse within us. The same is true of their other effects.

819. Some blessings are consecratory, such as the blessing of a church, and result in the permanent consecration of the object blessed; others are transitory, such as the blessing of Easter eggs. The consecration of an object prohibits the use of that object for any purpose other than the one for which it was consecrated.

Some blessings are reserved to the pope, like the blessing of the *Pallium* and of the *Agnus Dei;* others are reserved to the bishops. Among the latter some may never be delegated to an ordinary priest, like the blessing of the holy oils and holy chrism, and the consecration of churches; whereas others may be delegated. *Solemn* blessings of crosses are reserved to the bishop, although there is no precept to bless crosses or other sacred images to be set up in a church or even on an altar. (Can. 1147.)

820. The blessing of a new church, or of the corner-stone of a church, or of a cemetery, may be performed by any priest with the permission of the bishop or the vicar-general. Blessings, with the exception of those reserved to the Roman Pontiff, to the bishop or to others, may be given by any priest. Finally, pastors and rectors may bless the sacred vestments to be used in their churches.

The Ordinary of the diocese alone may licitly perform consecrations and blessings reserved to another with the permission of this other. If he has not the episcopal character, he must designate a bishop to perform these consecrations and blessings. The right to give the nuptial blessing, the blessing of houses on Holy Saturday, the blessing of the fruits of the earth and the fields, belongs to the pastor, and these blessings may not be given without his consent. As a general rule, one is not allowed to perform in the church of a pastor, without his permission, blessings which are not reserved, or to give public and solemn blessings without his permission in the territory over which he has jurisdiction.

A recent decree authorizes any priest to church a woman who so requests him, but he should apprise the pastor of his action.

821. A reserved blessing given by a priest without the necessary faculties, is valid, unless the Holy See explicitly states in the reservation that it cannot validly be given except to those to whom it is reserved or by those having special faculties. (Can. 1147.)

The use of the formulas prescribed by the Church is always required for validity. When giving blessings, the formulas of which are contained in the Ritual or the Roman Missal, the minister should, if possible, wear a surplice and a stole of the color of the day, unless another color is prescribed. In the blessing of a cross which bears the image of

Our Saviour, the formula to be used is that of the blessing of images. If no special formula is contained in the Ritual for the object one desires to bless, the formula *ad omnia* is used, or the sign of the cross is made over the object, with the words: *"In nomine Patris,"* etc., and sprinkling with holy water. (See no. 1167.)

Sacramentals may be given not only to baptized persons, but also to catechumens, and this publicly. Where there is no prohibition, they may also be given to non-Catholics, to obtain the light of faith and, together with it, bodily health. (Can. 1149.) A decree of the Holy Office of June 8, 1859, prohibits the administration to non-Catholics of sacramentals which are given publicly and individually in a church. A decree of the Sacred Congregation of Rites of April 26, 1924, authorizes the placement in the church of flags and banners, provided the latter be not those of societies antagonistic to the Church, that the rules and constitutions of these societies be not condemned, and that the banners themselves do not display forbidden or unworthy insignia. One may even bless such banners, if the request to bless them is made in deference to the Catholic religion.

822. Blessings are *constitutive* or *invocative*. The former render a person, object or place sacred, while the latter do not change the status of the person or object blessed, as, for instance, when a sick person or a house is blessed. Blessings are either *real* or *verbal,* according to whether or not the holy oils are used. When the holy oils are used in conjunction with the blessing, the latter is called a *consecration*. Consecrated objects, and objects rendered sacred by a constitutive blessing, must be treated with reverence, and may not be used for profane purposes or for purposes for which they are not intended.

Church bells which have been either consecrated or

blessed must not be rung for profane purposes, except in case of necessity and with at least the presumed permission of the Ordinary.

Furthermore, since an offense in this respect would not be grave, the pastor should be indulgent, rather than offend a whole population, especially if there is no danger of scandal or contempt. The following verse describes the different functions of the bells: *"Laudo Deum verum, plebem voco, congrego clerum, defunctos ploro, pestem fugo, festa decoro."*

823. Holy water should be blessed on all the Sundays of the year, with the exception of Easter and Pentecost, when the benediction of the baptismal font takes place. Salt which has been blessed in advance may be used, but not the salt blessed for the Sacrament of Baptism.

824. In cathedrals and parish churches the celebrant must sprinkle the people every Sunday at the principal Mass, even though this be not a High Mass, and even before the Blessed Sacrament exposed, except when the bishop is the celebrant.

825. The sacred vestments may be blessed at the altar, but all other objects to be blessed should be placed on a table at the epistle side.

SECOND SECTION

THE SACRAMENTS IN PARTICULAR

We shall devote a special treatise to each one of the seven Sacraments.

FIRST TREATISE

BAPTISM

826. There are three kinds of Baptism: Baptism of desire, Baptism of blood, and Baptism of water.

Baptism of *desire* is merely the desire to receive the Sacrament. The implicit desire which is found in perfect contrition suffices. Moreover, the desire for Baptism coupled with perfect contrition justifies. This is *certain.* "If any one love me," says Our Lord, "my Father will love him." (John 14, 13.) For this reason, the Church has condemned the following proposition of Baius: "Charity is not always joined with the remission of sins." However, Baptism of desire does not, as a rule, remit all the punishment due to sin, nor does it imprint the sacramental character upon the soul. The mere desire for Baptism, without perfect contrition, would not suffice for justification. Manifestly, also, children are not capable of Baptism of desire.

827. Baptism of *blood* or martyrdom justifies children *ex opere operato.* Does it justify adults in the same manner? Some authors reply in the affirmative, requiring of the subject faith accompanied by merely imperfect contrition. Other writers (*e. g.,* St. Alphonsus) require also perfect contrition.

"He that shall lose his life for me, shall find it." (Matt. 10, 39.)

If all the required conditions are present, martyrdom produces all the effects of Baptism save the sacramental character. But neither the Baptism of desire nor martyrdom imprints the sacramental character and neither excuses one from receiving the Baptism of water, whenever this is possible.

828. The theological concept of *martyrdom* includes four distinct elements: (1) violent death, or cruelties which would naturally cause death; (2) the endurance of these things for a holy cause, as, for instance, for the Catholic faith or for the practice of some supernatural (and more probably natural) virtue; (3) the voluntary acceptance of death without resistance; (4) the presence of dispositions required for the reception of grace.

829. Baptism of *water* is a true Sacrament. This is an article *of faith*. (See no. 756.) Baptism is defined as the Sacrament of regeneration by water and the word. We were all made sinners and children of wrath in our earthly father Adam, and we are all reborn saints and children of grace in Our Lord Jesus Christ. (Rom. ch. 5.)

We shall treat first, of Baptism in itself; secondly, of the minister of Baptism; and thirdly, of the subject of Baptism.

CHAPTER I

BAPTISM IN ITSELF

Art. I. Matter and Form.

830. *The Matter*. The *remote* valid matter of Baptism is natural water. This is *of faith:* "If any one saith, that true and natural water is not of necessity for Baptism and, on

that account, wrests to some sort of metaphor those words of Our Lord Jesus Christ: 'Unless a man be born again of water and the Holy Ghost;' let him be anathema." (C. of Trent, Sess. 7, can. 2.)

The *licit* matter, outside of cases of necessity, is water blessed for this purpose. Ordinary holy water may not be used in solemn Baptism. In the absence of consecrated water, or in a case where the consecrated water is spoiled, the priest should bless other water, using the special short formula to be found in the Roman Ritual.

A quantity of ordinary water less than the actual amount of baptismal water on hand, may be added to the latter when a deficiency threatens. Such water should not be added to baptismal water that is already corrupted, because corrupted baptismal water may not be used, except in cases of necessity, under pain of grievous sin. When it is not possible to consecrate other water, it would be better to use unconsecrated and preferably holy water, instead of baptismal water that is corrupted. In winter it is lawful, and even a command of prudence, to add to the baptismal water a small quantity of warm water. But if the child were at the point of death, one would be permitted to use cold water if no warm water were available, even though the child's death would be hastened by a few seconds. The Sacred Congregation of Rites has stamped as an abuse the failure to consecrate baptismal water twice a year, on Holy Saturday and on the Vigil of Pentecost.

It is probable that the use of baptismal water is not of obligation in private Baptism; ordinary holy water suffices; and in case of necessity, ordinary and even doubtful water may be used, when none other is available. When making use of doubtful water, Baptism must be administered conditionally.

831. The *proximate* matter is the application of the water

to the subject. This application is called ablution and involves a contact that is physical and successive between the subject and the matter. Several drops of water must flow to constitute an ablution. The application of the water to the head or forehead of the subject must be made by the minister himself, and directly. In cases of necessity, when the application cannot be made to the head or forehead, the water may be applied conditionally to any other part of the body, even to the hair, provided it be renewed conditionally later on the forehead. While pouring the water with the right hand, it is prudent to wash the forehead of the child with the left, in order to make sure that the water actually touches the body. If the water came in contact only with the skin which covers the child's head in the absence of hair, the Baptism would not be certain; it would be invalid, if it touched merely the garments. If the child is born enclosed in the membrane, and fear is entertained that if this be broken, the child will die, the application of the water should be made conditionally first to the membrane, and then to the head.

832. It is *certain*, and even *pertaining to faith*, that Baptism may be administered validly in three different ways. First, by *immersion*, as was the custom during the first centuries; secondly, by *aspersion*, according to the common practice of St. Francis Xavier in the missions; and thirdly, by *infusion*, as is the common practice today. Each church should administer the Sacrament according to its tradition. The Roman Ritual prescribes a triple infusion under pain of mortal sin.

Some writers opine that Baptism by immersion is doubtful if the subject is not withdrawn from the water. It would seem, however, that this method might be used if the one to be baptized were about to breathe his last and there were no other way of baptizing him except by throwing him in the water. Baptism in this case would be valid, provided the words of the form were all recited before the end came. This opinion is defended by Lehmkuhl, but St. Alphonsus would not permit throwing a dying child into a stream in an effort to baptize him.

833. *The Form of Baptism.* The form of Baptism consists in the words: *"N., ego te baptizo, in nomine Patris, et Filii, et Spiritus Sancti."* This *belongs to the domain of faith,* from the words of the Council of Trent. (Sess. 7, canons, 3 and 4.) All the words in this formula are essential except *ego* and the first *et.* The form is valid in all languages, and it is expedient that simple folk pronounce it in their native tongue. The English formula is: "N., I baptize thee in the name of the Father, and of the Son, and of the Holy Ghost."

The Greek formula runs as follows: *"Baptizetur servus Christi in nomine,"* etc. Baptism administered in the name of Jesus Christ or in the name of the Blessed Trinity would be at least doubtful and consequently gravely illicit.

Art. II. Divine Institution.

834. It is *certain* that Jesus Christ instituted Baptism immediately, according to the more common teaching of theologians, at the time when He Himself was baptized by St. John the Baptist in the Jordan. From this time on the Apostles began to baptize. Baptism became a *conditio sine qua non* of salvation when Jesus Christ said: "Going therefore, teach ye all nations; baptizing them in the name of the Father, and of the Son, and of the Holy Ghost." (Matt. 28, 19.)

Theologians have raised the question whether or not the Apostles were themselves baptized. Some deny this, but Hurter says we must believe that they were.

Baptism became obligatory for the Jews dwelling in the

Holy Land from Pentecost day on; and for Gentiles from the time of the revelation made to St. Peter calling them to the faith.

After the promulgation of the Gospel among the Jews and Gentiles, circumcision and the means at the disposal of infidels to obtain remission of original sin became obsolete. There are some writers, however, who hold that nations to whom the Gospel has not yet been preached are still governed by the regulations laid down for infidel adults and children before the advent of Jesus Christ.

Art. III. Effects of Baptism.

835. Baptism blots out all sins and all punishments due to sins. It confers sanctifying grace and imprints a sacramental character. This was defined as *of faith* against the Protestants. The Decree of the Council of Florence for the Armenians explicitly states: "The effect of this Sacrament is the remission of every sin, original and actual, and all punishments due to sin." And the Council of Trent formulated the following anathema: "If any one denies, that, by the grace of Our Lord Jesus Christ, which is conferred in Baptism, the guilt of original sin is remitted; let him be anathema." (Sess. 5, can. 5; see also no. 781.)

836. The Decree for the Armenians adds that, through Baptism, we become members of Jesus Christ, and are incorporated into His Church. Through Baptism we are rendered capable of receiving the other Sacraments. It also has the power of annulling the penalties of this life, such as sickness and disease. It does not achieve this result in this world, in order that we may more closely resemble Jesus Christ, for if we suffer with Him, it is meet that we should be glorified with Him. Baptism will produce all these effects at the general resurrection, as stated in no. 5454.

CHAPTER II

THE MINISTER

Art. I. The Minister Himself.

837. *The extraordinary minister.* "In case of necessity," says the Decree for the Armenians, "not only a priest or a deacon, but even a layman or woman, nay, even a pagan and a heretic, may baptize." The following, however, would be guilty of grave sin: (1) The priest who, even in case of necessity, would baptize in the presence of his pastor without his permission; (2) the layman who would baptize in the presence of a priest in good standing even in case of necessity; (3) the priest who would consent to such an action on the part of a layman; (4) parents who would baptize their own child in the presence of another.

The layman who baptizes in the presence of a deacon would probably sin only venially; but the layman who baptizes outside a case of necessity would sin grievously, although the Baptism would be valid.

In missionary countries, where only a few priests are scattered through extensive territories, the Sacred Congregation of the Penitentiary has authorized catechists or laymen in good standing to administer Baptism even to healthy children in the absence of a priest. The same line of conduct has been permitted by the S. Congregation in the case of insane or dying persons.

No one may administer Baptism to himself. Whoever fails to administer this Sacrament to others in case of necessity, commits a mortal sin.

The following signs may prove useful in ascertaining whether or not there is danger of death for a newly born infant: if it does not utter any cries at birth, nor shed any tears; if its respiration is weak; if its head is soft and its face livid; if over-strenuous efforts are required on the part of physician or midwife to deliver the child, or if it is born before the seventh month.

838. Because all may be called upon at some time or other to administer Baptism, all are obliged to acquaint themselves with the matter and form of this Sacrament. Moreover, there is a serious obligation binding all pastors to explain these matters from the pulpit, and upon confessors to instruct women, and especially midwives, in the confessional.

839. *The extraordinary minister of solemn Baptism.* If, with Suarez and other theologians, we except the case of necessity, a deacon would sin grievously, and, according to common opinion, incur an irregularity, if, with or without grave reason, he administered solemn Baptism without the permission of the pastor or the bishop.

The deacon who would administer Baptism with permission could not bless the water or the salt.

840. *The ordinary minister of solemn Baptism.* The priest is the ordinary minister of solemn Baptism, provided he acts with the permission of the bishop or the pastor. The pastor has the right to administer Baptism to his subjects and to delegate others for that purpose. However, neither the bishop nor the pastor may administer Baptism without permission outside the confines of their own diocese or parish, even to their own subjects. Neither may they baptize without permission, even within the confines of their diocese or parish, strangers who could obtain the Sacrament easily and without delay in their own respective diocese or parish. Parents are guilty of sin, therefore, when they bring their children into other parishes to receive Baptism without the permission of the pastor, and the priest sins gravely who, outside of cases of necessity, baptizes such children even

privately without express or at least reasonably presumed permission of the pastor.

May several ministers administer Baptism to one subject at the same time? They can neither administer the Sacrament validly nor licitly, if they have the intention of administering the Sacrament in common, even though they use the formula in the plural: *"Te baptizamus."* St. Thomas teaches that since there is but one Christ, there can be but one minister. If, however, they were to baptize at the same time, each having an intention independent of the other, the Baptism would be valid. Except in cases of necessity, the same minister may not baptize several subjects at the same time. Canon 744 states that, where it can be conveniently done, the Baptism of adults should be referred to the bishop in order that he himself or his delegate may confer Baptism with greater solemnity.

Art. II. Circumstances Attendant Upon the Administration of Baptism.

841. *The place of Baptism.* Children must be baptized in the parish where their parents have their residence or quasi-residence. Quasi-residence is the place where the parents live or have the intention of living the greater part of the year. Vagrants who have no domicile, may have their children baptized in the place where they actually reside. If a woman gives birth to a child in a parish far removed from her place of residence, she may have the child baptized where he was born, unless the Sacrament could be obtained easily and without delay in her home parish.

842. Solemn Baptism should be administered in the parish church or in some other church possessing a baptismal font. Canon 774 states that the bishop, for the convenience of the people, may allow or demand that baptismal fonts be placed also in other churches and public oratories within the

limits of a parish. If distance or other circumstances prohibit the administration of solemn Baptism in the parish church or in some other church possessing a baptismal font, the pastor may and should administer it in some nearby church or public oratory within the limits of his parish, even though the latter does not possess a baptismal font. Canon 774 also safeguards the right of having baptismal fonts in churches situated outside the limits of the parish. It would be a grievous sin to administer Baptism outside of any church or any public oratory without reason.

Solemn Baptism may not be administered in private houses except under the following conditions:

1. If those to be baptized are the children or grandchildren of the ruler of a country or the successor to the throne, if they lawfully ask for the favor. This favor is granted also to presidents of republics.

2. If in some extraordinary case the Ordinary prudently and conscientiously judges fit to grant the favor.

In both these cases, Baptism must be administered in the private chapel or in some other becoming place, and baptismal water is to be used. (Can. 776.)

In case of urgent necessity, private Baptism may be given at any time and in any place. If the minister is neither a priest nor a deacon, he must limit himself to the bare essentials, that is, pouring the water and pronouncing the words. If the minister is a priest or a deacon, he must perform the ceremonies which follow upon Baptism and omit those which precede. The latter must be supplied as soon afterwards as possible in church. In private Baptism the priest should wear a white stole. Private Baptism may be administered even when death is not imminent, but in that case the bishop may not permit its administration unless there is question of conditionally baptizing an adult heretic.

843. *The time of Baptism.* Infants should be baptized as

soon as possible, and, according to a decision of the Holy Office, their Baptism should not be deferred beyond three days. However, a delay of eleven days would not constitute a grievous sin, except in danger of death. A delay of more than twelve days would be a grievous sin according to some theologians, but not according to others. (See no. 582.) According to Suarez, for the negligence to be grievous, Baptism would have to be deferred one month without reason, or two months with reason. It would be a mortal sin to refuse, or indefinitely to defer, the administration of Baptism without reason in the case of an adult, especially if he were in danger of death.

844. *The ceremonies of Baptism.* Outside the case of necessity, it would be a grievous sin to omit the ceremonies of Baptism. If they have been omitted, they must be supplied under pain of venial sin, according to some, and under pain of mortal sin, according to others.

When the ceremonies are supplied for an adult Catholic, the formulas used must be those contained in the Ritual for infant Baptism; and when the ceremonies are supplied for a heretic, the formulas used must be those prescribed for adult Baptism.

When Baptism is repeated conditionally, the ceremonies omitted in the first instance must be supplied, unless the bishop dispenses from them in the case of a heretic.

If the ceremonies were performed in the first instance, they may be repeated or omitted at will in the second. Should they be repeated if the first Baptism administered was certainly invalid? Some theologians answer this question in the affirmative, others in the negative, both opinions being probable. (St. Alphonsus, 114.)

It would be a serious fault not to use baptismal water. As a general rule, the same oils may not be used in the consecration of this water as were used the preceding year.

The anointings with chrism and the oil of catechumens oblige under pain of mortal sin. The Sacred Congregation of Rites looks with disfavor upon the practice of not distributing the holy oils until after Easter. The pastor should secure the oils before blessing the font. If he is unable to secure them before this time, he should omit to pour the oil into the font at the time specified by the Ritual, and pour in the new oils, when they arrive. If, however, it became necessary for him to administer Baptism in the meantime, he should pour in the old oils. This decision was rendered on January 31st, 1896.

It is not permitted to give to a child a mythological or ridiculous name, nor, *a fortiori*, an obscene one. If the parents insist on such a name, the priest should give another, *submissa voce*. Canon 761 places upon pastors the obligation to see to it that those whom they baptize receive a Christian name. It adds that if they cannot do this, they should add to the name given by the parents the name of some saint, and enter both names in the baptismal record. Any one may change the name he has received at Baptism, provided he notifies those who have the right to know of the change. (St. Alphonsus, 148.)

The priest must enter in the baptismal record the names of the persons baptized together with the name of the minister, those of the parents and godparents, and the time and the place when the sacrament was administered. If the child is illegitimate, the name of the mother should be entered in the record if the fact of her maternity is publicly known, or if she requests the same to be done in writing or before two witnesses. The name of the father is also entered if he asks for it in writing or before two witnesses, or if he is known as the father through some public document. In all other cases, the child is entered as being of a father or a mother or parents unknown.

The Pontifical Commission for interpreting the New Code stated on July 1st, 1922, that, in entering the names of illegitimate children in the baptismal register, every effort must be made to shield them from infamy and disgrace, especially if their case be somewhat out of the ordinary.

In very extraordinary cases recourse should be had to the Sacred Congregation of the Council. Other information to be entered in the baptismal register according to the station the candidate adopts in life, is the fact and date of his confirmation, reception of subdeaconship, solemn religious profession, marriage, declaration of nullity, and repeal of the marriage contract by the Holy See in the case of a nonconsummated marriage. Habitual failure to make these different entries would constitute a grievous sin. (St. Alphonsus, 159.)

If Baptism is administered by a priest other than the pastor, the former must inform the latter of his act as soon as possible, unless there is question of injury to a third party. (Can. 778.) One absolutely trustworthy witness or the oath of the one baptized, if an adult, is sufficient for proof of Baptism. (Can. 779.)

A child must be baptized according to the rite of the father, unless other rules and regulations have been passed. If only one of the parents is a Catholic, the child must be baptized in the rite of the Catholic party. (Can. 776.) If, because of some urgent necessity, the child has been baptized in another rite, he must be reared in the rite of his father. The blessing *post partum* should not be given to the mother of an illegitimate child; it may be given to other mothers, but no one is obliged to ask for it.

845. *The Godparents.* Godparents or sponsors are spiritual parents who engage themselves to watch over the spiritual interest of the baptized. In order to act *licitly* as a sponsor:

1. One must be fourteen years of age, unless, for a just reason, the minister selects persons who are younger.

2. One must not be under excommunication for a notorious crime, nor excluded from legal actions, nor suffer from infamy of law, even though no sentence has been pronounced, nor must one be under interdict, or a public criminal, or disgraced by infamy of fact.

3. One must know the rudiments of the faith.

4. One must not be a novice or professed member in any religious organization, unless there is no other person available to act as sponsor and permission is granted by at least a local superior.

5. One must not be in sacred Orders, unless he has the express permission of his own Ordinary to act as sponsor. (Can. 766.)

If doubt exists as to whether one may validly or licitly act as sponsor, the pastor should, time permitting, consult the Ordinary. Spiritual relationship is contracted with the baptized one by the minister and the sponsor. It is the duty of the sponsors, by virtue of their office, to take an interest in their godchild and to see to it that he is instructed in the duties of the Christian life and lives up to these duties, as he solemnly pledged himself to do in the ceremony. This duty ceases only at the death of the child. (Canons 767 and 769.)

In order to act validly as a sponsor:

1. One must be baptized, have reached the age of reason, and have the intention of assuming the obligations involved.

2. One must not belong to any non-Catholic sect, nor be excommunicated, nor suffer from infamy of law, nor be excluded from legal actions by a condemnatory or declaratory sentence, nor be a deposed or degraded cleric.

3. One must not be the father or mother of the child, nor married to the person to be baptized.

4. One must be designated either by the person to be baptized, or by the parents or guardians, or, in their default, by the minister of Baptism.

5. One must physically hold or touch the one baptized or receive him immediately after Baptism from the sacred font or from the hands of the minister. The contact must be physical and must take place in the act of Baptism. (Can. 765.)

When a priest has to deny a person the right to act as sponsor, he should proceed with the greatest precaution in order to avoid more serious evils. It is a good policy never to refuse this privilege to any one who is not publicly recognized as unworthy. If such persons are notorious sinners, it is best to warn them (not in public, but privately) not to present themselves as sponsors, but merely as witnesses. One might even admit them as witnesses, and then not allow them to carry out the functions of sponsors, for it would be better in this case for the child not to have any sponsors at all. When more serious evils are to be feared from the denial of this right to unworthy sponsors, the laws of the Church do not oblige *cum tanto incommodo*.

According to a decision of the Holy See, a Catholic is never permitted to act as sponsor for a child baptized by a heretic. Such a sponsor would be required to seek Baptism for the child from a minister who could not administer it without committing grievous sin, a step which would not be permitted, the opinion of St. Alphonsus to the contrary notwithstanding.

846. In solemn Baptism the child should have, whenever possible, either a godfather or a godmother. This precept is commonly regarded as binding under pain of mortal sin. The New Code suggests that a sponsor be had also in private Baptism, whenever feasible. If no sponsor was present at the private Baptism, one should be present in supplying the

ceremony, but in that case he would not contract any spiritual relationship. (Can. 762.)

Should it be necessary to repeat Baptism conditionally, the same sponsor, if possible, should act who was present at the first Baptism. Aside from this case, there is no need of a sponsor in conditional Baptism. If Baptism is repeated conditionally, neither the sponsor of the first nor the sponsor of the second Baptism contracts spiritual relationship, unless the same sponsor was present at both. (Can. 763.)

In order not to multiply spiritual relationships without necessity, the Church forbids under pain of mortal sin the use of more than one sponsor of either sex, so that if two sponsors are used, they must be of different sexes. There are authors who deny that any spiritual relationship is contracted in private Baptism, but the majority of theologians hold that there is.

847. A pastor would sin grievously if, without reason, he refused to accept the sponsors designated by the parents, or admitted sponsors who were not designated. Care should be taken, therefore, to have the parents designate the godfather and the godmother. The pastor may designate the sponsors only in the default of parents or guardians. In a decree issued on November 25th, 1925, the S. Congregation of the Sacraments reminded the faithful of the obligations of sponsors, who in the eyes of God and the Church vouch for the children whom they present.

CHAPTER III

THE SUBJECT OF BAPTISM

Art. I. Who Is This Subject?

848. Any unbaptized man in the wayfaring state, be he adult or child, is a fit subject for Baptism. This is an article

of faith, defined by the Council of Trent (Sess. 5, canons 3 and 4.) Moreover, Baptism really received, or at least implicitly desired, is a necessary means of salvation for all.

849. Hurter distinguishes two kinds of necessity of means in the supernatural order. The first he calls *privileged,* and such would be a necessary means established by God to attain eternal happiness, but replaceable by another means. Baptism of water is such a means, since it can be replaced by Baptism of desire. The second he calls *absolute,* and such would be a means which God never dispenses with, although He has the power to do so. Faith and grace are such means, from which God never dispenses.

850. Baptism of water is necessary, therefore, as a *privileged* means, and Baptism of desire, coupled with perfect contrition, as an *absolute* means, when Baptism of water is not possible. The Council of Trent explicitly states that "the translation to the state of grace . . . cannot be effected without the laver of regeneration, or the desire thereof, as it is written: 'Unless a man be born again of water and the Holy Ghost, he cannot enter the kingdom of Heaven.' " (Sess. 6, ch. 4.)

851. What we have said of the necessity of Baptism applies also to the children of infidels who have never heard of revelation. There are some writers, however, who claim that infidels cannot be subject to a law of which they are totally ignorant.

According to canon 88, paragraph 3 of the Code, all who have not yet reached the age of reason are to be regarded as children with respect to Baptism, and it puts in the same class all persons who have not had the use of reason from infancy, no matter what their age. Adults are those who have the use of reason, and for their admission to Baptism it is sufficient that they ask for the Sacrament of their own free will. (Can. 745.)

852. Baptism, therefore, is of obligation for adults. To delay its reception beyond a certain time would constitute a mortal sin. The seriousness of this sin is to be measured chiefly by the reason for the delay. If the reception of the Sacrament is deferred out of contempt, or for some similar motive, the sin is grievous. An instance of a motive similar to that of contempt would be that of a person who would defer Baptism in order to allow himself greater freedom and claim exemption from the duties and obligations of the Christian life. There exists a grave obligation for parents to have their children baptized, and not to defer this action beyond a reasonable time limit. "If any one saith . . . that it is better that the Baptism of little children be omitted, than that, while not believing by their own act, they should be baptized in the faith alone of the Church; let him be anathema." (C. of Trent, Sess. 7, can. 13; see also no. 843.) Children who have been baptized are members of the Church and subject to her laws. This is *of faith,* from the words of the same Council. (Sess. 7, can. 8.)

853. The obligation of administering Baptism to little children gives rise to the further obligation of performing a Cæsarean operation on a deceased mother, if some hope is entertained that her child is still living, or even if one has good reasons to suppose that she had conceived a short time before her death. The obligation to perform such an operation is grave, both for the parents and for the physician, and a pregnant woman, when dangerously ill, should be persuaded to make known her condition to some discreet person who will extract and baptize the child after the mother's death. The pastor should have the operation performed by some one other than himself; but if no one is willing or able to do so, he himself, if able, would be bound *in principle* to extract the child, unless he feared that scandal or contempt for religion would arise from his action. (See nos.

2434 and 3680.) In a case of this kind it would be well to have some one else verify the decease of the mother, if there is no danger that the child will die in the meantime, in order not to expose himself to prosecution. Since, however, the good of the individual must always yield to the good of the community, a priest is never permitted to perform such an operation if there is any danger of scandal. For this reason, the Sacred Congregation of the Holy Office has forbidden missionaries to perform the Cæsarean operation or even to order that it be performed. They must content themselves with instructing the surgeons, and leave the rest to them.

854. There is a grave obligation to have the Cæsarean operation performed upon a living woman if she cannot be delivered otherwise, and if there is hope of being able to baptize the child without endangering her life. If there is danger of causing or precipitating the mother's death, the operation must not be performed. If, on the other hand, the mother is certain to die, and there is no hope of being able to deliver her, the operation must be performed, provided some hope be present of being able to baptize the child; if not, the obligation of performing the operation ceases. It ceases, too, if the mother alone risks her life, even though the child is destined to survive her, or hope is entertained that it will survive her.

The mother should not be informed of this hard duty, if she is in good faith and if it can be foreseen that she will not consent to the operation. In a case of this kind one should be content with gently trying to persuade her to have the operation performed. The same line of conduct should be followed in regard to an unmarried girl who is pregnant. (See no. 853.)

If it is impossible to perform the Cæsarean operation either before or after the death of the mother, care should at least be taken to administer Baptism, or have it administered, to the child, by means of an instrument introduced into the womb. However, Baptism administered in this fashion is doubtful, and according to a decision of the Congregation of the Council, the Sacrament must be re-administered conditionally if possible, even though the only attainable part of the child's body be the upper portion of the head. In matters of this kind the safest course should always be followed.

855. Canon 747 of the Code insists that every fetus born prematurely, no matter at what stage of pregnancy, be baptized absolutely if alive, and conditionally if life is doubtful. The verdict of modern embryology on this subject is that the embryo is animated from the first moment of its conception, and that three days after conception it has the outlines of a human body. The embryo or fetus must not, however, be confused with solid pieces of flesh and blood, to which Baptism should not be applied as a general rule. The fetus is enclosed in a membrane of the same color as the intestines and is very soft to the touch. In case of doubt, the safest course must be followed and Baptism administered to whatever one could reasonably suppose to be a fetus. The procedure in such cases is to administer conditional Baptism with lukewarm water, if possible, before breaking the membrane, then carefully to break open the membrane in a dish containing lukewarm water, in order not to expose the fetus to the fatal influence of the air, drain off the water contained within the membrane, and then baptize the fetus a second time conditionally, by plunging it into the lukewarm water and withdrawing it in such a way that a real ablution takes place. (See nos. 831 and 832.) Lehmkuhl reminds us that a fetus may live for several days after it has been expelled from the womb, and the only sure sign that it is dead is apparent putrefaction. He adds that pastors have a *grave* obligation to instruct physicians, midwives, and mothers on

these matters. The reader will, therefore, pardon us for entering into these details.

856. It is not permitted to baptize an infant while still enclosed in its mother's womb, as long as there is a probable hope that it can be baptized when born. If only the head protrudes, and there is imminent danger of death, Baptism should be administered unconditionally upon the head. If any other limb protrudes, Baptism should be administered conditionally upon that limb when there is immediate danger of death, and Baptism conditionally repeated when the infant is born alive. Any fetus baptized in the mother's womb, must be rebaptized conditionally after birth. (Can. 746.)

857. Misshaped children (*monstra*) should always be baptized, at least conditionally. When in doubt as to whether the fetus is one or several human beings, one should be baptized absolutely, the others *conditionally*. (Can. 748.)

If, for example, a *monstrum* has one head and two chests, Baptism should be administered unconditionally upon the head and conditionally upon each one of the chests. If it had two heads and two chests, there would certainly be two human beings, and both should be baptized *absolutely*.

858. Foundlings must be baptized *conditionally*. (Can. 749.) A written statement attesting their Baptism would not be a sufficient proof.

As a general rule, infants baptized by Catholic midwives should not be re-baptized unless there is a prudent doubt as to the validity.

859. An adult must not be baptized without his knowledge or consent, and only after due instruction. Moreover, he is to be admonished to repent of his sins. In danger of death it is sufficient that he assents in some way to the principal mysteries of the faith and earnestly promises that he will keep the commandments of the Christian religion. If he is in no position to ask for Baptism, but has either before, or in

his present condition, manifested the intention of receiving Baptism, he may be baptized conditionally. If he recovers his health later on, and there remains doubt as to the validity of the Baptism conferred, he may be baptized again conditionally. (Can. 752.)

Both the priest who is to administer Baptism to an adult, and the adult who is to be baptized, if in good health, are advised to remain fasting.

Unless there are grave and urgent obstacles, the baptized adult should assist at Mass immediately after Baptism and receive Holy Communion. (Can. 853.)

860. An infant of infidel, heretical, schismatic or apostate parents can be lawfully baptized, even though the parents object, in danger of death or if in such condition that it can be prudently presumed that the infant will die before reaching the age of reason.

Outside of the danger of death such an infant may be lawfully baptized if at least one of the parents or guardians consents, or if there are no parents (father or mother, grandfather or grandmother) nor guardians, or if they have lost the right to the child, or cannot exercise that right. In all these cases, however, there must be some guarantee that the child will be reared in the Catholic faith. (Canons 750 and 751.) Pastors should see to it that such children receive a Catholic education.

Insane and delirious persons must not be baptized unless they have been in this condition from birth, or became such before reaching the age of reason. In these cases they should be baptized like infants. If they have lucid moments, they may be baptized in one of these, if they so desire. If they showed some desire for Baptism before becoming insane, they should be baptized in imminent danger of death. The same rule must be followed in regard to those who are in a coma or delirium. (Can. 754.) Heretics should not be rebaptized if it can be established with certainty that their former Baptism was valid, something which is ordinarily very difficult.

861. According to the old Canon Law, a child born of Christian parents and educated as a Christian could be presumed to be baptized. The New Code no longer recognizes such a presumption, though Noldin and Vermeersch still uphold it.

According to canon 779, one absolutely trustworthy witness, or the oath of the one baptized in adult age, is sufficient proof of the Baptism, where the interest of no third party is involved. (Can. 779.)

Art. II. Dispositions Necessary in the Subject.

862. No dispositions are required in children or persons who lack the use of reason. In those who possess the use of reason, at least the habitual intention of receiving Baptism is required for *validity*.

For *liceity*, faith is required. An adult, before receiving Baptism, must explicitly believe in all the truths necessary by necessity of means, and implicitly in all the truths necessary by necessity of precept. Explicit belief must also be professed in Our Lord Jesus Christ. Therefore, one would not be permitted to pass over in silence the mysteries of the faith, and merely stress sorrow and confidence, for fear lest a dying infidel, who had not yet lost consciousness, might change his mind. If such an infidel did not understand these mysteries, or only believed in them in a doubtful way, he should be baptized unconditionally if, in the hour of death, his intention of receiving Baptism is certain, since this intention is sufficient for validity, but conditionally if his intention is doubtful.

Missionaries are bound to instruct all infidels not in danger of death in all the precepts of the positive divine law.

(Holy Office, March 30th, 1898.) They must also explain to them the mystery of the Holy Eucharist, according to a decision of the S. Congregation of the Propaganda. Such infidels must also pass all the tests prescribed by the statutes of the diocese. They must have hope and a beginning of charity, if they are without actual sins, and attrition, if their souls are stained with sins, especially if these sins be grievous. (See no. 813.)

863. In this age of religious indifference Christian parents sometimes neglect to have their children baptized. A zealous priest will take cognizance of the births which occur in his parish and remind the parents of their duty. A pastor who would not use all his ingenuity to remedy such an evil would have cause to worry about the state of his own conscience.

SECOND TREATISE

CONFIRMATION

864. Confirmation is a Sacrament of the New Law in which, through the imposition of hands, prayer and anointment of the bishop with holy chrism, the newly baptized are given increase of grace and strength to preserve and profess their faith.

It is an article of faith defined against Martin Luther and John Calvin, that Confirmation is a Sacrament. (See no. 756.) In the following three chapters we shall treat: (1) of Confirmation in itself, (2) of the minister, and (3) of the subject.

CHAPTER I

CONFIRMATION IN ITSELF

865. *The Matter.* According to the Decree for the Armenians, the *remote matter* of Confirmation is chrism, blessed by the bishop, and made of oil, which signifies purity of conscience, and balsam, which signifies the good odor of an upright life. It is *certain* that for *validity* oil is necessary, and for *liceity, sub gravi,* balsam be mixed with the oil, and the mixture blessed by the bishop.

866. Authorities are not agreed on the following questions: (1) Is balsam required for validity? (2) Is it necessary for validity that the holy chrism be blessed? (3) Is it necessary for validity that it be blessed by the bishop?

(4) Must the oil also receive the special blessing given by the bishop to holy chrism?

To the first question some reply in the negative, others, more probably, in the affirmative. In danger of death, Confirmation could be administered to a sick person with oil blessed by the bishop, in default of holy chrism.

To the second question some reply in the negative, but the opinion of those who reply in the affirmative must be followed.

Several theologians are of the opinion that the Pope could give to a simple priest the power to bless the holy chrism, but in practice the contrary opinion must be followed as being the safer of the two.

Some require the special blessing given by the bishop to holy chrism for validity; others affirm with some degree of probability that the Sacrament would be valid if administered with the oil of the sick or the oil of catechumens. Outside of cases of necessity, chrism that antedates that blessed on the last Holy Thursday may not be used under pain of mortal sin.

867. There are three opinions in regard to the *proximate matter* of Confirmation.

The first opinion claims that the proximate matter is the imposition of hands which the minister gives to those whom he is confirming at the very beginning of the ceremony, when he recites the prayer: *"Omnipotens sempiterne Deus,"* etc. This imposition is at least a very important part of the ceremony, and all those who are to be confirmed should be present when it is given.

The second opinion claims that the proximate matter is twofold: the first imposition of which we have just spoken, with the corresponding oration for the form, and over and above this the anointing with holy chrism together with the words: *"Signo te signo crucis et confirmo te chrismate salutis, in nomine Patris et Filii et Spiritus Sancti,"* or according to the Greek formula, *"Signaculum doni Spiritus Sancti."*

The third opinion, which St. Alphonsus calls *quite certain,* is that the anointment with holy chrism, together with the imposition which this anointment presupposes, is the sole matter of the Sacrament, and that the words which accompany this anointment constitute the sole form. Candidates who were not present at the first imposition of hands need not be re-confirmed.

868. It is of the essence of the Sacrament: (1) that the anointing be made on the forehead of the candidate according to the more probable opinion; (2) that it be made in the form of a cross, and (3) that it be made by the minister's hand and not by means of some instrument. Moreover, the minister must anoint with his right thumb. This is not necessary for validity, although some theologians claim that it is binding under pain of grievous sin. If the minister cannot use his right thumb, there are some authors who say he may use one of his fingers.

869. *The Form.* The same controversy exists in regard to the *form* of the Sacrament, but, according to the Decree for the Armenians, the form consists in the words: *"Signo te,"* etc. Therefore, these words constitute the sole form of Confirmation. To omit the invocation to the Holy Trinity or any one of the following words: *Signo, confirmo, te, signo, crucis, chrismate, salutis,* would constitute a substantial change in the form. Authors generally regard the Greek formula as valid.

Art. I. Divine Institution.

870. It is commonly believed that Confirmation was instituted at the Last Supper because the chrism is blessed on Holy Thursday.

Art. II. Effects of Confirmation.

871. Confirmation gives second grace and, *per accidens,* first grace. This follows from what we have said in no. 775. Over and above these graces, this Sacrament also confers the right to receive from time to time supernatural aids to assist us in preserving and professing our faith. In addition, it confers in plenitude of the Holy Spirit like unto that received by the Apostles on Pentecost day. It, therefore, infuses into the soul a greater amount of sanctifying grace than Baptism, which already gave us the Holy Spirit. Finally, it imprints upon the soul the character of a soldier of Jesus Christ, as we had occasion to remark in no. 781. In regard to the gifts and fruits of the Holy Ghost, we refer the reader to no. 2089. (See also nos. 2028 and 2036.)

Pastors should be particularly careful that their parishioners receive this Sacrament in proper time, for, although it is not absolutely necessary as a means of salvation, no one should neglect to receive it when the occasion presents itself. (*C. J. C.,* can. 787.) Theologians are not agreed as to the seriousness of the sin of negligence in this respect.

CHAPTER II

THE MINISTER

Art. I. The Minister Himself.

872. The ordinary minister of Confirmation is the bishop. This is *of faith.* "If any one saith, that the ordinary minister of holy Confirmation is not the bishop alone, but any simple priest soever; let him be anathema." (C. of Trent, Sess. 7, can. 3.)

The extraordinary minister is a priest who either by common law or by special indult from the Holy See has received the faculty to confirm. (Can. 782.) Without this faculty, or outside of these cases, a priest would confirm both illicitly and invalidly. A priest of the Latin rite who has received this faculty by virtue of an indult, can validly confer Confirmation on Catholics of his own rite only, unless the indult expressly allows more; and a priest of the Oriental rite who has the faculty to give Confirmation together with Baptism, cannot confirm infants of the Latin rite. (Can. 782.)

In virtue of a tacit privilege all priests belonging to Oriental rites have a general delegation from the Sovereign Pontiff to confirm the faithful of their rites.

Art. II. Necessary Conditions in the Minister.

873. *For validity*. The episcopal character, or the priestly character together with a delegation from the Holy See.

For liceity. The bishop may lawfully confirm his subjects within his diocese. Outside of the same he may confirm his subjects privately, without crozier and mitre. (Can. 783.) If he wishes to confirm a subject or a stranger outside of his own diocese in a solemn manner, he must have the at least presumed permission of the local Ordinary. As a general rule, a priest who confirms by virtue of an indult or special privilege, does so validly only within the territory designated, whereas a bishop confirms validly no matter where he is. Within his own diocese the bishop may lawfully confirm all strangers, unless there is an express prohibition to the contrary. The same is true of a priest who confirms in virtue of an indult or special privilege.

Confirmation may be administered at any time of the day, and at any season of the year, but preferably during the week of Pentecost. For a good and just cause, it may be administered in any becoming place, but the proper place is a church, even though it be in an exempted place. (Can. 792.)

874. The Church requires a sponsor at Confirmation for all candidates, and this sponsor must be of the same sex as the person to be confirmed, unless the minister has a good reason for accepting a sponsor of the opposite sex. A sponsor should not stand for more than two candidates, unless the minister for a just reason allows him to stand for more. The sponsor must be designated by the confirmandus or by his parents or guardians. In case they neglect or refuse to designate a sponsor, the minister or pastor may designate him. The sponsor must touch the confirmandus either in person or through a proxy in the very act of Confirmation. (Can. 795.) A sponsor who was not lawfully designated or who did not touch the candidate physically would not be a valid sponsor. For the rest, the same conditions governing the validity and liceity of sponsors in Baptism govern those of sponsors in Confirmation. The same sponsor should not serve at Confirmation as served at Baptism, unless there is a good reason, according to the judgment of the minister of Confirmation, or unless the Sacrament is given immediately after Baptism. A spiritual relationship (not an impediment to marriage) arises between the confirmandus and his sponsor, and the latter is obliged by his office to interest himself in the spiritual welfare of the confirmandus and provide for his Christian education. (Can. 797.)

875. In administering the Sacrament of Confirmation, the bishop should wear the amice over the rochet, or if he is a religious, over the surplice, then the stole, the white cope, the mitre and the crozier. Strictly speaking, the stole suffices, although it would be a sin not to wear any of the above vestments. It is not a grievous sin to omit the blow on the cheek or the use of the lighted candle; but the omission of all the prayers preceding Confirmation would constitute a mortal sin. A priest delegated to administer this Sacrament must wear the alb and the stole and, before proceeding to

administer Confirmation, must read the letter delegating him, aloud, in the vernacular, to the people. He is forbidden to wear any pontifical insignia.

The pastor should take care to enter the names of those confirmed, together with those of their sponsors, in the baptismal register.

Art. III. The Obligation of Administering Confirmation.

876. The local Ordinary must administer Confirmation at least once every five years in every part of his diocese. If he is reasonably prevented from doing so, or if he has not the power to confirm, he should see to it that the Sacrament is administered by some one else within the same time limit.

Some theologians would make it a mortal sin for a bishop not to administer Confirmation to a dying person who requests it of him, others excuse him from all sin in a case of this kind.

CHAPTER III

THE SUBJECT OF CONFIRMATION

Art. I. Who is the Subject?

877. Every baptized person is a subject for Confirmation, but only the baptized can receive this Sacrament. Children and persons who have not the use of reason may be confirmed validly. Insane persons may, nay, must be confirmed. Today one may not, except for some grave cause, licitly confirm children who have not yet reached the age of reason. Such a reason would be danger of death or the fact that the bishop was unable to return for a long time. "Though it seems that one should not wait to the age of twelve," says the Catechism of the Council of Trent, "it certainly is proper not to give Confirmation before the age of seven." The prac-

tice of not administering Confirmation until after First Communion, says Leo XIII, is not in agreement with the ancient and constant practice of the Church, nor does it correspond to the needs of the faithful. Children carry within themselves the elements of the passions, which if not promptly eradicated, will gradually grow. The faithful, therefore, from their tenderest years, need to be strengthened from on high. Confirmed in grace at an early age, children will be better able to understand the maxims of the Gospel, and better disposed to receive Holy Communion, which in turn will be of greater benefit to them.

One whose Confirmation is doubtful may receive the Sacrament a second time conditionally; but the doubt must be of a more solid nature than in the case of Baptism.

Art. II. Dispositions Required in the Subject.

878. Nothing is required of children or persons who lack the use of reason. Adults must have the proper intention to receive Confirmation *validly*. (See no. 812.) For *liceity*, the subject does not have to be fasting, but he must be in the state of grace and instructed in the elements of the Christian religion.

An intolerable practice exists in certain countries where Confirmation is administered to children before they make their First Communion. The pastors do not take the trouble to prepare the children for the reception of the Holy Spirit by confession, or if they do hear their confessions, do not give them absolution. It is difficult to explain such negligence, which may result in many sacrileges.

If several candidates for Confirmation present themselves from one or several parishes, all must be present at the first imposition of hands and must remain until the end of the ceremony. The pastor must inscribe in a special book the names of the confirmandi, the minister, parents, and sponsors, as well as the day and the place of Confirmation. He should also enter this information in the baptismal register.

If the pastor of the confirmandus was not present at the ceremony, the minister must apprise him of his action.

When the rights of others are not at stake, the testimony of one trustworthy witness or the sworn statement of the person confirmed, are sufficient evidence of the receipt of Confirmation, unless the Sacrament was administered in infancy. (Can. 800.)

THIRD TREATISE

The Holy Eucharist

As the Holy Eucharist is both a Sacrament and a sacrifice, this treatise will comprise two parts, the first dealing with the Sacrament and the second with the sacrifice.

PART ONE

THE EUCHARIST AS A SACRAMENT

879. The Holy Eucharist is defined as a Sacrament of the New Law, instituted by Our Lord Jesus Christ, to be the spiritual food of souls, and in which His body and blood are truly, really, and substantially present under the appearances of bread and wine.

880. It is an article of faith that the Holy Eucharist is a Sacrament. (See no. 756.) The sensible signs are the appearances of bread and wine, which remain after the consecration and signify the spiritual food, and which, according to some theologians, constitute the essence of the Sacrament; whereas, according to others, whose opinion is more probable, the essence comprises both the appearances and the body of Christ, which, signified by the appearances, in turn signifies grace. Holy Communion does not belong to the essence of the Sacrament, but is only the indispensable condition of its effects.

881. Jesus Christ is present in this Sacrament *truly*, not merely in a figurative manner, *really*, not merely by faith, *substantially*, not merely by His power, as taught by the

74

Sacramentarians. The real presence of Our Lord Jesus Christ in the Holy Eucharist is an article of faith, defined against Berengarius and a large number of Protestants. "If any one denieth, that in the Sacrament of the Most Holy Eucharist are contained truly, really, and substantially the body and blood together with the soul and divinity of Our Lord Jesus Christ, and consequently the whole Christ; but saith that He is only therein as in a sign, or in figure, or virtue; let him be anathema." (C. of Trent, Sess. 13, can. 1.) "Jesus took bread . . . and said: 'Take ye, and eat. This is my body.' " (Matt. 26, 26.) The Fathers of the Church unanimously profess the same truth, and all the ancient liturgies attest it, as well as the practice of preserving the Holy Eucharist in a fit receptacle and carrying it to the sick.

In virtue of the words of consecration, the body alone should be present under the appearances of bread. As a matter of fact, if the Apostles had consecrated during the three days that Our Lord was in the sepulchre, only His body and His divinity would have been present under the appearances of bread. Since the Resurrection, however, the body of Christ can no longer be separated either from His blood or from His soul; and hence Jesus Christ is present wholly in the Eucharist and under each species.

This has led several theologians to advance the view that the entire specific reason of the Sacrament is in only one species. Others more probably contend that it is in both species at once, because both the bread and the wine are necessary to signify the spiritual banquet which Christ has prepared for us.

Whence does the Sacrament derive its numerical unity? Some say from the unity of the body of Our Lord; others, from the physical union of each part of the species taken together; still others, from the moral union of the species, which, in so far as they are together on one altar, constitute only one Sacrament, and in so far as they are placed on different altars, or distributed to several persons, constitute several Sacraments.

882. Our Lord, therefore, must be worshipped in the Holy Eucharist. This is an article of faith. "If any one saith, that in the Holy Sacrament of the Eucharist Christ, the only-begotten Son of God, is not to be adored with the worship, even external, of *latria;* and is, consequently, neither to be venerated with a special festive solemnity nor to be solemnly borne about in processions, according to the laudable and universal rite and custom of Holy Church; or, is not to be proposed publicly to the people to be adored, and that the adorers thereof are idolators; let him be anathema." (C. of Trent, Sess. 13, can. 6.) This truth is a direct consequence of what we stated in nos. 608 and 881.

883. *How is Jesus Christ present?* Not, as Osiander maintained, by *impanation,* or a personal or hypostatic union into which the Godman enters with the bread; nor by *consubstantiation,* as maintained by Martin Luther, whereby Christ would co-exist with the bread and wine; but by *transubstantiation,* whereby the substance of bread is changed into the substance of the body of Christ. This is *of faith,* otherwise the words "This is my body" would be meaningless.

The Fathers of the Church have compared the Holy Eucharist to the change of water into wine at the marriage feast of Cana. "If any one saith, that in the sacred and holy Sacrament of the Eucharist the subtance of the bread and wine remains conjointly with the body and blood of Our Lord Jesus Christ, and denieth that wonderful and singular conversion of the whole substance of the bread into the Body, and of the whole substance of the wine into the Blood—the species only of the bread and wine remaining—which conversion indeed the Catholic Church most aptly calls Transubstantiation; let him be anathema." (C. of Trent, Sess. 13, can. 2.)

Hence, the substantial form of the bread no longer remains, and apart from Durandus, all theologians agree that even the prime matter of the bread ceases to exist. The bread is not annihilated, but its whole substance is changed into the body of Christ, who can undergo no change, since He is neither engendered, nor changed, nor increased, but remains whole and entire in His substance.

884. The Holy Eucharist is not, therefore, a *creation out of nothing*, nor is it brought down from Heaven, as contended by several writers, or effected by a *union* between the body of Christ and the species, but by *transubstantiation, i. e.,* the substantial change of the bread into the body and the wine into the blood of Our Lord, which thus become present.

885. Jesus Christ is wholly present under each species and in each particle of both species after division. This is *of faith*. (C. of Trent, Sess. 13, can. 3.) Christ, being immortal, can suffer no partition. He is, therefore, wholly present wherever His substance is found; and since He is present in the host by consecration and not by division, theologians argue (although this is not of faith) that He is whole and entire in each host and whole and entire in each particle of the host before division, somewhat as the soul is present whole and entire in the whole body and in each part thereof. (However, Cardinal Billot maintains with other theologians, that Jesus Christ is not present in each portion of the host before the division.)

886. "If any one saith, that, after the consecration is completed, the body and blood of our Lord Jesus Christ are not in the admirable Sacrament of the Eucharist, but [are there] only during the use, whilst it is being taken, and not either before or after; and that, in the hosts, or consecrated par-

ticles, which are reserved, or which remain, after communion, the true Body of the Lord remaineth not; let him be anathema." (C. of Trent, Sess. 13, can. 4; see also no. 879 ff.) This canon is aimed at the teaching of Martin Luther. Jesus Christ, therefore, remains present under the appearances of bread and wine until they change, which, in the stomach of an ordinary man, takes about a quarter of an hour. A few writers hold that corruption ordinarily takes place in about one-half hour, but in certain stomachs it requires several hours. Some consideration should be given this opinion in cases of vomiting. (See no. 922.)

Some writers maintain, against St. Thomas, that if the species of wine were mixed with a large quantity of wine, it would undergo no essential change. Because of this opinion, priests should use more water than wine at the last ablution, in order that the chalice may be certainly purified.

887. Jesus Christ is not present in the Holy Eucharist in a natural way, as He is in Heaven, but *sacramentally,* in the manner explained in no. 885 ff. The accidents of the bread and wine do not inhere in the body of Christ, for this would be an imperfection in His adorable body. For the same reason, they are not sustained by this body, but, "inhering in no subject, they subsist in themselves," by the power of God. (Catechism of the Council of Trent.)

888. Some theologians maintain that the species must be adored together with the body of Christ, just as the royal purple is honored together with the king, whereas others maintain that they must not. The former opinion would seem to be the true one. When corruption sets in, a new substance succeeds that of the body of Christ, and this substance is probably the same as that which would be there if no consecration had taken place. According to St. Thomas, the species at the moment of consecration receive from God the power to become the subject of all the forms which fol-

low corruption, and, therefore, anything which could be produced by the substances of bread and wine, were these substances present, can be produced by the dimensive quantity of the bread and the wine, not by a new miracle, but in virtue of the miracle previously performed. (*S. Theol.*, 3a, q. 77, art. 5.)

After these preliminary considerations we proceed to discuss: (1) the Sacrament of the Holy Eucharist itself, (2) the minister, and (3) the subject.

CHAPTER I

THE SACRAMENT ITSELF

Art. I. Matter and Form.

889. *Matter and form of the Sacrament in fieri.*—The matter of the Holy Eucharist is twofold, according to the Decree for the Armenians, namely, *wheaten bread,* and *wine of the grape.* The obligation to use both bread and wine is so rigorous that, according to the teaching of all theologians, one would not be permitted to consecrate one species alone in order to bring the Holy Viaticum to a dying person. St. Alphonsus goes so far as to assert that this precept is of *divine right.* The common opinion of theologians, from which only a few writers dissent, is that not even the Pope could dispense from it. Moreover, several theologians affirm that the consecration would be invalid if a priest consecrated one species without having the intention of consecrating the other, because it is probable that the Sacrament cannot exist outside the sacrifice. Common opinion, however, holds that in such a case the consecration would be valid.

It is certain that the consecration of one species is valid if the consecration of the other is not purposely excluded, as would happen, for instance, if a priest were threatened with death and had to take to flight after consecrating the bread. On the other hand, if a priest were threatened with death in case he did not consecrate one species, or a species that was doubtful, he would not be permitted to do so. Canon 817 forbids, even in extreme cases of necessity, to consecrate one species without the other, or both outside of Holy Mass.

890. For validity the bread and the wine must be present and determined as required by the words of the form— "*hoc est.*" If, therefore, the two substances were over twenty steps away from the priest, the consecration would be invalid, or at least doubtful. It would be invalid also if the priest said: "I wish to consecrate one host out of these twenty," without specifying which one.

Before celebrating Mass, the priest will do well to formulate his intention of consecrating all the hosts lying before him on the corporal. However, this intention would not dissipate all doubt as to the validity of the consecration of a host which had escaped notice. If, after the consecration, he notices that he has consecrated two large hosts instead of one, he should consume both at the Communion. If he notices the presence of a second large host after the offertory, he should set it aside and consume it with the Precious Blood. The priest should not have the intention of consecrating drops of wine outside the chalice, as this would be grievously sinful. It matters little in practice whether he has or has not the intention of consecrating such drops adhering to the inside of the chalice.

The consecration of a closed ciborium or a covered chalice is certainly valid; but the consecration of a ciborium which is outside the corporal is doubtful, unless the priest formulates a specific intention to this effect before Mass. It is certainly invalid if the priest explicitly intends to consecrate only what is on the corporal. Hosts that have been doubtfully con-

secrated should be consumed after the first ablution. Some
theologians authorize the priest to consecrate them conditionally at the next Mass, but St. Alphonsus does not approve of this practice, except for a just cause.

If consecrated hosts are mingled with unconsecrated, they
should all be reconsecrated conditionally (*"si non sint con-
secratae."*)

891. The priest is permitted to consecrate hosts which are
brought to him at the altar before the Canon by a mental
offering. He could do so even after the beginning of the
Canon if several persons would be deprived of Communion
otherwise. If only one or two persons would be deprived, he
could distribute to them particles of the large host. It would
be a grievous sin to repeat the words of consecration over a
ciborium brought to the altar after the first consecration.
Care should be taken not to consecrate more hosts than are
required, to avoid the danger of corruption.

892. *The Bread.* For validity, the bread must be made of
wheaten flour and natural water. "We define," says the Council of Florence, "that the body of Our Lord is truly rendered
present by the consecration of wheaten bread, whether
leavened or unleavened, and that the priests must use the
one or the other according to their rite." (Denziger-Bannwart,
no. 692.)

Greek priests who are traveling in the West may probably use leavened or unleavened bread, according to their
good pleasure, in places where there is no church of their
rite. The same rule holds for priests of the Latin rite traveling in the East. *A fortiori* one may consecrate with leavened
bread in the East, in order to complete a sacrifice which
would otherwise remain incomplete. All writers are agreed
on this point, but aside from this case, it is not permitted
to consecrate with leavened bread in the West even for the
purpose of taking the Viaticum to a dying person. This is the

prevailing opinion of theologians, although some disagree. (See no. 911.)

893. It would be a grievous sin to use a host that is considerably mutilated or badly stained. If the stains or mutilations are but slight, the sin in turn is slight. A priest could even consecrate a seriously mutilated or stained host without committing any sin, if he noticed its condition only after the offertory, provided there were no danger of scandal. In churches of the Latin rite the hosts must be round, and that used by the celebrant larger than the others. In default of a large host, however, a priest who celebrates privately, or who has to say Mass on a feast day, may consecrate with a small host, provided there be no fear of scandal. (St. Alphonsus, 204, 205.) In default of small hosts, the priest may consecrate several large hosts and break them into pieces for distribution. Altar breads should not be more than fifteen days old, and at most one month. According to a decision of the S. Congregation of the Sacraments (Dec. 7th, 1918), it would be a serious abuse to use hosts over two or three months old, and if the pastor is neglectful in this respect, the other priests attached to the church may not follow his example.

894. *The Wine.* Only grape wine is valid matter for the Eucharist. If the wine is completely soured, corrupted, or made of unripe grapes, or if so great a quantity of water has been added to it that its substance is changed, the consecration is invalid. (Rub., tit. 4, n. 1.)

If, after the consecration, the priest doubts whether he has consecrated wine or vinegar, he should consecrate some real wine conditionally, if the doubt arises before he has consumed the host. If the doubt arises *after* he has consumed the host, he should take a new host with some wine, to which he has added a few drops of water, and begin again at the words: *"Qui pridie."* (See no. 948.) This is the safest course;

however, the rubrics allow a priest to consecrate only the wine (beginning with the words: *"Simili modo"*) if there is danger of scandal.

If all the wine were spilled after the consecration in a manner that would prevent the celebrant from receiving the Eucharist under this species; or if the celebrant clearly recalled having omitted (even culpably) the words of one of the forms, he should follow the same course as above, and, moreover, make an act of contrition if he was at fault.

If, after laying aside the sacred vestments, and within less than one hour after coming from the altar, the priest recalls that he did not consecrate the wine, he should, according to the safer opinion, from which several writers dissent, repeat the consecration, either by returning to the altar or by consecrating upon an altar stone in the sacristy.

If the priest should notice before Communion that both consecrations were invalid, in default of matter or form, he should repeat the consecration. If he notices his mistake only after Communion, he may leave the altar, or if a number of persons were deprived of Communion as a consequence of his mistake, he could reconsecrate the species.

895. If the wine is frozen, one would certainly not be permitted to consecrate it, but if one happened to consecrate it, the consecration should be considered valid, since there would be no probable reason for doubt.

If a priest consecrated musty wine which was becoming sour or bitter, or if he added no water whatsoever, or again if he added a small quantity of rose water, the consecration would be valid, but he would sin grievously. (Rub.)

In default of any other kind, a priest could use a wine which was not altogether sour, and in case of necessity he would even be permitted, according to several writers, to use wine that was already quite sour, provided it was still wine.

According to a decision of the S. Congregation of the Propaganda, a priest would be permitted to use wine made out of dry raisins, provided that its taste and color would indicate it to be real wine. These raisins should not be cooked, and care should be taken not to add too much water.

One would be permitted also to add to a very weak white wine a small quantity of alcohol (distilled from grapes rather than raisins), to prevent it from souring, provided the alcohol is mixed with the wine whilst the latter is fermenting, and that it be not added in a quantity exceeding twelve per cent.

Non-alcoholic wine is invalid matter for consecration.

Priests should exercise the utmost care in procuring the matter for the Holy Eucharist from reputable merchants, lest they celebrate Mass invalidly.

896. It is probable that Our Lord at the Last Supper consecrated wine to which He had added a small quantity of water, and the Church has ordained that a few drops of water be added to the wine in the chalice before the consecration. This precept is so binding that, in default of water, one would not be permitted to continue the Mass, except for fear of giving scandal, even though it were a question of bringing the Viaticum to a dying person. If, however, the priest has omitted to add water to the wine before the consecration, he should not do so afterwards.

The water added to the wine is symbolic of the union of the faithful with their spiritual head, Jesus Christ, and also reminds us that water and blood flowed from the heart of Our Divine Saviour on the cross.

One or two drops of water is all that is required, but the priest should be careful not to add more than one-fifth part water, unless the wine be very strong. Too much water might render the matter doubtful or even invalid. This water is changed into the body and blood of Christ—immediately, according to some, mediately, according to others, *i. e.*, after being changed into wine (Catechism of the Council of Trent.) Both opinions are regarded as probable by St. Alphonsus.

897. *The Form.* According to the Decree for the Armenians, the form of the Holy Eucharist consists in the words of Our Saviour, through which He Himself instituted the Sacrament. But it is not enough to pronounce these words *historically;* they must also be uttered *significatively, i. e.,* their signification or meaning must be applied to the matter present.

The words which Our Lord pronounced over the bread, *"Hoc est enim corpus meum,"* alone constitute the form of the first consecration, according to a common and very probable opinion. Therefore, if one said, *Hic est,* etc., using the word *hic* adverbially, the consecration would be invalid. St. Alphonsus is adverse to classifying as improbable the opinion which maintains that the form begins with the words: *"Qui pridie."* In cases where the consecration was invalid, the rubrics require that the priest re-begin with the words: *"Qui pridie."*

898. The same controversy exists touching the words: *"Simili modo,"* etc. The common opinion among theologians is that the essential form is wholly contained in the words: *"Hic est enim calix Sanguinis mei,"* while a probable opinion maintains that the words: *"Novi et aeterni Testamenti,"* which follow, also pertain to the essence of the Sacrament. If they have been omitted, therefore, the whole form should be repeated conditionally from the words *"Simili modo"* on. The words: *"Haec quotiescumque,"* etc., are *not* an essential part of the form.

The voluntary omission of the word *"enim"* would constitute a serious offense, according to several authors, and a priest would surely sin grievously if he added to the form, even though the words added did not change the meaning. A priest who does not remember whether he recited the *whole* form, is not obliged to repeat it; but a priest who entertains a serious doubt concerning the omission of essential words, must repeat the form conditionally.

899. Is it necessary for valid consecration that the one who pronounces the words of the form should hear himself pronounce them?

Most authors answer this question in the negative, but since the opinion of those who reply in the affirmative is probable, the safer course must be followed in practice. According to an answer issued by the Sacred Penitentiary, it is sufficient if the form is pronounced loud enough to be heard, even though, as a consequence of some foreign noise, or a defect of hearing, the priest did not actually hear them. In a case of this kind, a priest would be guilty of sin if he repeated the consecration.

900. Even though there are in the Holy Eucharist two matters and two forms, there is in reality but one Sacrament, because there is only one thing signified, namely, the spiritual nourishment of the soul.

Matter and form of the Sacrament in facto esse

All we have said so far touching the matter and form of the Eucharist, relates to the Sacrament *in fieri*. In regard to the Sacrament *in facto esse*, or the consecrated hosts, some theologians claim that the union of the species and the body of Jesus Christ is, as it were, the matter of the Sacrament, while the sacramental signification or the nourishment of the soul is, as it were, the form. Billot is of the opinion that the permanent matter of the permanent Sacrament is the species, and that the permanent form are the words of consecration, which, once pronounced, denominate the consecrated species and remain intentionally attached to them, somewhat like the words of the priest remain attached to the holy water he has blessed. And indeed, the species of the Sacrament signify the spiritual nourishment of our souls only because of the words of the consecration, which alone give us to understand that they contain the body and blood of Jesus Christ. The species thus consecrated by the form are, therefore, the *Sacrament alone,* while the body of Jesus Christ is both the *thing and the Sacrament.* (See no. 781.) This Sacrament is formally the same wherever the consecrated species are present, since it is everywhere the same body of Christ, but it is numerically multiple in proportion to the number of species separated by moral distance.

Art. II. Divine Institution.

901. It is certain that Christ instituted this Sacrament on the evening of the Last Supper. (See no. 769.) St. Thomas raises the question whether or not Our Lord administered Communion to Himself and answers in the affirmative. Our Lord set the example and then taught us to imitate it. (3a, q. 81, art. 1.)

Art. III. Effects of the Holy Eucharist.

902. The remission of mortal sins is neither the sole nor the principal effect of the Holy Eucharist. This is an article of faith, defined against Protestants by the Council of Trent (Sess. 13, can. 5), although one of the accidental effects of the Sacrament is the remission of these sins. (See no. 776.)

The Holy Eucharist remits venial sins. According to the more probable opinion it remits these sins mediately, *i. e.,* by means of the charity which it excites in the heart.

In the same manner, and *ex opere operato,* it remits the temporal punishments due to the just. It preserves from mortal sin. It gives an increase of grace and virtue. It establishes a closer union between the recipient on the one hand and Jesus Christ and His members on the other. It affords comfort and solace to the soul. It is a pledge of eternal life. It sanctifies the body by allaying concupiscence and gives it a claim to immortality. Experience proves that frequent Communion is the most effective means of triumphing over the passions.

903. The Sacrament produces its effects as soon as it is taken, *i. e.*, in passing from the mouth to the stomach. For this reason the sacred Host should not be kept in the mouth, but swallowed as quickly as possible. Were the species to undergo a substantial change while in the mouth, it is commonly held that, morally speaking, one would not have received the Sacrament. It is probable, too, that communion under both species, or with a large host, is productive of greater grace than communion under one species or with a small host, because this Sacrament produces its effects after the manner of food. (See no. 912.) A person who receives sacrilegiously, but makes an act of contrition before the species change their nature, probably receives the effect of the Sacrament, which, according to sound opinion, persists as long as the species are not corrupted.

Holy Communion offered up for others does not produce its effect for these others *ex opere operato,* although it is certain that it can profit both the living and the dead *ex opere operantis,* by way of impetration and satisfaction.

CHAPTER II

THE MINISTER OF THE HOLY EUCHARIST

We shall speak first of the minister and secondly of his duties.

Art. I. The Minister.

We must distinguish between the minister who consecrates the Holy Eucharist and the minister who dispenses it to the faithful.

904. The minister who consecrates the Holy Eucharist must be a priest. This is *of faith*. "If any one saith, that by those words, *Do this for the commemoration of me* (Luke 22, 19), Christ did not institute the apostles priests; or did not ordain that they and other priests should offer His own body and blood; let him be anathema." (C. of Trent, Sess. 22, can. 2.)

If several priests consecrate the same matter together they consecrate validly; and newly ordained priests who celebrate their first Mass together with the consecrating bishop, may, according to a number of theologians, accept a stipend for this Mass. They must take care, however, to complete the form at the same time as the bishop, and especially not to utter it before the bishop does so, otherwise the latter would not consecrate. Before the consecration of the chalice they should take care not to have the intention of consecrating the wine if they did not consecrate the bread, otherwise the sacrifice would be incomplete.

A blind priest may not celebrate Mass without a special indult from the Holy See.

905. The ordinary minister who dispenses the Holy Eucharist is also the priest, and any priest who has permission to celebrate Mass in a church is presumed to have permission to dispense the Holy Eucharist to the faithful. Strange priests may administer Holy Communion even outside of Mass, provided they have at least the presumed permission of the pastor or rector of the church.

906. Holy Communion should be brought to the sick publicly, unless good reasons make private administration

advisable. (Can. 847.) The right and duty to carry Holy Communion publicly to the sick, even to non-parishioners in the parish, belongs to the pastor. Other priests may do so only in case of necessity or with the at least presumed permission of the pastor or the Ordinary. (Can. 848.)

For a just and reasonable cause any priest may bring Holy Communion to the sick privately with the at least presumed permission of the priest to whom the custody of the Blessed Sacrament is entrusted. A just and reasonable cause would be fear of irreverence, but other inconveniences could also be accounted as such. A decree of the Sacred Congregation of the Sacraments, January 3rd, 1928, reserves to the bishop the right to declare whether or not there is a just and reasonable cause for carrying Communion to the sick privately, but he should take care not to lay down general regulations that would deprive the sick of the benefit of the Sacrament.

A person in good health must not receive Holy Communion in a private house where Communion is brought to some one who is sick. The case would be different if the bishop had given his permission to celebrate Mass in such a house.

When Holy Communion is carried to the sick, the greatest reverence and respect must attend its ministration. The priest should wear a white stole and hang the burse over his breast. He should also choose a Catholic companion, and both should observe strict silence and concern themselves with nothing else.

The superior of a religious house of clerics, the confessor in a convent of religious, strictly so called, or his substitute, and the pastor or his assistant in the religious houses of brotherhoods, have the right and the duty to carry the Holy Viaticum to any and all sick persons who dwell day and night in these houses. The bishop may exempt such institutions from the jurisdiction of the pastor. The reader is referred to no. 926 for the pastor's rights in regard to First Communion.

907. Pastors should realize the importance of the duty incumbent upon them to prepare children for their first Holy Communion. The most efficacious means is to give them the opportunity of frequent confession, as soon as they are able to offend God. In this way they will shield them against impurity and render them fit receptacles for Our Lord Jesus Christ when He comes into their hearts the first time. In both parishes and religious institutions it is important to have the children make a short retreat in preparation for this great event. The pastor should see to it at this time that the children are provided with an extraordinary confessor.

No bishop may forbid a priest to admit to the Sacred Table a child who is under age, but who, in the judgment of the pastor, is sufficiently instructed and prepared. (See no. 2996.) There is a grave obligation for all pastors, and at least a duty of charity for all other persons, to seek out children who have reached or passed the required age limit for admittance to Holy Communion, but who have failed to give this matter due thought.

908. The *extraordinary* minister of distribution is the deacon, given the permission of the Ordinary or the pastor. This permission must not be granted except for a grave reason and in case of necessity. It may, however, be presumed. In case of necessity, the deacon is *obliged* to administer Communion, and St. Alphonsus deems it probable that, under such circumstances, a layman (and *a fortiori* an ordinary cleric) could administer Communion to himself and to others. It is expedient also to follow this opinion if the dying person has only attrition and can receive neither absolution nor Extreme Unction, for in this case Holy Communion becomes the indispensable means of enabling him to pass from

attrition to contrition. The minister of the Sacrament in this case should, however, take care to excite the penitent to an act of perfect contrition.

It is probable also that a priest and a deacon may administer Communion to themselves in default of any other minister, if they were to risk being deprived from Communion for a length of time. Some writers hold that a priest may administer Communion to himself as an act of devotion.

In case of urgent necessity, when no priest of another rite is to be had, a priest of the Oriental rite may administer Holy Communion to the faithful of the Latin rite, and *vice versa*. In this case each priest is to observe the ceremonies proper to his own rite. (Can. 851.) The faithful of either rite may even receive Holy Communion out of devotion either in fermented or unfermented bread.

The Viaticum must be received in one's own rite, but in cases of urgent necessity it is lawful to receive it in any rite. The faithful are to be advised, however, that each should receive Easter Communion in his own rite. (Can. 866.)

Art. II. Duties of the Minister.

909. *In Consecrating.* (See no. 787 ff.) For *validity*, it is required to have the virtual intention of consecrating a specified matter present before him. (See no. 890.) Priests do well to renew their intention every day before celebrating Mass.

For *liceity*, the priest must be fasting (see no. 938) and free from censure and non-confessed mortal sin. (See no. 798.) Moreover, he must consecrate with attention (see no. 802) in a place designated by the canons, a matter placed on the corporal and on an altar stone. The last condition obliges *sub gravi*. Finally, the matter must be uncovered and offered to God at least mentally before the Canon. (See no. 890.)

910. *In Administering the Holy Eucharist.* For *liceity*, he

must, according to the more probable opinion, be in the state of grace. Some writers do not require this condition for liceity, because to administer Communion is not *conficere sacramentum*. Communion is only the *conditio sine qua non* of the effect of the Holy Eucharist. All writers agree that it is not necessary to confess even a mortal sin before administering Communion—supposing, of course, that the minister has perfect contrition. (See no. 798.)

The minister must be free from censure, but a priest whose excommunication has not been inflicted by condemnatory or declaratory sentence, neither sins nor incurs irregularity in administering Communion when requested to do so by the faithful.

911. It is not necessary to administer Holy Communion under both species. This has been defined as *of faith* against Hus and the Protestants by the Council of Trent (Sess. 21, canons 1 and 3.) It follows from what we have said in no. 885. Jesus Christ is whole and entire under each species.

912. There is a grave ecclesiastical precept to administer Holy Communion only under the species of bread to laymen and clerics who do not consecrate, and it is *of faith* that the Church has made no mistake in requiring this practice. (*Ibid.*, can. 2.) According to common opinion, to which very few would take exception, Holy Communion may not be administered without sin to a dying person who is unable to swallow the host. In a case of this kind a small part of the host may and should be dissolved in a little water or wine, and the sick person made to swallow it. However, a layman may and should consume the species of wine if he fears profanation, and the Code makes no restriction concerning the reception of Holy Communion, even from devotion, under both species in another rite.

The hosts used should be whole and entire. However, for a slight reason the small hosts may be divided, and even a fragment of the large host used by the celebrant may be given to the laity. It is forbidden, under pain of venial sin, to give several hosts or a larger one than is customary, to foster some special devotion. The case would be different were the purpose to renew the supply of consecrated hosts.

913. How should the Holy Eucharist be administered? With the thumb and the index finger. If the minister is unable to make use of these two fingers, he may not, under pain of venial sin, administer Communion except for a sufficient reason.

Some writers authorize the practice whereby the plague-stricken administer Communion to themselves by taking the host on a clean piece of paper, which is then burned.

The rules and regulations laid down by the Roman Ritual must be followed minutely. They vary according as Communion is administered in church or carried to the sick. A priest would sin grievously if, outside of necessity, he administered Communion without any sacred vestment, and venially if he administered it without a white stole or a stole of the color of the day. During, and immediately after or before Mass, Holy Communion may be administered with the vestments used at Mass, even though they be black. During the Paschal season, when Holy Communion is administered with black vestments outside the Mass, the alleluia must be omitted. Opinion is divided on the question whether another priest may distribute Communion to the faithful with a ciborium which the celebrant has just consecrated, before the latter has himself received.

914. It is forbidden under pain of venial sin to transfer the Holy Eucharist from one altar to another without donning any sacred vestment, and to administer Communion without a lighted candle or a stole, or without reciting the *Confiteor*. Communion may be given without an altar boy and with only one lighted candle. A woman must not recite

the responses, and if no one else be present, the priest is to answer all the prayers himself. In administering Communion to nuns, the priest should be turned towards them when he recites the *Misereatur* and the *Ecce Agnus Dei*, but he should first give Communion to the servers, and then from left to right along the Communion rail, passing each time before the center of the altar. The verse and the oration after Communion are of precept, as well as the antiphon *O sacrum convivium*. When Communion is administered immediately before or after Mass, the priest should give the blessing, except it be a Mass of *Requiem*.

In distributing Communion during Mass the priest must not withdraw so far that he loses the altar entirely from view.

915. The regulations for the ministration of Communion to the sick are found in the Roman Ritual. In cases of necessity, Communion may be carried to the houses of the sick without the use of any sacred vestments, save a small white stole, but the ciborium or the pyx should never be entrusted to a layman. In order not to frighten the sick, the priest may recite the words *"Accipe viaticum"* in a low tone of voice; these words are not absolutely indispensable. After Communion, the priest may either give the ablutions to the sick person, or cast them into the fire, or bring them back and pour them into the sacrarium. It is never permitted to bring the Holy Eucharist to a sick person unable to receive it, and for the sole purpose of veneration.

A deacon who administers Holy Communion in case of necessity, must follow exactly the rite prescribed for priests, using the stole peculiar to his office. But he must omit the blessing at the end, though he may bless the assistants with the Blessed Sacrament.

916. If, when Communion is given to the faithful, one of the hosts falls inside a woman's clothing, she should extract

it and give it back to the priest. If it falls on the ground or on the altar cloth, the place should be noted and afterwards carefully washed. The obligation of washing the place is slight, if it be a question of the sacred host, but grave if it be a question of the Precious Blood. If the host falls on the beard or the clothing of any one, there is nothing to do but to pick it up. If the Precious Blood is spilled, the priest should do his best to recover the same by wringing the cloth or carefully licking the spot. The obligation of washing the spot afterwards binds *sub gravi*.

917. To whom must the Holy Eucharist be administered? Priests engaged in the work of the sacred ministry are obliged by reason of their functions, and if they are salaried, by an obligation of justice, to administer Communion to their charges every time the latter reasonably request it. Refusal can easily become matter of grievous sin, except when Communion is requested by public sinners or idiots. The Holy Eucharist should not be refused to a secret sinner who requests it publicly.

If, after bringing the Viaticum to a dying person, the priest finds that he is not properly disposed, he should try to persuade him to declare before the people of the house that he does not wish to receive Communion. If the sick person refuses to do this, the priest should give him Communion. To avoid such an inconvenience, the priest would do well to bring Communion only after hearing the sick man's confession, unless it is imperative for him to act otherwise. It is not proper to carry Communion to immoral women in the place where they ply their trade. Neither is it permissible to administer Communion to persons who have lost consciousness in the very act of sin, unless they give signs of repentance. (See, however, no. 930.)

Is a priest bound to administer Communion to the plague-stricken? Some answer this question in the affirmative, others reply that he is bound to administer only Baptism and Penance. Both opinions are probable, but a devout priest will follow the former, at least in practice. A pastor is even obliged to seek out the sick in his parish who do not ask for Communion, in order to minister to their needs.

918. When may Communion be administered? Canon 867 permits the distribution of Communion on every day of the year, except Good Friday, when it may be given only in the form of Holy Viaticum. On Holy Saturday, Communion cannot be given to the people except in the Mass of the day, or immediately after the Mass is finished. Holy Communion is to be distributed only during those hours of the day when the celebration of Holy Mass is allowed. According to canon 846, a priest may distribute Holy Communion in the Mass, that is, immediately after the communion of the celebrant, and also immediately after or before a privately celebrated Mass. Holy Communion should not be distributed at an altar where the Blessed Sacrament is exposed, except in case of necessity or by reason of an Apostolic indult. A reasonable cause is required to administer Communion after dusk, and during the night it may be administered only in the form of Holy Viaticum. In religious communities it is permitted to administer Holy Communion shortly after midnight to persons who are unable to fast.

919. Where may Communion be administered? To the sick in their houses, and to others in the places designated in no. 906 f.

920. *Reservation of the Holy Eucharist.* If there is a person in charge and a priest says Mass at least once a week in the place, the Holy Eucharist must be preserved (1) in the cathedral church; (2) in the principal church of an abbey or prelacy *nullius,* a vicariate or prefecture apostolic; (3) in all parochial or quasi-parochial churches, as well as

in all churches attached to houses of exempt religious men and women.

With the permission of the Ordinary, it may be kept: (1) in collegiate churches; (2) in the principal, public or semi-public oratories of religious houses and charitable institutions; as also (3) in ecclesiastical colleges in charge of either diocesan clergy or religious.

In other churches and oratories it may be kept only by indult of the Holy See. The Ordinary may for a good reason grant this permission to a church or public oratory for a special occasion, but not permanently. (Can. 1265.)

Churches in which the Blessed Sacrament is kept, especially parochial churches, should be open to the faithful for at least a few hours each day. (Can. 1266.)

In religious houses or pious institutions the Blessed Sacrament may not be kept except in the church or principal oratory, and in the monasteries of nuns with solemn vows it may not be kept inside the choir or enclosure. All privileges to the contrary have been revoked. (Can. 1267.)

The Blessed Sacrament may not be kept on more than one altar of a church, and as a rule this should be the main altar. In cathedral, collegiate, and conventual churches, in which choral functions are conducted at the main altar, it is more convenient not to keep the Blessed Sacrament on the main altar, so that the latter may be free for pontifical functions.

The Blessed Sacrament must be kept in an immovable tabernacle, placed in the middle of the altar. The tabernacle should be well constructed, securely closed, free from all other objects, and well guarded, so as to prevent all danger of profanation. Unless the tabernacle be of marble, or of some other more precious material, it is fitting that the outside of it be gilded. If the inside is not gilded, it should be neatly hung with white silk. The tabernacle should be covered with a white canopy, or a canopy of the color of the day. At Masses for the dead, the canopy should be violet.

The hosts for distribution among the faithful should be kept in a ciborium of solid and becoming material. This ciborium must be blessed, clean, well enclosed, and covered with a veil of white silk. (Can. 1270.)

The tabernacle should also be blessed and contain a corporal upon which to place the ciborium. Nothing must rest on the tabernacle except the cross, and nothing must ever be placed in front of the tabernacle for the veneration of the faithful. The tabernacle door must be left open when the Blessed Sacrament is not there.

Before the tabernacle at least one lamp should burn day and night, fed with either olive oil or bees' wax. Where olive oil is not easily obtainable, the bishop may allow the use of other, preferably vegetable, oils. (Can. 1271.) In case of necessity he may even allow the use of an electric light. (S. C. R., Feb. 23rd, 1916.) It would be a serious fault to allow the "perpetual light" to remain extinguished for a period of twenty-four hours.

Sleeping apartments should not be located above the room wherein the Holy Eucharist is kept.

For a grave reason, and with the approval of the bishop, it is lawful to remove the Blessed Sacrament from the tabernacle over night, and keep it in a safe and decent place, on a corporal, with a light burning before it.

The key of the tabernacle in which the Blessed Sacrament is kept must be carefully guarded; this duty binds the conscience of the priest who has charge of the sanctuary under pain of grievous sin. (Can. 1269.)

921. *When is it allowed to expose the Blessed Sacrament?* Canon 1274 distinguishes between *private* exposition, with

the ciborium, and *public* exposition, with the ostensorium. In churches and oratories that have permission to preserve the Blessed Sacrament, the former kind of exposition may be held for any good reason, with the permission of the Ordinary. Public exposition may be held in all churches on the feast of Corpus Christi and during the octave, both at Mass and at Vespers. At all other times public exposition may be held only for good and sufficient reasons and with the permission of the Ordinary. This permission is required even in churches of exempt regulars.

The minister of exposition and reposition is either the priest or the deacon, but the priest alone can give benediction with the Blessed Sacrament. The deacon is allowed to do so only when he takes the Viaticum to the sick.

During the exposition of the Blessed Sacrament some worshippers should always be present in church.

During public or solemn exposition twelve wax candles must be lighted, and during private exposition, six. It is lawful to add stearine candles to this number. (Decrees of the S. C. R., Sept. 16th, 1843, and Sept. 4th, 1875.)

No relic or image should be exposed on the altar during the exposition of the Blessed Sacrament.

According to a decision of the S. C. R., of Feb. 4th, 1871, the host must not touch the glass in the pyx.

It is not against the spirit of the Church to expose the Blessed Sacrament frequently, provided it is always done with due reverence.

The clergy should not fail to admonish the faithful, both by word and example, to make frequent visits to the Blessed Sacrament.

According to several decisions issued by the S. C. R. it is not lawful to use gas or electric light instead of, or in addition to, the wax candles prescribed by the rubrics, for the sole purpose of adding splendor to the ceremony, no matter whether these lights are on the table of the altar, on the tier above the table, or on the inside or the outside of the repository.

922. What is to be done with hosts or particles of hosts that are found? If a layman finds such particles, he should immediately inform some priest. If no priest is available, the finder should place the particles on a clean piece of paper by means of a pin and keep them in a safe and decent place until he is able to find a priest.

If a priest finds a host that is certainly consecrated, but not corrupted, he should consume it before the ablutions or give it to some communicant. If it is doubtfully consecrated or doubtfully corrupted, he should consume it before the ablutions. If, in the two preceding cases, the host is so soiled that the priest would become nauseated if he tried to consume it, he should place it in the tabernacle until it becomes totally corrupted and then destroy it.

If he finds small particles left over from the sacrifice which he has just offered, he may consume them before and even after the ablutions, or even in the sacristy, if he has not yet removed his vestments. If he has removed his vestments, he may enclose the particles in the tabernacle or entrust them to a priest who is to celebrate Mass after him. If neither of these courses of action is feasible, he may consume the particles himself.

If particles are left over from a Mass other than his own, he may consume them only before the ablutions. Only the fear of grave inconvenience would warrant him in consuming them while not fasting.

If a sick person rejects the sacred species, they should be gathered into some suitable vessel and destroyed when they have become totally corrupted. If the sick person vomits them up with other food, the whole should be gathered by means of pads of cotton or similar material, burned, and the ashes poured into the sacrarium.

923. When must the sacred species be renewed? Every eight, or at least every fifteen, days. A priest who would fail to renew them at the risk of their becoming corrupted, would sin grievously, and one who, in renewing them, would leave hosts or particles in the ciborium at the risk of their becoming stale, would not entirely escape fault. The old hosts should be consumed before the ablutions. In purifying the ciborium, a priest may either empty the particles into the chalice or pour wine into the ciborium, then transfer the contents to the chalice and consume it.

CHAPTER III

THE SUBJECT OF THE HOLY EUCHARIST

Who is the subject of the Holy Eucharist? What obligation has he of receiving this Sacrament, and what dispositions must he bring to its reception?

Art. I. Who is the Subject?

924. Only those who have been baptized may receive the Eucharist *sacramentally, i. e.,* as a Sacrament. That the reception of the Eucharist may certainly be a Sacrament, it must be received after the manner of food or drink, but probably it would suffice to introduce the sacred species by means of an instrument into the stomach of one who could not receive them in any other way. However, this manner of administering Communion is not obligatory, except perhaps in the case of a dying person who could receive no other Sacrament. It is lawful to use this method as long as there is no law against it.

Infidels can receive the Eucharist only *materially,* as he would do who consumed a host which he thought unconsecrated, but which in reality was consecrated.

Properly disposed Catholics receive the Eucharist both sacramentally and spiritually, *i. e.,* they receive at once the Sacrament and the effects of the Sacrament, whereas sinners receive the Sacrament, but not its effects.

Art. II. What Obligation is There to Receive the Holy Eucharist?

925. It is certain that there exists an obligation *of divine right* at least for adults to receive the Holy Eucharist. Children who have not yet reached the age of reason, are forbidden to receive the Sacrament, even though it is capable of producing grace in their souls. It is even forbidden *sub gravi* to administer it to them in the form of Holy Viaticum, but when they have reached the age of reason, even though they be only seven years old, there is a grave obligation to administer it to them as Viaticum. And because the obligation to receive Communion is of divine right, the priest should administer it to children who have reached the age of reason, even though they are not yet seven years old. (See no. 2010.) Communion may be administered to them also in case of doubt.

The divine precept obliges *in articulo mortis,* unless because of delirium or for some other serious reason, a person is unable to receive. The obligation exists also when death is imminent, either as a consequence of sickness, or by reason of a conflict, or a perilous journey. (See no. 1404.) The precept obliges *per accidens* also when, *e. g.,* the Holy Eucharist is the only means of overcoming great temptations. Those who comply with the ecclesiastical precept of receiving Communion at Easter time sufficiently fulfill the divine precept, and those who fail to receive it in times of great temptations do not sin against the precept of receiving the Holy Eucharist, but against the particular virtue which is exposed to danger. By divine precept also, only priests who celebrate Mass have to receive Communion under both species. (See no. 912.)

926. There exists, by ecclesiastical precept, an obligation binding all the faithful who have reached the age of reason to receive Communion once a year at Easter time.

Taking its inspiration from the decree *"Quam singulari"* of August 8th, 1910, and a few older documents, the Code enumerates some rules governing the First Communion of children (canon 854):

1) Children who, on account of their age, have not yet a knowledge of, nor a desire for, this Sacrament, should not be given Communion.

2) In danger of death, Holy Communion may be administered to young children, if they know enough to distinguish the Holy Eucharist from ordinary bread, and reverently adore it.

3) Outside the case of danger of death a more comprehensive knowledge of Christian doctrine and a more careful preparation are required. The children must know, to the extent of their ability, at least those mysteries of the faith which are necessary as means of salvation, and they must approach Holy Communion with as much devotion as may be expected at their age.

4) The confessor of the children as well as their parents, or those who take the place of the parents, are to judge whether the children are sufficiently disposed.

5) It is the duty of the pastor to see to it that children do not approach the Sacred Table before they have attained the use of reason or acquired the proper dispositions. But he should also see to it that the children who have attained the use of reason and are sufficiently instructed are strengthened

as soon as possible by this divine food. (Can. 854.) The law presumes (can. 88) that a child has the use of reason when fully seven years of age.

927. The ordinary period set aside for the Easter Communion extends from Palm Sunday to Quasimodo, inclusively. Ordinaries may make exceptions to this rule in favor of both persons and places, but in no case may the period begin before the first Sunday in Lent or extend beyond the feast of the Blessed Trinity.

The faithful should be advised to make their Easter duty in their own parish church, and those who have done so in another church, are advised to inform their pastor of the fact. If for any reason one has not made his Easter duty within the prescribed time, he is bound by the precept until he does so. (Can. 859.) The duty to see to it that children below the age of puberty make their Easter duty rests with those who are responsible for them, *i. e.*, the parents, guardians, confessors, teachers and pastor. (Can. 860.)

Canon 861 calls attention to the fact that the precept of receiving the Holy Eucharist is not satisfied by a sacrilegious Communion. However, if a dying person were to receive the Holy Viaticum in the state of mortal sin, it would be better in our opinion to leave him in good faith than to inform him of his obligation to receive Communion again, if it could easily be foreseen that he would not comply with the demand. In danger of death, no matter from what cause this danger arises, the faithful are bound by the precept of receiving Holy Communion. (Can. 864.) A person who has already received the Holy Viaticum in the same dangerous illness, and relapses into grievous sin, need only confess his fault and is not obliged to receive communion again. One who has received the day before he became dangerously ill, must receive again; those who have received the same day, are strongly advised to receive again, if they become seriously ill in the course of the same day. (Can. 864.) While the danger of death lasts, the Holy Viaticum may, according to the judgment of the confessor, be administered repeatedly for several days, but not several times the same day. It should not be deferred too long, and those who have the care of souls should see to it that the sick receive it before becoming unconscious. (Can. 865.)

928. Is Communion necessary for salvation by necessity of means? No, and this is *certain* for all the faithful and *of faith* for children, according to the words of the Council of Trent (Sess. 21, can. 4.) Is the desire to receive this Sacrament necessary as a means of salvation for adults? Some theologians reply in the negative, others more probably affirm that at least an implicit desire is necessary.

929. Should Communion be administered to persons who are subject to coughing spells? Yes, if the cough is not violent enough to prevent the recipient from swallowing the host. Persons who vomit should be made to wait one or two hours, given a little food, and if they are able to retain it, be permitted to receive Communion. If there is doubt whether or not they are able to retain the Host, they should not be given Communion. (See no. 922.)

930. Communion should not be administered, even in the form of Holy Viaticum, to those who have never had the use of reason.

Insane, delirious, obsessed or epileptic persons who have lucid moments, may be given Communion during these intervals; but they should never be allowed to receive while subject to attacks. Persons who have lost the use of reason after having possessed it, should be given Communion if they have led a Christian life, unless it is certain that they lost the use of reason in the act of committing a mortal sin. The same rule is to be followed in regard to those who have lost the use of their senses, provided they are able to swallow

the host without danger of irreverence. According to Lehmkuhl, Communion may be administered even to those who
became unconscious in the act of mortal sin, if they are
unable to receive any other Sacrament; according to a regulation of Propaganda, it should be administered to any one
who is reputed worthy of absolution.

931. Holy Communion must be administered to semi-
idiots as well as to the deaf and dumb, when it is of precept,
provided they are able to distinguish the Eucharist from
ordinary bread; it may be administered more often, if they
exhibit greater lucidity. Communion may be administered to
the deaf, dumb and blind if they have the use of reason and
can be instructed sufficiently, as is possible at the present day.

932. In regard to condemned criminals the custom of the
locality in which one lives should be followed, but the practice of administering Communion to them would seem to
be more in keeping with Christian mercy and piety. St. Alphonsus contends that they should be allowed to receive,
even though not fasting, if it is impossible to defer the time
of their execution.

Art. III. Dispositions of Soul and Body.

933. The dispositions of soul required partly concern
sacramental, partly spiritual Communion. Those required
for frequent Communion differ from those required for ordinary Communion.

For ordinary Communion faith does not suffice. "If any
one saith, that faith alone is a sufficient preparation for receiving the Sacrament of the most Holy Eucharist; let him
be anathema." (C. of Trent, Sess. 13, can. 11.)

The state of grace is also required, or at least one must
prudently believe himself to be in the state of grace. Without
this disposition, Communion would be sacrilegious. A person
whose conscience is burdened with one mortal sin, com-

mitted since his last confession, may not receive, even though he have perfect contrition, but must have recourse to the Sacrament of Penance, unless it be difficult for him to find a confessor or to approach him, and at the same time he is obliged to receive. A person would not be justified in such a course of action simply because his ordinary confessor was not available. Any duly authorized priest, *qui non sit complex in materia turpi,* is an available confessor.

A feast, an indulgence to be gained, a Mass promised for some special intention, or mere devotion, are not sufficient reasons for celebrating Mass in the state of mortal sin. The obligation to receive or administer the Holy Viaticum, serious danger to one's reputation if one did not celebrate or fulfill one's Easter duty, the duty to complete an incomplete sacrifice, and, according to a probable opinion, to fulfill one's Easter duty, would constitute sufficient reasons. A priest, therefore, who could not neglect to celebrate without giving scandal, or, according to several writers, without causing his parishioners to miss Mass on a holyday of obligation, would be permitted to say Mass after making an act of perfect contrition. The foregoing regulation does not apply to one who is not a parish priest.

A priest who has begun Mass and who, after the first consecration, recalls a grievous sin committed since his last confession, or one who commits a mortal sin after the consecration, may continue with the Mass after exciting himself to contrition. But if a priest has sinned grievously before the consecration, he should have recourse to the Sacrament of Penance, or leave the altar, if he can do so without fear of scandal or serious detriment to his reputation. If he had sins reserved to the pope, he should go to confession; if he had sins reserved to the bishop, he should comply with the regulations laid down in no. 1282.

A layman who recalls some grievous sin committed since

his last confession when he is already at the altar rail, may receive Communion, if it is impossible for him to withdraw without seriously impairing his reputation. However, he should make an act of contrition if he has the time.

According to several theologians, a person in the state of mortal sin would be permitted to consume the sacred species in an effort to save them from profanation.

A priest who receives under these conditions is bound by ecclesiastical precept to go to confession *as soon as possible, i. e.,* within three days, supposing that he does not have to receive before that time. If he has to receive before the three days, he is obliged by divine right to go to confession first. "He who would communicate," says the Council of Trent, "ought to recall to mind the precept of the Apostle: 'Let a man prove himself.' Now ecclesiastical usage declares that necessary proof to be, that no one conscious of mortal sin, how contrite soever he may seem to himself, ought to approach the sacred Eucharist without previous sacramental confession." (C. of Trent, Sess. 13, ch. 7.)

The duty of going to confession *as soon as possible* may become binding immediately, as, for instance, if a confessor happened along and one foresaw that another might not be available for some time to come.

According to common opinion, a sacrilegious celebration of the Holy Sacrifice, without necessity or with necessity but without confession when the latter was possible, does not render sacramental confession obligatory *as soon as possible,* unless one were obliged to celebrate or receive again. The obligation does exist, if in case of necessity and in default of a confessor, a priest celebrated Mass without having previously made an act of contrition.

934. A doubtful mortal sin does not oblige one to have recourse to sacramental confession before receiving Holy Communion. According to a few authors, a person whose

conscience is burdened with such a sin, would be obliged to make an act of perfect contrition; according to others it suffices that he is probably in the state of grace. In all cases of this kind, confession should be recommended to those whose conscience is lax. A mortal sin, involuntarily forgotten in confession, does not prevent one from receiving or celebrating, nor does it render sacramental confession obligatory as soon as possible. Inclination toward venial sin does not deprive one of all the effects of Holy Communion, although it does tend to diminish them.

935. According to the decree *"Quam singulari,"* freedom from mortal sin and the right intention give one the right to receive Holy Communion every day. It is not necessary to perform the penance imposed in confession before receiving. However, since attachment to venial sin tends to diminish the principal effect of the Holy Eucharist in the soul, we should do our best to rid ourselves of it. Canon 863 suggests that the faithful be admonished according to the decrees of the Holy See to receive the Eucharistic bread frequently, nay, even daily.

936. *Frequent Communion.* By frequent communion we are not to understand weekly Communion, but Communion several times a week. "The sacred and holy Synod would fain indeed that, at each mass, the faithful who are present should communicate, not only in spiritual desire, but also by the sacramental participation of the Eucharist." (C. of Trent, Sess. 22, ch. 6.)

"It will, therefore, be the duty of the pastor," says the Catechism of the Council of Trent, "frequently to admonish the faithful that as they deem it necessary to give daily nutriment to the body, they should also be solicitous to feed and nourish the soul every day with this heavenly food." St. Alphonsus de' Liguori, following the Council of Milan, denounces persons who go about preaching against frequent Communion as slanderers. The confessor alone is to judge whether or not a person (even a nun) should receive daily. Pious communicants should be urged to spend some time in thanksgiving, and the confessor should set a good example in this respect.

937. *Spiritual Communion.* Spiritual Communion is nothing else but a pious desire to be united with Jesus Christ. It should be recommended to the faithful, especially when they assist at Mass and make visits to the Blessed Sacrament, because they can derive many spiritual advantages from this practice. They can receive spiritual Communion every day, everywhere, and at every hour of the day, but especially each time they assist at Mass. To receive spiritual Communion it is enough to perform the same acts one would perform in receiving sacramentally, *i. e.,* acts of contrition, humility, faith, desire, and love; and then to make an act of thanksgiving, just as if one had really received.

938. *Dispositions of the body.* The natural fast requires that the recipient abstain from everything in the nature of food or drink, even in small quantities, from the previous midnight. This precept obliges under pain of mortal sin and is traceable to early Apostolic ordinances. One is permitted, but not obliged, to follow any clock, even though it may not be correct.

The fast is broken: (1) if something is swallowed that comes from outside; (2) if it is taken in the form of food or drink, and not in the form of saliva or respiration; (3) if it can be considered as food or drink and is susceptible of being assimilated by the stomach.

939. Small particles of food which cling to the teeth do not break the fast if swallowed involuntarily. If swallowed voluntarily, some theologians hold that they break the fast, while

others teach that they do not. The Catechism of the Council of Trent does not make this distinction, but simply says that they do not break the fast.

If a person voluntarily swallowed a few drops of some liquid he was tasting, the fast would be broken. It would not be broken if, against his intention, he swallowed a small quantity together with the saliva. The fast is not broken by particles of tobacco dust inhaled through the nose, by tobacco smoke, or even by tobacco juice, when the latter is involuntarily swallowed together with the saliva. A person who is in doubt as to whether or not he has taken some food before or after midnight, should not hesitate to receive Holy Communion. One who, because of dry mouth, is obliged to take a little water or liquid in order to swallow the host, does not break the fast, even though he swallows a few drops of the liquid before swallowing the host. Hence, Communion may be administered to a sick person in a little water or wine. One is not forbidden to take food or drink immediately after receiving, although it is better to wait a little while. One is allowed to spit, provided no portion of the host remains in the mouth. (See no. 912.)

940. One is permitted to receive Communion without fasting:

a) In probable danger of death, no matter from what cause the danger arises. Communion may, therefore, be administered to a criminal condemned to death, and every day to a sick person in danger of death, even though they be not fasting. A priest may celebrate Mass after breaking his fast, if he be required to do so under pain of death, provided the threat to kill is not made in contempt of religion.

b) If the Holy Eucharist is exposed to destruction or profanation, in which case even a layman may consume it.

c) If scandal would arise through the omission of Mass or Communion. In cases where no scandal arises and no serious dissatisfaction is expressed by the congregation, the fact that the people would otherwise miss Sunday Mass would not be a sufficient reason. If there were danger of scandal, a priest who, before consecration, remembered that he was not fasting, could go on with the Mass. If he remembered the fact after the consecration, he *must* go on.

d) If it is necessary to complete an incomplete sacrifice.

e) Probably also if it is necessary to administer the Holy Viaticum to a dying person, and, according to common opinion, if it is necessary to administer it to oneself, and, finally, according to several writers, to escape death when neither scandal nor contempt for the faith are to be feared. One would also be obliged to celebrate Mass when not fasting in order to administer the Holy Viaticum to a person incapable of receiving any of the other Sacraments.

f) Communion may also be administered to converts who have tasted of the salt in Baptism. (S. C. of the P., 1806.)

941. *The outward appearance of the body.* No blemish or mark on the body can render a Communion bad. Nevertheless, obvious stains or marks should be removed whenever possible, and if they are to disappear shortly, one should refrain for that length of time from receiving, unless forced to do so by some special reason. The faithful should approach the Sacred Table with modesty and reverence. Communion should be refused to women whose dress is scandalous, for instance, if they would come to the rail *denudatis omnino uberibus.* On the other hand, the poor should be encouraged to receive without fear, even though they are poorly clad, provided they are clean. Soldiers should lay aside their arms, and priests are bound at least to wear a stole.

942. *Pollutio nocturna, si est involuntaria, nec sacrum nec communionem sequente die impedit; imo, de consilio confessarii, nec pollutio voluntaria et quodcumque peccatum*

mortale, absolutione secuta. Nec amplius valent quae the-
ologi olim de tempore menstrui vel purgationis aut de debito
conjugali sentiebant. Haec omnia judicanda sunt ad normam
decreti "Quam singulari."

Canon 858 states that the sick who have been confined
to their bed for a month without certain hope of a speedy
recovery, may, if the confessor deems it prudent, receive
Holy Communion once or twice a week, even though they
have taken medicine or some liquid food. By liquid food we
understand anything which is drunk, even though it be taken
in the form of food, such as milk, coffee, chocolate, tea, raw
(but not cooked) eggs, flour mixed with water or some other
liquid, but still in the state of a beverage. It is the common
teaching of theologians that those who have made lawful use
of this privilege may receive several times more during the
week if they are willing to observe the law of fasting on
these occasions. And those who have observed this law do
not thereby lose the right to receive once or twice without
fasting. By the sick we are to understand here not only those
who are bedfast, but also those who cannot lie in bed, or who
rise from their bed occasionally.

Sick persons who are not obliged to take to their beds or
stay in their room, and who are unable to keep the fast, are
not included in this privilege, except perhaps when they
make their Easter duty. Permission for them to use this
privilege must be specially obtained from the Holy See.
If necessary, Holy Communion may be administered to such
persons shortly after midnight. Benedict XV has explicitly
stated that the Holy See is ready to grant to Ordinaries the
faculty to dispense from the fast sickly priests who are
obliged to binate. Priests who are obliged to travel a considerable distance between two Masses may also avail themselves of this dispensation by applying to the Ordinary. An
important letter from the Holy Office, dated March 22nd,

1923, explains the conditions under which Ordinaries may grant this dispensation to priests who have to binate or say Mass at late hours, and gives them the necessary powers for all urgent cases. (*Acta S. Sedis*, X, V, 151–152.) Priests who are dispensed from fasting for the second Mass, may take the ablutions at the first. (*Ibid.*, 585.)

PART TWO

THE EUCHARIST AS A SACRIFICE

943. As a sacrifice, the Eucharist consists in the sacrificial act. This act is transient, and therefore differs from the Sacrament, which is permanent. Moreover, the sacrifice requires the presence of two species, is intended for the masses of the people, and has for the primary purpose of its existence the worship of God. The Sacrament, on the other hand, is whole and entire under each species, has for the principal reason of its existence the sanctification of souls, and operates *ex opere operato* only in the recipient.

The sacrifice of the Holy Eucharist usually goes under the name of Mass. This name has been assigned to the sacrifice either because Jesus Christ, who is immolated on the altar, is the victim *sent* (*missus*) into the world by the Father, or because formerly the deacon at the dismissal of the catechumens said: "*Ite missa est.*"

In the following two chapters we shall treat, first, of the sacrifice itself, and, secondly, of the minister of the sacrifice.

CHAPTER I

THE SACRIFICE ITSELF

We shall deal: (1) with the existence of the sacrifice; (2) with its nature and essence; (3) with its efficacy.

944. *Existence.* Sacrifice in general is the oblation of a sensible gift, which is destroyed, or at least subjected to an appropriate transformation, by an authorized minister, in recognition of God's supreme dominion over the human race. (See no. 633.) St. Thomas teaches that, just as natural reason apprises us of the duty to offer sensible objects to an earthly lord or master in recognition of his authority, so the same reason reminds us of the necessity of offering up to God sensible gifts in recognition of the honor and submission which are His due. (*S. Theol.,* 2a 2ae, q. 85, art. 1.)

Sacrifices have always existed, both under the natural and the Mosaic laws. Sacrifices, must, therefore, exist also under the New Law. The Holy Eucharist is the sacrifice of the New Law. This is *of faith,* against Protestants. "We have an altar, whereof they have no power to eat who serve the tabernacle." (Heb. 13, 10.) "If any one saith, that in the Mass a true and proper sacrifice is not offered to God; or, that to be offered is nothing else but that Christ is given us to eat; let him be anathema." (C. of Trent, Sess. 22, can. 1.) All religious rites have had their sacrifices, and sacrifice pertains to the natural law; how then could the only true religion be without a sacrifice?

945. *Nature and essence of sacrifice.* The sacrifice of the Mass is the same as that of the Cross. "It is one and the same victim, it is the same person who offered Himself on the Cross, who now offers Himself through the ministry of the priests." (C. of Trent, Sess. 16, ch. 17.) The differences between these two sacrifices are only accidental. On the Cross, Our Lord offered Himself *immediately* and in a bloody manner; on the altar, He offers Himself *mediately* through the ministry of the priests, in an unbloody manner. On the Cross, He merited; on the altar, He applies His merits. The sacrifice of the altar differs also from that of the Last Supper, in that on the altar Jesus Christ is impassible and immortal,

whereas at the Last Supper He was passible and mortal. Again, on the altar He offers to His Father also His mystical body, which is the Church.

946. Some Catholic authors maintain that the sacrifice of the Mass is merely a commemoration of that of the Cross, and relative to it, *i. e.*, that Jesus Christ, really present on the altar, represents thereon, in a living manner, the sacrifice of the Cross which He offered for the same purposes as any sacrifice is offered. Others more probably maintain that the sacrifice of the Mass is all these things, but that over and above that, it is really and truly an *absolute* sacrifice, because in a sense the victim really undergoes destruction. The body of Our Lord is present on the altar in such a way that it cannot carry on the ordinary functions of a human body. As a matter of fact, it can be put to uses very different from those of the body, since it is assumed in the form of food. The change effected in the body of Christ, therefore, is more notable than that which took place in sacrifices where wine was poured out in libations. Moreover, the sacramental separation of the body and blood of Christ is a kind of mystical immolation, which gives Him the appearance of being in the state of death.

947. The sacrifice of the Mass has all the qualities of the ancient sacrifices. Some of them were *latreutic,* their purpose being to render homage and worship to God and recognize His supreme dominion over all things; others *eucharistic,* or offered up in thanksgiving; others *propitiatory,* or offered up in expiation of sin; and, finally, others *impetratory, i. e.,* intended to obtain favors.

It is *of faith,* from the words of the Council of Trent, that "the sacrifice of the Mass is not only a sacrifice of praise and thanksgiving, but that it is also impetratory and propitiatory for both the living and the dead." It is the means by which the merits and satisfactions of the Passion of Christ are applied to our souls, and since it is latreutic, it can be offered to God alone. However, the Council adds: "If any one saith, that it is an imposture to celebrate masses in honor of the saints, and for obtaining their intercession with God, as the Church intends; let him be anathema." (Sess. 22, can. 5.)

948. In the act of sacrifice certain elements are integral, in the sense that without them the sacrifice exists, although in an imperfect manner, whilst others are essential, in the sense that without them there is no sacrifice.

Opinions are divided as to which elements are essential to a sacrifice. Some writers place the essence of sacrifice in the offering or oblation, which is probably only one of the integral parts. By this offering some understand the oblation which is made at the offertory, others, with more reason, that which is made after the consecration in conjunction with the words: *"Unde et memores."* Hurter and many other theologians maintain that this opinion is obsolete and erroneous.

Others place the essence of the sacrifice in the Communion of the priest, but it is more probable that Communion is but an integral part.

Others more probably assert that the consecration alone is essential; some among them contending that the consecration of only one species suffices, while others, more commonly and more probably, aver that both consecrations are essential.

Therefore, if one of the two matters were missing before the consecration, the priest could not continue with the Mass, but if he noticed its absence after the consecration, he should have the other matter brought to him. If the missing matter could not be found, or if it could not be procured within the space of one hour, the priest should proceed with the Mass, in order not to inconvenience the congregation, and omit all the signs to be made over the missing matter. If, after taking the two species, the priest should notice that one or even both were doubtful (without being certainly invalid), he should immediately consecrate both species conditionally, using the formula: *"If this be necessary to complete the sacrifice."* If the priest had consecrated the wine in an absolute manner, and the first consecration, although doubtful for the celebrant, was valid in the eyes of God, this new sacrifice would be incomplete.

Finally, a fourth opinion, which is the safest of all, and which must, therefore, be followed in practice, asserts that both consecrations and Communion are essential parts of the sacrifice of the Mass. If, therefore, a priest should die after one or other of the consecrations, another priest should take up where he left off. (See nos, 977, 979, 1026 ff.) The Communion indeed is necessary to effect the change which the followers of the third opinion deem sufficient without Communion, because the words of the consecration separate the body from the blood of Christ.

According to the fourth opinion, therefore, the priest must receive with the same species which he consecrated at the Mass, and this rule holds even in regard to the host. A priest, therefore, unless he be in danger of death, is never permitted to consecrate one species without the other, even to give the Holy Viaticum.

From what we have said in no. 789, it is manifest that the action of the minister, who consecrates with the at least virtual intention of doing what the Church does, is also essential to the sacrifice.

949. *The efficacy of the sacrifice of the Mass.* The sacrifice of the Mass, like that of the Cross, has an infinite intrinsic value, both for the honor of God and for the sanctification of men. But the intrinsic value or efficacy which the Holy Sacrifice derives from the dignity of Jesus Christ considered both as priest and victim is quite different from the

fruit or blessings which God bestows upon men as a consequence of the Mass and which differ from the intrinsic value of the sacrifice as the effect differs from its cause.

While acknowledging that the intrinsic value of the Mass is infinite, a few theologians hold that, in its application *ex opere operato,* it is limited by the will of God. The *common* opinion, however, denies such a limitation, holding that even the extrinsic value of the Mass is infinite. This extrinsic value is infinite both in an *intensive* manner, for each individual to whom it is applied, and in an *extensive* manner, in such wise that when the Sacrifice is offered for several, it benefits each one of them as much as if it were offered for him alone. Accordingly, the only limitations that can be placed on the value of the Mass are those caused by the individual's own, more or less perfect dispositions, or his ability to apply it to his soul.

950. There is question here, of course, only of the effects produced *ex opere operato* by the sacrifice, in virtue of the merits of Jesus Christ, and not of the effects *ex opere operantis* or the prayers of the Church and the devotion of the celebrant. These last effects are manifestly limited, and hence the Church forbids a priest under pain of mortal sin to celebrate only one Mass for several stipends received. Moreover, the opinion that a Mass said for several benefits each one individually in the same manner, is not certain. In strict justice, therefore, a priest may not apply to several persons a Mass he has agreed to offer for one, unless he does so on this condition: If it is in no way detrimental to the person who furnished the stipend. However, a priest may apply to several persons Masses for which he has received no stipend, or even those which he is obliged to celebrate by reason of some gratuitous promise, or out of obedience to a superior or to the constitutions of his Order. (See no. 966.)

If a priest celebrated Mass in the state of mortal sin, the *ex opere operato* effects of the Mass would be the same, as would also the effect of the prayers of the Church, unless the celebrant were excommunicated by name, for the Church is always agreeable to God.

951. *Division of the fruits of the Mass.* If the fruit of the Mass is considered in relation to those to whom it is applied, it is divided into general, less general, special, and very special. The *general* fruit is that which is applied in every Mass to all the faithful living and dead, and for the salvation of the whole world. The *less general* fruit benefits principally those who serve or assist at Mass, according to their dispositions. This fruit does not decrease in proportion to the increase in the number of persons assisting. The *special fruit* of the Mass is that derived by those for whom the Mass is offered, and it is a doctrine *bordering on faith* that the priest may offer the sacrifice for certain specified persons, so that they alone gain this special fruit. Finally, the *very special* fruit goes to the celebrant. It is not certain that he may apply this fruit to others, but it *is* certain that he cannot demand a stipend for applying it.

952. If the fruit of the Mass is considered in the ends which it attains, it is divided into latreutic, eucharistic, expiatory, and impetratory. The *latreutic* and *eucharistic* effects of the Mass are produced infallibly and immediately.

As for the *expiatory* effect: the Mass does not pay to God the price of our redemption, but it applies to us the price that was paid on the Cross.

a) The Mass does not *immediately* remit mortal or venial sins, although it may remit them *mediately* by obtaining for the persons guilty of them the grace of conversion.

b) The Mass immediately remits the punishment due to forgiven sins only in the just, whether living or deceased, and it does this infallibly, *ex opere operato;* but in the living it remits them according to their dispositions, and in the dead, according to the good pleasure of God.

c) The Mass averts plagues, calamities, public and private evils, but especially spiritual punishments, which are far more to be dreaded, and which God inflicts for sin committed and unatoned for.

Catholic piety attributes special efficacy to the Gregorian Masses, in the matter of delivering some particular soul from Purgatory. These thirty Masses must be said on thirty consecutive days for the same soul. Some theologians hold that an involuntary interruption would not make it necessary for the celebrant to begin the series over again, especially if he is able to make up for any deficiency by indulgences gained at a privileged altar. It is certain that the three last days of Holy Week would not interrupt the Gregorian Masses. A decision of the S. Congregation of Indulgences declares that the thirty Masses need not be said by one and the same priest nor at the same altar. The Gregorian Masses may be offered for the dead only.

953. The *impetratory* effect. The Mass does not immediately and infallibly produce an increase in sanctifying grace, nor does it immediately and infallibly produce all spiritual blessings. The reason is that men may place an obstacle in the way of these blessings or graces. But in those for whom the Mass is said it immediately and infallibly produces a certain number of actual graces.

It obtains temporal blessings immediately, but not infallibly. The Mass obtains graces after the manner of a prayer *ex opere operato,* in virtue of the supplications of Jesus Christ, though some theologians deny the *ex opere operato* part of this statement.

To obtain a grace infallibly through the Mass two conditions are required: perseverance and that the things be proper and useful to salvation. Consequently, one should not hesitate to have several Masses said to obtain the same grace. The Mass also obtains graces *ex opere operantis* because of the prayers of the Church and of the celebrant, if he is worthy.

Which is the more useful: to assist at Mass, or to have a Mass said? This question cannot be answered with precision. If one is in the state of grace and wishes to obtain some spiritual favor for himself, it will be more to his advantage devoutly to assist at Mass; but for the deceased the application of the special fruit of the Mass is more effective. The satisfactory and the impetratory fruit of the Mass can be of benefit to all the souls of Purgatory, but it is not certain that the expiatory fruit benefits infallibly and *ex opere operato* persons who died without Baptism and were justified by perfect charity.

CHAPTER II

THE MINISTER OF THE SACRIFICE

954. The principal minister of the Mass is Jesus Christ. This is an article of faith. "Jesus Christ offers through the ministry of His priests," says the Council of Trent.

Strictly speaking, the priest alone is the secondary minister. (See no. 104.) It is *certain* and *bordering on faith*, that the faithful who assist at Mass are not, strictly speaking, priests. It is only in an improper sense that they may be given this name, because they supply the offering or give the stipends, and because the priest, as a public minister, acts in their name.

We must treat here of the obligation of priests in regard to the Mass. First, we shall deal with the celebration of Mass; and, secondly, with the application of its fruits.

Art. I. The Celebration of Mass.

We shall speak first of the obligation to celebrate Mass, and, secondly, of the circumstances attendant upon the celebration.

955. *The obligation to celebrate.* Is the priest obliged by divine law, and under pain of grievous sin, to celebrate Mass at least now and then? Some theologians answer this question in the negative, on condition that such a priest would give no scandal. But since omission to say Mass would almost invariably cause scandal, their opinion is of little value in practice. A priest who failed to say Mass for a whole year would seriously scandalize persons who had knowledge of the fact. Unless there were attenuating circumstances justifying his action, the people would readily suspect that he was in a state of sin, led a disorderly life, or had no respect for his office. The majority of theologians reply in the affirmative.

The divine law does not specify how many times a year a priest should say Mass, but in our opinion a priest would be guilty of venial sin whenever he neglected to say Mass out of sheer laziness.

956. The ecclesiastical law, as formulated in canon 805, obliges every priest to say Mass several times a year. By the same canon, the bishop or the religious superior must see to it that the priests under their charge say Mass at least on all Sundays and holydays of obligation. It is *of faith,* that Masses in which the priest alone receives Communion are licit.

957 *By reason of his functions.* By divine law, pastors who hold their office by *divine institution,* are certainly obliged to celebrate Mass now and then for their people. It is not certain that the same holds true for pastors who hold their office by purely *ecclesiastical institution.* By *ecclesiasti-*

cal law all pastors in charge of souls are obliged to say Mass for their congregation on all Sundays and holydays of obligation, even though suppressed. These days are: Christmas, New Year, Epiphany, Easter, with the Monday and Tuesday following the feast, Ascension, Pentecost, the Monday and Tuesday after Pentecost, Corpus Christi, the Finding of the Holy Cross, the Purification, Annunciation, Assumption, and Nativity of the Blessed Virgin Mary, the Dedication of St. Michael, the Nativity of St. John the Baptist, all the Feasts of the Apostles, St. Stephen proto-martyr, the Holy Innocents, St. Lawrence, St. Sylvester, St. Joseph (March 19th), St. Anne, All Saints, the Patron of the country or locality, the Immaculate Conception. These Masses must be said for the people, and the special fruits applied to them.

The following are obliged to say Mass for the people on these days: Diocesan bishops, capitulary vicars, abbots or other prelates who have charge of a certain territory, secular and regular pastors, and those who take their place.

Vicars Apostolic, Prefects Apostolic and quasi-pastors, are obliged to celebrate Mass for their congregation at least on Christmas, Epiphany, Easter, Ascension, Pentecost, Corpus Christi, Assumption, Immaculate Conception, St. Joseph, the Feast of SS. Peter and Paul and All Saints.

It is doubtful if priests are obliged to celebrate for the people on these days, whose parishes have not been canonically erected, and who minister independently to Catholics scattered throughout non-Catholic localities.

With the exception of diocesan bishops, all pastors must celebrate Mass for their people in their own parish churches. If a holyday of obligation is transferred, the obligation to celebrate Mass for the people is also transferred, when such a transfer affects both the divine Office and the Mass, as also when it carries with it the duty to assist at Mass and abstain from servile work. In all other cases the obligation is not transferred. If a pastor has either culpably or inculpably failed to celebrate Mass for the people on a prescribed day, he should offer another for the same intention at his earliest convenience. The circumstance of time and place obliges *sub gravi*. A priest would be guilty at most of venial sin, however, if he failed occasionally to comply with this regulation, or if he had a sound reason for acting otherwise. A pastor who is legitimately absent from his church, may fulfill the obligation either himself or by proxy. Priests in charge of two or more parishes are obliged to say only one Mass for them all.

958. Titular bishops are not obliged, but urged, to offer the Holy Sacrifice from time to time for their dioceses. By *ecclesiastical law* religious superiors are not obliged to say Mass for their subjects, although by divine law they are in duty bound to pray for and to offer the Mass for them. It is not certain, however, that they are obliged to apply to them the special fruit of the Mass.

959. *By reason of the stipend received*. St. Paul says that the laborer is worthy of his hire. Even a wealthy priest, therefore, may receive a legitimate stipend for the Masses he says. This stipend is not to be regarded as the price of the Mass, but as a means of subsistence afforded the priest. It is probable that a priest who celebrates merely because of the stipend he receives is not guilty of simony, although he is certainly lacking in piety.

960. The Church has always shown the greatest concern in seeing to it that Masses for which the faithful have made an offering are duly said. Besides the encyclical *"Quanta cura,"* issued by Benedict XIV, eight decrees of the S. C. C. regulate this matter. These decrees are still in force, in spite of the more recent legislation of the Code, as may be gathered from the second, third, and fourth sections of canon 6. However, some of the penalties inflicted upon transgressors

have in some cases been abrogated (can. 6, §5.) The Code has about the same things to say in regard to this matter as the decree *"Ut ubi"* issued by the Sacred Congregation of the Council, May 11th, 1904, and the decree *"Ut ubi"* merely repeated, confirmed, and specified more exactly regulations that had been observed throughout the centuries. According to ecclesiastical regulations, the obligation to celebrate Mass for stipends received binds under pain of mortal sin.

The Code distinguishes between *manual Masses,* for which the faithful offer stipends, as it were with their own hands (*manus*), out of devotion, or from some obligation; and quasi-manual Masses or Masses *ad instar manualium,* for which foundation stipends cannot be applied in the church where they were made, or not by those who should say them, and which may by law be given to other priests to say; and *foundation Masses,* for which a fund has been established. (Can. 827.)

961. Any kind of negotiations or trading with Mass stipends is strictly forbidden; one would not even be permitted to enter into such trading to the extent of accepting Masses. Even the appearance of commercialism must be avoided. The decree *"Ut ubi"* forbids one to give stipends to others, even priests, who will not say the Masses or have them said by others.

In the matter of manual or quasi-manual Masses one is forbidden to separate the stipend from the celebration, or to diminish or change it in any fashion. A priest would not, therefore, be permitted to solicit Masses, and then have them said by other priests and use the stipends for some other purpose, even though it were a pious cause.

It is not permitted to give Mass stipends to newspaper publishers, booksellers, or dealers in ecclesiastical goods, no matter how pious their institutions or how conscientious their personnel may be. There is nothing, however, to prevent one from making an offering in the form of books or other articles for Masses said at one's own expense and for one's own intentions, provided the practice does not become habitual and all appearance of trafficking is avoided. On the other hand, it is not permitted to withhold a certain amount from stipends received and give the balance together with the intentions to some other priest, no matter how worthy the cause for which the subtracted amount is intended.

There are, however, exceptions even to this last rule. One would be the case of a priest who willingly, and without being asked, consented to part with a portion of the stipend; another, that of a priest who, in transferring Mass intentions, retains the portion of the offering which is in excess of the amount stipulated by the diocese, when it is plainly evident that this amount was meant as a personal gift to him. In the case of Masses *ad instar manualium,* the amount in excess may be retained, if such was the clear intention of the founder, or if, in the intention of the founder, some institution or work of charity was to be benefited by the excess. The Ordinary may not forbid priests to accept stipends over and above the amount stipulated by the diocese, if such stipends are freely made, but he may forbid priests to accept any below this amount. And yet, even in this last case, it would be permissible to return to the poor a portion or the whole offering in the form of an alms.

It is the duty of the Ordinary to determine the amount of the stipend, and it is preferable that he do so in diocesan synod. Both the secular and regular clergy must conform to his regulations, and the obligation binds *sub gravi.* A priest who exacts a higher stipend is guilty of an injustice and bound to restitution, although he does not commit simony. Regulations regarding Mass stipends made by the Ordinary seem to regard only those Masses offered by his subjects.

If he has made no regulations, the priests should abide by the custom and traditions of the locality.

The executor of a will is not permitted to have Masses left by the deceased celebrated in a locality where the diocesan tax is less and appropriate the balance to his personal needs, but the heir who has the obligation of seeing that the Masses are said, may give them to any priest, if the place and the tax have not been designated. Administrators of churches who give Mass intentions to priests desiring to celebrate Mass, are not permitted to deduct from the stipend the amount necessary to defray expenses; on the other hand, they are not obliged to permit a priest to say Mass who is not willing to meet these expenses. Canon 1303 states that if a church is very poor, the Ordinary may permit a moderate fee to be levied on priests who say Mass there.

Bishops are no longer permitted to use a portion of the stipends received in extraordinary quantities at famous shrines to defray the expense of decorating these shrines.

Concina would not hold a priest guilty of mortal sin who exchanged an intention, retaining the amount in excess of the stipulated stipend. Noldin and others would excuse him if he had a good reason for acting thus, and if his action did not cause serious annoyance to the donor. As an habitual practice such a course of action is forbidden.

If a pastor has some other priest celebrate a nuptial or funeral Mass for which he has received a larger stipend, he may retain the amount in excess, unless it was offered because of the singing or some other extraordinary feature.

962. A priest is not permitted to take two stipends, one for the celebration of the Mass, the other for the special fruit attached to the Mass, unless it is certain that the donor requested only the celebration and not the special fruit. A priest is also forbidden to accept more than one stipend for

the same Mass, or a stipend for a Mass he is required to celebrate. Neither is he permitted to celebrate Masses in advance for stipends he may receive later.

If a person gives a sum of money for an indeterminate number of Masses, the number to be said should be determined by the diocesan tax, unless it is known that the donor intended otherwise. A priest is obliged *sub gravi* to celebrate as many Masses as he has received stipends, even though these stipends are less than the amount prescribed by the diocese. He would not be obliged *sub gravi* to celebrate all the Masses if he happened to notice that the stipend was far below that amount. A priest who does not celebrate as many Masses as he has received stipends, sins grievously against justice, and if the sum he has thus appropriated is considerable, he is bound *sub gravi* to make restitution.

A priest may celebrate Mass only once a day, but for a grave reason, the Ordinary may permit bination. He may not permit him, however, to accept a stipend for each Mass, nor even for one of them, if the other is to be said *pro populo*. A priest who offends against this regulation sins grievously, although it is not certain that he is bound to restitution.

Because of extra efforts concerning time or locality a priest may ask for something over and above the diocesan tax. This rule applies also to the second Mass in bination and to the second and third Mass on the second of November. The decree of the Sacred Congregation of the Council of Oct. 15, 1915, forbidding one to receive some compensation from an extrinsic title on the occasion of the second or third Mass on All Souls' Day, has been abrogated by the New Code. (Can. 824.) This has been expressly stated by the President of the Pontifical Commission for the interpretation of the New Code, issued Dec. 13, 1923. It is still forbidden to receive more than one stipend for several Masses said on the same day, except on Christmas. In some dioceses, however, in virtue of an indult of the Holy See, a priest may receive a stipend even for the second Mass in case of bination, except on Nov. 2, but the stipend must be sent to the Ordinary and applied to the needs of the seminary.

It is not forbidden to offer a second Mass, for which one cannot receive a stipend, for an intention prescribed by some society to which one belongs. An obligation of justice cannot be fulfilled by the second Mass of bination, either by oneself or by another.

The person who gives the stipend is supposed to want only the application of the special fruit of the Mass. If, however, he should specify certain circumstances of time, place, or kind of a Mass, the priest must fulfill these conditions once he has accepted them, especially if he would cause serious annoyance to the donor by not doing so. The loss of a stipend does not release one from the obligation of saying the Mass.

963. A priest who has a number of Masses which he is free to give to others, may give them to any priest he wishes, provided he has moral certainty that that priest is trustworthy. Unless he is in the possession of an indult to that effect, the Ordinary may not forbid priests to send Masses which they are allowed to give to others outside the diocese. (Can. 838; also S. C. C., Feb. 19, 1921.) He who transmits Masses to others must not deduct anything from the stipends, not even if they exceed the diocesan tax, unless it is certain that what was offered above the usual stipend was intended as a personal gift. A priest who retains part of such a stipend is bound to make restitution to the priest who says the Masses. (Can. 840.) When sending away Masses, one may always deduct the expense entailed in sending them. The obligation to say Masses sent to another priest, ceases

upon receiving the latter's acknowledgment. A written attestation that the Masses have been said is no longer required.

A priest who transmits Masses to others must send them without delay, and this obligation becomes binding from the moment the others accept the Masses.

All Mass intentions for churches of the Oriental rite must pass through the Sacred Congregation of the Propaganda, or through the Apostolic delegates, and should be accompanied by a note indicating the number of Masses and stipends. They may also be forwarded through any prelate with ordinary jurisdiction.

If a priest receives a definite sum of money for services rendered, say, at a funeral, or during a triduum, etc., with the request to offer one or two Masses at his convenience, he may give these Masses to another priest, and remit to him only the ordinary diocesan tax.

The Church has the right to reduce and even completely to abolish the stipends for Masses, supplying them from her spiritual treasury. Reduction of the number of Masses is in order when, by reason of the times, the revenue from foundations becomes insufficient for all the Masses stipulated. The reduction of Masses is, however, reserved to the Pope, unless the founder has conceded this right also to the Ordinary. Noldin is of the opinion that the bishop may, without an Apostolic indult, reduce the number of Masses to the diocesan tax, if an insufficient legacy has not yet been accepted. Other theologians do not agree with him, basing their opinion on a decree of the S. C. C. The complete annulment of Masses is also reserved to the Holy See, in which case the Church declares the obligation to say the Masses no longer binding, making up for the deficiency out of her own spiritual treasury. Ordinarily, the Church grants such a favor to a priest who has not said and cannot say all the

Masses which he has accepted and who has not the means to supply the deficiency. Petitions for the reduction of Masses should be addressed to the Sacred Congregation of the Council; petitions for their abolition, to the Sacred Penitentiary.

964. A priest may be obliged to say Mass by reason of a simple benefice, in which case he must say Mass every day, or on a certain number of days of the year, according to the stipulations of the foundation. These Masses are called "perpetual foundation Masses." Perhaps the founder had nothing more in mind than to have a certain number of Masses said each year, or it was his obvious intention that the people be given the opportunity to hear Mass on certain days. The simple beneficiary is bound in justice to say the number of Masses stipulated, and he is obliged *sub gravi* to respect any other conditions laid down by the founder in regard to the kind of Mass, as well as the time and place of their celebration. In a word, he must respect all the conditions which the founder laid down for serious reasons. The bishop may dispense from these conditions only in cases where the reason for their existence has ceased.

The beneficiary should obtain a list of the foundation Masses and hang it up in a conspicuous place as a constant reminder. As a rule the beneficiary is not obliged to say the Masses himself, but if this condition is stipulated by the founder, the obligation is grave. He would not be guilty of mortal sin, however, unless he would make it a habit of requesting others to say the Masses without sufficient reason.

At times the intention of the founder is not indicated, in which case the Masses must be said for his presumed intention. If the beneficiary who is bound to say Mass every day, does not have to celebrate all the Masses himself, he may not omit any one of them, but must have those which he cannot say himself said by another. On the other hand, if he is obliged to say all the Masses himself, he may omit celebrating from time to time for a sufficient reason without obtaining a substitute. According to ecclesiastical legislation such a sufficient reason would be a short illness lasting not more than fifteen days. A lengthier illness would not dispense him from the obligation of obtaining a substitute, unless the beneficiary is without means of subsistence and has been ordained *titulo beneficii*.

The annual clergy retreat dispenses from such an obligation. A beneficiary who must apply the Mass for the founder on holydays, must also celebrate Mass for his intention on suppressed holydays.

965. Local Ordinaries and superiors of religious orders may require their subjects to celebrate Mass and apply the fruits of their intention. Conventual Masses in cathedral and collegiate churches as well as in the churches of religious who are obliged to recite the office in choir, are instances in point.

966. A priest who seriously promises to say a Mass gratis, is obliged *sub levi* to apply its special fruit for him to whom the promise was made. He would be obliged *sub gravi*, if he intended to bind himself *sub gravi*, or if he had taken upon himself to fulfill a grave obligation which was binding upon another. A priest who has doubtfully consecrated is obliged to offer another Mass for the same intention. (See, however, no. 2710.) Wedding Masses, and Requiem Masses *praesente corpore*, do not require that the special fruit be applied to the person or persons in question, except when one has received a stipend. There are certain days on which Requiem Masses are not permitted unless the special fruit is applied to the deceased person whose funeral is being held.

967. The omission of certain ceremonies in the celebration of Mass does not entail the obligation of making restitution, unless it were the explicit will of the donor that these be

carried out. If the priest accepted this obligation together with the stipend, he would be obliged *sub levi,* or *sub gravi,* according to the case, to make up for his deficiency. If there were no way in which he could do this, he might be obliged to offer a second Mass conformably to the conditions agreed upon.

A priest who says a Mass other than the one requested, is, generally speaking, guilty of venial sin, but since every Mass is substantially the same, he is not bound to make restitution. And if he has a good reason for saying another Mass, he probably does not commit any sin at all. If, on the other hand, the rubrics permit a votive Mass, and a person made an offering for a Mass in honor of some special saint or mystery, explicitly asking that the votive Mass be said, a priest would hardly be justified in saying the Mass of the day. A priest satisfies his obligation of offering Mass for the dead by saying the Mass of the day, unless the donor explicitly requested a Requiem Mass. If a priest has received an intention with the explicit request that the Mass be said at a privileged altar, he cannot fulfill his obligation by offering the Mass at an ordinary altar unless he is in possession of a personal privilege in this respect. But if he has failed to fulfill this condition in good faith, he may, according to a Roman decree, make up for the deficiency by gaining the same number of indulgences by some other prayers. Generally speaking, however, an ordinary plenary indulgence is not equal to the indulgence gained at a privileged altar, so that a priest would not be permitted to suit himself in this regard.

According to a decree of the Holy Office, Feb. 20, 1913, it is no longer required to say a Requiem Mass, or in default of this, the Mass of the feria or vigil, with the oration for the deceased, in order to gain the indulgence of a privileged altar. It suffices to say the Mass of the day, or, if the rubrics permit, a votive Mass, with the intention of gaining the indulgence. Noldin is of the opinion that, in the regulations concerning the time when Masses are to be said, the distinction between Masses for the living and Masses for the dead, even those recently deceased, need no longer be made.

968. To allow one month to pass before saying a Mass for which a definite date was set, would be a mortal sin according to the common opinion of theologians. The executor of a will who, in this capacity, must see to it that a certain number of Masses are said for the intentions of the deceased, may give these Masses to whomsoever he pleases within the space of one year, provided nothing in the will of the testator and no canonical prescription is opposed to this course of action. Once this period has elapsed, he must send the intentions to the Ordinary of the diocese.

969. Here are some of the regulations of the New Code of Canon Law regarding the time within which Masses must be said:

1. If a day has been specified by the donor, Mass must absolutely be said on that day.

2. If the donor specified no time for saying the Masses, the priest may say them at a convenient time.

3. Masses requested for an urgent cause must be said as soon as possible, and a priest who neglects to say them within the *tempus utile* is bound to restitution, even though he celebrates them later.

4. In all other cases the time accorded for saying manual Masses is measured by the larger or smaller number of stipends received. Authors are generally agreed in allowing one month for saying one Mass, two months for twenty Masses, three months for forty, etc., always supposing that the stipends were all given by the same person.

5. If the donor of the stipend expressly left the time for

saying the Masses to the judgment of the priest, he may say them at his convenience. (Can. 834.)

Canon 835 forbids a priest to accept more Masses for himself than he can say within a year. This canon does not apply to a priest who receives more Masses than he could possibly say within a year from the same person, because it is evidently the intention of the donor that he take more time to fulfill his obligation.

In churches where stipends for Masses are offered in such numbers that it is impossible to say all of them in that church within the required time, the faithful should be notified by a notice conspicuously posted that the Masses will be said either in that church, if convenient, or elsewhere. (Can. 836.)

970. All who, for any reason, are obliged to attend to the saying of Masses for which stipends have been offered, whether they be clerics or laymen, must at the end of each year send to their Ordinaries the stipends which they have not yet satisfied, according to the manner to be specified by the Ordinary.

This rule is to be understood in such a way that, for quasi-manual Masses, the obligation of sending them to the Ordinary begins with the end of the year during which they should have been said; and for manual stipends, one year from the day on which they were received, unless the donors intended it otherwise. (Can. 841.)

The right and the duty to see to it that the obligation of Mass stipends is carried out in secular churches belongs to the Ordinary, and in churches of religious, to their superiors. (Can. 842.)

Rectors of churches and other pious places, both secular and regular, in which Mass stipends are usually received, must keep a book in which they accurately enter the number, intention, amount of stipends, and the celebration of the

Masses received. The Ordinaries are obliged to inspect these books at least once a year, either in person or through some one else. (Can. 843.)

Ordinaries of dioceses and religious superiors who give Masses to their subjects or to others to say, must enter these Masses together with the amount of the alms in a special book in the order in which they receive them, and see to it that these Masses are said as soon as possible. Every priest, whether secular or regular, must keep an accurate record of the Mass intentions which he receives.

971. *The circumstances attending the celebration of Mass. The time.* Holy Mass may be celebrated on all days except the three last days of Holy Week. On Holy Thursday, only one Mass is permitted in the same church, and only where the Blessed Sacrament is kept and the ceremonies of Holy Week are carried out. These ceremonies must be carried out according to the regulations of the Missal or the *Memoriale* of Benedict XIV in country churches which do not have the proper facilities.

In parish churches in which the ceremonies of Holy Week do not take place, the bishop may permit the celebration of one low Mass for the convenience of the people. Even in churches where they do take place, he may permit the celebration of a low Mass before the high Mass, for the purpose of distributing Holy Communion, and if it is a holyday of obligation, several Masses may be permitted. In order to grant this permission to non-parochial churches or public oratories where the ceremonies of Holy Week take place, the bishop must be in possession of an indult. In practice, however, these kinds of permission are presumed in many places where there is a resident priest and the Blessed Sacrament is kept.

Superiors of religious houses who do not carry out the ceremonies of Holy Week in their churches or oratories, may say one low Mass on Holy Thursday, in order to distribute Easter Communion to their subjects.

On Good Friday, the Mass of the Presanctified may and must be said in all churches wherever the ceremonies of Holy Thursday were held the day before. It is forbidden *sub gravi* to say an ordinary Mass on this day, except to give the Viaticum, and it would be a grievous sin to distribute Communion except as Viaticum to the dying.

In parish churches possessing baptismal fonts, the ceremonies of Holy Saturday are obligatory. In other churches or oratories they may be omitted, even if the ceremonies of the two preceding days were carried out.

On this day, Holy Communion may be distributed both during and immediately after Mass.

972. Except by virtue of a privilege or because of particular circumstances, Mass may not be begun earlier than two hours before dawn, nor later than two hours after midday. This law binds under pain of mortal sin. A more serious reason is needed to celebrate Mass before the appointed hour in the morning than to retard it after noon. Canon 821 allows Mass to be begun one hour before dawn and one hour after midday.

Mass may be begun any time after midnight if the purpose be to administer the Viaticum. One would be justified also, it seems, in advancing or retarding the celebration of Holy Mass by twenty minutes, even on weekdays, in order to give the working classes an opportunity to assist. The same rule holds good for a priest who is traveling and who could not say Mass otherwise. In countries where there is no dawn, one should substitute the hour at which the inhabitants are accustomed to rise.

On Christmas the conventual or parochial Mass may be begun at midnight. No other Mass may be begun at midnight without an Apostolic indult. (Can. 821.)

In religious houses or pious institutions possessing an oratory where the Blessed Sacrament is ordinarily kept, one priest may say all three Masses or only one at midnight; In the latter case, the obligation of hearing Mass will be satisfied by all who assist. Holy Communion may be distributed at this Mass to all who wish to receive. (Can. 821.) After the midnight Mass or Masses, one is not permitted to begin the celebration of another Mass or the distribution of Communion until one hour before dawn. Every priest may say two or three Masses at Christmas if he wishes. If he says only one, he must take the one corresponding to the hour at which he is celebrating. A priest who has a perpetual indult to say the Mass of the Blessed Virgin, may say this Mass three times on Christmas day. (S. C. R., Jan. 12, 1921.) On Nov. 2 he may say three times the *Missa Quotidiana* with only one oration.

973. Outside of Christmas and the second of November, on which latter day each priest may say three Masses, one for all the deceased, the other for the intentions of the Sovereign Pontiff, and the third for his own intention, no one is permitted to say more than one Mass on the same day without an Apostolic indult or the permission of the local Ordinary. The Ordinary can grant the permission to binate only if a considerable portion of the faithful would otherwise have to miss Mass on a Sunday or holyday of obligation. It is not in the power of any bishop, however, to allow a priest to say more than two Masses on one day. (Can. 806.) In giving permission to binate, the Church no longer requires that there be only one priest in the locality, or that the same priest say the two Masses in two different places. One may probably say a second Mass in order to administer the Viaticum to a dying person.

974. If the second Mass is to be said in another church, the priest should say the prayer *"Quod ore sumpsimus"* with

his hands joined after drinking the Precious Blood, and then purify his fingers in a cup saying, *"Corpus tuum,"* etc. He should then cover the chalice as usual and leave it upon the unfolded corporal. After the last Gospel, he should take care to consume the few drops of the Precious Blood which may still remain in the chalice, rinse the chalice with a little water, re-cover it, and carry it into the sacristy. This same water may be used on the following day in the place of the ablutions, allowed to dry in the cup, or poured into the sacrarium.

When the second Mass is to be said with the same chalice and in the same place, the new rubric inserted in the Roman Missal for 1920 must be carefully observed. This rubric forbids one to purify or dry the chalice after drinking the Precious Blood. The priest should leave the chalice on the corporal just as it is, cover it with the pall, and then with joined hands recite in the middle of the altar the prayer *"Quod ore sumpsimus."* He should then purify his fingers in a cup and dry them, saying the prayer, *"Corpus tuum."* The chalice is left on the corporal and prepared for the second Mass in the usual way, *i. e.*, by covering it first with the purificator, then with the paten and the host, then with the pall, and finally with the veil. This rubric must be observed also on All Souls' Day. Care should be taken not to allow the purificator to dip into the chalice.

In case the second Mass does not follow immediately, and it is not convenient to leave the chalice on the altar, the priest should carry it into the sacristy, always being careful that it is placed on the corporal.

975. It is a slight sin to celebrate Mass before Matins and Lauds without reason, but it is no sin at all to do so with a reason. The conventual Mass must be celebrated after Lauds, *sub gravi*, except for a good reason.

976. St. Alphonsus would hold a priest guilty of mortal

sin who celebrates Mass in less than fifteen minutes. Yet every priest should, as a rule, complete his Mass within thirty minutes, in order not to tire the faithful. Every good priest makes a thanksgiving of at least fifteen minutes after celebrating; St. Alphonsus requires half an hour.

977. It is permitted to interrupt Mass after the Gospel or before the Communion, in order to preach. If the priest has not yet begun the Canon, he may also interrupt the Mass to receive a bishop or ruler or a group of pilgrims, or if there is no other possible way of ridding the church of a person publicly excommunicated. Once a priest has entered upon the Canon of the Mass, however, he may not make an interruption without a grave reason. To make an interruption after the consecration, he must have a *very* grave reason, such as the obligation to administer Baptism or Penance to a dying person, or Extreme Unction if a person is unable to confess. He would not be permitted to make an interruption to administer the Holy Viaticum, unless he could do so without removing his vestments or losing sight of the altar, and unless it were impossible for him to administer another Sacrament validly.

978. After the reason for the interruption ceases, the priest should resume the Mass at the place where he left off, if both consecrations have already taken place. If only one consecration has taken place, he should resume Mass at the second, except if the interruption lasted more than one hour, in which case he should begin all over again. In this latter case, he would do well to consecrate the second host with the condition: "If there is no moral union." (See no. 948.) Upon leaving the altar, he should lock the Blessed Sacrament in the tabernacle.

One is never permitted to interrupt the consecration purposely. In case of fire or other similar danger, the priest should consume the consecrated host as quickly as possible, or carry it to a safe place to consume it there. The same rule applies to the consecrated wine.

979. If a priest becomes ill *before* the consecration, there is nothing to do. If this happens *after* the consecration, another priest should be called in, who, even though he be excommunicated, must continue and complete the Mass, if he can do so without too great inconvenience. He would be obliged to do this, even though he were not fasting and the Precious Blood alone remained upon the altar, but not after one hour had passed, because, according to the more probable opinion, there would no longer be a moral union after the lapse of an hour. In this case he should simply lock the sacred species in the tabernacle. There are some authors, however, who hold that the moral union persists for the entire day, and therefore, insist that in this case a priest should complete the sacrifice.

If a priest who completes a sacrifice has to begin before the consecration of the chalice, he must apply the fruits of the Mass to the same ends which the priest had who was taken ill, and he must give part of the consecrated host to him if possible. In all such cases a priest should take care not to consume at his own Mass species consecrated by a fellow-priest who became ill at the altar, except after a protracted period of time.

If a priest who is called in to complete a sacrifice is unable to ascertain at what part of the Mass his fellow-priest became ill, he should make the act of oblation mentally and begin at the first consecration, conditionally. A priest who has completed a sacrifice begun by another is not permitted to celebrate Mass again the same day.

980. *The place.* The Holy Sacrifice is ordinarily celebrated in a church or an oratory. There are several kinds of churches. Some are called basilicas, because it is to these churches the Pope was accustomed to repair. Among these,

four are called major basilicas in honor of the four great
patriarchates. They are: St. John Lateran, St. Peter at the
Vatican, St. Paul outside the walls, and St. Mary Major, all
in Rome. All other basilicas to which the Holy Father has
given this title by decree are called minor.

981. The principal object of a church is to serve the faithful at large as a house of worship, whereas that of an oratory
is to serve only a limited number, a family, an institution,
etc. No one, not even the vicar-general, may erect a church
or an oratory without a special mandate from the bishop.
The bishop must not give this permission if he foresees that
the church will be turned over to profane uses, and he must
not consecrate such a church if it has already been erected.
Before giving his permission the bishop must make sure that
the necessary funds are available for the maintenance of the
edifice.

The permission to establish a house given to any clerical
religious institute carries with it the right to have a church
or public oratory. (Can. 497.) But if the religious intend to
build a church, the bishop's approval of the location must
be sought. (Can. 497.)

Before giving his consent to the building of a church, the
bishop should, as a rule, consult the pastors and rectors of
the neighboring churches who are concerned, in order that
the new church may not jeopardize the interests of churches
already established, without a proportionate spiritual benefit accruing to the faithful. (Can. 1162.)

The *blessing* and laying of the cornerstone of a *church*
belongs either to the local Ordinary or to the major religious
superior if the church is annexed to an exempt religious
order. (Can. 1163.) Both the Ordinary and the religious superior may delegate a priest for this function.

The *consecration* of churches of both seculars and exempt
regulars belongs to the Ordinary of the diocese in which

these churches are located. If this Ordinary has not the episcopal character, he may delegate any bishop of the same rite. (Can. 1155.)

Cardinals have the privilege of consecrating churches and altars of their rite.

The right to *bless a sacred place* which does not belong to an exempt religious institute of clerics, belongs to the local Ordinary. If it belongs to an exempt religious institute of clerics, the right of blessing it appertains to the major superior. Both the Ordinary of the diocese and the religious superior may delegate another priest for the purpose. (Can. 1156.)

There must be no doors or windows in the church opening into a layman's house, and the space in the basement or above the church must not be used for purely profane purposes. (Can. 1164.)

A church must at least be blessed before divine worship can be held in it.

982. Solemn consecration ought to be given to cathedral churches and, as far as possible, also to collegiate, conventual, and parochial churches. A church constructed of wood or metal cannot be consecrated. An altar may be consecrated without consecrating the church, but if a church is consecrated, at least the high altar (or if this is consecrated, another altar) must be consecrated with the building. (Can. 1165.)

The consecration of a church must take place during Holy Mass. The consecrating bishop and those who have petitioned for the consecration must fast the day before (can. 1166.) The priests in charge of the church which is to be consecrated must say the office of the dedication of a church as a double, beginning with Tierce. If the recitation of this office is impeded by the feast of the day on which the church is consecrated, a commemoration should be made of the dedication and the office transferred to the first free day beginning at Vespers.

The anniversary of the dedication of a church is celebrated each year. It is customary in some dioceses to celebrate this dedication on the same day. The feast of the title which the church receives when it is either blessed or consecrated, must also be observed each year. The title of a consecrated church cannot be changed. The title of a church must be that of a saint or a mystery; no church may be dedicated in honor of a beatified person without a special indult from the Holy See. (Can. 1168.)

The church bells must either be consecrated or blessed. They are exclusively under the jurisdiction of the Church authorities, and, with the exception of conditions stipulated by the donor with the approval of the Ordinary, must not be rung for purely profane purposes, except in case of necessity, or with the permission of the Ordinary, or in accordance with lawful custom. Persons authorized to consecrate or bless churches are authorized also to consecrate or bless church bells. Doubtful blessings or consecrations may and must be repeated.

983. A document testifying to the fact of blessing or consecration must be drawn up and one copy kept in the episcopal archives and another in the archives of the parish. The consecration or blessing of a church is sufficiently attested to by one trustworthy witness, provided his testimony is not injurious to any one.

A church does not lose its consecration or blessing unless it is totally destroyed, or the larger portion of its walls collapse, or it is reduced to profane purposes by authority of the Ordinary. (Can. 1170.)

984. A church is desecrated by the following crimes, provided they are certain, notorious, and committed in the building itself: (1) homicide; (2) the sinful shedding of

human blood in considerable quantities; (3) godless and sordid purposes for which the Church was used; (4) burial of an infidel or of an excommunicated person. (Can. 1172.)

If the church is desecrated, the cemetery adjoining it is not thereby desecrated, and *vice versa*. (Can. 1172.)

It is forbidden to hold divine services, to administer the Sacraments, and to hold funeral services in a desecrated church.

If the desecration takes place during divine services, they should be discontinued immediately. If during Mass, before the beginning of the Canon or after Communion, Mass must be discontinued at once. In all other cases a priest should continue until the Communion. (Can. 1173.)

A desecrated church must be reconciled as soon as possible. If the desecration is doubtful, reconciliation is permitted *ad cautelam*. (Can. 1174.)

A church that has been blessed may be reconciled by its rector or by any priest delegated by him. The reconciliation of a consecrated church belongs either to the bishop or to the major religious superior, according to canon 1156. If, in case of urgent necessity, the bishop cannot be reached in time, the rector of a consecrated church may reconcile it and then notify the Ordinary of his action. (Can. 1176.)

The reconciliation of a blessed church is effected with ordinary holy water, but the reconciliation of a consecrated church requires holy water specially blessed for the purpose with the ceremonies prescribed by liturgical law. (Can. 1177.) Any priest who knowingly celebrates Mass in a desecrated or polluted church is guilty of a mortal sin.

985. All persons in charge of a church must see to it that the building is kept clean, as becomes the House of God. The administration of goods intended for the upkeep and decoration of the church belongs, with the exception of special cases and privileges, to the Ordinary and his chapter, if it

be question of the cathedral church; to the collegiate
chapter, if the church be collegiate, and to the rector in the
case of other churches.

986. The offerings made to a parish or mission, or to a
church situated within the confines of the parish or mission,
are administered by the pastor of the church or the rector
of the mission, unless there is question of churches possessing an administration of their own, distinct from that of the
parish or mission, or unless some special law or legal custom
exists to the contrary.

987. The pastor, missionary, or rector of a church, both
secular and regular, must administer the offerings in accord
with the regulations of the sacred canons, and give an account thereof to the Ordinary of the diocese. (Can. 1182.) If
other persons, either cleric or lay, are admitted to the administration of the goods of any church, they must act as an
administrative council under the presidency of the pastor.
The members of this administrative council are to be chosen
by the diocesan Ordinary, unless special laws provide otherwise, and may be removed by him for any grave reason.
(Can. 1183.) The duty of the council is to see to the proper
administration of the church revenues, but it must in no way
interfere in spiritual functions.

The sacristan, the singers, the organist, the choir boys, the
workmen for the cemetery, and all others serving the church
in an inferior capacity, are appointed by the rector, unless
lawful custom or the right of the Ordinary decree otherwise.
Moreover, they exercise their functions under his supervision
and can be dismissed by him.

Unless special customs or laws exist, or special burdens
are placed upon individuals by civil law, the obligation of
maintaining the cathedral church building rests, *first,* with
the administrative council of the cathedral parish. If the
church has revenues, these must be used for the repairs of

the church edifice, but the revenues necessary to carry on divine worship and the ordinary administration of the church must not be touched. The obligation rests, *secondly*, with the bishop and the canons of the cathedral, who must defray the expenditures for repairs in proportion to their income, but are entitled to that part of their salary which is considered necessary for their proper sustenance. It rests, *thirdly*, with the people of the diocese, who must be invited to contribute according to their means.

The duty of repairing the parish church rests, first, with the administrative council; secondly, with the patron; thirdly, with those who derive some income from the church; and, fourthly, with the parishoners. These rules, *mutatis mutandis*, apply to all other churches. (Can. 1186.)

988. If a church can no longer be used for divine worship, and no means are available for repairing it, the bishop may assign it to some decent profane use. The rights and obligations must be transferred to another church by the Ordinary, and if this church be a parochial church, the title must also be transferred.

989. Oratories are of three kinds: public, semi-public, and private. An oratory is *public* if it has been erected principally for the convenience of some establishment, or for some private individuals, but in such wise that all the faithful have the right to worship therein, especially at the time of divine services. An oratory is *semi-public* if it has been erected in such wise that not all the faithful have access to it. It is *private* if erected in a private home for the benefit of some family or private individual. (Can. 1188.) Chapels erected in a cemetery are to be treated as private oratories.

Public oratories are governed by the same laws as churches, and all the sacred functions, except those forbidden by the rubrics, may be held in them. Semi-public oratories cannot be erected without the permission of the

Ordinary, and the latter must not give this permission until he has inspected, either in person or through some one else, the place where the oratory is to be erected, and has convinced himself that the place is well suited for that purpose. Once this permission has been granted, the oratory cannot be turned over to profane purposes without a new permission from the same Ordinary. The Ordinary should not authorize the erection of secondary oratories in colleges and other institutions for the education of youth, high schools, castles, barracks, prisons, hospitals, etc., where a principal oratory already exists, unless necessity or great utility makes it advisable to do so.

The Ordinary may permit the celebration of several Masses in sepulchral chapels; in other private oratories he may allow only one Mass for some extraordinary occasion, but not habitually. He may not give this permission before he has inspected the oratory either in person or through some one else. To celebrate Mass habitually in a private oratory, one would have to be in possession of an indult from the Holy See, and a similar indult would be required to erect a private oratory in a convent for the convenience of a sick priest. Even with an indult from the Holy See, one is not permitted to celebrate Mass in private oratories before the bishop or his delegate has visited the place, unless the indult expressly states the contrary. The Pope does not permit the celebration of High Masses in private oratories, and only one Mass can be celebrated therein each day. All other ecclesiastical functions are barred. Generally speaking, Mass should not be said in private oratories on solemn feast days, but for good reasons other than those for which the indult was granted, the Ordinary may permit the celebration of Holy Mass even on these days, by way of exception in particular cases. (Can. 1195.)

Private and semi-public oratories cannot be consecrated

or blessed after the manner of churches, but only with the ordinary blessing for a house. Whether blessed or not, however, such oratories must be exclusively reserved for divine worship. (Can. 1196.)

990. The privilege of the *portable altar* bestows the faculty to say Mass in any decent and respectable place (except at sea) and on a consecrated stone. The local Ordinary, or when there is question of an exempt religious house, the major superior, may for a just and reasonable cause give permission to celebrate Mass outside the church or oratory, but on a consecrated stone and in a decent place, never in a bedroom. (Can. 822.) The Sacred Congregation of the Sacraments has issued orders to the Italian bishops not to permit the celebration of Holy Mass outside a church or oratory without first consulting the Congregation.

Holy Mass may never be celebrated in the churches of heretics or schismatics, even though these churches were properly consecrated at some previous time. If a priest has no altar of his own rite, he may celebrate on an altar consecrated according to another Catholic rite, following his own rite, but he may not celebrate on the Greek *antimensia*, which are made of canvas. No one is allowed to celebrate on papal altars without an Apostolic indult. (Can. 823.)

The privilege of the portable altar is granted either by law or by an Apostolic indult. One of the privileges granted to cardinals by the New Code is to celebrate Mass on a portable altar not only in their own residences, but wherever they are, even at sea, with all necessary precautions. They may even allow others to say Mass in their presence in all these places. Canon 349 concedes this same privilege to bishops, diocesan and titular. The oratories of cardinals and bishops, though private, have the same privilege as semi-public oratories.

991. *The manner of celebrating Mass.* We shall consider,

first, the requisites for celebrating Mass, and, secondly, the prescribed rubrics.

The requisites for celebration. The first requisite, which binds *sub gravi,* is an altar of stone consecrated by a bishop. This altar must have a sealed sepulchre containing the relics of several martyrs. To these relics may be added those of confessors. The relics must be fragments of the bodies.

An altar is either *fixed* or *movable.* It is considered fixed if the upper table together with its support is consecrated as a whole, and movable, if the stone, which is usually small in size, is consecrated alone. Consecrated churches must possess at least one fixed altar, but in blessed churches all the altars may be movable. (Can. 1197.)

The mensa of a fixed altar must consist of one piece of solid, natural stone. It must cover the entire altar and be properly cemented to the supports. The supports, or at least the sides or columns on which the table rests, must be of stone. The altar stone must be sufficiently large to hold the host and the larger portion of the chalice. On altars nothing must be placed except what is ornamental or serves the purpose of the sacrifice. An antipendium must hang before the altar, unless the front is painted or carved, or has the form of a tomb. If possible, this antipendium must be of the color of the day, but it should always be white when the Blessed Sacrament is exposed.

Any bishop may lawfully consecrate movable altars or altar stones; but the consecration of fixed altars is reserved to the local Ordinary, who, if he is not a bishop, must delegate a bishop to perform the consecration.

The consecration of an altar may take place on any day, but for that of a fixed altar a Sunday or holyday of obligation should preferably be chosen. The same rule holds for the consecration of churches.

A fixed altar loses its consecration if the table becomes

separated from its supports, even though it be only for a moment. In this case the Ordinary may permit a priest to re-consecrate the altar with the shorter formula.

A fixed altar, as well as its stone, lose their consecration:

1. If they are *seriously* fractured, seriously referring either to the size of the break, or the place where it occurs, *i. e.*, at the anointed parts.

2. If the relics are removed, or the cover of the sepulchre is broken or removed, unless either the bishop or his delegate remove the cover in order to repair, fasten, or replace it, or in order to inspect the relics. A slight fracture of the cover does not induce desecration, and any priest may fill the crack with cement. (Can. 1200.)

A fixed altar does not lose its consecration by being de-placed, as long as the table is not separated from the sup-ports. A church may be desecrated without the fixed or movable altars being desecrated, and the altars may be dese-crated without the church being desecrated, but fixed altars are always desecrated and reconciled together with the church or oratory to which they belong.

Every altar, at least every fixed altar, should have a title. The principal title of the main altar should be the same as that of the church. The same title may not be given to sev-eral altars in the same church or oratory. With the permis-sion of the Ordinary the title of a movable altar may be changed, but never that of a fixed altar. Churches and altars may not be dedicated to *Beati* without an indult from the Holy See.

It is not permitted to celebrate Mass on an altar under or near which lies the body of a deceased person. *Near* is to be taken to mean three feet away.

992. The altar must be covered with three blessed altar cloths. A priest would be guilty of mortal sin if (except in case of grave necessity) he celebrated Mass without any

altar cloths, and of venial sin if he celebrated with two, or one, or even three unblessed cloths. There are some authors, however, who hold that the blessing of the altar cloths is not of precept.

The cloths may be of linen or hemp, but never of cotton, and the same holds good of the alb, the amice, the purificator, the pall, and the corporal, which latter must be entirely white. With the permission of the Ordinary, the alb may be of cotton from the waist down. It is more fitting that the cincture be of linen, though it may be of wool or silk.

993. There must be a crucifix upon the altar. This obligation binds *sub levi*. By a crucifix we mean a cross with a corpus. This crucifix must be large enough to be seen by the people, unless there is above the main altar a painting or a piece of sculpture representing Christ crucified. It is not necessary that the cross and other images placed upon the altar be blessed. When the Blessed Sacrament is exposed, the cross may be removed or allowed to stand, according to local custom. (S. C. R.)

The crucifix must be placed between two candle-sticks. It is a grievous sin to celebrate Mass without lights, even in order to give the Viaticum, although some theologians exempt a priest from sin in this latter case. Some writers hold a priest guilty of mortal sin who celebrates Mass with tallow or stearine candles except for a grave reason. One would, however, be permitted to celebrate Mass, even out of pure devotion, with one wax candle, and some theologians go so far as to say that, for the same reason, one would be permitted to celebrate with a stearine candle or even an oil lamp, if no wax candles were available. These same authors aver that one would be justified in continuing the Mass even though the two candles became extinguished after the offertory.

994. The S. C. R. approved the practice of certain bishops

who, in case of urgent necessity, permitted the use of tallow or stearine candles and electric light at Mass, and of only two wax candles for the benediction of the Blessed Sacrament.

More than two wax candles may be lighted on the altar at a low Mass if the feast of the day warrants it, but never more than two to honor the celebrant, unless he happens to be a bishop. (See no. 921.) There is nothing to prevent the addition of stearine candles. The rubrics prescribe that an additional wax candle be lighted at the consecration, but this is no longer of precept.

The Paschal candle and the candles blessed on Candlemas day must also be of wax.

995. The obligation of using a Roman missal containing at least the canon, obliges *sub gravi.* As a general rule, a priest who celebrates Mass in a strange church must use the Roman missal, even though he uses a missal of his own at home. If a Roman missal cannot be found, he may use the particular missal of that church, provided, of course, that it be approved.

A priest could celebrate Mass without any missal at all if he could not find a Roman one and was sure that he would not make any mistakes. In churches administered by regulars, a secular priest may make use of the missal proper to the Order, but not their rites. A priest who is entirely blind may not celebrate Mass without a dispensation from the Pope (see no. 973), and a priest who, because of poor eyesight, has permission to say the Mass *de Beata* may say the one prescribed from Pentecost to Advent at any time.

The altar cards, the bell, the biretta, the glass dish, the veil and the burse are fitting, but not required. There is no obligation to bless the veil, the burse, the lavabo towel, and the antipendium.

996. The sacred vessels required for the sacrifice are the chalice and the paten; without them it would not be per-

mitted to celebrate, except in case of extreme necessity. These vessels must be made not of copper or bronze, but of gold or silver. They may be of tin or aluminum, mixed with other metals in the proportions indicated by the S. C. R., but it is required *sub gravi* that they be consecrated and gilded.

Sacred vessels that have been blessed or consecrated lose their blessing or consecration:

1. If they are so damaged or changed that they lose their original shape, and are no longer fit for the purpose for which they were made;

2. If they have been used for unbecoming purposes or put up for public sale.

The chalice and the paten do not lose their consecration when the gold plating wears off or is renewed, but there is a grave obligation to have this gold plating renewed when it does wear off. (Can. 1305.)

997. The ciborium and the ostensorium must be of decent and solid materials, but the cup of the ciborium and the lunula of the ostensorium must be of the same material as the chalice and the paten. The ciborium and the lunula must be blessed and this suffices, but it is not prescribed, although it is quite fitting, that the ostensorium be blessed also. These vessels lose their blessing in the same manner as the chalice and the paten, and when they do, they must be blessed again by a priest who has faculties to bless sacred vestments. It would be a venial sin to touch these vessels even when they do not contain the sacred species, but clerics who have received the order of acolyte may do so without sin. In places where the custom exists, even simple clerics, brothers or nuns who have charge of a sacristy, may handle the sacred utensils without sin. A layman may touch the ciborium and the lunula even after they have been blessed, but he may not do so after they have been used to contain the Holy Eucha-

rist. He may touch the ostensorium, but not consecrated things like altars.

998. Care must be taken that the unpurified chalice, the paten, unwashed purificators, palls and corporals, are not touched except by clerics or those who have charge of these utensils. Purificators, palls, and corporals used in the Holy Sacrifice must not be given to lay persons, even religious, to be washed, until they have first been rinsed by a cleric in major Orders. The water of the first washing must be poured into the *sacrarium*, or if there is no sacrarium, into the fire. (Can. 1306.)

Silversmiths may touch the sacred vessels when repairing them.

999. The corporal, the pall, and the purificator are accessories. Nevertheless a priest would be guilty of mortal sin if, except in case of grave necessity, he said Mass without a corporal, or with a corporal that was not blessed, or with a corporal that was not clean. A priest may not use a corporal that is torn at the spot where the sacred host is laid. (See no. 992.) Theologians are not agreed as to whether or not a priest sins grievously by celebrating Mass without a pall or with one that is not blessed. In default of a pall, one may probably use the burse, the purificator or the corporal. Like the purificator and the corporal, the part of the pall which touches the chalice must be of linen or hemp, except in India, where it may be of silk. The top part of the pall may be of silk and of any color except black. The purificator need not be blessed and a priest would be permitted to celebrate without one.

1000. *The sacred vestments*. Aside from cases of grave necessity, a priest would be guilty of mortal sin, according to all theologians, if he celebrated without any sacred vestment, or even without the alb (see no. 922), or without a chasuble, or without stole and maniple, or with vestments that were not blessed. It is probable that he would not sin if he celebrated without either the stole or the maniple, or either one of them were not blessed. One is not bound *sub gravi* to use the amice and the cincture.

Theologians are divided on the question whether or not a priest may celebrate Mass without any sacred vestment, or without an altar or a chalice, if threatened with death. All are agreed that he would *not* be permitted to do so even in order to administer the Viaticum to a dying person.

1001. The following persons have the right to bless sacred utensils, linens, and vestments:

1. All cardinals.

2. All local Ordinaries, for the churches and oratories of their own territory.

3. All pastors, for the churches and oratories within the limits of their parish, and rectors for their respective churches.

4. All priests delegated by the Ordinary, within the limits of the delegation and the jurisdiction of the delegating Ordinary.

5. All religious superiors and priests of the same Order delegated by them, for their own churches and oratories, and for the churches of nuns subject to them. (Can. 1304.)

There is a serious obligation to have the sacred vestments blessed, but in administering the Holy Viaticum, one may dispense with this blessing. Reuter is of the opinion that a priest would be permitted to celebrate without a blessed alb, in order not to deprive the people of a sacrifice at which they were bound to assist. It is a mistake to believe that unblessed vestments that have been used at Mass do not need to be blessed afterwards.

Sacred vestments lose their blessing when they are torn or have lost their original shape. The blessing may be safe-

guarded by repairing them as soon as a tear becomes notice-
able. After they have become torn to the extent of losing
their blessing, they may be used to repair other vestments,
and the remaining portions destroyed by fire. It would be a
serious sin to use these parts for profane purposes. The same
is true of the sacred linens.

The sacred vestments must not be of painted cotton, canvas or wool, but of any other fitting material. A textile fabric
of silk may be used, even though it be derived from the
leaves of the mulberry-tree, provided no foreign materials
are interwoven with it. According to a decision of the Congregation of the Council, the lining of vestments may be of
wool, cotton or linen in poorer churches, provided it is completely covered with silk.

1002. It is required *sub levi* that the sacred vestments be
of the colors prescribed, *i. e.,* white, red, green, purple, black,
and rose. One is not permitted to make use of vestments in
which one of these colors does not predominate. Gold vestments may be used, provided they be not substituted for
purple or black.

1003. According to a decision of the S. C. R. of Dec. 9th,
1895, both secular and regular priests who celebrate Mass
in a church, public oratory, or oratory used by a congregation of men and women, must do so in conformity with the
office of this particular church or oratory when the feast is
that of a double. This rule must be observed even when the
office is that of a *Beatus,* or of a saint or *Beatus* proper to
the Order, whether the office is in the Roman Missal or not.
In all these cases, the priest must not use the rites peculiar
to the Order or congregation.

If the feast celebrated in these churches or oratories is inferior to that of a double, each priest may say the Mass of
his office at his own good pleasure, but not as a votive Mass.
He may also say a Requiem Mass, the Mass of the *feria,* or

any votive Mass, except on days when the rubrics of the Missal or the decrees of the Congregation forbid the saying of votive Masses.

On the feast of a double, he does not have to make commemoration of his office when he says Mass in any such church, but if he says Mass in a church other than his own on Sunday, he must make commemoration of a double or an octave of his own office. It would seem that he should do likewise when he celebrates a votive Mass in a church other than his own.

If the office of the celebrant is that of a *Beatus,* he may not say his Mass in a church where this cult is not authorized.

When a priest celebrates Mass in a private oratory, the Mass must always coincide with the office of the celebrant, even though it be the feast of a *Beatus* whose Mass may not be celebrated in another church.

1004. The vestments must be put on in the sacristy, or if there be no sacristy, on the gospel side of the altar.

The celebrant must (*sub levi*) wear a cassock beneath the alb. The statutes of some dioceses enjoin this practice more strictly. A priest would be guilty of mortal sin if, without papal dispensation, he wore a skull-cap or a wig during the entire Mass. To remain covered until the time of the consecration would constitute a venial sin, but an aged or sickly priest might be excused from any fault in this case. A priest is forbidden *sub levi* to celebrate Mass bare-footed.

1005. A priest is obliged *sub gravi* to have a server, and this server must be a man and not a woman. A woman may answer the responses from a distance, if no male server is available, but she may not approach the altar without committing serious sin. A priest may say Mass without a server if the people or the priest himself would otherwise have to miss Mass on a holyday of obligation. If the server leaves the church after the Mass has begun, the priest may continue, especially if he is past the offertory. A priest should supply the deficiencies in the responses of an inefficient server. He should not have more than one server, although two or more may be permitted at the principal Mass.

A priest who is about to celebrate a private Mass should prepare the chalice himself, even though the server is in sacred orders.

St. Alphonsus is of the opinion that it would not be permitted to serve the Mass of a priest who is positively known to be in the state of mortal sin, except for a grave reason.

1006. *The rubrics.* The rubrics derive their name from the red color (*ruber*) in which they are usually printed. We have already indicated their sources in no. 803. They are: the Roman Missal and Ritual, the Ceremonial of Bishops, and the decrees of the Sacred Congregation of Rites, which are binding in all places unless a custom approved by Rome exists to the contrary. These decrees lose none of their vigor by reason of some well-established custom; on the contrary, they rescind contrary customs, even those that exist from time immemorial.

Some rubrics are directive, others preceptive. Authors are not always agreed as to which ones are obligatory, but St. Alphonsus and a number of others opine that rubrics regulating functions other than those of the Mass and the administration of the Sacraments, are merely directive. Nevertheless, it is commonly held that a priest is guilty of venial sin who neglects to say the prayers while vesting, or to wash his hands before celebrating. A priest might even be guilty of mortal sin in this latter case if his hands were extremely dirty. One could scarcely excuse from some kind of sin a priest who habitually makes no preparation whatever for celebrating Mass.

1007. The rubrics which regulate the celebration of Mass

or the administration of the Sacraments are preceptive and bind either *sub gavi* or *sub levi,* according as to whether the matter involved is grave or slight. Nothing may be added to and nothing substracted from these rubrics. Ignorance of what one must know as a matter of duty does not excuse. Priests should be enjoined to read the rubrics of the Missal and those of the Breviary at their annual retreats. They should be urged also to study the *Cæremoniale,* wherein may be found the decrees of the S. Congregation of Rites which they should know and which are not found in the rubrics.

1008. Authors are not agreed as to whether the rubrics of the Mass intended for inferior ministers such as the deacon and the sub-deacon are of precept.

The same controversy exists in regard to the rubrics of the High Mass, but the opinion of those who hold to the affirmative is substantiated by a decree of the S. Congregation of Rites.

1009. In differentiating between grave and slight omissions in the matter of rubrics, one must distinguish between what is said every day at Mass and what is sometimes omitted. The omission of what is said every day is grievous, unless the matter itself be slight. Thus, a priest would be guilty of mortal sin if he purposely omitted the prayers at the foot of the altar, the epistle together with the tract and the gradual, or the gospel—but not the last gospel—two of the first collects, one of the orations of the Canon, eight or ten names of saints from the Canon, or even one word of the Canon upon which the remaining words depend for their meaning. A priest is not guilty of mortal sin if he omits the gospel or the epistle, when the latter are sung by some inferior minister at High Mass.

The name of the local Ordinary must be inserted in the Canon. One should not repeat after omitting some non-essential words.

"If any one saith, that the rite of the Roman Church, according to which a part of the canon and the words of consecration are pronounced in a low tone, is to be condemned; or that mass ought to be celebrated in the vulgar tongue only; let him be anathema." (C. of Trent, Sess. 22, can. 9.) It would be a venial sin to pronounce in a low tone of voice what should be uttered aloud, but it would be a mortal sin to recite the words of the consecration or the Canon in such wise that they could be heard forty steps away. According to St. Alphonsus, only an insane person would speak that loud, and so outside this case, he fails to see how in this matter any one could commit a mortal sin. The priest must be able to hear words which he is supposed to pronounce in a low tone of voice, and he would sin grievously if he pronounced the words of consecration without being able to hear them himself. (See no. 899.)

1010. It is a venial sin to omit a blessing or a genuflection, but if a priest omitted a considerable number of them, he would be guilty of mortal sin. It is a grievous sin not to elevate the host or the chalice, or not to drop a portion of the host into the chalice and not to purify the chalice and the paten. It is a venial sin to omit one of the ablutions.

Sickly priests who are unable to carry out the principal functions and ceremonies of the Mass should abstain from celebrating; but a priest who cannot genuflect may say Mass, and may even use a walking-stick to support himself at the altar. A priest who is unable to elevate the host and must support himself with both hands, may celebrate Mass in private, and even in public if he explains his action to the people.

1011. It is not permitted to omit prayers and ceremonies that are prescribed. It would be a venial sin to omit parts of the Mass that are not always said, like the *Gloria* and the *Credo,* although a priest might be guilty of mortal sin even in this case, according to the amount of matter omitted. The omission of parts that are always said at Mass is grave, unless the amount omitted is too small to constitute sufficient matter. The omission of the last gospel is commonly regarded as a venial sin. It is forbidden *sub gravi* or *sub levi*, according to the case, to add prayers or ceremonies to those which are prescribed. It would be a grievous sin to add the *Gloria* and the *Credo* to a Requiem Mass. It is forbidden to displace or change prayers, *sub gravi*, if the displacement or change effects a notable difference in the rite. Thus, it would be a grievous sin to recite the gospel before the epistle, but only a venial sin to say one preface instead of another.

Only the names of residential bishops are to be inserted in the Canon, and not those of vicars Apostolic or other prelates. Except on the vigils of Christmas and Pentecost, on Palm Sunday, on doubles of the first class and in Requiem Masses a priest may, on the anniversary of his ordination, add to the prescribed collects one for his own intention. If he is prevented by the rubrics from doing so on that day, he may add the collect on the following day, or on the first free day, provided it be not a double of the first class.

In all Masses sung before the Sacred Host exposed, the prayer to the Blessed Sacrament must be added to the other collects, and if it is a double of the first or second class, this oration must be recited under one conclusion with the first. A priest who says a private Mass before the Blessed Sacrament exposed, may make commemoration of the Blessed Sacrament, except on a feast of the first or second class. The last gospel is never that of the Mass in honor of the Blessed Sacrament.

1012. Votive Masses are either solemn or private. They are solemn if, by order or permission of the Ordinary, they are celebrated with chant, before the assembled congregation, for some grave and public cause. A religious profession, the first Mass of a newly ordained priest, or perpetual adoration would not constitute grave and public reasons. The bishop's permission must be sought in every individual case. Solemn votive Masses are prohibited on Sundays, first-class feasts, the vigils of Christmas and Pentecost, Ash Wednesday, all the days of Holy Week, and the second of November.

1013. The *Credo* is always sung at solemn votive Masses, but the *Gloria* is omitted on days when the priest wears purple vestments. The only commemorations made are those of a double of the second class, a Sunday, a major *feria*, the Rogations, and a privileged vigil or octave. If the Mass has no special preface, the priest should follow the ordinary rubric. If the solemn votive Mass is celebrated at a time which calls for a special *Communicantes,* this prayer must be said, even though it does not correspond with the preface.

At the end of the Mass the priest sings the *Ite Missa est* or the *Benedicamus Domino* according as to whether or not he was obliged to sing the *Gloria.*

The last gospel is ordinarily that of St. John, but when at the Mass of the day commemoration has been made of the Sunday, even an anticipated one, a *feria* during Lent or on ember days, the second *feria* of the Rogations, that of the vigil and octave of Epiphany, a privileged octave of the first class, or a feast which has a special gospel, the last gospel must be that of the office or feast commemorated.

1014. Private votive Masses are those celebrated not for some grave and public cause, but for some other reasonable cause. They may be read or sung, but when they are sung, the priest should use the ferial tone without the *Gloria,* unless the Mass be that of the Holy Angels or of the Blessed Virgin Mary *in sabbato*. The *Credo* is never sung.

Chanted votive Masses are forbidden on the following days: (1) all Sundays, even though they be anticipated or transferred, and all double feasts; (2) Ash Wednesday and all days of Holy Week; (3) the vigils of Christmas, Epiphany, and Pentecost and during privileged octaves or those of Christmas, the Epiphany, Easter, the Ascension, Pentecost, and Corpus Christi; (4) Rogation days in parishes where the procession takes place and where there is but one Mass; (5) All Souls.

Low votive Masses are forbidden on the following days: (1) all Sundays, even though they be anticipated or transferred, and the day when one must celebrate a Mass prevented by the Sunday office; (2) all double feasts; (3) during privileged octaves; (4) ember days; (5) the *feriae* of Advent from the 17th to the 23rd of December, inclusively; (6) all the days during Lent; (7) the Monday of Rogations; (8) all vigils; (9) the Tuesday of the Rogations in parishes where the procession takes place and where there is but one Mass; (10) the day of a simple octave, if commemoration is made of it at least in the office; (11) the second of November.

Votive Masses may be said of all the saints whose names appear in the Breviary or Martyrology, all the Blessed, whose office is permitted by the diocese, and all the mysteries which have a special Mass in the Missal. In celebrating a votive Mass of one of the saints, the priest reads the special Mass, if the saint has one, if not, a Mass taken from the *Commune*. A priest who wishes to say a votive Mass in honor of the Blessed Virgin, may take either one of the five *de Beata,* or that of the Seven Dolors, or that of the Immaculate Conception.

A priest who, because of poor eyesight, has an indult to say the Mass of the Blessed Virgin, must observe the rules laid down by the S. C. R. on Jan. 12, 1921. He may always say the Mass prescribed from Pentecost to Advent; he may say it three times on Christmas day, but he may not say it

on the last three days of Holy Week. He must recite the
Gloria and the *Credo,* each time the Mass of the day calls
for their recitation in the church where he is celebrating,
and on the anniversary of his ordination. He must also recite
the *Gloria* on all Saturdays and during the entire octave,
even simple, of the Blessed Virgin. If the office does not call
for any orations *de tempore,* he has only to say one oration,
otherwise three: *de Beata, de S. Spiritu* and *pro Ecclesia* or
pro Papa. At the preface, he must say *et te in veneratione,*
unless a special feast or an octave of a feast of the Blessed
Virgin is being celebrated that day.

On days when the Mass *Quotidiana pro defunctis* is permitted in the church where he is celebrating, the priest who
possesses such an indult may say or sing the Mass. On the
second of November, he may say this Mass three times with
the one oration *Fidelium.* On other days, he recites only one
oration, if his Mass takes the place of a Mass at which only
one oration is prescribed, otherwise he must say three orations, the first two of which he may select at his discretion.
He is always dispensed from the *Dies irae,* but if he sings
the Mass, the choir is not exempt.

1015. The *Missa pro Sponsis* is a votive Mass and may
neither be said nor sung on a Sunday or feast of ecclesiastical
precept, even if suppressed, on a double feast of the first or
second class, during the octaves of Epiphany, Easter,
Corpus Christi, and Pentecost, on the second of November,
or on privileged *feriæ* and vigils. The privileged *feriæ* are
those of Ash Wednesday, and the Monday, Tuesday, and
Wednesday of Holy Week. The privileged vigils are those
of Christmas, Epiphany, and Pentecost. On these days the
priest says the Mass of the day, adding the oration *pro
Sponsis* and the nuptial blessing. If the nuptial blessing may
not be received, either because the woman has already received it at a previous marriage ceremony, or because it

is prohibited by the season, the oration *pro Sponsis* may not be added to the Mass. According to a decree of the S. C. R., issued in 1911, the same rule holds if the two spouses are not present. A decree of the same Congregation issued in 1918 declares that if the nuptial blessing be given on Christmas day, Epiphany, Easter Sunday, Pentecost, Trinity Sunday, or Corpus Christi, the oration *pro Sponsis* must be said with one conclusion with the first.

The rite of the *Missa pro Sponsis* is simple and, therefore, the priest should always add the orations *pro Tempore*, unless the Mass is said on the day of a double feast. Canon 1108 states that marriage may be contracted on any day of the year, and the bishop may even permit marriages in seasons when the solemn blessing is forbidden without the nuptial blessing, if the parties refrain from too much pomp. A woman who has received the nuptial blessing once, may not receive it again at a subsequent marriage. (Can. 1143.)

The solemn blessing of marriage is forbidden from the first Sunday in Advent to Christmas, inclusively, and from Ash Wednesday to Easter Sunday, inclusively. (Can. 1108.)

1016. A Requiem High Mass sung on the day of death or burial, and those which, for just reason, are substituted in their stead, the corpse being present or absent, buried or awaiting burial, may be celebrated on all days except the following: (1) double feasts of the first class, not including, however, the Monday and Tuesday after the feasts of Easter and Pentecost; (2) the days of dedication or titular feast of the church, or the feast of the principal patron saint of the locality; (3) the three last days of Holy Week; (4) all Sundays and feast days even when suppressed, including the second of February, if candles are blessed on that day; (5) Ash Wednesday; (6) the feast of St. Mark and the Rogation days, if there is a procession and only one Mass is celebrated in the parish church; (7) the vigil of Pentecost, if only cne Mass is celebrated in the parish church; (8) during the exposition of the Blessed Sacrament.

When a Requiem Mass is prohibited by the rubrics, it may be transferred to the first free day. If the day of the burial coincides with the feast of All Souls, the priest says one of the three Masses of the day, adding the oration *de Die Obitus* under one conclusion.

1017. A Requiem High Mass is always permitted on the third, seventh, and thirtieth day after the death or burial of a deceased person, or on the anniversary—whether it be the exact day, or the one selected by those who have the right, or the most fitting day that can be selected after his decease has become known—except on the following days: (1) all the days indicated in no. 1016; (2) the second of November; (3) the Monday and Tuesday after the feasts of Easter and Pentecost; (4) all the days of Holy Week; (5) all double feasts of the second class; (6) the vigils of Christmas and Pentecost; (7) the octaves of Christmas, Easter, the Epiphany, the Ascension, Pentecost, and Corpus Christi.

When this Mass is prohibited by the rubrics, it may be anticipated or transferred to the nearest free day.

Some anniversaries are anniversaries only in the broad sense of the term, because they do not fall on the exact day of the person's death or burial. Such anniversaries are those which chapters, communities, confraternities, and other societies set apart each year to commemorate the death of their departed members. The privileges of ordinary anniversaries extend also to these, and during the octave of All Souls these offices may be celebrated to satisfy the piety of the faithful.

1018. Requiem High Masses for the deceased are permitted on all days of the year except the following: (1) the days indicated in the two preceding numbers; (2) days that have a double office; (3) anticipated Sundays, or Sundays on which the office is transferred; (4) all privileged *feriæ*, vigils, and octaves. The Holy See has issued an indult to some dioceses in virtue of which three of these Masses may be sung or said weekly, irrespective of whether or not there is a double feast.

1019. Low Masses of Requiem that are said for poor persons as funeral Masses are permitted under the same conditions as funeral High Masses.

Low Requiem Masses for the burial of a deceased who is not poor are permitted on the same days as those indicated for Masses on the third, seventh, thirtieth, and anniversary days. These Masses may not be said if the special fruit of the Mass is not applied to the deceased, and are permitted only in the church where the burial service together with the funeral Mass takes place on the same day. In private, but not in semi-public oratories, Requiem Masses may be said on all the days between the death and burial of the deceased, except on days when it is forbidden to say a private burial Mass in the church. This Mass is not permitted if the body of the deceased is not present. In churches or public oratories attached to seminaries, colleges, or religious communities, a private Requiem Mass for a deceased may be said once between the dates of his death and burial. In cemetery churches or chapels, private Requiem Masses may be said on all days except Sundays and holydays of obligation (even suppressed), on double feasts of the first and second class, and on privileged *feriæ*, vigils, and octaves.

Private Masses of Requiem for the third, seventh, and thirtieth days after the death or burial of the deceased are permitted on all days when Requiem High Mass is permitted. These Masses may not, however, be anticipated or transferred when prohibited by the rubrics.

1020. The low Requiem Mass is forbidden on the same

days as the High (see no. 1018); also: (1) all during Lent, except the first day of each week not prevented by a double feast, the Ember Days, or a vigil; (2) on a day when one is required to say a Mass transferred from the preceding Sunday; (3) on all Ember Days; (4) on the first day of the Rogation; (5) from the 17th to the 23rd of December, inclusively; (6) on all vigils; (7) on the eighth day of a simple octave.

The absolution may only be given after a Requiem Mass.

When the rubrics do not permit a votive Mass or a third oration *ad libitum,* the priest may not add another oration at his own discretion. The oration commanded by the Ordinary must be added to the orations prescribed by the rubrics. Unless the foregoing oration is commanded for a grave reason, it must be omitted: (1) on double feasts of the first and second class; (2) on Sundays of the first and second class; (3) on the vigils of Christmas and Pentecost; (4) during the octaves of Christmas, the Epiphany, Easter, the Ascension, Pentecost, and Corpus Christi; (5) on days when there are more than three orations prescribed by the rubrics.

1021. According to a decree of June 30, 1896, the following orations are to be said at Masses of Requiem. On the second of November, the day of the decease or the funeral, in solemn and low Masses on the third, seventh, and thirtieth days, on the anniversary of death, and every time a solemn Mass is celebrated for the dead with a rite which corresponds to that of a double office, only one oration is to be said. An example of the last point in question would be days when one would learn of the death of a person, or anniversaries which are not strictly speaking, anniversaries of the deceased.

In all daily Masses for the deceased, whether chanted or said, the first oration must be recited for the deceased, the second *ad libitum,* and the third for all the faithful departed.

In all Masses celebrated for the faithful departed in general, the orations must be taken from the *Missa Quotidiana* in the order indicated. If the celebrant wishes to add other orations, he may do so only at low Masses, in which case he must see to it that an odd number of orations are said and that the last is for all the deceased.

The priest must recite the *Dies Iræ* every time he says only one oration, even though the Mass be a High Mass. In the other Masses he may recite or omit the hymn *ad libitum*. Purple vestments may never be used at Requiem Masses.

1022. The singing of certain parts of the Mass may not be curtailed in any way, even on weekdays. All the strophes of the *Dies Iræ* must be sung, and the entire *Credo*. No priest should take it upon himself to go on with the Mass before the *Credo* is completed, and the singers should not begin the chant before the priest has reached the altar.

1023. It is the wish of the Holy See, clearly expressed in decrees of the S. C. R., that the Gregorian Chant be used everywhere.

1024. The singing of hymns in the vernacular is forbidden at solemn High Mass. It is not forbidden before the Blessed Sacrament exposed, provided the songs be not translations of the liturgical hymns or prayers. (S. C. R., Feb. 27, 1882.) The bishop may permit the singing of hymns in the vernacular during low Mass, but never during a solemn or High Mass. (S. C. R. Jan. 31, 1896.) No music may be used at the Mass or offices of the dead. The bishop should see to it that all unbecoming music be excluded from the churches. One should avoid also accommodating the words of the liturgy to the music at the risk of displacing the words or changing their meaning.

1025. The organ may be played on all Sundays and holydays of obligation, except the Sundays of Lent and Advent. The organ may, however, be used on *Lætare* and *Gaudete* Sundays.

1026. Every priest should read attentively the rubrics in regard to the defects which may occur in the celebration of Mass. Here are some of the more important points to be remembered:

If, after the consecration, and before he has consumed the Precious Blood, the priest cannot find the host, or discovers that it is completely altered, he must take another, offer it mentally, and, beginning with the words: *Qui pridie,* consecrate it *absolutely,* if the first consecration was certainly invalid, and *conditionally* if there is doubt. He then consumes the host with the Precious Blood. (See nos. 948, 977, 978, and 979.)

1027. If the priest discovers that the host is corrupted after he has consumed the Precious Blood, he must repeat the two consecrations (conditionally, if he is in doubt), and then receive. He must act similarly if, after the consecration, he discovers that the host and the wine have been poisoned.

1028. Besides the Roman liturgy, there are several other liturgies substantially the same, but different in details. In the East, we have the liturgies of St. Mark and St. James, of which the liturgies of St. Basil and St. John Chrysostom are merely abbreviated forms. In the West, we have the Ambrosian liturgy, which does not differ essentially from that of Rome, and the Gallican, which bears some resemblance to the liturgies of the East, having been brought from there by St. Pothinus and St. Irenaeus. Finally, we have the Mozarabic liturgy in Spain, which resembles the Gallican. The right to pass regulations regarding liturgies is reserved to the Holy See, and even Oriental bishops must have their liturgical books revised at Rome.

Art. II. Application of the Fruit of the Sacrifice.

1029. There is no question here of the general, less general, or very special fruits of the Mass (see nos. 951, and 1737 ff.), but only of the special fruit, which benefits the person to whom it is applied more than any one else.

1030. *Who may and must apply this fruit?* The application of the fruit of the Mass is an act of priestly power; the celebrant, therefore, may and must apply it. If he fails to do so, the fruit reverts to the treasury of the Church, as also when he applies it to a person who is incapable of profiting by it. There are some authors who are of the opinion that this fruit reverts to the priest if he fails to apply it, or to those for whom he is especially obliged to celebrate. For this reason a priest is advised to make a conditional application of the fruit to other persons of the family of the person from whom he has received a stipend, if he has received one, or to himself or his own parents, if he is saying the Mass *gratis*. Finally, it would be a very good practice to apply the special fruit to those for whom the Mass is said; and conditionally, but without detriment to those persons, to one's friends and benefactors, to all sinners and just, and to all the souls in Purgatory. (See no. 949.)

1031. *How must this application be made?* It must be made before the consecration. If it were made after the first consecration, it would no longer be certain, because some theologians are of the opinion that the essence of the sacrifice is constituted by only one consecration. If the priest made the application of the fruit after the consecration of the bread, therefore, the sacrifice would have already produced its effect, according to this opinion and, therefore, no further application of it could be made. This fruit may not be reserved at one's own discretion, and for this reason one may not receive a stipend for a Mass that has already been said.

1032. The actual application of the fruit is not necessary, although virtual application is required by some authors. Virtual application demands so little effort that one should not omit it in his preparation for Mass or at the *Memento* of the living. Habitual application suffices, and by habitual, we understand an application that has been made on some previous occasion and never retracted. It is necessary, how- ever, that this habitual application be well-determined; if one had received stipends from ten different persons and applied the fruit to one of the ten without distinction, the application would be null and void. It would be valid, how- ever, and more often than not licit, if during ten days, one applied the fruit of the sacrifice each day to the ten persons taken together. An implicitly determined application suffices, and so one would be permitted to apply the fruit to the person a superior had in mind, to the person who made the offering, to the person who made the offering first, to the person who stands most in need, to the most abandoned soul in Purgatory, or to the soul that is most pleasing to God. The application of the fruit would not be valid if the priest said, "I offer the sacrifice and leave it to God or to the Blessed Virgin to apply the fruit."

1033. One cannot make the application under a condition which has not yet been fulfilled. Thus a priest would not be allowed to offer the sacrifice of the Mass for the first person who dies, or for the first person who offers him a stipend. Even though it were valid, such an application has been prohibited by Pope Clement VII. A priest who has applied the fruit of the Holy Sacrifice to a deceased person for whom he knows he will receive a Mass stipend, may accept such Mass stipends when they are offered him, and not be obliged to repeat the Masses. On the other hand, if a priest received Mass stipends with the instruction that the Masses be said after the person is deceased, and he celebrated such Masses while the person was living, thinking him dead, he would be obliged to repeat the Masses. Some theologians regard this decision as somewhat too severe, because the satisfactory fruit of the Mass may be applied to a living person. (See no. 792.)

May a priest apply the impetratory fruit of the Mass to one person and the satisfactory fruit to another? Not when he has received a stipend, because the special fruit of the Mass goes entirely to the person who has given the stipend. The common opinion of theologians is that he may do so in Masses for which he has received no stipend.

1034. *To whom must this application be made?* For this question we refer the reader to what we have said regarding persons who have charge of souls and persons who have received stipends. (See nos. 960–974.)

1035. *To whom may this application be made?* It is *of faith* that the Sacrifice of the Mass must be offered for the living and the dead.

The dead. It is certain that the Holy Sacrifice of the Mass may be applied to the saints only as an act of thanksgiving, since they have no need of expiating for their sins. It may not be applied to the souls of the damned or to children who have died without Baptism and whose supernatural status is settled. It is *of faith* that the Holy Sacrifice may be offered for the souls in Purgatory, although some theologians claim that the Mass does not benefit them *ex opere operato* in virtue of an infallible divine promise, but only by way of impetration or prayer. The opinion of those theologians who assert that the Mass benefits the poor souls *ex opere operato* is more probable.

By *divine right* a priest may celebrate Mass for all the souls in Purgatory who are able to benefit by it. By *ecclesiasical right* he may offer the Holy Sacrifice publicly for all those who died in communion with the Church, and privately, if there is no danger of scandal, for excommunicated persons, provided the sentence was not passed by a judge. He may not offer the Holy Sacrifice either publicly or privately for persons who died in the very act of mortal sin without giving signs of repentence.

1036. *The living.* A priest may say Mass for any living person, but the Church forbids him to do so for excommunicated persons who have been formally sentenced, unless it be to obtain their conversion. She authorizes him to say Mass for *excommunicati tolerati,* such as heretics, schismatics, and apostates, but only on condition that it be done in private and that there be no danger of scandal (see canons 809 and 2262.) She does not forbid him to say Mass for infidels, provided there be no danger of scandal and no error, evil or superstitious notions on their part as to why he says Mass for them. (Holy Office, July 12, 1865.)

FOURTH TREATISE

Penance

1037. As a moral virtue, Penance is an offshoot of justice. It inclines man to repair by sorrow and satisfaction the offense which sin gives to God. (See no. 2067.) As a Christian virtue, it is supernatural because, without grace, man cannot repent of his sins as he ought. It necessarily presupposes sorrow for the past and a firm purpose of amendment for the future. It does not merely mean a change of life, as was taught by Martin Luther.

1038. Penance, as a Sacrament, is defined as a visible sign which consists partly in the acts of the penitent and partly in the act of the priest lawfully absolving the penitent in the form of a judgment. It is *of faith* that Penance is really and truly a Sacrament.

We shall treat, first, of the Sacrament itself; secondly, of the minister; and thirdly, of the subject.

CHAPTER I

THE SACRAMENT ITSELF

We shall divide this chapter into three articles: 1. Matter and form; 2. Divine institution; 3. Effects.

Art. I. Matter and Form.

1039. *The matter.* The remote matter, or rather the matter to be removed by the Sacrament, is either necessary or not necessary. The *necessary* remote matter are all the mortal sins committed after Baptism and not yet submitted to the power of the keys. This is *certain*. It is also the common opinion of theologians that sins committed in the reception of Baptism belong to the remote matter of the Sacrament of Penance. There are, however, some theologians who deny this.

A person whose Baptism is doubtful, must first be rebaptized conditionally, then confess all the sins he has committed, at least since the time of his doubtful Baptism, and finally be given conditional absolution. If such a person has already confessed his sins and received absolution before his second Baptism, he would not be bound to confess them afterwards, because, if the second Baptism were valid, it would be because the first was valid, and the confessions which preceded the second Baptism would also be valid. Such a person should, however, confess all the sins committed between the last absolution and the second Baptism, although there are some theologians who would not require even this, since the first Baptism is still doubtful. It is for this reason that Ballerini holds that one should urge, but not compel, converts to make this confession, especially if, by compelling them, one would jeopardize their conversion. In the U. S. confession and conditional absolution of converts is of precept (Pl. Council of Baltimore.)

1040. The remote matter which is *not necessary* are all venial sins committed since Baptism and all mortal sins already submitted to the power of the keys. This is also *certain*. Doubtful sins are only doubtful matter and do not warrant the administration of the Sacrament, unless there is a sufficient reason for giving it conditionally. Imperfections are not matter for the Sacrament of Penance.

1041. The *proximate* matter are the acts of the penitent. These acts are: contrition, confession, and satisfaction. This is the common opinion of theologians against Scotus, who regards absolution as the proximate matter. The common opinion of theologians is that of the Church in general, explicitly affirmed in the Roman Ritual, and it is *of faith* that these three acts are the *quasi-matter* of the Sacrament of Penance. (Trent, Sess. 14, can. 4; see also no. 811.) The Council calls these acts the quasi-matter of the Sacrament, not because they are not the true matter, but because they are not physical matter like the water in Baptism.

1042. *Contrition.* Contrition may be defined as a profound sorrow of the soul, coupled with a detestation of sin committed and the firm purpose of sinning no more. We shall deal, first, with contrition in general; secondly, with contrition in particular; and thirdly, with the purpose of amendment.

Contrition in general. Does contrition consist in sorrow? This question is controverted, but there is no doubt that both sorrow and detestation are necessary requisites for contrition, and that one is contained within the other. A person who is sorry for his sins necessarily detests them, and he who detests them is necessarily sorry he ever committed them.

1043. Contrition must be *internal* and *true.* "Rend your hearts, and not your garments." (Joel, 2, 13.) The remedy must be applied to the source of the trouble, and sin is in the will. To become the matter of the Sacrament of Penance, however, contrition must be manifested externally, either by confession or by some sensible sign. According to some theologians, whose opinion must be followed in practice (*ante factum,* or before confession, as below, n. 1066; not *post factum*), the penitent must direct his sorrow towards the Sacrament of Penance, in other words, make an act of contrition in view of confession. According to these authors, an act of contrition made without the intention of going to confession would not be matter for the Sacrament.

1044. Contrition must be universal, *i. e.*, it must extend to all mortal sins. The remission of sins, writes St. Thomas, cannot be effected without sanctifying grace (*S. Theol.*, 3a, q. 87, art. 4), and one mortal sin for which a person has no contrition would exclude grace. Unless there is a special reason for detesting some particular sin, it is not necessary to recall all sins one by one and express sorrow for each, but it suffices to have sorrow for them all from some general motive.

If a person has committed both mortal and venial sins, it suffices that he have contrition for the mortal sins, which alone exclude grace, although he will not be forgiven venial sins for which he has not some kind of sorrow. If he has only venial sins to confess, he must have contrition for at least one of them, otherwise there will be no matter for the Sacrament. Sorrow for one of them suffices for the validity of the Sacrament, although the others are not forgiven unless they are repented of in some manner or other. It is the teaching of all theologians that, as it is the will that has offended God, the will must make amends by detesting each and every sin. (See no. 1045.)

Some authors are of the opinion that the sorrow one has for several venial sins in general would not constitute sufficient matter for the Sacrament of Penance. According to them, the penitent must have sorrow for at least one or several of these sins in particular. For this reason penitents who frequently lapse into the same venial sins, and who consequently give grounds for doubting their sincerity, should be strongly urged to accuse themselves of some mortal sin of their past life, upon which they may focus their contrition. And yet even an accusation of this kind would be without value if the penitent did not endeavor to excite himself to contrition for this particular sin. In accusing himself of this sin, the penitent need not go into details, but merely make mention of the special virtue against which he offended in the past.

Many confessions run the risk of being null and void by reason of negligence in this respect. Priests should guard themselves against such a danger. (See no. 1087.) If the penitent is unable to recall any sins of his past life, the priest should assist him by asking him questions in regard to definite sins. If he still appears helpless, the priest should aid him by means of a question such as the following: "Do you wish to accuse yourself of some sin of anger committed in your past life?" If he answers in the affirmative, the priest should excite him to contrition for this one sin, and then give him conditional absolution, when he would otherwise be deprived of the grace of the Sacrament for a long time. The priest should always make allowance for the ignorance of penitents in these matters.

1045. No venial sins can be forgiven if a person has not obtained the remission of his mortal sins, or of original sin—assuming that it is possible to have only venial sins on one's conscience together with original sin, which St. Thomas denies. Mortal sins and certain venial sins may be forgiven without other venial sins being remitted also. A penitent, therefore, who has both venial and mortal sins on his conscience, cannot obtain forgiveness of the former unless he has either perfect contrition outside of the Sacrament, or attrition *with* the Sacrament. (Even perfect contrition does not efface all venial sins if it does not exclude attachment to sin.) Attrition suffices for the remission of venial sins in Baptism, Penance, and Extreme Unction, and if one be in the state of grace, it suffices without any Sacrament, and even without the wish to receive a Sacrament. This is at least the more probable opinion. It is even more probable that a prayer in which a person begs pardon for his venial sins, or an act of virtue opposed to the sins he has committed, suffices to obtain forgiveness. Theologians more commonly teach that the four other Sacraments (which we have not mentioned above) may also remit venial sins, provided one places no obstacle in the way of their efficacy.

1046. Contrition must also be *sovereign.* This sovereignty need not be one of intensity and duration, although both of these are very desirable, but of appreciation, in the sense that the penitent must have the right appreciation of sin as the greatest of all evils, repent of his sins and be ready to suffer anything rather than offend God. God is the sovereign Good, and sin, even venial sin, is the sovereign evil. It is not necessary that the penitent picture to himself other kinds of evil, in order to ascertain whether or not he is willing to suffer them rather than offend God; it suffices that he be resolved to offend God no more, no matter what happens.

1047. Time is no element in contrition, because the will can turn away from sin in an instant. Nevertheless, it is good to aim at a contrition which perseveres. "My sin," says David, "is always before me." (Ps. 50, 5.)

1048. Finally, contrition must be *supernatural,* either in its principle, which is grace, and without which man can do nothing in the order of salvation; or in its motive, which determines the soul to detest sin. This is *certain.* Innocent XI condemned the proposition that a natural attrition suffices, provided it be honest. Faith furnishes several kinds of supernatural motives of a nature to help us detest sin. It is faith which makes known to us the ugliness of sin, hell, and the other punishments with which God visits the sinner, Heaven, of which sin deprives us, the many benefits we receive from the hand of God if we refrain from sin, and the sovereign perfections against which we offend by sin. These diverse motives give rise to different kinds of contrition.

1049. *Contrition in particular.* If we repent of sin because of the divine perfections which sin outrages, we have contrition properly so called; if we repent from some other motive, we have imperfect contrition or attrition.

1050. *Perfect contrition.* Theologians agree in teaching that contrition is perfect when inspired by perfect charity, or by the love of God because of His intrinsic perfections, made known to us through faith. The love which we have for God because He has been good to us does not suffice for perfect contrition. This is *certain.*

Would the love of a single one of God's perfections, such as His justice or goodness, known to us through faith, suffice for perfect contrition? Some theologians answer this question in the affirmative, others more probably in the negative, asserting that we must have a love of God's intrinsic goodness, which is the source and consummation of all His perfections.

1051. There are two ways in which we may make an act of perfect contrition. We may contemplate the infinite goodness of God and then say: "O my God, thou art infinitely perfect, I love Thee above all things, and for the love of Thee I repent of having offended Thee." Or, we may consider the perfections of God without making an act of love, and sincerely repent ever having offended against these perfections. Some theologians claim that perfect contrition requires an act of love, others are of the opinion that we may dispense with it, as in the second instance. The second opinion is more probable, although the first is safer. When it is a question of the matter of a Sacrament, or of things necessary for salvation, we are not permitted to follow even a more probable opinion.

On the necessity of perfect contrition. Could God forgive us if we did not repent? Writers of note have claimed that He could, but as a matter of fact, perfect contrition is necessary.

Perfect contrition is *necessary as a means* for all those guilty of mortal sin who cannot receive Baptism or Penance. This is *of faith.* "Except you do penance, you shall all likewise perish." (Luke, 13, 5.) The Council of Trent says: "Penitence was indeed at all times necessary to obtain grace and justice for all those who had defiled themselves by a mortal sin." (Sess. 14, ch. 1; see no. 1043.)

Explicit contrition is not always necessary, but implicit contrition, as found in an act of charity, may suffice in the case of one who does not advert to his sins. He who loves God becomes the friend of God, and God will not damn His friend. Outside the Sacrament of Penance and the case of necessity, certain authors require that perfect contrition attain a certain degree of intensity in order to remit sin, but this opinion does not appear very probable, and St. Alphonsus even looks upon it as improbable.

1052. A person who has only original sin does not have to have contrition. Original sin was contracted through no fault of ours, and consequently we are not required to repent of it. Nevertheless, it is quite evident that an infidel who is unable to receive Baptism, and who has no mortal sins on his conscience, cannot be justified except through perfect charity. Contrition is not necessary by necessity of means for a person who has only venial sins, because such a person is already in the state of grace.

1053. Contrition is necessary by necessity of precept in order to reconcile to God a person in the state of mortal sin, when such a person is in danger of death or insanity. All writers agree that in such cases, a person who receives the Sacrament of Penance with attrition is most certainly justified. Is such a person bound to make a perfect act of contrition once he has been justified in this way? Several authors answer in the negative, but St. Alphonsus and a large number of theologians reply in the affirmative. Such a person, they say, is certainly obliged to elicit an act of perfect charity, and how is he to do this if, when adverting to his sins, he does not detest them from a motive of charity? We recommend the second opinion, and in the hour of death, confessors should do their best to excite the dying person to acts of perfect contrition.

1054. Does the precept of contrition oblige outside the danger of death in such a way that any delay in this matter constitutes a grievous sin? Some reply in the affirmative, others in the negative. In opposition to other theologians St. Thomas teaches that final impenitence is not a special sin. St. Alphonsus is of the opinion that, *per accidens,* no one who delays his conversion over a notable period of time can escape serious fault. But what are we to understand by a notable period of time? Some writers say a week, others a whole year. St. Alphonsus does not subscribe to the latter view and says that the precept of contrition obliges *per accidens:* (1) when the precept of charity obliges, if one adverts to one's sins; (2) when a person in the state of mortal sin is called upon to receive or administer the Sacraments; (3) when without this contrition a person would be exposing himself to grave temptations.

1055. *The efficacy of perfect contrition.* When coupled with the vow or desire to receive the Sacrament, perfect contrition always effaces all sins, even outside the danger of death, and when one does not receive the Sacrament. This is *certain* from the *tenets of our faith.* The same is true of perfect charity in the case of a person who does not advert to his sins, since an act of perfect charity contains contrition implicitly. The Church has condemned the proposition of Baius that "charity is not always joined to the remission of sins."

1056. It is *certain* from the words of the Council of Trent (Sess. 14, ch. 4) that the desire for the Sacrament is necessary for justification, but must this desire be explicitly expressed or need it only be implicitly contained in the desire to do whatever is necessary for salvation? Some writers require that it be explicitly expressed, others more probably hold that it must be implicitly contained in this more general desire.

1057. Because contrition remits mortal sin, it remits also the eternal punishment due to sin, but if it is very intense, it may remit all temporal punishment due to sin, and even the residue of sin, or the natural infirmity of the soul in regard to virtue.

1058. *Attrition.* Attrition is the detestation of sin from a supernatural motive other than perfect charity. It is necessary by necessity of means, together with the Sacrament, for all those who are in the state of grievous sin and have not perfect contrition. This is *certain* from what we stated in no. 1051.

Coupled with the Sacrament of Penance, attrition reconciles the soul with God. This is *certain.* "Attrition," says the Council of Trent, "disposes the sinner to obtain the grace of God in the Sacrament of Penance." (Sess. 14, ch. 4; see no. 1043.)

1059. A special preparation is required in order to dispose the sinner to receive grace either through perfect contrition, or through attrition coupled with the Sacraments of Baptism or Penance. The Council of Trent describes this supernatural operation which takes place in the soul of the sinner as follows: "Conceiving faith by hearing they are freely moved towards God, believing those things to be true which God has revealed and promised, especially this, that God justifies the sinner by His grace, through the redemption that is in Christ Jesus; and when, understanding themselves to be sinners, they, by turning from the fear of divine justice whereby they are profitably agitated, to consider the mercy of God, are raised unto hope, trusting that God will be merci-

ful to them for Christ's sake; and they begin to love Him
as the fountain of all justice." (Sess. 6, ch. 6.)

1060. In connection with this important teaching of the
Council of Trent, theologians have raised the question
whether or not the acts of faith and hope which prepare for
justification must be explicit. Some reply in the affirmative,
others, like St. Alphonsus, more commonly and more probably, in the negative. A sinner who sincerely repents of his
sins performs implicit acts of faith and hope, even though
he does not advert to them. Regarding the virtue of hope, we
must observe with St. Francis de Sales that a person who
tends towards God merely from love of self is guilty of sin.
It is one thing to say: "O my God, I love Thee as my sovereign Good," and another to say: "O my God, I love Thee
only for my own sake." The first act is good, the second
impious.

1061. What theologians call *servilely servile fear* does not
suffice for attrition. This fear consists in the dread of sin on
account of the punishments which it entails; one would be
disposed to sin, were there nothing to fear. *Servile fear,*
which causes one to avoid sin because of the punishments
attached to it, but which would not dispose one to commit
sin were there no punishments, is a gift of God. This is *of
faith.* (C. of Trent, Sess. 14, ch. 4, can. 4.) This kind of fear
supplies a sufficient motive for attrition. St. Alphonsus observes that instead of saying: "I am sorry for my sins because I have deserved hell," we should say: "I am sorry for
having offended God, because by doing so I have deserved
hell."

According to a very common and morally certain opinion,
the fear of Purgatory is a sufficient motive for attrition. (St.
Alphonsus, 452.)

Is the fear of temporal punishments, in so far as they are
inflicted by God, a sufficient motive for attrition? Some

writers answer in the affirmative, holding their opinion to be morally certain; others reply in the negative. St. Alphonsus observes that since the second opinion is not lacking in probability, it should be followed in practice.

Filial fear, which causes us to dread not the punishment, but the offense done to God, is much more perfect than servile fear. It is one of the fruits of the virtue of charity and increases with that virtue. Servile fear, on the other hand, decreases as charity increases, although it persists as part of the virtue of charity, being the legitimate love of self.

1062. What are we to understand by the words: "They begin to love God as the fountain of all justice"? Some writers understand these words in the sense of a love of God for Himself, but not above all things. This opinion appears false, because such a love would tend to offend rather than to placate God. Others interpret the words to mean a love of God for Himself and above all things, but only in a very feeble degree. This opinion must also be rejected, because the lowest degree of perfect charity suffices for justification outside the Sacrament of Penance. (See no. 1051.) Lehmkuhl is of the opinion that this love is a certain kind of affection for, or complacency in, God, which is not yet perfect charity, but accompanies the sinner's desire to become reconciled with God, and his hope of obtaining pardon for his sins. Other writers make this love identical with attrition, plus faith, hope, and fear, because "the fear of the Lord is the beginning of love." (Eccles. 25, 16.) St. Alphonsus regards this last opinion as *morally certain,* but adds: "It is to the best advantage of penitents that they make every effort to elicit a perfect act of contrition, and the confessor should do all he can to excite them to it. The more difficult it is for ignorant penitents to make an act of perfect charity without the assistance of the priest, the more strongly do we recommend this course of action, because, in the opinion of some writers, they are bound to elicit such an act once every month." Nevertheless, the confessor should not regard as indisposed a penitent who has attrition only.

If one commits a mortal sin, the special malice or shame of which is known to him through faith, and accuses himself of this sin with a sorrow generated by this special motive, his confession is good, but he should be advised to rest his sorrow on some other universal motive, for otherwise it might be insufficient to cover a sin of another kind which he may have forgotten to confess.

1063. We must not forget that an implicit act of contrition or attrition, such as is found in the act of charity, cannot serve as matter for the Sacrament of Penance, even though one accuses himself of venial sins only, no more than wheat can serve as matter for the Holy Eucharist. This is the common opinion of theologians.

1064. Speculatively speaking it suffices that attrition or contrition exists at the time the priest gives the absolution; but in practice attrition or contrition should precede this act, for fear there be no matter present when he applies the form. A penitent acts imprudently, therefore, when he delays exciting himself to sorrow for his sins until he is in the confessional, and a confessor acts just as imprudently when he gives absolution before the penitent has made the act of contrition.

1065. It is necessary also (see no. 1043), that the penitent make an act of contrition in view of receiving the Sacrament or as a preparation for it. St. Alphonsus regards this opinion as probable. (See no. 1072.) How long does the influence of such an act persist in such a way that there is still a moral union between the act itself and the reception of the Sacrament? Some writers are of the opinion that such an influence persists for a whole day, provided the act of contrition was made in view of the confession and was not retracted by sin.

Other writers would not extend its influence that far, although they would be willing to concede that the influence of an act of contrition made in the morning would persist until that same evening, and certainly for the space of one hour. Others extend its influence beyond one day, so that in justice to all three opinions, penitents should be advised to renew their act of contrition shortly before going to confession. (St. Alph., 447.)

Does the influence of an act of contrition made from a universal motive for venial sins which one is about to confess, persist after a new venial sin has been committed? It is not certain that it does, but Lehmkuhl is of the opinion that it perseveres if the new venial sin is slighter than the others. It is certainly revoked by a new mortal sin.

If a penitent requests absolution for some forgotten sin after he has been granted absolution, some writers are of the opinion that he need not make another act of contrition, others require him to make another act of contrition, and in practice their opinion is to be followed.

1066. *The purpose of amendment.* The purpose of amendment is as necessary as contrition and attrition. This is *certain* from the *tenets of our faith.* No contrition could be sincere without a firm purpose of amendment, because he who repents of his sins, implicitly desires not to commit them again, even though he does not explicitly promise or think of promising it.

Does an implicit purpose of amendment suffice? Not if the act of contrition was made from some special motive; if the act of contrition was made from a universal motive, the question is controverted. Some theologians are of the opinion that it does; others, that it does not; others, again, that it does in cases where the penitent has no thought of the future. Since it is question here of the matter of the Sacrament, the safest opinion must be followed. It is the duty of the confessor, therefore, to excite penitents whose dispositions appear doubtful to a firm purpose of amendment. *Post factum,* however, he should not require that confessions in which the purpose of amendment was not explicit, be repeated. (See nos. 1293 and 1313.)

1067. The purpose of amendment must be (1) *interior* and *firm;* a slight desire does not suffice. He who is convinced that he will certainly relapse into sin, has no firm purpose of amendment, but the mere fear of a relapse would not prevent one from having a firm purpose. We must all entertain the hope that with the help of grace we shall persevere. (2) It must be *universal,* and unlike contrition, which extends only to the sins which one is confessing, it must extend to all possible mortal sins. In the words of the Council of Trent, we must have the *firm purpose of sinning no more.* In the case of venial sins, however, it suffices that the penitent resolve to avoid one among them. (3) The purpose of amendment must be *sovereign* and *supernatural* like contrition and for the same reasons. (See no. 1044 ff.) (4) It must be *efficacious,* not indeed in the sense that the penitent will never relapse into the same sins, but in the sense that he is ready, not only to avoid them, but also to use the means necessary to break his bad habits, and especially to avoid the occasions of sin. (See no. 1329 ff.) However, a relapse is not always an indication that the firm purpose of amendment was lacking, although an easy relapse immediately after confession would certainly point in this direction.

1068. *Confession and the examination of conscience. Necessity of confession.* By divine law confession is necessary for all those who have fallen into mortal sin after Baptism. This is *of faith.* "Whatsoever thou shalt bind upon earth, it shall be bound also in heaven, and whatsoever thou shalt loose on earth, it shall be loosed also in heaven." (Matt.

16, 19.) Jesus Christ appointed His Apostles as judges and physicians of souls, and they cannot act in this capacity without a knowledge of the sins of their subjects, *i. e.*, without confession. The Council of Trent states: "If any one saith, that in the Sacrament of Penance it is not necessary, of divine right, for the remission of sins, to confess all and singly the mortal sins which are remembered after due and diligent meditation, even those [mortal sins] which are secret, and those which are opposed to the two last commandments of the Decalogue, as also the circumstances which change the species of a sin . . . ; let him be anathema." (Sess. 14, can. 7.)

1069. By divine law all those who are in the state of mortal sin are obliged to go to confession when in danger of death and especially at the hour of death. Consequently, there is a grave obligation to confess one's sins before a serious operation, before a difficult childbirth, before undertaking a long sea voyage, and before engaging in battle. Is there any time when this obligation arises outside the danger of death? Some theologians say no, while others maintain that God has left it to His Church to determine the time when the divine precept binds. The Church has decided that it binds once a year.

According to the common opinion of theologians, this obligation does not *per se* bind a person to confess immediately after he has committed some grievous sin, although *per accidens*, it does bind (1) him who, being in the state of mortal sin, must receive Holy Communion, or, possessing only attrition, must administer or receive a Sacrament; (2) him who cannot overcome serious temptations without confession, (3) him who otherwise must remain in the state of mortal sin for a long time. Bucceroni does not think it advisable to instruct the faithful on the second point, although the priest should not fail to preach frequent confession, and point to the Sacrament as the most efficacious means of overcoming one's vices. (See nos. 748, 1054, 2990.)

1070. *The Qualities of Confession.* Confession must be: oral, private, sorrowful, and sincere. Confession must be *oral.* This is prescribed by the custom of the Church, and any one who would make his entire confession by letter or by signs would sin grievously, unless he did so in good faith. If he acted in good faith, his confession would be valid, provided the confessor was present when the confession was presented to him. If the confessor were absent and read the confession afterwards, the confession would be invalid, even though he were present to absolve the penitent.

The following persons are not bound to make an oral confession: those who suffer from a serious impediment of speech, timid young girls, scrupulous persons, and deaf-mutes. The latter are obliged to make their confession in writing if they can, though a few theologians exempt them even from this obligation. Those who do not know the language of the confessor must confess their sins by signs whenever the precept to confess obliges. Apart from this case, it is probable that they may be absolved when they would have to go a long time without a confessor who would understand them, even though they are able to express themselves only by signs or in broken language. The same rule holds good for deaf-mutes (see no. 1094), but the confessor may not oblige them to confess through an interpreter. If they ask for this favor the confessor may allow them to use an interpreter, always taking care, however, that they answer by signs which the interpreter is not able to see.

1071. Confession must be *private, i. e.,* made to the priest alone. The obligation to confess one's sins publicly, as before a battle, in a shipwreck, or in cases of sickness where the patient is surrounded by physicians and others who cannot leave him alone, or where the aid of an interpreter is indispensable, binds only *in articulo mortis,* and even in that case it binds only those who are not sure that their contrition is perfect. In public confessions of this kind, however, one does not have to safeguard the material integrity of the confession, but it suffices if he accuses himself of one venial sin for which he has attrition. (See no. 1096.)

1072. Confession must be *sorrowful.* Therefore, it is not enough merely to enumerate one's sins, to boast of them, or to indicate them by way of a historical narrative; but the penitent must confess his sins in view of the Sacrament. According to the common opinion of theologians, which several call *quite certain,* this is sufficient. A few, however, require that contrition precede confession. It is for this reason that St. Alphonsus in his *Praxis* suggests that, before giving absolution and after the penitent has made an act of contrition, the confessor ask him to renew the accusation of his sins by saying to him: "Do you accuse yourself of all the sins which you have related to me?" In his Moral Theology, the Saint is not quite so formal, but merely says that confessors are in the habit of requiring this general accusation before giving absolution in order to allay all fear on the part of scrupulous persons. A general accusation of this kind would be necessary in the case of a penitent who had first related his sins in a purely historic fashion, without any intention of receiving absolution, but who, after enumerating his sins, had come to repent of them from some supernatural motive. In this case the confessor should excite the penitent to contrition, and if he clearly remembered all that was told him, require him to make a general accusation and then give him absolution. If the confessor does not remember the penitent's confession, he should make him repeat it by means of a series of pertinent questions, and then give him absolution.

1073. Confession must be *sincere,* at least in regard to

mortal sins for which one has not as yet received absolution. The penitent should not exaggerate his faults, but truthfully confess all that he has done.

We said that confession must be sincere *at least in regard to mortal sins,* because an untruth told concerning a venial sin cannot be grave *in se.* Such an untruth might, however, be a grievous sin in the mind of the penitent, in which case his act of contrition bearing on his venial sins might be invalid. (See no. 1065.) *A fortiori,* an untruth of this kind would not be grave if it referred to things which do not strictly belong to confession, as, for instance, a name, a country, etc.

A person who dissimulates his voice in order not to be recognized by the priest, does not sin grievously, unless he resorts to this ruse to obtain an absolution which otherwise he would not secure. On the other hand, it is a serious sin for the penitent to lie to the priest when the latter questions him in regard to a habit of mortal sin, an occasion of mortal sin, or a point of information which it is necessary for the confessor to know in connection with the actual confession. Lack of sincerity in these matters renders it impossible for the confessor to exercise his functions of judge and physician. A lie told in confession is a double mortal sin, because it is an offense against truth and religion.

The confession must be sincere, at least in regard to mortal sins *for which one has not as yet received absolution,* because there is no obligation to accuse oneself of sins that have already been forgiven.

A penitent who knowingly exaggerates the number of his mortal sins, or who confesses as mortal, sins that are only venial, or who confesses as certainly grave, sins that are only doubtfully so, commits a grievous sin, unless he acts thus because of scruples or because he fears that his confession is not as it should be. Scrupulous persons who have exagger-

ated their sins are not obliged to repeat their confession
when they come to realize their mistake, and neither are
persons who have exaggerated or diminished their venial
sins. In practice, the confessor should advise his penitents
to tell rather more than less in their confessions when they
are not sure, in order that they may be at ease.

1074. The penitent should tell everything that it is necessary for the confessor to know. This is what is known as the
material integrity of confession; or at least, of all the sins
he must confess, given the particular circumstances in which
he is, and omitting certain faults which he cannot *per accidens* confess; and this is what is known as the *formal integrity* of confession.

To safeguard the *material integrity* of confession, the
penitent must accuse himself of each and every mortal sin.
This is *of faith* from the words of the Council of Trent. (See
no. 1068.) He must accuse himself also of the kinds of sin,
and this is *certain* from the *tenets of our faith*. The Council
of Trent states that the accusation must be *in specie* (Sess.
14, ch. 5) and all agree that it is question here of the lowest
species, which is the only species properly so called. A person who does not know the species of his sin, must tell its
genus, and if he does not know the genus, he should at least
say whether the sin was mortal or venial.

1075. The penitent must, therefore, tell the number of his
sins in as precise a manner as possible. If he cannot remember the exact number of times he has sinned, he should add
the word "about." When he says that he sinned *about* five
times, he should mean that the number of times was between
four and six; and when he says that he sinned *about* ten
times, he should mean that it was between eight and
twelve, and so forth. If, later on, he remembers the exact
number of his sins and finds that they were comprised
within the number indicated, he need not make any further

mention of them in confession. If, on the other hand, he indicated the exact number of times he committed a certain sin and later on recalls another or several others, he should mention this fact in a subsequent confession. All theologians agree that a person who has contracted a sinful habit need only indicate the duration of said habit, and the approximate number of times he has fallen per month, per week, or per day. St. Leonard of Port Maurice, whose orthodoxy no one may contest, says that the confessor who cannot obtain from such a penitent either the exact or the proximate number of sins, may content himself with an enquiry concerning the duration of the habit, unless it is question of sins like theft, which have special consequences. His reason for prescribing such a line of conduct is the same as that advanced by the Angelic Doctor, namely, that God does not demand more of man than that of which he is capable. A confessor, however, who would take advantage of such a ruling to cut short the confessions of some of his penitents, under the pretext that many others are waiting, would be guilty of grievous sin.

A penitent who omits one mortal sin, or wittingly diminishes the number of his mortal sins by one, commits a sacrilege. The same is true of a penitent who confesses some of his mortal sins to one confessor, with the intention of confessing the others to another. The case would be different if he confessed all his mortal sins to one confessor, who gave him absolution, and all his venial sins to another.

If the confessor happens to notice the penitent's action, he should not appear concerned, and yet he should exhibit some solicitude for the contrition of the one who confesses only venial sins. Priests need to be solicitous also for the contrition of penitents who are constantly changing confessors because they are unwilling to give up some bad habit or some occasion of sin.

1076. Theoretically speaking, there is no obligation to confess mortal sins regarding which one is in doubt, or which have certainly been committed, but concerning the grievousness of which one has either positive or negative doubts. Positive doubt is founded on probable reasons. Negative doubt admits of reasons both for and against. This doctrine may be helpful to persons who are able to form their own consciences, but in practice, penitents should be advised to rid their souls even of doubtful sins. Penitents with a lax conscience who accuse themselves of doubtfully committed mortal sins, must be presumed to have sinned grievously; those whose consciences are scrupulous should be presumed to have sinned venially. It is even advisable to forbid scrupulous persons to confess doubtful sins. (See no. 934.)

On the other hand St. Alphonsus teaches that *in articulo mortis* a penitent who entertains a positive doubt as to whether or not he has committed a mortal sin is certainly obliged to excite himself to perfect contrition, or have recourse to absolution by confessing some other sin of which he is certain.

1077. Penitents who fail to remember whether they have confessed mortal sins which they certainly committed, are obliged to submit such sins to the power of the keys, if they have no reason to believe that they have already confessed them. If they have a probable reason for thinking they have confessed them, they are still obliged to submit them to the power of the keys, according to some theologians, but probably not, according to others. In cases of this kind, it is best to presume that timorous and (*a fortiori*) scrupulous persons need *not* repeat such confessions.

1078. Is there an obligation to confess a sin formerly regarded as doubtful, but now known to be certain? The more common and more probable opinion holds that there is; another, which is probable enough, states that there is not. All agree that if a sin has been confessed in its entirety, without either the penitent or the confessor being cognizant of its grievousness, the penitent is not held to repeat this sin if he later finds out that it was mortal. For the question of mortal sins certainly committed but forgotten, or omitted for good reasons, we refer the reader to nos. 934 and 1097.

1079. If a penitent, after he has received absolution, mentions some mortal sin which he had forgotten, he must repeat his act of contrition and the priest must absolve him anew. This is the common opinion of theologians and must be followed in practice. If the penitent was in the habit of confessing to the same priest, the latter might defer absolution until the next confession, although it would be better for him to administer absolution immediately, because the penitent might confess to some other priest the next time.

1080. It is *of faith*, according to the Council of Trent (see no. 1068), that circumstances which change the nature of sins must be mentioned in confession. Sins have both a theological and a moral species. Therefore, there is an obligation to confess circumstances which change the theological species of a sin, rendering a venial sin grave, and *vice versa* (see no. 1073), and to confess circumstances which change the moral nature of a sin, rendering a sin specifically different from other sins of the same kind. The confession of a penitent who accused himself of striking a man would not be sufficient if the man he struck happened to be his father. This rule applies only to grave circumstances and grievous sins; and hence one would not be obliged to confess having stolen a penny from a church, or having struck a relative, if the person happened to be one's cousin. (See no. 2399.)

For the specific and numerical distinction between sins we refer the reader to nos. 2114 and 2122.

1081. According to common opinion one is obliged to confess hatred of a relative only if the person is in line direct, of first degree in line collateral, a godparent, a godchild, a spouse or a relation in the first degree. Hatred of other relations is merely an aggravating circumstance. *Nec teneris dicere, si peccata contra castitatem confiteris, te esse religiosum vel sacerdotem, vel confessarium complicis, nisi scandalum dederis, vel nisi occasione confessionis sollicitasses, aut absolvisses illum; sed dicere debes te habere votum castitatis, vel te peccasse cum habente hoc votum, vel te esse pastorem ovis quam perdidisti vel eius directorem, si hoc officium suscepisti.*

1082. A person who accuses himself of a sin of incest is obliged to tell whether he sinned with a spiritual or blood relative, because sin committed with a spiritual relative is a species of sacrilege. According to a probable opinion, a penitent is not bound to tell whether the relationship arose from consanguinity, affinity or legal parenthood; neither is he obliged to state the degree of relationship between himself and his accomplice, unless he be related in the first degree of affinity or consanguinity in direct line, or in the first degree of collateral line.

Some authors claim, *fratrem non teneri dicere se peccasse cum sorore, dummodo dicat se peccasse cum consanguinea.* In regard to the degree of natural or legal affinity, there are some authors who maintain that even the first degree in one or other of these lines does not change the species of a sin, neither in the matter of incest, nor in that of hatred, nor in that of injuries done to relatives, without mentioning the degree.

On the other hand, a penitent may be obliged to mention other circumstances, not on account of the incest itself, but on account of being a superior or having other obligations. Thus the sin of a father who seduces his daughter, or his daughter-in-law, differs from the sin of a son who seduces his mother, mother-in-law, or step-mother. The same is true of a person who sins with a pupil towards whom he is fulfilling the duties of a father. A son who commits sin with his step-mother must also state if his father is living, because of the serious injustice he would do him if he were. (See no. 2536.)

A penitent is not bound to confess his sex, state of life, or position unless he has failed in his duties. Pastors, parents or teachers who scandalize their parishioners, children or pupils, respectively, commit a special sin against the duties of their state. *Per se,* a penitent is not bound to state that he committed fornication with three different persons, but may merely assert that he committed the sin three times, without going into any explanations as to whether his accomplices were women of evil repute or otherwise. But he must state these facts at the request of the confessor, because the confessor has the right and the duty to question the penitent in order to ascertain whether or not he is in a proximate occasion of sin.

Per se, a penitent does not sin grievously who accuses himself of a recently committed sin, as if it had been committed some time back, or who makes no distinction in his confessions between sins of which he has never accused himself and sins he has already confessed. He must enter into these distinctions at the request of the confessor who questions him to ascertain a habit of sin, also if his recently committed sin is reserved or a circumstance of time changes the species of the sin, because of a vow taken or a marriage contract entered into. The habit of committing sin does not change the species of the sin, unless it ensues in disobedience, contempt or other faults of this kind, or unless it constitutes a proximate danger of deliberate or indeliberate sin for the party involved. All are of the opinion that the penitent is bound to confess a habit of sin, if the confessor insists that he do so.

1083. According to the more common and more probable opinion, *aggravating circumstances* need not be made matter of confession. By aggravating circumstances we understand circumstances which change neither the theological nor the moral species, nor the number of sins committed, but which do render the sin more or less grave. These circumstances must be confessed, according to all writers, if they are such as to place the penitent under censure, or if they make the sin reserved, or if the confessor questions the penitent in these matters in order to prescribe a remedy or require restitution, or if the duration of the sin leads to other sins such as hatred, etc.

According to all theologians, the external sin must also be confessed. It would not suffice, therefore, to say: "I desired to eat meat on Friday" if one had voluntarily eaten it.

Is one obliged to tell the effect of one's sin, if such an effect takes place some time after the sin has been committed? For instance, is one who administered poison to another for the purpose of killing him, obliged to accuse himself of homicide if the poison took effect three days later? Some theologians claim that a penitent is obliged to accuse himself of this sin, if he did not retract his evil intention before the poison took effect; others claim that he is bound not *per se,* but only *per accidens,* because of the damage done or the censure incurred. (See nos. 1826 and 2097.)

In practice, the penitent should accuse himself of anything that disturbs his peace of conscience, but the confessor should gently dissuade him from entering into useless details concerning sins against chastity.

1084. *Attenuating* circumstances, or such as diminish the guilt of a sin, must be mentioned in confession only when they render venial a sin which would otherwise be mortal.

1085. *General* circumstances, such as ingratitude towards

God, etc., which are found in all sins, need not be confessed except when the penitent has attended to them in a formal and deliberate way.

1086. *Formal integrity.* All that we have said so far has reference to the material integrity of confession. Since, however, God does not ask the impossible, and material integrity is in many cases an impossibility, formal integrity suffices, *i. e.,* the penitent need only confess what he can and must under the existing circumstances.

It is certain that the intrinsic difficulty experienced in the act of confession does not excuse the penitent from material integrity; he can dispense with this only when it is physically or morally impossible for him to tell all. Moral impossibility admits of the omission of those sins only, the mention of which would entail serious inconvenience. Even in this case, it is required that there be no other confessor available to whom the penitent could conveniently confess, and that he be obliged by precept to confess and receive Communion or be forced to remain two or three days (many say, one whole day) in the state of mortal sin. When the moral impossibility ceases, the penitent is obliged, *sub gravi,* to mention all the omitted sins in his next confession.

1087. *Physical* impossibility dispenses dying persons from the material integrity of confession. It suffices for the validity of the Sacrament that they give signs of repentance in the presence of the confessor, in which case they should be absolved unconditionally. It is proper, says St. Alphonsus, to absolve such persons every time they give signs of repentance.

Would these same signs of repentance suffice for the validity of the confession of a person who has no mortal sins on his conscience, but who is anxious that his contrition and the priest's absolution bear on the mortal sins of his past

life; and would it suffice in this case that the penitent give
signs of repentance for these past sins without confessing
any one of them in particular? The more common opinion
is that these signs of repentance suffice. Since, however,
some theologians disagree, it is safer, in practice, to require
the mention of some specific sin against some specific virtue.
(See no. 1044.)

1088. If a dying person gives signs of repentance in the
absence of the confessor, or if he gives no signs whatever,
but has always led a Christian life, he should be given conditional absolution. A priest should administer *conditional*
absolution also to a dying person whose disposition appears
doubtful. If the dying person has not led a Christian life, or
if he lost consciousness in the very act of sin, even the sin of
refusing the Sacraments, it is probable that he may still be
given conditional absolution. *Sacramenta propter homines.*
"In cases of this kind," writes Billot, "it is not necessary
that the priest base the validity of his act on a probability
properly so called; it suffices that he rest it even on an
unlikely possibility. Must we not try everything when a soul
is in danger of eternal damnation?" On the other hand, it is
certain that a priest may not give absolution to a sick person
who, while in his right mind, refuses his ministrations or ex-
hibits no attrition.

1089. It is useless for a confessor to request a dying person,
who is not yet unconscious, to give some ostensible sign after
he has lost the use of his speech, in order to manifest his intention of accusing himself of some sin of his past life, for
which he is sorry and wishes to obtain absolution.

A priest may give conditional absolution several times to
a dying person who has lost the use of his senses. St.
Alphonsus advises that it be given every three hours and
even oftener when death approaches, whether the dying man

was able to confess beforehand or not. If he were not able to confess beforehand, he is all the more in need of the charity of the priest who ministers unto him.

1090. The following are the signs of approaching death: a missing pulse; a pulse which beats intermittently; painful respiration; eyes that are hollow, glassy, or staring; a pinched and whitish nose; a yellowish face; cold sweat; excessive heat around the heart while the extremities are cold.

The signs of imminent death are: intermittent respiration; missing pulse beats; contraction and grinding of the teeth; a slight sigh or moan; one lonely tear; contortions of the mouth, eyes, or body. The confessor should not delay, therefore, because it is better that the dying person receive the Sacraments while conscious, than to aim at a complete confession and fail to be absolved. The priest should impress upon the mind of the patient the necessity of as rapid a confession as possible, adding that if he ever recovers, he can spend more time on the examination of his conscience and the confession of his sins. The confessor might even suggest that the penitent relieve his mind of any further disquietude after he has received the Holy Viaticum, because if it became impossible for him to confess all his sins, God in His mercy would forgive them nevertheless.

1091. Confessors should be mindful of the admonition of St. Alphonsus: "The priest should never leave a sick person in his death agony." A priest may have other important duties to attend to, but he should remember that a man dies only once. He should see to it, also, that good parishioners be trained to assist him by exciting the dying to acts of perfect contrition in the hour of death. He himself should exhort the sick to perform these acts, stressing their efficacy and that of prayer, and urging them to pray and perform these acts when they lose consciousness.

1092. It is true that canon 731 forbids priests to administer the Sacraments of the Church to heretics and schismatics, even though they ask for them in good faith; yet it would seem that this rule applies only to non-Catholics who are not in immediate danger of death. If, therefore, the dying person is a heretic or a schismatic and is deprived of the use of his senses, the confessor should seek to have him elicit acts of the theological virtues, at the same time suggesting to him in a loud tone of voice the various motives to be borne in mind. If Baptism is doubtful, a priest, and for that matter any man, may administer this Sacrament conditionally, after which the confessor may conditionally absolve the dying person from excommunication and all his sins. If such a person has not yet lost the use of his senses, and accepted conditional Baptism, believing in good faith that sacramental confession is not essential, the confessor could still absolve him conditionally, provided he showed signs of repentance and a resolve to sin no more, especially (this is a condition required by Lehmkuhl) if the penitent made known his desire to be assisted by the priest in making his peace with God. (See nos. 1367, 1404, and 2235.) At this very critical time the priest should be on his guard and not condemn too overtly the sect of which the dying person is a member, in order not to rob him of his good faith and create for him a well-nigh insurmountable temptation.

1093. Let us not forget, either, and let us be emphatic in our teaching, that any heretic, and for that matter any infidel, may be justified by an act of perfect charity and perfect contrition, coupled with faith and hope. No one of the Sacraments of the living or of the dead can justify an adult who has not at least attrition, coupled with faith and hope. It is a mistake, therefore, for priests to imagine that they have done everything when they have administered absolution and Extreme Unction to a dying person, without suggesting to him these acts, to which more often than not even heretics

do not object. It is upon this ground that we may meet non-
Catholics, and so we should not fail to take advantage of
such an opportunity. What we have said regarding the dying applies also to children who have not yet reached the age
of reason. (See nos. 1334 ff. and 1387.)

1094. Deaf-mutes must confess their sins in their entirety
by means of signs, if the confessor is acquainted with the
sign language; and it is probable that they must confess
their sins in writing if they know how to write. Some theologians maintain, however, that they have no such obligation, hence, the confessor may dispense with asking them
questions in writing, the sole purpose of which is to secure
the integrity of their confession. For illiterate deaf-mutes it
is enough if they manifest in a general way some sin they
have committed, or even merely indicate that they have
sinned. The same holds of those who do not know the language of the confessor. (See no. 1070.) All such persons
should be absolved when they are bound by the precept of
confession or when they would otherwise be in danger of remaining for a long time in the state of mortal sin. It is better,
however, to instruct such persons beforehand, and to impart
to them, through modern methods, all the information they
need concerning motives, theological virtues, attrition, etc.
Work of this kind should be entrusted to persons whose
judgment is sound; too much attention should not be paid
to manuals of piety, which, as Lehmkuhl remarks, are often
deficient in this respect. If such persons fail to accuse themselves of any specific sin, it is better to give them conditional
absolution. The confessor may question in advance persons
who associate with deaf-mutes concerning their habits of
living, in order to be in a better position to discover their
sins. One is not warranted in refusing them Holy Communion, or the Sacrament of Matrimony, unless they are
born blind and deaf and dumb, and even then they should

be given Confirmation and Extreme Unction if they show any signs of reason.

1095. The deaf are obliged to accuse themselves of all the sins they remember, but the confessor is not bound to question them, if it is hard for them to hear him, or if he would run the risk of violating the seal in questioning them. He should absolve them either absolutely or conditionally, according to the dispositions which the confession reveals. (See no. 1387.) It is not at all proper to hear the confessions of deaf persons in an ordinary confessional, where they cannot hear the confessor, because they may drift into a complete ignorance of the things necessary for salvation. They cannot hear sermons and often enough are unable to read. Moreover, if they have some vicious habit, how are they to rid themselves of it without the assistance of the confessor? They should, therefore, be urged to make their confessions in the sacristy, or at a time when there are no other persons in church, unless it be question of women whose lives are open to suspicion. It would not be out of place to have an ear-trumpet in every sacristy for the benefit of these unfortunates.

1096. The following are to be considered as morally unable to observe the law of integrity in the matter of confession:

1. Those who are in danger of death, *e. g.*, soldiers on the eve of a battle, shipwrecked persons, sick persons who are surrounded by physicians and nurses. All these may be given absolution as we have stated in no. 1071, provided they accuse themselves of one venial sin, or better still, a mortal sin that persons in these conditions can be presumed to be able to confess. A large number of such persons may be absolved *in globo* by means of the formula, *"Ego vos absolvo."* A priest may even absolve a whole group conditionally in case of shipwreck or before battle, even though he is unable to

obtain any kind of confession; but in that case it is best to ask the penitents to signify their contrition by a sign such as the raising of the hand. In times of pestilence, a confessor who fears contagion is not obliged to secure the integrity of the penitent's confession, although he should advise the diseased to complete their confessions at their earliest convenience.

2. Those who are in danger of becoming insane, or of incurring some other grave inconvenience, as is the case with certain scrupulous persons.

3. Those who are in danger of either falling into sin themselves, or of giving scandal, e. g., *si paenitens aliqua peccata revelando timeret ne confessarius secum caderet.*

4. Those who cannot reveal a sin without violating the seal of confession.

5. Those who are exposed to the danger of losing their good name. Thus, a priest would be excused from the law who, just before celebrating Mass, needed to make a general confession, yet could not do so without arousing suspicions concerning his life and conduct. A dying person would be excused who just before receiving the Holy Viaticum needed to make a lengthy general confession; a parishioner who at the time of a general communion in church needed to make a similar confession; and finally, a penitent whom the confessor is reprimanding in such a way that he can be overheard by persons outside the confessional. If such a penitent calls the confessor's attention to this fact, and he refuses to take cognizance of it, the penitent is excused from the law if he fears that by confessing a sin, his reputation will be seriously compromised.

Is the penitent excused from the law of integrity in order to safeguard the reputation of another, let us say, an accomplice? Some theologians assert that he *is*, others claim that he is *not*, but that the penitent is obliged to find a confessor who does not know the accomplice. This obligation of finding another confessor is grave only if there is question of a serious crime, and a penitent is not obliged to confess elsewhere if he has hopes of gaining some extraordinary indulgence, or of obtaining better advice from the priest who knows the accomplice. Manifestly, one may not make known the sin of another when accusing himself of some venial fault or of some mortal sin already forgiven.

1097. When the reasons for curtailing a confession cease, all sins that have been omitted for the reasons we have just mentioned, as well as all mortal sins involuntarily forgotten, must be submitted to the power of the keys. This is certain and beyond controversy.

1098. A confessor who threatens to refuse absolution unless the penitent reveals the name of his or her accomplice, sins grievously, unless he acts without reflection and no scandal or defamation of the person's character results from his action. Nevertheless, the confessor has the right to question the penitent concerning occasions of sin, in order to deter him from entering into them, even thought such information would reveal to him the name of the accomplice. He may and must exact of the penitent that he or she reveal, not to him, but to some one who is in a position to put an end to the abuse, the name of a college student, for instance, who is leading his fellow-students astray, or that of a physician, pharmacist, or midwife who is procuring abortions. There is no legislation to prevent penitents from revealing the names of such persons to the confessor of their own free will. Nevertheless, the confessor should make it a point to receive such information only outside the Sacrament of Penance. One would be permitted even to request the name of the accomplice, together with permission to make use of such information, if there were no other way, not only of furthering the good of the community, but of forestalling a public calamity. (See no. 1303.)

1099. When must confessions be repeated? We shall first treat of such confessions in general, and secondly, we shall say a word in regard to general confession.

A confession is invalid *on the part of the minister,* if he has no jurisdiction, if he does not pronounce or mispronounces the words of absolution, if he does not hear any of the sins confessed to him, or if he remembers nothing at the time when he gives the absolution. A confession is invalid *on the part of the penitent,* if he has not the necessary dispositions, if he is ignorant of the truths which are necessary by necessity of means, if he has seriously neglected to examine his conscience, and if he is lacking in sincerity, attrition, or firm purpose of amendment. If the penitent is not aware of his lack of disposition, his confession is null and void; if he is aware of it, it is sacrilegious. A confession which is certainly null and void must be repeated just like a sacrilegious one, but a sacrilegious confession that has not been repeated renders all subsequent confessions equally sacrilegious. A possible exception to his rule would be the confessions of a penitent made in good faith and with good dispositions, but in complete forgetfulness of past sacrilegious confessions. If the penitent omits to tell in confession something which does not impair validity, he has only to tell this in his next confession (see nos. 1079 and 1097), but if he notices that the confessor is distracted, or has not heard any one of his sins, he must repeat them all before receiving absolution. If the confessor happened to be distracted during the confession of only two or three of the penitent's sins, the latter should repeat these before receiving absolution. If he does not remember them, he must repeat his entire confession if it is short. A penitent who in good faith has confessed his sins to a confessor who is ignorant of their gravity does not need to repeat his confession, but a penitent who does this in bad faith must repeat his entire confession to another priest.

All invalid confessions must be repeated. If they are repeated to the same confessor, it is not necessary, according to the more probable opinion, to repeat everything, even though the confessor remembers nothing from the previous confession, but it suffices that the confessor have some vague idea of his penitent's former state of conscience, and that the penitent accuse himself in a general way of the sins mentioned in his former confession, making an explicit mention of all those he omitted to tell. According to a few distinguished theologians, it suffices that the confessor have some recollection of the penance he gave in the first confession, but if he remembered nothing of this, his absolution would be invalid, according to the more common opinion, although some writers claim that a generic confession would suffice even in this case. What we have said applies also to a penitent, the absolution of whose sins has been deferred, and the confession of whose sins has been forgotten by the confessor. A good rule for the confessor in these cases is to administer a penance which both he and the penitent will remember. (See no. 1151.)

1100. A confession repeated to another confessor must be repeated in its entirety. A penitent must repeat also all sins of which he accused himself in a purely narrative way if the confessor has no distinct recollection of what was told him. If the confessor has a distinct recollection of the sins confessed to him, it suffices for the penitent to say: "I accuse myself of all the sins of which I told you." It is probable even that a generic accusation of this kind would suffice even though the confessor had no distinct recollection of the sins confessed to him, if in listening to the account of the person's life, he entertained a hope of inducing him some day to make a sacramental confession. There are some theologians who claim that a generic accusation suffices even outside of this case.

1101. In assisting persons whose habits are regular to repeat the confessions of a whole lifetime, the confessor need only to insist on a confession of one year, especially if such persons are extremely ignorant. He has then only to reckon their age and ask them to say at the end of their confession: "I accuse myself of about these same sins each year of my life." He could not remain content with such a procedure if, at the end of their accusations, he clearly perceived that the previous confession was of no avail, unless he had a distinct recollection of their annual confession.

1102. Confessions that are doubtfully null or invalid need not, strictly speaking, be repeated, but are presumed to be valid.

1103. *General confession.* It is customary to distinguish between a complete general confession, in which the penitent repeats all the sins of his past life, and a *partial one,* in which he repeats the sins of one year or several years only. When confessions have been null or invalid, general confession becomes imperative (see no. 1099), but only in these cases must it be enjoined upon the penitent. If the penitent has a mortal dread of such confessions, if his life is regular, or if he is ignorant, the confessor may inquire into his exact age, and then have him make a confession extending over one year of his life, asking him at the end to accuse himself of these same sins for the rest of the years of his life, and assuring him that he will be forgiven for all.

1104. Even when a general confession is not necessary, the confessor should *advise* one, if the penitent is not given to scruples, and if there is some question of the validity of his previous confessions. (See no. 1102.) It is a good prac-

tice to advise other persons (except the scrupulous) to do
the same, if there are good reasons for believing that they
will derive real profit therefrom. This is the case with persons who have never made a general confession before, or
who have made one only during their childhood days, before
reaching adolescence. Penitents should be strongly advised
to make a general confession when they reach certain land-
marks in their lives, e. g., First Communion, the choice of a
state of life, a jubilee or a mission, the beginning of widowhood, and, finally, the hour of death. This is the advice given
by the majority of theologians and masters of the spiritual
life, and should be preached from both confessional and
pulpit, because general confessions which were thought to
be merely useful in the beginning, have turned out to be
necessary from more than one viewpoint afterwards, as St.
Leonard of Port Maurice says and as experience teaches.

1105. The number of souls lost through sacrilegious confessions is incredible, not only among women, but also, as
St. Leonard remarks, among men, whose pride is greater and
whose faith is weaker. In view of this fact, St. Alphonsus,
as bishop, decreed that several times during the year the
priests of his diocese should call in other priests to act
as extraordinary confessors. At least once a year, during the
holy season of Lent, every pastor should invite a neighboring priest, or, better still, a priest located some distance
away, to hear the confessions of his parishioners, and he
himself should return the service. St. Alphonsus advised that
a mission be preached in every parish once every three years,
and St. Vincent de Paul, once every five years. One of the
best precedents a pastor could possibly set is a mission in his
church once every five years, for in the opinion of all the
saints and all good men of experience, there is no better
means of arousing the lukewarm and converting sinners.
Pius VI condemned the doctrine of the synod of Pistoia

which called a mission "a vain noise," and St. Alphonsus spoke these harsh words: *"Parochus ille, qui rejicit missiones, magnam ingerit suspicionem probitatis suae."*

1106. A confessor who is reluctant about allowing his penitents to confess elsewhere, sins. If he learns that they have done so, he should rather show himself well pleased with their conduct. He would even do well to require that those of his penitents who are not scrupulous confess from time to time to other priests, and during the time of the mission, he should refuse to hear confessions himself. His advice to mothers should be that they leave their sons and especially their daughters absolute liberty in the matter of selecting a confessor. If there is more than one priest in the parish, boys, for instance, should not be obliged to confess to the assistant, and the girls to the pastor, but all should be allowed complete liberty.

1107. St. Leonard of Port Maurice censures confessors who condemn general confession on principle, who refuse to hear a general confession, or who, as soon as they are asked to hear one, want to know if the penitent ever wilfully concealed a sin in some past confession, and if he did not, reply that such a confession is altogether unnecessary, just as if lack of sincerity alone makes general confession indispensable. Are not such confessors aware that a question put so bluntly may provoke a lie from penitents, who more often than not must be gently persuaded before they will make a complete avowal of sins which they have purposely concealed? (See no. 1130.)

1108. To forestall scruples, however, the same Saint advises that confessors never allow penitents to make a complete general confession, if they have made one satisfactory general confession after reaching the age of twenty. If these penitents are not scrupulous, they may be advised to make a general review of their life from the time of their last general confession, and incidentally tell what they may have omitted at that time. General confessions are useless and even disastrous in the case of scrupulous persons, who should, therefore, be deterred from making them.

1109. When, as during a mission, a large number of persons are waiting to go to confession, it is well nigh impossible to allow all to make a general confession. In this case, it suffices to ask those penitents who have no real need of making a general confession, to mention the sins of their past life which are causing them disquietude, and when they have mentioned these, the confessor may say: "You accuse yourself also of all the sins of your past life, in thought, desire, word, and act." He should then tell them to feel perfectly at ease in regard to the rest, and give them absolution. Failure to do this might throw these souls into a state of mental turmoil; and then they will either remain in this state, or they will seek some other confessor and take up his time.

1110. Confessors should not, however, too readily persuade themselves that general confessions are impossible when large crowds are waiting. All those who feel a real need of making a general confession should be encouraged to do so, as well as they can. It is true that, when a general confession is not necessary, it need not be complete, and the penitent should be advised of this. However, the more perfect the general confession, the more abundant the fruits that will accrue to the soul.

1111. It is easy to make a general confession (see no. 1101); a penitent can make one as quickly as he can make a confession covering one year. The penitent need not first tell the sins he has committed since his last confession, but may include them all at one time. He should be informed about this before he begins. He need make no mention of venial sins, he can dispense with the history of each and every one of his mortal sins, and there is no need of him dividing his confession into a certain number of parts corresponding to certain periods of his life, as is suggested rather uselessly and imprudently by certain pious writers, against whom St. Leonard of Port Maurice justly protests. It is sufficient if the penitent, with the assistance of the confessor, or better still the confessor himself, rapidly runs over the commandments of God and the Church, and the confessor asks the penitent at what age he began to break this or that commandment, and how many times he did so per month, per week, etc. (See no. 1075.) Before beginning the confession, the priest should ask the penitent in what year he was born, because if an elderly woman be asked her age, she will seldom tell the truth. If the penitent does not know the year of his birth, the confessor should ask him how old he was when he married, how long he lived with his first wife, how long with his second, how long he has been a widower, etc. Sins against chastity are of a different species according to whether they are committed before or after marriage, consequently, they must be distinguished in confession. (See no. 1125.)

1112. *The examination of conscience. Its necessity.* It is *certain from the tenets of our faith* that we are obliged *sub gravi* to examine ourselves in the matter of our mortal sins. (See no. 1068.) How, indeed, are we to know and recall the number and kind of our sins, as well as the circumstances which change their nature, unless we diligently examine ourselves beforehand? Therefore, a penitent sins grievously if, knowing that he is obliged to examine his conscience, he fails to do so when he has several mortal sins to confess, and if, as a consequence of his negligence in this matter, he omits something which he is obliged to tell, his confession is invalid. A penitent who has committed only two or three mortal sins would not sin grievously in failing to examine his conscience, if he had these sins clearly in mind; but one who had a number of mortal sins to confess, and who exposed himself to omitting one or two of them, would not be free from blame, even though he succeeded in telling all, because a serious thing like confession should be given serious attention. This attention need not, however, be minute and strained, but it should be reasonable, so as not to render confession too burdensome. There is no obligation to write out one's sins. Forgetfulness is not always a sign that one has been neglectful in examining his conscience, and moreover, slight negligence in these matters does not render confession invalid.

1113. There is no obligation to examine oneself with regard to venial sins or to accuse oneself of them in confession. Pious penitents are advised not to spend too much time on this examination, five minutes at the most, and scrupulous persons should be commanded not to pay any attention at all to venial sins. A serious mistake is often made by pious persons who spend a great deal of time on their examination of conscience, but very little in exciting themselves to sorrow and a firm purpose of amendment. Persons who are in the habit of going frequently to confession need not spend as much time on their examination of conscience, even though they have lapsed into mortal sin, as persons who remain away from the Sacrament for a long time. Less diligence is required of an ignorant than of an educated person, and less of a sick than of a healthy one. It is often better for the confessor himself to examine persons who are incapable of making such an examination, and especially the sick, whom it is better to absolve after an incomplete confession than expose to eternal damnation. In certain cases, a confessor may tactfully advise educated persons who present themselves unprepared, to examine their consciences a little better and then return for absolution, but today especially, it is safer for the confessor himself to examine them, and then allow them a few instants for further examination before giving them absolution. (See no. 1320.)

1114. *Manner of making the examination of conscience.* After invoking the aid of the Holy Spirit, the penitent should try to recall the places where he was each day and the circumstances in which he sinned by thought, desire, word, action and omission, although in lengthier confessions it is advisable that both the confessor and the penitent follow a definite order and plan: the commandments of God, the precepts of the Church, the capital sins, the obligations of the penitent's state of life, etc. With this in mind, we subjoin an examination which may prove of use in lengthy and especially general confessions; the confessor will select those questions which he deems best suited to the conditions of his penitent.

1115. The confessor may begin by saying to the penitent: "If there is anything in your past life which worries you, do not be afraid to tell me, because I am here to assist you. Have you failed in some of your past confessions to excite yourself to sorrow for your sin? Have you been neglectful in the examination of your conscience? Have you relapsed into sin shortly after confession?" These questions should be put to every penitent whom the confessor meets for the first time. Often enough he will not succeed, even by means of these questions, in uncovering a sacrilege, and yet his gentleness and kindness will eventually bring the penitent around to the accusation of sins which he did not at first confess.

We herewith append a list of the principal questions which the confessor may put to the average penitent. Some of these questions will not fit all cases, and a prudent confessor will use discretion and omit them when indicated. Every priest should know the different kinds of sins of which penitents may accuse themselves, and since this list is not exhaustive,

it becomes imperative for him to study the different treatises
on sins. (See no. 2094; the virtues, no. 2022; the Ten Commandments, no. 2185, and the precepts of the Church, no.
2976.)

1116. The *First Commandment. Faith.* Have you forgotten some of the truths which it is necessary to know?
Have you entertained doubts in regard to some of the truths
of the faith? Have you denied them in your mind? How
often? (Unless there are special circumstances, it is advisable not to question the penitent concerning exterior sins
against the faith, when he has not consented to interior ones.
Nevertheless, it is worth remarking that many ignorant persons have no conception of what an evil thought is and deny
having consented to any when they have indulged in sinful
external actions.) Have you revealed to others your doubts
concerning the faith, or your lack of faith? Have you indulged in, or listened to, talk against your religion? Have
you read books or periodicals directed against the faith?
(Penitents should be advised to destroy all such literature,
to refuse to accept it, and to avoid bad company.)

1117. To obviate a sacrilege, the confessor should not put
the questions negatively, otherwise the penitent might be
tempted to answer in the same way, and thus violate the
truth. All questions should be asked in the affirmative, and
upon receiving an answer, the confessor should add a word
intended to inspire the penitent with courage and confidence.
In questioning the penitent concerning the number of his
sins, it is better to act as if one expected it to be greater than
it actually is. He should say: "Did you sin twenty times a
day?" if he fears that the penitent sinned ten times. The
penitent will invariably find it easier to diminish the number
suggested than to add to it. For the same reason the confessor should ask: "Did you fall back into this sin today?"
in order to urge him to admit that he did so yesterday; and

if the penitent has not been to confession for a long time, the priest should ask: "Is it all of fifty years since your last confession?" in order to make it easier for him to admit that it was twenty or thirty years. If the confessor entertains any misgivings as to the sincerity of the penitent who answers his questions concerning the commission of certain sins in the negative, he may ask how many times the penitent committed such a sin. If the penitent indicates the number, he evidently confesses that which he formerly denied.

Every effort should be made to assure the penitent that he is unknown to the confessor. If he does not answer his questions immediately, the confessor should not hurry him, for instead of gaining time, he will only seal his lips. The confessor should not adopt too high a tone in hearing confessions, even though he speaks of extra-confessional matter, otherwise penitents will fear that their confessions are overheard. The suggestions we have just indicated will prove of value in preventing sacrilegious confessions.

1118. *Hope*. Have you ever despaired of your salvation? Have you ever despaired of being able to correct your faults? Have you murmured against God in adversity? Have you sinned by presumption? Have you exposed yourself to occasions of sin by deferring the time of your conversion or sinning with greater ease because you knew God is merciful, or because you imagined you could save your soul without good works?

1119. *Charity*. Have you ever hated God, or have you grown disgusted in His service?

1120. *Religion*. Have you ever indulged in superstitious practices, putting faith in dreams or fortune-tellers? Did you do these things with the intention of harming your neighbor? Have you committed certain mortal sins in church? Have you mistreated persons consecrated to God or entertained a desire of sinning with them? Have you ever received Communion when not fasting? Have you neglected to say your prayers or to pray for those under your care?

1121. The *Second Commandment*. Have you uttered injurious or blasphemous words against God and His saints? (Confessors should be careful to put this question not only to women and little boys, but also to little girls, who easily conceal this sin.) Have you uttered false or unjust oaths? In doing so, have you harmed your neighbor? Have you neglected to carry out the oaths and vows which you lawfully made?

1122. The *Third Commandment*. Have you engaged in servile work for a long period of time and without necessity on Sundays and holydays of obligation? Have you compelled others to work on these days? Have you missed Mass? Have you arrived at Mass late? Have you allowed or made others miss Mass?

1123. The *Fourth Commandment*. Have you fostered hatred against your parents, your superiors, your wife, your husband? Have you contemned or despised them? Have you threatened or struck them? Have you disobeyed them? Have you ill-treated your children, your students, your servants, your wife? Have you exposed them to occasions of sin? Have you neglected to correct them? Have you given them a bad example? Have you failed to make known to them their religious duties? Have you failed to make them fulfill these duties? Have you hated, contemned, ill-treated or insulted your brothers and sisters?

1124. The *Fifth and Eighth Commandments*. Have you lied? Have you wished that grave evil might befall yourself and others? What was this evil? Have you rejoiced in the misfortunes of your neighbor? What were these misfortunes? Have you grieved at his prosperity? Have you held a grudge against any one? Have you insulted any one? Have you made known some real or imaginary fault of theirs? Have you struck any one? Have you ever occasioned the death of any one? (The penitent should forgive everything, be willing to render service to all, and be on good terms with all, accept excuses and repair calumnies and pernicious lies.) Have you misjudged others? Have you made known the secret sins of others or read secret and important letters addressed to them?

1125. The *Sixth and Ninth Commandments*. The confessor should take care in his efforts to secure the integrity of confession and the penitent's peace of mind not to apprise him of sinful practices with which he has no acquaintance. Sins against the sixth commandment are most likely to disturb the penitent's mind when he has not confessed them. The questions asked should be brief and to the point.

1126. Have you taken pleasure in evil thoughts? Have you read obscene literature? Have you passed such literature on to others? Have you looked upon obscene things? Have you desired to see such things? Have you rejoiced upon seeing them? (According to St. Leonard, the best means of bringing the penitent to accuse himself of unchaste desires is to question him concerning the sins we have just indicated, and then ask him if he ever wished to commit them. The same holds true of the pleasure derived from sins committed.) Have you avoided evil conversation? Have you avoided wicked companions? Have you spoken of unchaste things with evil thoughts in your mind, before persons who might be scandalized thereby? Have you sung or listened to suggestive songs? Have you taught such songs to others? Have you committed impure actions alone, either before or after being married; either before or after taking the vow of chastity? Have you experienced pleasure as a consequence of these actions? How old were you when you began to experience these pleasures?

1127. If the penitent is making a general confession, he

should mention all the sins which he has committed since his childhood days, *i. e.*, since the age of three or four. If he does this he will have no qualms of conscience later on. Let the confessor question him on this point.

1128. *Tactus habuisti erga alios ejusdem sexus, cum manibus, et etiam alio modo, cum iisdem voluptatibus malis? Erant consanguinei? Conjugati? Deo consecrati? Erga alios etiam alterius sexus oscula habuisti et tactus? Erant consanguinei? Conjugati? Deo consecrati? Actum conjugii cum illis fecisti? Quoties? Habuisti filios ex hoc consortio, quid de illis? Si non habuisti, modo prohibito conceptionem impedisti? Vel abortum procurasti? Complices manetne in domo tua?—Si poenitens puer sit, quære cum quo dormiat: removenda est occasio. Uxoribus: Obedivisti marito in rebus licitis? Ambobus conjugibus: Numquid desiderasti alium vel aliam quam conjugem? Habesne in matrimonio aliquid quod te molestet? Si respondent: Bene concordamus, adde: Aliquidne fecistis contra castitatem? Fortasse accusabunt onanismum. Aliquid aliud habetis? Si hæsitant, adde: Extra actum conjugii malas libertates sumpsisti, tactu? alio modo, cum malis voluptatibus? An in vase indebito? Omnibus post prædicta: Si quid adhuc habes, quod non postulaverim, dic bono animo, adjuvabo te; et deinde potes, si poenitentem anxie hærentem vides, interrogare, prasertim si sit rudis, vel pastor, an peccaverit cum animalibus tactu vel alio modo?* The confessor should not put too much faith in the statements of married persons who feign ignorance concerning the sinfulness of certain actions. He should ask them if they would want to die without telling him, or if they would rather not be questioned concerning these matters. If they accuse themselves of sins which are only slight, he should reassure them, at the same time asking them if these very same things caused them to worry in their former confessions. The confessor should not be afraid to praise their straightforwardness; it is often possible to rectify sacrilegious or doubtful confessions by this means.

1129. The *Seventh and Tenth Commandments*. Have you injured your neighbor by stealing from him, by deceiving him in transactions, by advancing him money at too high a rate of interest, by underpaying your employees, or wilfully retaining valuable objects that you have found? How many persons have you harmed in this way? Have you desired to steal? Have you made restitution of stolen goods?

1130. At this juncture, the confessor may offset the possibility of a bad confession by saying to the penitent: "You have confessed your sins to me very frankly. Did you ever explain them so well before? Have you ever had any qualms of conscience?" If the penitent replies in the affirmative, the confessor should ask him how long he was in this frame of mind. He might add: "I am very happy that you opened your heart to me. Do not be afraid to confess all the sins of your past life, because I am here to help you." A suggestion of this kind may induce the penitent to make a general confession, something which, perhaps, he refused to do before. If it is plain to the confessor from the beginning that the penitent is in need of a general confession and if, while the latter was recounting to him the sins he had committed during his past life, the confessor was careful to apply what was said to the penitent's entire life, he might be content to add: "You accuse yourself, of course, of having committed these same sins practically throughout your whole life." This statement will suffice if the confessor knows the age of the penitent.

1131. If the penitent has never made a satisfactory general confession, and if he is not given to scruples, it is best to allow him to confess the sins of his entire life rather than those committed since a certain time in that life, if he wishes to do so. It often happens that a penitent who says that his qualms of conscience date back to the time of his marriage, finally discovers that they antedate his first Communion. The confessor can gain time, therefore, by immediately requesting the penitent to confess the sins of his entire life.

1132. The *Commandments of the Church*. Have you failed to perform your Easter duty? How many times did you go to confession and receive Communion while you had qualms of conscience? Were you confirmed and were you married in this state of mind? Do you accuse yourself of not receiving these Sacraments with the right disposition? Always confess all your sins, and if you experience any difficulty in telling them, ask your confessor to help you. If need be, make your confession to another priest rather than conceal any of your sins. Have you observed the laws of fasting? Have you eaten meat on days of abstinence?

1133. The *Capital Sins*. Did you ever drink to excess? When drunk, did you grow angry or entertain impure thoughts?

1134. *Duties of one's state of life*. According to St. Alphonsus de' Liguori, it is not enough to ask the penitent if he has fulfilled all the duties of his state of life. The confessor should question him in regard to the principal obligations of that state, especially if he has a lax conscience.

In hearing the confession of another *priest*, the confessor should ask whether he has recited his Office, whether he has said the Masses he was supposed to say at the specified time, whether he has been negligent in the matter of hearing confessions, whether he has studied his theology, whether he has failed to absolve children who were capable of offending God, whether he disregarded the regulations concerning the absolution of backsliders and those who live in the occasion of sin.

1135. In hearing the confession of a *pastor*, the confessor should ask whether he sought to reconcile to God those of his parishioners who had gone astray, whether he has seen to it that all made their Easter duty, whether he ever refused the Sacraments to those who asked for them, whether he has been faithful in his services to the dying, whether he duly prepared his instructions for Sundays and holydays of obligation, whether he instructed the children and the ignorant in the principal mysteries of the faith, whether he unduly deferred the First Communion of the children of his parish, and whether he issued letters of recommendation to undeserving *ordinandi*. (See no. 3671 ff. on the duties of bishops; also no. 3452 ff.)

1136. In hearing the confession of a nun, the confessor should ask whether she has kept her vows, whether she has entertained dangerous affections in her heart. If she is a *superior,* the confessor should ask whether she has enforced all the regulations of her Order, because a superior can sin mortally by tolerating even slight abuses.

1137. In hearing the confession of a *judge,* the confessor should ask whether he has allowed prejudice to influence his decisions, whether he has deliberately protracted a case or failed to ponder the evidence sufficiently before passing sentence.

1138. In hearing the confession of a *lawyer,* the confessor should ask whether he has defended unjust cases, whether he has undertaken cases though deficient in legal knowledge, and whether he has exacted excessive fees.

1139. In hearing the confession of a *bailiff* or *sheriff,* the confessor should ask whether they have exaggerated or diminished the testimony of witnesses, whether they have engaged in unjust actions or in just actions without complying with the proper legal procedure, whether they have entrusted such actions to incompetent subordinates. (See no. 3717.)

1140. In hearing the confession of a *physician*, the confessor should ask whether he has seriously studied difficult cases, whether he has given proper medical attention to the sick, and especially to the poor, whether he has administered dangerous drugs without necessity, whether he has been too lenient in excusing his patients from fasting, whether he has urged them to have their prescriptions filled at a druggist's whose stock had lost some or all of its medicinal value, and whether he has warned his patients of the imminent danger of death.

1141. In hearing the confession of a *pharmacist,* the confessor should ask whether he has sold contraceptives and overcharged his customers (see no. 3744 ff.)

1142. In hearing the confession of *voters,* the confessor should ask whether they have cast their ballots in favor of unworthy candidates, or have aided in the election of unworthy men, actively or by failing to vote.

In hearing the confession of *merchants,* the confessor should ask whether they unduly raised the price of their goods, especially when selling on credit, when they were certain of being paid.

1143. In hearing the confession of *salesmen,* the confessor should ask whether they retained for themselves, without just reason, part of the price of the commodities they handled.

In hearing the confession of s*aloon-keepers,* the confessor should ask whether they sold intoxicating liquors to minors or habitual drunkards, whether they tolerated immoral and scandalous practices in their places of business, etc. (See no. 2478 ff.)

1144. *Satisfaction.* Satisfaction is the voluntary compensation made by man to God to repair the injury done Him and to expiate for the temporal punishment due to sin. Satisfaction, therefore, is a part of the Sacrament of Penance. Baptism cancels all the temporal punishments due to sin, but this is not always the case with the Sacrament of Penance. "If any one saith that God always remits the whole punishment together with the guilt, and that the satisfaction of penitents is no other than the faith whereby they apprehend that Christ has satisfied for them; let him be anathema," says the Council of Trent. (Sess. 14, can. 12.) What is this punishment due to sin? God alone knows. Undoubtedly it depends upon the grievousness of the sins forgiven and the more or less perfect character of penitence. "If any one saith that satisfaction for sins, as to their temporal punishment, is nowise made to God, through the merits of Jesus Christ, by the punishments inflicted by Him, and patiently borne, or by those enjoined by the priest, nor even by those voluntarily undertaken, as by fasting, prayers, almsdeeds, or by other works of piety; and that, therefore, the best penance is merely a new life; let him be anathema." (C. of Trent, Sess. 14, can. 13.) It is *of faith,* therefore, that there exists both a sacramental and an extra-sacramental satisfaction.

1145. *Sacramental satisfaction.* According to some authors, the wish to satisfy to God or the desire to accomplish the penance imposed by the confessor, a desire made sensible through the imposition of the penance and its acceptation by the penitent, is of the essence of the Sacrament of Penance, though in reality the satisfaction itself or the actual performance of the penance is an *integral* part of the Sacrament, so much so that the Sacrament is valid even though the penance be not performed, but would be invalid if the penitent did not have the firm purpose of performing it. Other writers are of the opinion that not even the wish to make satisfaction is of the essence of the Sacrament, but is only an integral part thereof. We should be mindful, however, that the Council of Trent calls the acts of the penitent the quasi-matter of the Sacrament of Penance, and that these acts include satisfaction. (See no. 1152; also C. of Trent,

Sess. 14, can. 4.) Whatever view one may hold, it is certain that sacramental penance remits *ex opere operato* a greater or less portion of the punishment due to sin, according to the greater or less perfections of the penance imposed or the dispositions of the penitent; and that it has a greater value in satisfying for sins than if the penitent imposed upon himself some equivalent good deed. Some theologians even hold that satisfaction confers an increase of grace, but others deny this. Among the latter, several teach that satisfaction confers *ex opere operato* supernatural helps that will enable the penitent to avoid sin. We shall treat, respectively, of the imposition, the acceptation, and the commutation of penance.

1146. *The imposition of penance.* It is certain that confessors are under grave obligation to impose serious penances for mortal sins, unless they have good reason for acting otherwise. The Council of Trent is explicit in this matter: "The priests of the Lord ought, as far as the Spirit and prudence shall suggest, to enjoin salutary and suitable satisfactions, according to the quality of the crimes and the ability of the penitent . . . and they should have in view that the satisfaction which they impose be not only for the preservation of a new life and a remedy against weakness, but also for the avenging and punishment of past sins." (Sess. 14, ch. 8.)

Several reasons may authorize the confessor to lessen the penance which he is obliged to impose, even in the case of mortal sins. When the penitent is seriously ill, it suffices to have him repeat the names of Jesus and Mary; when his dispositions are so imperfect that it can be foreseen that he will not accept a hard penance, he may be given an easier one, as also when there is an indulgence to be gained or when the confessor himself intends to make up for the deficit. When in doubt as to whether there is a sufficient reason for diminishing the penance, the confessor, other things being equal, may always favor the penitent. St. Alphonsus instructs the confessor to give a light penance to sick persons and to add to it when they have fully recovered. A dying person who has lost the use of his senses may be absolved without imposing any penance whatever.

It is the more probable and more common opinion of theologians that the words, *"Passio Domini nostri Jesu Christi,"* etc., raise the good works of the penitent to the dignity of a sacramental satisfaction.

1147. For a just reason, the confessor may impose a grave penance for mortal sins with the intention of obliging the penitent only *sub levi*. This follows from what we have said in no. 1146. According to St. Alphonsus, however, against several other theologians, the confessor may not impose a penance which obliges neither *sub gravi* nor *sub levi,* but is ordinarily bound to impose a serious penance for mortal sins.

Before imposing the penance, the confessor should ask the penitent whether he is willing to perform it, and then, if need be, he may change it. Penances are considered serious or grave when they are equivalent to works enjoined by the Church *sub gravi,* such as attendance at Mass, the recitation of five decades of the beads, but not the recitation of the Psalm *"Miserere."*

Does the confessor sin gravely when he fails to impose a penance upon persons who are guilty of venial sins only? Some theologians answer this question in the affirmative, others in the negative. Would he sin in imposing a penance to be said by the penitent in case of a relapse into the same sin? He probably would if this were the only penance he imposed, but not if he made one penance absolute and another conditional. Several writers, however, are of the opinion that he does not sin in imposing a conditional penance.

As a rule, the confessor should impose the penance before

giving absolution, but if he has failed to do so, he may and must impose it afterwards. There is no sin in reversing this order, especially if it can be foreseen that the penitent will comply with the confessor's instructions.

1148. *Qualities of the penance.* The penance imposed must be *in proportion to* the sin committed. A confessor should not impose a public penance for secret sins, neither should he impose such a penance for public sins, if the penitent has a dread of such penances. Scandal can be atoned for in many other ways, as, for instance, by the public reception of the Sacraments. It is out of place, therefore, to require of a child that he apologize to his parents or superiors.

The penance imposed must be suited to the penitent; hence, it should not inspire him with contempt nor be too burdensome. It is unreasonable to impose a penance extending over a period of several months; it would be imprudent to require children or persons in poor health to fast, ordinary working men to recite long and difficult prayers, or ignorant persons to say Latin prayers.

1149. Above all, the penance must be *medicinal, i. e.,* apt to cause the penitent to amend his life. Some penances are intended to cure the ailments of the soul, like the avoidance of occasions of sin, the frequentation of the Sacraments, assisting at sermons and church services, spiritual reading, frequent examination of conscience, the Way of the Cross, visits to the Blessed Sacrament or to an altar of the Blessed Virgin Mary, the recitation of three Hail Marys morning and evening for the gift of perseverance—a penance which St. Alphonsus imposed on all his penitents—an act of contrition morning and evening, coupled with the resolution to avoid sins against such or such a commandment, mental prayer for pious persons and wholesome reflections before retiring for the ignorant and the illiterate, accompanied by a short prayer morning and evening, or during the week. The confessor may also enjoin the daily recitation for a definite period of time of the Our Father, the Hail Mary, the Creed, the Commandments of God and the Church, and an act of contrition. He may also enjoin assistance at Mass on two Sundays, for it is quite permissible to impose something which is already prescribed. A person who failed to perform such a penance, would commit two sins. St. Alphonsus is of the opinion that one and the same act prescribed in a previous confession may not be given as a penance in a second one, but De Lugo and other authors dissent from this view. In practice, a second penance should be enjoined on those to whom one has given a second absolution for sins forgotten, although some writers claim that this is not absolutely necessary.

1150. Besides these general medicinal penances there are others which aim at curing special ailments of the soul. Contraries are cured by contraries, and so the confessor should enjoin the recitation of acts of faith upon those whose faith is weak; ejaculatory prayers upon the lukewarm; acts of hope upon those who are tempted to despair, and the recitation of the invocation "Praised be Jesus Christ" upon those who blaspheme. He may enjoin assistance at week-day Masses upon persons who often miss Mass on Sunday; internal and external acts of charity upon those who harbor ill-feelings; privations in food, drink or sleep, or bodily mortifications upon persons given over to the pleasures of the senses, almsgiving upon thieves and misers, and acts of humility upon the proud.

1151. If the confessor is obliged to refuse absolution, he should impose a penance, the nature of which will serve him as a reminder of the penitent's spiritual status and help him to determine later on whether or not the penitent should be absolved. (See no. 1099.) One or more of the medicinal penances we have cited will help him to recall whether the penitent has one or several bad habits. If the penitent is in an occasion of sin *in esse,* or if he is under obligation to make restitution, the confessor would do well to add to the above penances some special prayer (like the act of contrition) calculated to recall these circumstances. The confessor should take care not to multiply penances at the risk of the penitent's forgetting to perform them; he should make sure that the penitent has understood the penance, otherwise the latter will perform a penance which has not been imposed.

1152. *Acceptance of the penance.* It is certain that the penitent must accept a just penance imposed by the confessor. The Fourth Lateran Council states explicitly that "the penitent should do all in his power to perform the penance imposed by the confessor." However, if the penance were altogether out of proportion with the sin confessed, it is probable that the penitent could withdraw with impunity before receiving absolution. If the penance were fair and within reason, the penitent could not refuse to accept it, or could not insist on a lighter penance without committing a mortal sin.

1153. *Performance of the penance.* It is certain that the penitent is bound *sub gravi* to perform a grave penance imposed for mortal sins, unless it should happen by way of exception that the confessor enjoined the penance upon him only *sub levi.* Grave penances issued for venial sins or sins already confessed probably oblige *sub levi.*

1154. It is a mortal sin to omit a notable portion of the penance, or unnecessarily to delay for a lengthy period of time performing a grave penance imposed for mortal sins. Theologians are divided as to what constitutes such a delay. Some regard a delay of two months as serious; others a delay of one year. It is certain that if the penance were of a medicinal character, a much shorter delay would involve mortal sin. If a penitent fails to accomplish his penance within the prescribed time, he is not thereby excused from performing it at a later date. A slight penance can never oblige *sub gravi*, even though it be imposed for grave offenses. If the confession is null and void, the penance is likewise so, except in the following cases: (1) if the penance is medicinal in character and calculated to preserve the penitent from relapse; (2) if the penitent fails to receive absolution several consecutive times, and the confessor imposes a penance each time, intending in the end to enjoin a much lighter penance.

1155. The penitent is obliged to attend to the circumstances of the penance prescribed by the confessor, and this *sub gravi*, if his offenses were grave. Penances may be recited during attendance at Sunday Mass or, in cases of prayers, by alternating with another person. Penitents who relapse into the state of mortal sin and then perform their penance, satisfy their obligation according to the common opinion of theologians.

Does a penance performed in the state of mortal sin satisfy the justice of God? Some theologians deny this, others reply that it does, provided the penitent has no further attachment to mortal sin, and finally, some are of the opinion that such a penance produces its effect only after the mortal sin has been forgiven. It is certain that the penitent cannot delegate another to perform his penance, but he may probably do so if the confessor gives him express permission.

1156. Must the penitent perform his penance with the intention of satisfying for his sins? This question is controverted by theologians; some claim that such an intention is not necessary; others, like Lehmkuhl, claim that it is; others, finally, go so far as to say that the penitent satisfies by performing the act prescribed with the formal intention of doing it out of devotion. The following proposition has been condemned by Pope Alexander VIII: "Those who claim the right to receive Holy Communion before accomplishing their penance are to be regarded as guilty of sacrilege." *A fortiori*, one is not bound to perform his penance before receiving absolution. According to common opinion, a penitent who has forgotten his penance, even through his own fault, is not obliged to repeat his confession; nevertheless, according to some theologians, he is obliged to seek out his confessor, if he can do so without too great inconvenience, and if he thinks that the priest will recall the penance imposed. Authors are not agreed as to whether or not he himself may substitute another penance for the one he has forgotten, if he is unable to find his confessor.

1157. The Roman Catechism suggests that, to excite the faithful to penance, pastors should explain to them the penitential canons of the early Church. At the beginning of Lent, all penitents presented themselves before the bishop at the entrance of the church, barefooted and clothed in sackcloth. The bishop, reciting the seven Penitential Psalms, ushered them into the church, sprinkled ashes upon their heads, informed them that he was about to expel them from the Church in the same manner that Adam and Eve were put out of the Garden of Eden. The bishop's assistants then proceeded to expel the penitents from the sacred edifice, saying as they did so the words of Holy Scripture: "In the sweat of thy brow," etc. The early penitents were divided into four classes. There were the Weepers, the Hearers, the Prostrate, and the Standers. The Weepers (*flentes*) remained in the atrium, or portico, dressed in mourning and begging those who entered the church to intercede for them. The Hearers (*audientes*) stood in the ante-nave and withdrew after the reading of the Scripture and the preaching of the sermon. The Prostrate (*prostrati*) knelt at the entrance of the nave and were dismissed when the Mass of the faithful was about to commence. The Standers (*consistentes*) stood in the nave, separated from the rest of the faithful; they were allowed to assist at Mass, but not to receive Communion. The canons prescribed a penance of two years for a wicked desire, of seven years for adultery, of three years for disrespect towards one's parents, and of five years for consulting fortune-tellers.

1158. *The commutation of penance.* According to common opinion, a penitent who is morally unable to perform the penance enjoined on him, or who can perform it only with great inconvenience, may not assume to change it, even for one that would be more salutary. The confessor alone may change a penance which he has imposed. However, any duly authorized priest may change a penance if he fears the penitent will not perform it, even though the penitent himself does not request the favor.

May a priest of a lower rank change a penance imposed for reserved sins by a priest of a higher rank? This question is controverted; some affirm that he may, but St. Alphonsus does not seem to favor this view. The Saint adds, however, that in practice one may follow the affirmative opinion, if it is impossible to have recourse to the superior, or if his permission can be reasonably presumed. Outside the tribunal of penance, only the priest who imposed a penance can change it, but he should do so very soon after confession, or before the penitent has withdrawn, according to St. Alphonsus. Some theologians show themselves more lenient in this matter, authorizing the priest to change the penance some time during the same day, or the same week.

Apart from these cases, a penance can only be commuted in the tribunal of penance. If the penitent who wants his penance changed has recourse to the same confessor, he need not repeat his confession. But if he seeks out another confessor, or if the confessor to whom he confessed the first time has no recollection of the case, the penitent, according to the majority of theologians, should repeat his confession, He is not bound to repeat it according to an opinion which St. Alphonsus calls probable, but is required only to inform the priest concerning his first penance.. The penitent whose penance has been commuted may always return to the former penance, but if he repeats his confession to another confessor for the sole purpose of obtaining a lighter penance, he would be still obliged to perform the first penance, if the confessor did not dispense him from it.

1159. *Extra-sacramental satisfaction.* This kind of satisfaction may be made by each and every one in the form of good works. We shall treat of it in no. 1741 ff. It may also be made by the works of the rest of the faithful who desire to apply to our souls whatever is satisfactory in the good which they do. (See no. 1734 ff.) It may be made, finally, by indulgences, of which we must say a word.

INDULGENCES

1160. We must first of all observe that the satisfaction made by Christ was more than ample, and that in virtue of His merits, from which the works of the just draw all their merit, the Blessed Virgin Mary, who had no need of satisfaction, and others among the saints have superabundantly satisfied for themselves. Through their merits, they have obtained both grace and glory, but the satisfactory and impetratory fruits of their good works are still present to the mind of God, who has graciously deigned to accept them, and constitute those heavenly treasures, the existence of which, according to the Council of Trent, is a *veritas proxima fidei.* (Sess. 1, ch. 2 ff.)

1161. An indulgence is a remission of the temporal punishment which remains due to sin after its guilt has been forgiven. This remission is effected through the power of the keys, by the application of the merits contained in the treasury of the Church. We shall treat, first, of indulgences in general; and, secondly, of some of them in particular.

1162. *Indulgences in general.* We shall deal first, with the granting of indulgences; and secondly, with the manner of gaining them.

The granting of indulgences. That the Church has the power to grant indulgences is an article of faith. "Whatsoever you shall loose upon earth, shall be loosed also in heaven" (Matt. 16, 19.) The Church has always understood this text to apply to indulgences, the existence of which the Waldenses were the first to deny. The Council of Trent anathematizes all those who say that indulgences are useless, or who deny that the Church has power to grant them. (Sess. 25.)

Jesus Christ has placed no restrictions on the power of His Church to bind and loose. Heaven is closed not only by sin, but also by the temporal punishments due to sin, and the Church can remove both guilt and punishment. She removes the bond of eternal damnation by sacramental absolution; she removes that of temporal punishment by indulgences. The granting of an indulgence is a real act of absolution, *i. e.*, of jurisdiction and payment at once for the living and for the dead, who are no longer subject to the Church.

1163. The Sovereign Pontiff alone has the power of granting indulgences throughout the Church and of dispensing the treasures of the Church.

Prelates inferior to the Pope may grant indulgences only when he gives them permission to do so, either by law or by indult. Canon 930 states that all indulgences granted by the Pope may be applied to the poor souls in Purgatory, unless the contrary is expressly stated. Other prelates cannot grant indulgences applicable to the souls in Purgatory.

Cardinals may everywhere grant to persons present an indulgence of two hundred days, which may be gained only once, but persons who live in institutions or places under the jurisdiction of a Cardinal, as well as those who are under his jurisdiction or protection, may gain this indulgence *toties quoties*. Archbishops may grant an indulgence of one hundred days in their dioceses or provinces, and residential bishops an indulgence of fifty days in their dioceses. Unless the contrary is stated in the grant, indulgences granted by a bishop may be gained by his subjects, even though they are actually absent from the diocese, and by strangers, *vagi*, and exempt religious actually present. The consecrator of a church or of an altar, even though he has no jurisdiction, may grant an indulgence of one year to those who visit the church or the altar on the day of its consecration, and an indulgence of fifty days to those who make this visit on the anniversary.

If the consecrator is an archbishop, he may grant an indulgence of one hundred days for the anniversary and two hundred if he is a Cardinal. After the promulgation of the New Code, Pope Benedict XV invested nuncios, pro-nuncios, and Apostolic delegates with new faculties relative to the granting of indulgences. These dignitaries now have the right to grant a plenary indulgence six times each year and also during the Forty Hours' Devotion. This latter indulgence may not be granted for an unlimited time, but must be restricted as the dignitary sees fit. These same dignitaries may grant a plenary indulgence to all converts from heresy and to all those who make a mission. They may grant an indulgence of two hundred days to those who assist at divine services held by them, and may decree that the indulgences granted by them are applicable to the souls in Purgatory.

The successor of a bishop may not, under the same conditions, attach a new indulgence to the same sacred place or thing to which his predecessor or the Pope has attached an indulgence, and neither can several bishops attach an indulgence to the same object. Particular councils, titular bishops, coadjutor bishops, bishops who have resigned their sees, prelates inferior to bishops, diocesan chapters during the vacancy of a see, and vicars-general may not grant indulgences, but a simple cleric who is capable of jurisdiction may, by special delegation from the Sovereign Pontiff.

1164. Prelates regular may not grant indulgences, but in certain religious Orders they may, even though only provincials, communicate the indulgences and suffrages of the Order to others by *letters of affiliation*. Some of them have the privilege of delivering from Purgatory by one Mass those who have obtained such letters and who, during their lifetime, were aided by the prayers and suffrages of the religious. The grantors of these letters cannot apply the past suffrages of their religious, since these have already reverted to the treasury of the Church, to which they do not have the key; but they *can* apply to them all future satisfactions, and this not by way of jurisdiction, since they have no jurisdiction over persons outside of their Order, but by way of solution.

1165. For indulgences to be validly and licitly granted, two conditions must be fulfilled: (1) a just and pious cause; and (2) some prescribed good work. If the grantor of an indulgence had no cause for bestowing such a favor, he would not be a faithful administrator of the treasures of the Church. Of course, he is the judge of what constitutes such a cause, not the faithful.

1166. To prevent apocryphal indulgences from being hawked about, it is forbidden to publish any notices regarding indulgences without the permission of the Ordinary. Moreover, no collections of indulgences, or translations of such collections into other languages, may be published without the permission of the Congregation of Indulgences. For collections, or translations of collections taken from books approved by this Congregation, the permission of the Ordinary suffices, unless a special prohibition exists to publish or translate some particular collection.

Generally speaking, the permission of the bishop is not required for the validity of an indulgence; but if the indult requires such a permission, the indulgence would be null and void without it. This permission of the bishop is not absolutely necessary, although it is better to ask for it in the case of personal indults authorizing one to bless crosses or granting the indulgence of a privileged altar, unless the indult specifies otherwise. This permission is necessary for the erection of Stations of the Cross and for the lawful application of Apostolic indulgences and of that of St. Bridget, which can be validly granted only by those who are approved to hear confessions. In cases where it is impossible to reach the bishop, his permission may be presumed. If the indult is marked *"privatim,"* the priest cannot bless publicly from the pulpit, nor after some Church function, pious objects placed upon the altar.

1167. In blessing such objects, it suffices to have the intention of granting the indulgences and to make the sign of the cross over the medals, crosses, or rosaries. But in blessing rosaries of St. Dominic and of Our Lady of Seven Dolors, a special formula must be used together with holy water.

On Nov. 23, 1918, the Sacred Congregation of Rites published a briefer form for the blessing of rosaries of St. Dominic with or without the stole or holy water. The formula is as follows: *"Ad laudem et gloriam Deiparæ Virginis Mariæ, in memoriam mysteriorum vitæ, mortis et resurrec-*

tionis ejusdem Domini Nostri Jesu Christi, benedicatur et sanctificetur hæc sacratissima corona; in nomine Patris et Filii et Spiritus Sancti."

1168. Pious objects may be blessed, no matter of what material they are made; but in order to attach indulgences to them, they must be of solid material. Crosses must be either of wood, ivory, iron or steel (but not of lead or tin.) Rosaries may be of wood and lead or even of solid glass. Indulgenced objects lose their indulgences if they are sold or completely destroyed, but not if they are lent or given away. These indulgences are not personal, but real.

A rosary loses its indulgences if most of the beads are lost or destroyed, but not if the small chain with the cross has been replaced, nor a crucifix, if the figure of Christ upon the cross is broken. If a priest purchases a quantity of crosses, attaches indulgences to them and then sells them, they lose their indulgences. At the time of missions, therefore, he should purchase the articles, sell them, and attach the indulgences to them afterwards.

1169. No medals may be indulgenced which do not bear, on one side at least, the image of a saint whose name appears in the Roman Martyrology. The indulgences of crosses applies also to crucifixes, consequently the material of the cross may be replaced. Several indulgences may be attached to one and the same crucifix. In order to gain these indulgences, the crucifix must be carried on one's person, or the prescribed prayers must be said before it. The indulgence ceases when the object to which it is attached becomes badly worn. However, indulgences attached to a church do *not* cease, even though a new church is built to replace the old one within a period of fifty years, provided the new church is erected under the same title and in approximately the same place, *i. e.*, at about twenty or thirty feet from the old site. An indulgence granted for a definite period expires at the end of that period, which must be computed from the day the letter granting the dispensation was mailed. If an indulgence is granted *in perpetuum,* or for an unspecified period of time, it does not expire at or after the death of the person who grants it, unless it is revoked by his successor. It is impossible to gain the same indulgence several times on the same day, even though one fulfills all the prescribed conditions, unless the contrary is expressly stipulated, and it is equally impossible to gain several indulgences by performing the same good work, even though several indulgences are attached to the same object or the same place for different reasons. The case would be different if the good work prescribed was confession or communion, or if the contrary is expressly stipulated. (*C. J. C.,* can. 933.)

As soon as they receive official notification of their canonical appointment, Cardinals may bless with the mere sign of the cross throughout the world, crosses, rosaries, medals, and statues, and attach to them all the indulgences which the Holy See usually attaches to such articles. In the same manner they may bless approved scapulars and invest persons with them, with one blessing, without entering their names, and erect Stations of the Cross in churches, oratories, and other places of devotion, attaching to them the usual indulgences. Bishops, even titular bishops, may do likewise, except that they must comply with the regulations laid down by the Roman Ritual. As a general rule, bishops may not habitually delegate Apostolic faculties.[1]

1170. *Manner of gaining indulgences.* Who can gain indulgences? Only a baptized Catholic, who is still a wayfarer, can gain indulgences, because he alone is capable of works of satisfaction, properly so called, and he alone can

[1] By decision of the S. Poenit. of July, 1919, a bishop may not delegate his faculties enumerated in can. 349, 1.

share in the treasures of the Church. This excludes the dead, infidels, heretics, schismatics, and all excommunicated persons.

1171. For whom may indulgences be gained? First, for the dead. This is *certain* from the time-honored practice of the Church, who grants indulgences applicable to the poor souls in Purgatory. The contrary assertion has been condemned in the writings of Peter of Osma. Since the dead are no longer subject to the jurisdiction of the Church, indulgences are applied to them not by way of absolution, but by way of solution. Bishops cannot grant indulgences that are applicable to the souls in Purgatory, and so the Church, in the person of her Sovereign Pontiff, lays at the feet of the Creator the satisfactions of Jesus Christ, petitioning Him to diminish the punishments of the poor souls in virtue of these satisfactions. But if it is certain that indulgences profit the souls in Purgatory generally, it seems equally certain that, all other things being equal, they can be applied to particular persons; otherwise the pious practice of applying indulgences to definite souls would be vain and futile. (See no. 1737.)

1172. The question whether indulgences assist the souls in Purgatory *ex congruo* or *ex condigno* is controverted. It is more probable, as we shall have occasion to show when speaking of suffrages, that they assist them *ex iustitia* and *de condigno*. (See no. 1737.) We must not, however, think that a soul to which we have applied a plenary indulgence is infallibly released from Purgatory, because we do not know if we have satisfied all the conditions required to gain the indulgence. In practice it is always best to apply our indulgences to our relatives, with the clause that if they cannot be of any help to them, they will benefit others.

1173. For indulgences to be of avail to the deceased, it is indispensable that they be applied to their souls, because those who gain indulgences may either reserve the fruits to themselves or apply them to others. The application of indulgences is an act of the will, which may be directed either to some determined person, or to the most abandoned souls, or to all the souls in Purgatory.

1174. The Sovereign Pontiff may grant the permission to apply indulgences to the living; but he is not in the habit of doing this because every Catholic should try to gain indulgences for himself.

1175. Indulgences are divided into partial and plenary. A *partial* indulgence is one that remits only a portion of the temporal punishment due to forgiven sins. Therefore, an indulgence of forty days remits as much temporal punishment as would have been formerly atoned for by a canonical penance of forty days. A *plenary* indulgence, which the Pope alone can grant, remits the whole of the temporal punishment due to sins. This proposition is *certain*. Moreover, it is a truth *proxima fidei* that an indulgence is not merely the remission of the penance imposed by the Church, but also of the temporal punishment due to God. The contrary doctrine has been condemned in the teachings of Martin Luther and those of the Council of Pistoia.

1176. *Conditions for gaining indulgences.* Canon 925 states that to gain indulgences it is necessary to have a virtual intention, at least in general. Therefore, it is a good idea to renew each morning the intention of gaining the indulgences of the day, and to renew also the application of these indulgences. Unless specified differently, the day runs from midnight to midnight.

A second condition for gaining indulgences is the *state of grace*. It is certain that no one can gain indulgences for himself unless he is in the state of grace, because the punishment due to sin cannot be remitted if the sin itself is not forgiven.

But can a person who is in the state of mortal sin gain indulgences *for others?* Some theologians answer this question in the affirmative; others, more probably, in the negative. It is safer, therefore, to perform all the prescribed works in the state of grace, although, according to common opinion, it suffices if the last work only is performed in the state of grace. Venial sin, or attachment to venial sin, does not prevent one from gaining a partial indulgence, for, although one venial sin may not be forgiven, other venial and mortal sins may. A venial sin does, however, prevent one from gaining an indulgence applicable to the temporal punishment due to this sin in particular, because if the sin is not forgiven, the punishment cannot be remitted.

1177. A third condition is the substantial fulfillment of the prescribed good works. A slight omission in this respect will not prevent the indulgence from taking effect, but a grave omission will. Besides the special works stipulated for the gaining of each indulgence in particular, more general ones are prescribed for the majority of plenary indulgences. They are: confession, Communion, vocal prayers for the Pope's intention, and sometimes a visit to a church.

Confession. This condition is indispensable, even though the person who seeks to gain the indulgence is not in the state of mortal sin, in which case, however, absolution is not required. According to the common law, the same confession suffices to gain the indulgences of the eight days preceding and the eight days following, so that a person who goes to confession twice a month is in a position to gain all the indulgences for which confession is prescribed, without making an additional confession. Canon 931 states, however, that indulgences of an ordinary or extraordinary jubilee, and those granted in the form of a jubilee, are excepted from this rule.

1178. *Communion*. The same canon states that Holy Communion may be received the day previous and also during the octave of the feast, and that furthermore, the faithful who receive Holy Communion daily in the state of grace, though they may abstain from receiving once or twice a week, can gain all indulgences without actual confession. Easter Communion suffices to gain the indulgence attached to Easter Sunday, but it does not suffice for the jubilee, unless the contrary is stated in the papal Bull.

1179. *Visits and prayers for the Pope's intention*. When an indulgence is granted for a visit to a church, it is not necessary that Holy Communion be received in that particular church, and when prayers are prescribed and not a visit, it is not necessary that they be said in the same church. These prayers need not be said after the prescribed reception of the Sacraments, but may be said beforehand, on the same day. The visit must be made and the prayers said as many times as a person wishes to gain the indulgences for which they are prescribed. If the visit is prescribed for a certain day, it may be made from noon of the day previous to midnight of the day prescribed. Canon 934 states that if prayer in general for the intentions of the Holy Father is prescribed for the gaining of an indulgence, purely mental prayer is not sufficient, and that any vocal prayer may be chosen by the faithful, unless particular prayers are assigned. Strictly speaking, one Our Father and one Hail Mary will suffice. If fasting is prescribed for the gaining of an indulgence, this good work suffices to gain all the indulgences for which fasting is prescribed on that day.

As a general rule, the work prescribed must be repeated, whenever possible, for every indulgence. Several indulgences may be gained the same day, if they are attached to the good works by different titles, or if the works to which they are attached differ, and even if these works are the same, provided they may be performed several times on the same day, and that the indult contains the words *toties quoties*.

A person who gains a plenary indulgence for himself cannot at the same time gain for himself another plenary indulgence, because, all the temporal punishments due to sin having been remitted, these same punishments cannot be remitted anew. If the same person, however, relapses into sin and receives forgiveness the same day, there is nothing to prevent him from gaining a second plenary indulgence for himself.

A plenary indulgence granted, either daily or perpetually or for some definite time, to those who visit some church or public oratory, can be gained only once a year, unless the indult states the contrary. (*C. J. C.*, can. 921.)

Plenary indulgences granted for the feasts of Our Lord and the Blessed Virgin Mary apply to those feasts only that are found in the universal calendar. A plenary or partial indulgence granted for the feasts of an Apostle can be gained only on the anniversary of his death. (Can. 921.)

Indulgences attached to feasts are transferred to the day to which the external solemnity of the feast is transferred. The same is true of sacred supplications and prayers in the form of novenas or those held for a week or three days either before or after the feast or during the octave. If the transferred feast has no external solemnity, the transfer of the Office and the Mass affects the indulgence only if the latter is perpetual.

Indulgenced prayers in the language of the people must be approved by the Sacred Penitentiary or by the Ordinary of the diocese where that language is spoken. The indulgence is lost if any addition, diminution, or interpolation is made. For the gaining of an indulgence it suffices to say the prayers alternately with others, or to follow them mentally while they are recited by another. But if one is alone, purely mental prayer does not suffice. Those who have received from the Holy Father grants of indulgences for all the faithful are bound to furnish the Sacred Penitentiary with an authentic copy of them, under pain of nullity. New indulgences, including those granted to churches of regulars, must not be promulgated without consulting the bishop, unless they have already been promulgated in Rome.

If the grant of an indulgence contains the words, *"in forma ecclesiæ consueta,"* this merely means that the only conditions required are contrition and the state of grace. If it contains the words, *"sub consuetis conditionibus,"* it means that, over and above these conditions, one must receive the Sacraments of Penance and the Holy Eucharist and recite some prayers for the Pope's intention. When there is question of attaching indulgences to certain articles, the formula *"applicandi in forma ecclesiæ consueta"* means that it suffices to have the intention and to make the sign of the Cross over the object without prayer or holy water.

Deaf mutes can gain the indulgences attached to the recitation of public prayers by assisting with the faithful at the services and raising their minds and hearts to God. If private prayers are prescribed, they may say them mentally, or by signs, or by perusing them with their eyes. (*C. J. C.*, can. 936.)

The faithful of either sex who, either for the sake of religious perfection, or for study, health or education, lead a community life in houses established with the consent of the Ordinary, and all other persons working in such houses, can gain indulgences for which the visit of some church or public oratory is required, by visiting the chapel of their own house, where they can by law satisfy their obligation of hearing Mass on Sundays and holydays of obligation, provided there is no public church or oratory attached to the institution, and that they perform the other good works prescribed for the gaining of these indulgences. (*C. J. C.*, can. 929.)

1180. The good works we have just referred to are not prescribed for all indulgences. They are not required for the Way of the Cross, for instance, or for the indulgences attached to the recitation of six Our Fathers and Glory be to the Fathers of the blue scapular.

1181. Confessors are authorized to commute the good works prescribed for sick persons who cannot perform them, even though such persons be living in community. It is better to do this in the tribunal of Penance, although several writers are of the opinion that this is necessary only when expressly enjoined. For the jubilee, it is necessary to have the good work changed every time one wishes to gain the indulgences, otherwise those who cannot perform the work prescribed do not gain the indulgences.

1182. *The jubilee indulgences.* The jubilee has been established by the Church in imitation of the jubilee year of the Old Testament. According to reliable authors, it dates back to Apostolic times. It would be a mistake to imagine that it was first established by Pope Boniface VIII; he merely decreed that it should take place every one-hundred years. Clement VI reduced the term to fifty years; Urban VI to thirty-three, and Paul II to twenty-five. A jubilee is a plenary indulgence accompanied with the power to absolve from reserved sins and censures, and to commute vows, provided the prescribed conditions are complied with. While the major jubilee is being celebrated at Rome, all other real or local indulgences granted by Sovereign Pontiffs for the living are suspended, except the indulgence *in articulo mortis,* the indulgences attached to the recitation of the Angelus, accompaniment of the Holy Viaticum, and visits to the Blessed Sacrament when solemnly exposed, and except indulgences granted by ecclesiastical dignitaries other than the Sovereign Pontiff. During this time are also suspended all powers to absolve from censures and reserved cases, and to commute vows, etc., except those held by bishops in virtue of their office, or for some individual cases by indult, and those which prelates regular possess for their subjects. All indulgences gained during the time of the jubilee are applicable to the dead.

1183. The jubilee which is published at Rome every twenty-five years is called *major;* that which is accorded for some particular occasion, as the crowning of a new Pope, an urgent need of the Church or State, etc., is called *minor*. The major jubilee is the *ordinary*, the minor, the *extraordinary* one. Jubilees are general or particular, according as they extend to the universal Church or to only a portion thereof.

1184. The ordinary conditions required to gain the jubilee are:

1. A strict fast on Wednesday, Friday, and Saturday of the same week. Commanded fasts do not satisfy this condition, unless the Sovereign Pontiff gives permission to select a period of time when fasting is obligatory. In places where it is extremely difficult to obtain fish, the bishops may permit the use of milk and eggs. Children and the aged are also obliged to fast, and consequently they do not gain the jubilee indulgence if they fail to have their fast commuted to some other good work. When the fast is prescribed for only two days, it is not necessary that both days occur within the same week.

2. Giving alms according to one's means. Religious, children subject to their parents, and servants satisfy this condition if to their knowledge, their superiors, parents or masters, respectively, give some alms in their name. The smallest alms will suffice in the case of the poor.

3. Visits to churches, accompanied by the usual prayers

for the intention of the Sovereign Pontiff. For religious, visits to their own church do not suffice. These visits may be commuted to some other good work for persons who are unable to comply with this condition, but the prayers for the intention of the Sovereign Pontiff may never be commuted. For the ordinary jubilee, but not for others, all the visits must be made the same day, from midnight to midnight, or from the evening preceding to the evening following, according to the wording of the Bull.

4. A confession and a Communion other than those which are of precept. It is possible, however, for any one wishing to gain the jubilee during the Pascal season, to defer his Easter confession and Communion until later, and to gain the jubilee by only one confession, although, as a rule, he should make two Communions. Confession is necessary, even though one may have no sins, in which case it is not necessary to receive absolution. However, the confessor should enjoin a penance in all cases. A confession made the day before the jubilee will not suffice, unless it was made after the first Vespers of the feast, and the jubilee starts at first Vespers. As a rule, confession and Communion may not be commuted into some other good work. The confessor may commute the other good works whenever the penitent is desirous of gaining the jubilee indulgence, provided the Bull states that the indulgence may be gained more than once.

Almsgiving and fasting are prescribed only for the extraordinary jubilee. Communion may be commuted to some other good work in the case of children and the sick, who could not gain the indulgence if it were not commuted. It is not necessary that the good works—fasting excepted—be performed during the same week, and no strict order is required in their performance. They may be performed everywhere, and it suffices that one is in the state of grace when performing the last. Confession is indispensable when one is not in the state of grace, for in this case contrition does not suffice. Unless the indult specifies other conditions, the above-mentioned four suffice to gain the ordinary jubilee indulgence.

1185. *Faculties which accompany the jubilee.* The first faculty is to absolve in the internal forum from all sins and censures, even those specially reserved to the Holy See, or to bishops, *a iure* or *ab homine*. This faculty is granted to every confessor, and during the time of the jubilee, all the faithful without exception may select any confessor approved by the Ordinary. Regulars may select any regular confessor approved by their superior, but if they so desire, they may obtain absolution from any approved confessor for all the sins reserved in their Order. Nuns with solemn vows may select any confessor approved for nuns, and nuns with simple vows, any priest approved for seculars. Unless the contrary is stated in the Bull, one may not absolve his accomplice during the jubilee, nor a priest who has absolved his accomplice more than twice, nor any one who has falsely accused a priest of having practiced solicitation in the confessional. One may absolve from the sins of external heresy; but one may not absolve excommunicated, suspended or publicly interdicted persons, unless they have made reparation during the time of the jubilee, or promise to do so, or are incapable of anything in that respect. As a rule, the faculty to dispense from irregularities other than those incurred occultly by the exercise of the power of orders, is not to be counted among the faculties conceded by the jubilee. Reserved cases must be handled in the confessional exclusively, and, according to a more probable opinion, the same rule applies to censures. It is certain that they must be dealt with in the confessional, if the Bull states this explicitly, and the same is true of commutations, etc.

1186. The second faculty is that of commuting all simple vows, even those reserved to the Holy See. Exempt from this rule are the vows pronounced in a Congregation, the vow of perpetual chastity, the vow to enter a solemn religious Order, a vow made in favor of a third party who has accepted its conditions, vows taken for the express purpose of avoiding sin, and vows taken unconditionally after sixteen years of age. It is probable also that if a person has forgotten to have such a vow commuted during the time of the jubilee, he may obtain this favor from any approved confessor at some later date.

1187. These faculties are granted only in favor of those who wish to gain the jubilee indulgence, and for one time only. Consequently, if one has no intention of making the jubilee, one cannot benefit by these extraordinary privileges; and if he relapses into sin or pronounces new vows, he cannot obtain absolution from his sins or dispensation from his vows, even though the wording of the Bull is to the effect that he may gain the indulgence as many times as he performs the work prescribed. Some authors are of the opinion that such a person may still be absolved if he relapses into these reserved sins before performing the last work prescribed. If, after he has received absolution, he fails to perform the remainder of the works prescribed, or renounces his intention of gaining the jubilee indulgence, he is absolved from his sins. A person who began his confession at the time of the jubilee, may be absolved from reserved sins when the jubilee has lapsed.

A penitent who has forgotten to confess some reserved sin, and probably also one whose confession was null and void (even sacrilegious according to some writers), may be absolved after the jubilee. (See no. 1287.) Writers are not agreed as to whether or not a person may be absolved from reserved sins in the preceding instances if he relapses into these sins after the jubilee. The safest course in this case would be to have recourse to one's ecclesiastical superior.

According to the more probable opinion, a confessor may substitute other good works for those omitted by the penitent, even through negligence, after the time of the jubilee, or may prolong the time of the jubilee in his favor. A person is permitted to perform the prescribed works in different places, and, if about to make a trip, may prolong the time of the jubilee until his return. One who makes no attempt to gain the jubilee indulgence does not sin grievously, unless he is inspired by contempt or gives scandal. It is, however, difficult to excuse from venial sin one who deprives himself of this grace through sheer laziness.

1188. The indulgence *in articulo mortis*. The faithful can gain this indulgence without the assistance of the priest, if they have the objects to which the indulgence is attached, provided they have received the Sacraments, or, if unable to receive them, that they are sorry for their sins, invoke the Holy Name of Jesus, and accept the pains of death with resignation and in expiation for their sins. The indulgence *in articulo mortis,* as contained in the Ritual, may be applied by any priest. He should use the formula prescribed, unless he is pressed for time, in which case it suffices to say: *"Indulgentiam plenariam et remissionem peccatorum tibi concedo, in nomine Patris,"* etc. The *Confiteor* must be recited, even though it has already been recited before the administration of Communion or Extreme Unction. Furthermore, the patient should be urged to make acts of contrition and resignation, invoke the Holy Name of Jesus, and enter into the dispositions referred to above. The dying person may receive the indulgence only once in danger of death. The priest may not grant the indulgence several times, even though he do so as a member of several confraternities or of several third orders, and even though the dying person received it for the first time in the state of mortal sin, relapsed into serious sin, or received anew the Sacrament of Extreme Unction. The reason for this is that the subject can gain this indulgence only at the moment he is about to die. The indulgence may be granted to those who have lost the use of their senses, *iis qui etiam culpabiliter non fuerunt ab incepto morbo sacramentis refecti, subitoque vergunt ad interitum,* to children who have attained to the age of reason, and to criminals condemned to death, on the day of their execution. The danger of death which suffices for the administering of Extreme Unction suffices also for the granting of this indulgence. Finally, the indulgence *in articulo mortis* attached to a cross does not cease when the owner of the cross applies it to himself, because the indulgence is real and not personal.

1189. The indulgence of the privileged altar. Any one who celebrates Mass at a privileged altar, or who has the personal indult of a privileged altar (see no. 1740), gains a plenary indulgence, *per se* capable of delivering a soul from Purgatory, if God in His mercy accepts it in its entirety. This indulgence is not dependent upon the dispositions of the celebrant, but to gain it, he must apply it to the soul of the person for whom he is offering the Mass, because, although the application of the fruits of the Sacrifice is *in se* distinct from that of the indulgence, the wording of the indults permits one to gain the indulgence only for the soul to whom the fruits of the Mass are applied. If the Mass is being offered for several deceased persons, the indulgence must be applied to one among them. This does not mean that no benefit is derived from the privilege when the celebrant fails to apply the indulgence, for in this case the indulgence reverts to some one soul in particular, or is divided among several, according to the good pleasure of God. On the second day of November all altars are privileged and the indulgence is not limited to the person for whom the Sacrifice is being offered. There are some writers, however, who would not subscribe to this latter view.

During the solemn celebration of the devotion known as Forty Hours, all altars are privileged. The celebrant may accept a higher stipend for celebrating Mass at a privileged altar, but he cannot gain the indulgence if he celebrates for both the living and the dead. Residential bishops, abbots and prelates who exercise quasi-episcopal jurisdiction over a given territory, vicars and prefects Apostolic and major superiors of exempt religious communities may single out an altar in their cathedral, abbatial, collegiate, conventual, parochial or quasi-parochial churches, respectively, and declare it to be privileged for all times and for all days of the year, provided there are no other altars there to which this same privilege is attached. This right does not extend to public or semi-public oratories, unless they are annexed to the parochial church or form one building with it. To indicate that an altar is privileged, it is enough to inscribe upon it these words: *"Altare privilegiatum perpetuum,"* or *"ad tempus, quotidianum,"* or *"non quotidianum,"* according to the circumstances. Nuncios, pro-nuncios, and Apostolic delegates have the same right in regard to churches located in their respective territories.

For an altar to be privileged, it is not necessary that it be fixed or consecrated; it is enough if it is immovable and the stone is consecrated. This stone may be changed and another put in its place without the altar losing the indulgence, and the altar together with the stone may be changed or constructed anew at the same place or at another place without losing the indulgence, provided the title remains the same and the altar is not transferred to another church. In requesting Rome for the indulgence of the privileged altar, the applicant should give the title of the altar as well as the name of the church. Finally, no one may accept the perpetual obligation of saying Masses at a privileged altar.

1190. *Indulgences granted to certain confraternities.*

Nothing is better suited to foster the piety of the faithful, encourage them to receive the Sacraments frequently, preserve them from falling into sin, and edify the rest of the congregation than the establishment in a parish of confraternities of young men and women, boys and girls. Hence, there is no work to which the pastor should devote more attention and zeal. However, confraternities are productive of fruit only if they are governed by regulations apt to help them attain their end. The principal obligations imposed upon the members should be:

1. To avoid occasions of sin and scandal;
2. Frequent reception of the Sacraments;
3. Regular meetings on certain determined days, at which the members have occasion to listen to an instruction by their spiritual director. The Sovereign Pontiffs have attached indulgences to all such confraternities, provided they have been canonically erected, and all members may gain these indulgences if they perform the prescribed good works.

Every pious confraternity must be erected or at least approved by the Church. The erection or approval of a new confraternity is obtained from the Sovereign Pontiff or the local Ordinary. If, by a special privilege, the confraternity is to be affiliated with some religious Order, the faculty of erection is obtained from the superior of the Order, with the consent of the bishop. That consent is valid only if issued in writing. The faculty to erect a convent includes that of erecting in the church a confraternity proper to the Order, provided the confraternity is not of the nature of an organic body.

1191. Canon 689 states that every society shall have its statutes approved either by the Holy See or by the bishop of the diocese. Statutes that have not been confirmed by the Holy See are subject to modification and correction by the bishop. All pious unions, except those established by exempt religious that do not possess a special privilege of exemption from the Holy See, are under the jurisdiction and vigilance of the bishop of the diocese, who has the right and duty to inspect them. But the bishop has no right to visit, in regard to internal discipline or spiritual direction, societies that have been erected by religious in their own churches in virtue of an Apostolic indult. A legally erected society may, unless the contrary has been expressly stated, possess and administer temporal goods under the authority of the bishop of the diocese, to whom it should render a financial statement at least once a year. This is to be done by the society itself and not by the pastor in whose parish the society is erected, unless the bishop has ordered the pastor to make such a report.

1192. The vicar-general or a vicar-capitular cannot erect pious societies, or approve their erection or aggregation, except by special mandate. The formulas prescribed for the erection of confraternities are obligatory for the regular superiors, but not for the bishops. Several different confraternities may be erected in the same church, but in one and the same town there should not be several confraternities of the same kind, unless the law or special regulations provide for an exception. In large cities, this whole matter is left to the discretion of the bishop.

Confraternities and pious unions should be erected only in churches and public or semi-public oratories. In churches and oratories of religious women, the bishop may allow the erection of societies for women, or of pious unions which meet only for the purpose of reciting certain prayers, and share spiritual favors with some confraternity. The religious superiors may give to the confraternities and pious unions erected by them only those indulgences which the Holy See has declared communicable, and they should be made known to all the members at the time of the erection of the confraternity. Members of such a confraternity are not allowed to wear in public ecclesiastical functions the habit or other insignia, without special permission of the bishop; neither may they change or abandon the habit or insignia proper to the confraternity without episcopal permission.

The foregoing rules and regulations apply also to confraternities erected by religious superiors, and no one is allowed to publish the list of indulgences granted to these confraternities without the permission of the bishop.

Non-Catholics who belong to a condemned society, persons publicly known to be under ecclesiastical censure, and, in general, public sinners, cannot be validly received into a confraternity or pious union. The bishop has the right to dismiss unworthy members. In order to participate in the rights, privileges, indulgences, and other spiritual favors of such a society it is sufficient that a person be validly received into that society according to its statutes, and that he has not been legally expelled. Expulsion from the society must be effected conformably to the statutes, and after the usual admonitions. Inscription into the membership records of the society is necessary for validity of admission, if there is question of a confraternity formally erected by ecclesiastical authority.

Confraternities must be formally erected by the Church, and not merely approved. When they have been formally erected, they enjoy the right of a legal person. Pious unions may content themselves with the approval of the bishop, but this approval does not give them the rights of legal persons, although they share in all the spiritual graces, especially the indulgences. No charges may be made for admission or enrollment beyond those permitted by the bishop or the statutes.

If confraternities wish to hold extraordinary meetings,

they shall advise the Ordinary or his delegate, otherwise the bishop has the right to stop the meeting and cancel its proceedings. They are fully authorized to meet for the purpose of appointing officers and administrators of their possessions. Aside from special Apostolic privileges, the moderator and the chaplain of societies which are either erected or approved by the bishop or by the Holy See, and of societies erected by religious in virtue of an Apostolic indult outside of their own churches, is to be appointed by the bishop of the diocese. For societies erected by religious in their own churches, the moderator and the chaplain are appointed by the religious. If, however, the superior should appoint a secular priest for these offices, the consent of the bishop of the diocese is required. The pastor is not by law the moderator or the chaplain of pious societies, unless this is expressly stipulated. For serious reasons the bishop may suppress societies erected either by himself or by religious superiors with his consent, but he cannot suppress societies erected or approved by the Holy See.

1193. There are three kinds of pious associations:

1. Third Orders Secular;
2. Confraternities;
3. Pious unions.

Canon 703 confirms the existing third orders, but forbids new ones to be established.

Superiors of religious orders may receive individuals into their Third Order if they possess one, but they cannot validly establish a new branch of Tertiaries in any church without the consent of the bishop. Persons who have taken either perpetual or temporary vows in a religious institute, cannot at the same time become or remain secular Tertiaries of the same. On March 20, 1922, Pope Pius XI forbade Tertiaries to wear a medal instead of the scapular. This decree was not, however, intended to interfere with the right of Franciscan superiors to dispense from the above-mentioned rule in particular cases and for just reasons.

1194. Associations of the faithful erected for the exercise of works of piety or charity are called pious unions. When such an association is established after the manner of an organic body, it is called a corporation. A corporation which has for its purpose the furtherance of divine worship is called a confraternity. The bishop has the right to preside at the meetings of confraternities, even in the churches and oratories of regulars, to confirm or reject the officers elected, and to approve statutes not yet approved by the Apostolic See. Confraternities or pious unions annexed to a religious Order cannot change their location without the consent of the superior.

1195. Corporations or confraternities which possess the right to affiliate other associations of the same kind are called Archconfraternities or primary unions, congregations or societies. No association can affiliate others without an Apostolic indult. Archconfraternities and primary unions may affiliate only such confraternities and pious unions as have the same title and the same purpose, unless the papal indult states otherwise. By such an affiliation all indulgences, privileges, and other communicable spiritual favors granted to the affiliating body directly and by name are communicated to the affiliated body, unless a restriction is made in the papal indult. Affiliating bodies do not acquire any right over the confraternity affiliated by the act of affiliation.

For an affiliation to be valid, the following conditions must be fulfilled:

1. The association to be affiliated must have been canonically erected.

2. The affiliation requires the written consent of the Ordinary, accompanied by testimonial letters.

3. The association must not have been previously affiliated to any other Archconfraternity or primary union.

4. The indulgences, privileges, and other spiritual favors communicated by the affiliation must be enumerated in a document which is to be submitted to the bishop of the diocese where the Archconfraternity resides, and be given to the affiliated society.

5. The affiliation must be issued in the prescribed form and for all time.

6. The letters of affiliation must be issued gratis.

The Archconfraternity or primary union cannot be transferred from its present to another place except by authority from the Holy See. (*C. J. C.*, canons 720–724.)

Confraternities of the Blessed Sacrament and of Christian Doctrine, when legally erected, are *ipso facto* affiliated with the Archconfraternities of the same name erected in Rome.

1196. The principal Confraternities are: (1) The Confraternity of the Blessed Sacrament; (2) The Confraternity of the Blessed Virgin Mary; (3) The Confraternity of the Holy Rosary; (4) Third Orders.

The *Confraternity of the Blessed Sacrament* is a most appropriate society for the men of a parish. According to canon 711, the Holy See desires that the bishops establish a Confraternity of the Blessed Sacrament in every parish, but the local Ordinary can comply with the wishes of the Sovereign Pontiff in some circumstances by merely creating a sodality, private association or even pious union of the Blessed Sacrament. (Decision of the Commission for the Interpretation of the New Code, March 6, 1927.) There is this difference, however, that Confraternities of the Blessed Sacrament are *ipso jure* affiliated with the Archconfraternities directed by the Cardinal Vicar at Rome, whereas the sodalities and pious unions are not.

1197. The *Confraternity of the Blessed Virgin Mary* is

enriched with countless indulgences and is most appropriate for young girls. If the parish is very small, the young girls and the women may all be inscribed in the Confraternity of the Holy Rosary, although it would be well to hold special meetings for the young girls.

1198. The *Confraternity of the Holy Rosary* deserves to be recommended to all the faithful. To become a member it is enough to have one's name and surname entered in the registers, and to gain the indulgences one has only to recite the rosary and meditate upon its mysteries. The right to attach to rosaries the indulgences of this Confraternity is vested only in the priests who possess that faculty, and they must make use of the formula prescribed *ad hoc*. An indulgence of one hundred days is attached to each Our Father and Hail Mary of the rosary (this indulgence may be gained without belonging to the Confraternity). These indulgences are not to be confused with those of St. Bridget, which may be attached to the same rosary, and are one hundred days for each Our Father, Hail Mary, and Credo.

1199. Pastors may receive as postulants into these Confraternities children of both sexes after their First Communion, reserving their final reception for some future time, dependent upon their perseverance in virtue.

1200. *Third Orders.* We call attention first to the formula of the plenary indulgence which any confessor may give to Tertiaries. This formula is not identical with that of the papal blessing which, according to the regulations of the Third Orders, may be given twice a year to the assembled Tertiaries. Neither is it the complete formula of general absolution which the priest must use when he gives this plenary indulgence outside the confessional. It is merely the formula which he must use in the sacred tribunal.

1201. The following are the days on which this indulgence may be granted: Christmas, Easter, Pentecost, the Feasts of the Sacred Heart, of the Immaculate Conception, of St. Joseph (March 19), of the Stigmata of St. Francis, of St. Louis of France, and of St. Elizabeth of Hungary. The indulgence may be given in the confessional on the day before these feasts.

1202. The formula of the plenary indulgence is as follows:

"Dominus noster Jesus Christus, qui beato Petro Apostolo dedit potestatem ligandi atque solvendi, Ille te absolvat ab omni vinculo delictorum, ut habeas vitam aeternam et vivas in saecula saeculorum. Amen.

"Per sacratissimam Passionem et mortem Domini nostri Jesu Christi, precibus et meritis Beatissimae semper Virginis Mariae, beatorum Apostolorum Petri et Pauli, beati Patris nostri Francisci, et omnium sanctorum, auctoritate a Summis Pontificibus mihi concessa, plenariam indulgentiam omnium peccatorum tuorum tibi impertior. In nomine Patris et Filii et Spiritus Sancti. Amen."

If time does not permit the recitation of the entire formula, the priest may omit the first part and begin with the words *"auctoritate a Summis Pontificibus mihi."*

No one may be a member of several Third Orders at the same time, and members of religious Orders and congregations approved by the Holy See or by the Ordinary cease to be Tertiaries when they make their profession. If their vows expire or are dissolved, their membership in the Third Order revives. It is permitted to pass from one Third Order to another for any just reason.

1203. *Scapulars*. In giving the scapular of Mount Carmel to St. Simon Stock, the Blessed Virgin Mary said: "Anyone dying with this habit shall not burn in hell. This habit will be unto him a sign of salvation, a shield in danger, and a pledge of peace and special protection." Commenting upon these words, Pope Benedict XIV says: "It is our belief that this vision must be regarded by all as genuine." In another apparition the Blessed Virgin promised Pope John XXII to alleviate the pains of those souls in Purgatory who died with her scapular, and to deliver them as soon as possible, especially on the Saturday after their death. To share in the promise made to St. Simon Stock it is sufficient to have been vested with the scapular by a priest who possesses this faculty, and to have one's name inscribed in the Confraternity of Mount Carmel. Formerly this last condition was not required, but now it is prescribed for the scapulars of Mount Carmel, that of the Blessed Trinity, and that of the Seven Dolors. The scapular of Mount Carmel must be given separately from the others.

In virtue of a decision of Pope Benedict XIV, members of the Union of the Clergy for missionary countries are dispensed from entering the names of those whom they invest with the scapular. Members of the Apostolic Union have the same faculty, but only on occasions when, because of large crowds, they impose the scapular *in globo,* in which case each person places the scapular upon his own shoulders while the priest recites the formula of reception.

1204. To gain the *Sabbatine Indulgence* it is required that one practice purity according to his or her station in life, and that he or she recite the Little Office of the Blessed Virgin or the canonical Office every day. Those who cannot read are allowed to substitute for the Office, fasts on the days prescribed by the Church, and abstinence on the Wednesdays, Fridays, and Saturdays of each week, or to have this abstinence commuted into some other good work.

1205. The *blue scapular* or *scapular of the Immaculate Conception* was revealed by Christ Himself to Venerable Ursula of Benincasa. It must be blessed and imposed by a priest who possesses this faculty. Persons invested with this scapular may gain a great number of plenary indulgences,

applicable to the souls in Purgatory, each time they recite
six Our Fathers, Hail Marys, and Glory be to the Fathers
in honor of the Blessed Trinity and the Immaculate Conception for the intentions of the Sovereign Pontiff. It is not
necessary to add any other prayers, nor to go to Confession
or Communion, and one does not need to have one's name
inscribed in the registers.

The scapular may be imposed upon the shoulders, as it is
often impossible to place it around the neck, especially in
the case of women who wear large hats. In receiving new
members, it is enough to hold the scapulars in one's hand
and to recite the formula once in the plural and then impose
them individually. When a scapular becomes worn or soiled,
another may be purchased and worn without being blessed.
The case would be different if one had renounced the scapular out of contempt or from some other unworthy motive.

Several decrees have been issued in reference to the different scapulars. We refer the reader especially to those of
May 16, 1882, December 14, 1904, and July 30, 1910. The
scapular of the Blessed Trinity requires no image, but a red
and blue cross—the arms of the cross being blue and the ver-
tical line red. According to a decision of the Holy Office issued
December 16th, 1910, the scapular may be replaced by a
medal.

1206. *The Way of the Cross.* No devotion can be of
greater profit to the living and the dead than the Way or
Stations of the Cross. To gain the many indulgences attached
to this most salutary devotion, it is enough to meditate, without moral interruption, upon each station successively. It is
better to do this by stopping before each station, but when
this cannot be done, it is enough to make a simple genuflection at one's place (S. C. R., Dec. 14, 1917), and at the same
time to meditate upon the Passion of Christ, or, better still,
upon that phase of the Passion which the particular station

recalls. Neither prayer, nor confession, nor Communion are prescribed for these indulgences, and, what is more, if it is morally impossible to make the Way of the Cross, it suffices to hold in one's hand a crucifix blessed for this purpose by a priest possessing the faculty, and to recite the Our Father, the Hail Mary, and the Glory be to the Father at each station, and at the end five Our Fathers, Hail Marys and Glory be to the Fathers in honor of the five wounds, and one Our Father, Hail Mary, and Glory be to the Father for the intentions of the Sovereign Pontiff. Persons who are grievously ill and who possess such a crucifix may gain these same indulgences if they have received the favor from the General of the Franciscan Order or a priest delegated by him, by reciting instead of these prayers one verse of the Te Deum, to wit: *"Te ergo quaesumus famulis tuis subveni,"* etc., and together with the act of contrition, whilst following mentally the recitation of three Our Fathers, Hail Marys, and Glory be to the Fathers by some other person. It is not certain that the indulgences of the Way of the Cross may be gained *toties quoties*.

To erect a way of the Cross, one must possess an indult from the Holy See and the permission of the local Ordinary. This permission must be in writing, under pain of nullity. For hospital chapels and convents of non-exempt religious, one must also have the written permission of the pastor and superiors of the church and convent. The indult from the Holy See merely authorizes the erection of Stations of the Cross in public churches and chapels; for private chapels one must possess a special rescript. The Stations of the Cross may not be erected in cloisters or cemeteries.[1]

1207. A plenary indulgence is attached to the papal blessing. The bishop may give this blessing twice a year within

[1] The Sacred Congregation of Indulgences has revalidated all Stations of the Cross erected before Sept. 10, 1883. See Appendix I.

the confines of his diocese by means of the prescribed formula. One of these days is Easter Sunday, the other, any solemn feast he may select. Abbots and other ecclesiastical dignitaries possessing jurisdiction over a certain territory, and vicars and prefects Apostolic, have the same faculty on one solemn feast day each year within the confines of their territory, even if they are not bishops. Regular superiors who are authorized to give the papal blessing, may give it only in their own churches or in those of religious subject to them or Tertiaries legally affiliated with their Order, provided the bishop is not giving the blessing on the same day and in the same place. Nuncios, pro-nuncios, and Apostolic delegates may give this blessing three times a year in different parts of their territory.

The Beads. A brief issued Sept. 4, 1927, grants for all time a plenary indulgence, *toties quoties,* to all the faithful who recite the beads, *i. e.,* one-third of the rosary, before the Blessed Sacrament exposed or preserved in the tabernacle, provided they fulfill the ordinary conditions.

Priests should recommend also the practice of ejaculatory prayers. An indulgence of one hundred days, *toties quoties,* is attached to the prayer, "My Jesus, mercy"; one of fifty days to the prayer, "Jesus, my Lord, I love Thee above all things"; an indulgence of fifteen days to the invocation of the holy names of Jesus and Mary, and one of seven years and seven quarantines to the invocation of the names of Jesus, Mary, and Joseph.

Having treated of contrition, confession, and satisfaction, which constitute the *matter* of the Sacrament of Penance, we must now take up the study of its *form.*

1208. *The Form of the Sacrament of Penance.* The Council of Trent has defined that the form of the Sacrament of Penance is contained in the words: *"Ego te absolvo a peccatis tuis.*" (Sess. 14, ch. 3.) The word *ego* is not essential, but according to a probable opinion the words *te* and *tuis* are. This opinion must be followed in practice. The words *"in nomine Patris,"* etc., are not essential, but the confessor may not omit them without committing a venial sin. In case of shipwreck, or on battle-fields, the priest may absolve several persons at once, using the formula. *"Ego vos absolvo,"* etc. The person who is to receive absolution must be morally present. By this we mean he must be at a distance at which persons holding conversation can hear one another. St. Alphonsus is of the opinion that twenty steps would be too far. This opinion would not hold, however, if it were a question of absolving several persons distributed over a distance of twenty steps. In case of necessity the priest may absolve, at least conditionally, any penitent whom he can perceive through one of the senses. Thus in case of a plague the priest may absolve a stricken person from an adjoining door or window. Absolution conferred by letter would be invalid, even though the penitent were present when he made his confession. Absolution by telephone is probably invalid, but one might give it conditionally to a person *in articulo mortis,* who would request it in this way because no other means was available. Absolution may not be given by signs. Sporer is of the opinion that a deaf-mute priest may give absolution conditionally in writing or by signs to a dying person.

It is certain that the elevation of hands and the sign of the Cross are not necessary for the validity of the Sacrament. According to common opinion, the priest may omit them without committing a grievous sin, and according to some authors, without committing any sin at all.

Since absolution is the form of the Sacrament, it must be united to the matter, *i. e.,* the acts of the penitent. The form could not be separated from the matter, therefore, for a period of more than one hour, but there is nothing to prevent separating it for a longer period of time, provided the penitent says some such words as the following: "Father, I accuse myself of all the sins which I stated to you formerly," and then makes his act of contrition. (See no. 1099.)

1209. May the form of this Sacrament be deprecatory? This form is certainly valid in the Greek Church, but its validity in the Latin Church is controverted. Some authors aver that it is valid, claiming that this was the formula used at one time in the Latin Church; other authors hold the opposite opinion. Probably the Church grants no jurisdiction to priests using the deprecatory form.

1210. The form prescribed by the rubrics is as follows: *"Misereatur tui,"* etc.; *"Indulgentiam,"* etc., which words the priest may omit without committing sin. From the word *"Indulgentiam"* on, the priest raises his hand: *"Dominus noster Jesus Christus te absolvat et ego auctoritate ipsius te absolvo ab omni vinculo excommunicationis, suspensionis et interdicti, in quantum possum et tu indiges."* According to several authors this latter formula obliges *sub levi,* but according to others it may probably be omitted without sin. It would be a mortal sin to absolve a penitent from excommunication after absolving him from his sins, if the priest knew that the penitent was excommunicated. While the absolution in this case would be valid, if the penitent were in good faith, it would be gravely illicit because of the prohibition of the Church. It would not be a mortal sin to absolve a penitent from his sins before absolving him from suspension and interdict, because the latter do not bar him from the reception of the Sacrament of Penance.

1211. The priest may validly absolve from censures, provided he has the intention of doing so, by the simple form: *"Deinde, ego te absolvo a peccatis tuis in nomine Patris et Filii et Spiritus Sancti."* In imminent danger of death, however, it is better to use the formula: *"Ego te absolvo ab omnibus censuris et peccatis tuis in nomine,"* etc. The words *"in nomine Patris,"* etc., are not essential, but according to common opinion a priest who would omit them would be guilty of a venial sin. The word *"Deinde"* is not essential either, although it is part of the form. The form is completed by the following words: *"Passio Domini nostri Jesu Christi, merita beatæ Mariæ Virginis, et omnium sanctorum, quidquid boni feceris et mali sustinueris, sint tibi in remissionem peccatorum, augmentum gratiæ, et præmium vitæ æternæ. Amen."* This part of the form may be omitted when the penitent confesses his sins frequently, but it is better not to omit it, except on rare occasions, according to the explanation given in no. 1146. Moreover, the priest is at liberty to recite this part of the form while the penitent is withdrawing from the confessional.

1212. The Sacred Congregation of Rites prescribes the use of the stole in the administration of the Sacrament of Penance. Aside from cases of necessity, it would be a mortal sin to hear the confession of women in some place other than the church or in some retired corner, because of the scandal that might result. It would not be a mortal sin to do this once or twice under circumstances where scandal is excluded. (See no. 1306.)

1213. Absolution with some present or past condition attached, is valid, according to all writers. This is *certain*. (See no. 792.) Again, according to all writers, absolution given with a condition, the fulfillment of which does not depend upon the confessor, is licit. Such a condition would be: "If thou art alive;" but according to some writers such an absolution would be illicit if the condition bore upon dispositions with which the confessor should be acquainted. This opinion, however, is neither intrinsically nor extrinsically probable.

The priest should bear in mind that he is not permitted to give conditional absolution for any reason. (See nos. 763, 767, and 792). When the penitent is well disposed, he should be absolved unconditionally, although the priest would not sin grievously in giving him conditional absolution. If the dispositions of the penitent are doubtful, the confessor should try to correct them, but if he does not succeed, he may and must give conditional absolution. This rule applies not only in cases of extreme necessity, as admitted by certain rigorists, but every time the priest runs the risk of rendering the Sacrament null and void by giving unconditional absolution, or exposes the penitent to some serious spiritual loss. The same is true if he exposes the penitent to the loss of some notable, although not indispensable, spiritual good, and hence the confessor may and must give absolution to the dying. (See no. 1087.)

The priest is bound to give absolution to a woman who is in danger at child-birth, to a sailor about to embark on a long voyage, and to a sick person about to undergo a serious operation. The priest should give conditional absolution to a penitent in the state of mortal sin who he fears has not been validly absolved, although the better course of action in this case would be for the penitent to renew his act of contrition, accuse himself anew of all his sins, and receive absolution without condition.

1214. The priest may and must give conditional absolution to idiots and children concerning whom he doubts whether or not they have reached the age of reason. He must follow this rule not only in imminent danger of death, but also every time the precept of annual confession obliges and even when these penitents accuse themselves of grievous sins. It is probable, too, that he may absolve them conditionally every three months, even though he doubts their disposition, in order not to deprive them of the fruits of the Sacrament for too long a period of time. For the same reason he may absolve conditionally every month pious penitents who have no certain matter for absolution.

1215. *A fortiori* the priest may absolve conditionally at Easter, during a mission, and before marriage, penitents who are doubtfully disposed and who he fears will withdraw from the Church if he refuses or defers absolution.

1216. The priest should say nothing about Communion to persons whom he absolves conditionally. When they ask if they may receive, he may answer: "If your conscience is clear and you are well disposed, you may go to Communion." In such cases good faith will save these persons from a sacrilegious Communion and, moreover, the reception of the Holy Eucharist may result in the remission of their sins. (See nos. 776 and 1232.) A penitent thus conditionally absolved is obliged to repeat his confession only if he is certain that it was null and void.

Art. II. Divine Institution.

1217. It is an article of faith that the Sacrament of Penance was instituted by Jesus Christ: "The Lord instituted the Sacrament of Penance especially when, after His resurrection from the dead, He breathed upon His disciples saying: 'Receive ye the Holy Ghost, whose sins you shall forgive, they are forgiven them, and whose sins you shall retain, they are retained.'" (*C. of Trent*, Sess. 14, ch. 1.)

Art. III. Effects.

1218. The Sacrament of Penance remits all sins committed after Baptism. This is *of faith* (Council of Trent, Sess. 14, can. 1.) It remits all sins because final impenitence alone renders sins irremissible. The Montanists, who taught that the power of the keys admitted of limitations, were condemned as heretics. It is *certain* that the Sacrament of Penance also remits the eternal punishment due to sin, for this cannot persist in the soul of a person from which all stain has been removed and who is now a friend of God and heir of His kingdom. This is also *of faith*. Although the eternal punishment due to sin is remitted by the Sacrament of Penance, there remains more often than not a temporal punishment, which must be remitted by some other means.

1219. The third effect of the Sacrament of Penance is the recovery of merits. Some of our works are deadly, others are dead, and still others are latent. *Deadly* works are sins. Dead works are those which, although good in themselves, are performed in the state of mortal sin, and hence cannot be revived nor merit eternal glory. They can, however, merit for us temporal blessings, train us in the practice of virtue, and, if performed with the aid of actual grace, merit *de congruo fallibili* the justification for which they prepare us. (See no. 744.) Others of our works were once alive, because performed in the state of sanctifying grace, but when grace was lost, they became latent, without being completely destroyed. They may be revived, and it would be sheer temerity to hold the contrary view. According to the more probable opinion, the Sacrament of Penance restores to the soul the same right to eternal glory and the same degree of sanctifying grace which it possessed before it lapsed into sin. We may thank the mercy of God that forgiven sins and the forgiven eternal punishment of sin do not revive. This is *certain* from the words of the Apostle, "For the gifts of God are without repentance." (Rom. 11, 29.)

1220. The Sacrament of Penance gives to the sinner first sanctifying grace and to the just second sanctifying grace. It remits part of the temporal punishment due to sin and sometimes, by reason of the profound contrition of the penitent, the whole of that punishment. (See no. 1057.) It confers sacramental grace or the right to receive, at the proper time, actual graces to avoid sin, overcome temptation, and regain the health of one's soul. Finally, it confers security and peace of conscience.

CHAPTER II

THE MINISTER

1221. We shall treat, first, of the powers of the minister and, second, of his duties. Concerning the obligation to administer the Sacrament of Penance, the reader is referred to nos. 1309, 1369, 2435, 3680.

Art. I. Powers of the Minister.

1222. *The Power of Orders*. The priest alone is the minister of the Sacrament of Penance. This is *of faith*. To the Apostles alone Christ addressed the words: "Whose sins you shall forgive, they are forgiven, and whose sins you shall retain, they are retained." The Council of Trent defined: "If anyone saith that priests have not the power of binding and of loosing; or, that not priests alone are the ministers of absolution; let him be anathema." (Sess. 14, can. 10.)

Through the Sacrament of Holy Orders the priest is made the instrument of Jesus Christ to impart grace to others and to administer the Sacraments, in particular, Penance. However, since this latter Sacrament was instituted after the manner of a judgment, the priest must, over and above the power of Orders, possess the competence required of a judge in passing judgment on those who appear before his tribunal. He may not make use, therefore, of his power of Orders unless, over and above this, he has received the necessary approbation and power of jurisdiction.

1223. *Approbation.* Approbation is the judgment which a prelate passes upon the capacity of a priest to hear confessions. This capacity comprises two things: sufficient theological knowledge and probity of life. The approbation must be given by the bishop, or the vicar-general, or the vicar-capitular, or an abbot possessing quasi-episcopal jurisdiction, or any other Ordinary of the place where the priest hears confessions. According to the present practice the approbation is always included in the power of jurisdiction.

1224. *Jurisdiction.* Jurisdiction is the power to govern subjects. It may be *external,* or *in the external forum,* and this pertains principally and directly to the public good of the Church. It is the power to enact laws, pass judgments, and procure redress of grievances. When such a power is exercised over subjects forcibly, as when they are made to conform to the law and judgment, it is termed *contentious;* when it is exercised to their advantage in such wise that they willingly receive it as a favor, it is called *voluntary.* The second kind of jurisdiction is *internal,* or *in the internal forum,* and it is concerned primarily and directly with the private good of each one of the faithful. Internal jurisdiction is subdivided into extra-penitential (the faculty to preach and dispense as possessed by a pastor), and penitential, of which there is question here, and this is the power to absolve in the tribunal of Penance. It is a truth bordering on the faith that jurisdiction is necessary to absolve from sin. The Council of Trent is explicit on this point: "Since the nature and order of a judgment require that sentence be passed only on those subject to that judicature, it has ever been firmly held in the Church of God, and this Synod ratifies it as a thing most true, that the absolution which a priest pronounces upon one over whom he has not either an ordinary or a delegated jurisdiction, is of no weight whatever." (Sess. 14, ch. 7.)

1225. *Ordinary jurisdiction* is that acquired by law in virtue of an office. The Sovereign Pontiff has ordinary jurisdiction in both the internal and the external forum for the entire Church. Cardinals also have ordinary and universal jurisdiction, but only in regard to the Sacrament of Penance. They may absolve anywhere from all reserved sins and censures, except those very specially reserved and those incurred by revealing a secret of the Holy Office. All prelates possessing the episcopal character may delegate jurisdiction for the absolution of themselves and their suite, including cases reserved to the Ordinary.

1226. The local Ordinary and his vicar-general have jurisdiction for both forums within the confines of their own territories. Pastors and other administrators of parishes or quasi-parishes possess ordinary jurisdiction for the sacramental forum in their respective territories. The jurisdiction for the sacramental forum possessed by the canon penitentiary of a cathedral or collegiate church for the entire diocese is also ordinary. Within the limits of their respective constitutions, superiors of exempt religious Orders possess ordinary jurisdiction in both forums over their subjects and over others actually living under their discipline.

A person acquires jurisdiction when he is inducted into office; he loses it when that office ceases or when he is deprived of jurisdiction by the sentence of a judge, by excommunication, suspension from office, or interdict. An office does not cease at the death, or resignation, or deposition of the person who has conferred it, unless the appointment contained the clause, *ad beneplacitum nostrum,* or some other clause of this kind.

1227. Any person possessing ordinary jurisdiction may delegate the same, with the exception of cardinals as such, canons penitentiary, and, according to an authentic interpretation of October 16, 1919, pastors and other administrators of parishes or quasi-parishes. Presumed or tacit jurisdiction does not suffice. Jurisdiction must be granted expressly, either in writing, or by word of mouth, and the person delegated must be notified in such a way that there can be no mistake as to his faculties. The acceptance on the part of the person delegated is also necessary for validity, but he who petitions for jurisdiction is reputed to have accepted it when it is delegated to him.

1228. *Simple jurisdiction.* The Ordinary of the place where confessions are heard may grant jurisdiction to both secular and religious priests, even those of exempt orders, to hear the confessions of both secular and religious persons, even those who are exempt. Within the limits of their constitutions, superiors of exempt religious Orders may also grant jurisdiction to any secular or religious priest to hear the confessions of those living under their discipline and for the time they continue to do so. Any person delegated by the local Ordinary may, therefore, validly and licitly absolve religious, even those who are exempt, and he may absolve them even from cases reserved in their Order. A religious priest to whom the local Ordinary has granted jurisdiction, must obtain the permission of his superior in order to exercise his faculties licitly. Local Ordinaries and religious superiors must not grant jurisdiction or permission to exercise jurisdiction except to priests whose ability is known to them from thorough examination or some other source. As a general rule, the bishop should not grant jurisdiction to religious priests who are not presented to him by their superiors. Once these subjects have been presented, however, he should not refuse them jurisdiction, except for serious reasons, but he always has the right to subject them to an examination.

According to an authentic interpretation of canon 130, the bishop may not require a religious who serves as pastor or assistant pastor in a parish, to undergo the examination which this canon requires of secular priests. Should a religious fail to take the examination required by canon 590 each year for at least five years after the completion of his course of studies, the local Ordinary should report the matter to the Sacred Congregation of Religious. As a general rule, the bishop and the religious superior may subject a priest who has jurisdiction to a new examination, if doubts arise as to his knowledge and competency. This rule applies even to pastors and canons penitentiary. It might be well to add that a religious superior may not suspend, and still less annul, the jurisdiction which his subjects hold from the local Ordinary, except if they have not obtained the at least reasonably presumed permission of the religious superior, which, as noted above, is required for the licit exercise of their faculties.

1229. The delegated jurisdiction which is necessary to hear the confessions of nuns with even simple and temporary vows and other pious women leading a community life is subject to special regulations. All universal or particular laws contrary to these new regulations have been repealed by canon 6 of the New Code. All priests except cardinals, both religious and secular, no matter what their dignity or office, require a special jurisdiction from the local Ordinary to hear the confessions of both professed nuns and novices. The competent Ordinary is the one in whose diocese the convent is located. Superiors of religious Orders must also secure this special jurisdiction.

1230. The local Ordinary must see to it that all the nuns in his diocese have an ordinary confessor. In answer to a letter from the Bishop of Luxemburg, Cardinal Gasparri, president of the Pontifical Commission for the Interpretation of the New Code, replied, January 16, 1921, that this law applies even to convents in which less than six nuns reside. Canon 520 states that in each house of religious women there should be appointed only one confessor for the whole community, unless two or more are deemed necessary because of the large number of religious or for some other just cause. Canon 521 states that each community of women is to have an extraordinary confessor, who shall repair to the convent four times a year, on which occasions all the Sisters must go to him, at least to receive his blessing.

The jurisdiction of the extraordinary confessor is not restricted to these four visits. While the extraordinary confessor is discharging his duties, the ordinary confessor may not come to the convent, but if he has his residence there, he is not obliged to leave, although he must not hear the confessions of any of the nuns or hinder his colleague in any way from performing this duty. The approbation of the ordinary as well as the extraordinary confessor is valid only for the nuns of the convent specified.

1231. Canon 524 states that the ordinary and extraordinary confessors of religious women should not interfere in any way in the internal or external government of the community. Generally speaking, the spiritual direction of the nuns belongs to the ordinary confessor, and the extraordinary confessor will do well not to concern himself with it. Should the Sisters seek his advice, however, he should endeavor to assist them by salutary counsels.

1232. For Sisters who are directly subject to the Holy See or to the local Ordinary, the obligation to select ordinary and extraordinary confessors and provide them with the necessary jurisdiction devolves upon the bishop. He may select secular priests and, with the consent of the superiors, religious priests. The ordinary confessor should be forty years of age or over, unless the bishop has good reasons to dispense with this requirement.

1233. The vicar-general cannot be either the ordinary or the extraordinary confessor of nuns. Every religious superior should present to the bishop the names of both the ordinary and the extraordinary confessor desired for the Sisters subject to him, and the bishop will give them jurisdiction. If the religious superior fails to present a candidate, the bishop himself should take care of this matter.

1234. The ordinary confessor should not exercise his office for more than three years, and cannot be appointed extraordinary confessor immediately after his term expires. The extraordinary confessor, on the other hand, can always be made ordinary confessor. These changes must be made even in convents where the personnel changes every three years. Again, an ordinary confessor cannot be reappointed to office except at least one year after the expiration of his term. The bishop may, however, reappoint him for a second and a third term if, on account of a scarcity of priests suitable for this work, he cannot easily appoint another, or if the majority of the Sisters by a secret vote, in which every Sister has a right to cast a ballot, express the wish to retain the same confessor. By a special indult from the Holy See, the bishop may reappoint the same confessor for a fourth and even fifth term, but the Sisters who dissent must be allowed to go to confession to some other priest. A chaplain who is not the confessor of the nuns does not have to be changed every three years.

1235. The local Ordinary may remove the extraordinary confessor and, for a grave reason, also the ordinary confessor, before the expiration of his term. He may also remove, for a grave reason, ordinary and extraordinary confessors of Sisters who are subject to a religious superior, even though these confessors be religious. Nor is the bishop bound to give the superior any reason for the removal;

the most he is obliged to do is to notify the regular superior to whom the Sisters are subject.

1236. The local Ordinary shall appoint several priests in the vicinity of each convent, who may hear the confessions of the Sisters in particular cases, without being required to obtain faculties each time. Should a Sister ask for any of these priests, no superior is allowed, either by herself or through another, either directly or indirectly, to inquire for the reason, or to refuse the petition by word of mouth or action, or to show dislike in any way whatsoever. The bishop should reprimand any superior who violates this rule, and if his words are of no avail, he should remove her.

1237. If any Sister, for conscience sake or to make greater progress in the spiritual life, should request a special confessor or director, the Ordinary must grant her request, taking care, however, that no misuse is made of this concession. Should abuses creep in, the bishop must eliminate them without jeopardizing the Sisters' liberty of conscience. Special confessors should not be appointed for a definite period of time, but for the entire duration of these conditions.

1238. If, notwithstanding the concessions of the foregoing ecclesiastical regulations, a Sister wishes to go to any confessor approved by the local Ordinary, in any church, or public or semi-public oratory, her confession is both valid and licit.

Observe that the condition of place specified by canon 522 is a requisite for validity. In making use of this permission, the Sister who does not need to go outside the convent, either because she is already outside, or because some priest is visiting the convent, is not obliged to apprise her superior of her actions. And neither may the superior either directly or indirectly inquire concerning this matter. It goes without saying that if the Sister is obliged to leave the convent in order to take advantage of this privilege, she must inform her superior.

Whenever a Sister is seriously ill, though there be no immediate danger of death, she may ask for any approved priest of the diocese to confess to him. During her illness she may confess to such a priest as often as she desires, and the superior cannot forbid it either directly or indirectly.

The New Code urges specially designated confessors prudently to dismiss Sisters who come to them for confession without just reasons. Generally speaking, Sisters should be instructed to confess to confessors other than their ordinary confessors only for the peace of their soul or greater progress in virtue.

In houses of religious congregations of laymen, extraordinary and ordinary confessors should likewise be appointed who, in this case, do not need any specially delegated jurisdiction. If a lay religious should petition for a special confessor, his superior must not inquire into the reason nor exhibit any displeasure at his request. In houses of non-exempt lay religious, the local Ordinary must designate the chaplain and the confessors. If the Order or congregation is exempt, the superior has the right to designate the priest, and if he neglects to do so, the local Ordinary. The right to delegate jurisdiction for the confessional always belongs to the bishop.

Although it is praiseworthy that religious of both sexes confide unreservedly in their superiors, the latter are forbidden to induce such intimate confidences.

A sufficient number of approved confessors should be appointed in each house of a religious clerical community to hear the confessions of the inmates. If the house is exempt, these confessors should have the power to absolve from reserved cases. It is for the superiors to designate the confessors. Any secular or religious priest approved by the local Ordinary has jurisdiction over religious, even exempt, and may validly and licitly absolve them from all censures and all sins reserved in their Order. Any religious may licitly confess to such a priest in order to quiet his conscience. The novices must also have their ordinary confessor, who, in clerical religious communities, must reside in the novitiate, and in lay religious communities must frequently visit the novitiate. Besides the ordinary confessors, several other confessors should be appointed, to whom the novices may freely repair in particular cases. At least four times a year, the novices shall be provided with an extraordinary confessor, to whom all shall present themselves, at least to receive his blessing.

1239. The master of novices and his associates, as well as the superior of a seminary or college, shall not hear the confessions of those in their charge, except in particular cases, when a novice or student, for grave and urgent reasons, of his own accord asks them to hear his confession. Any attempt to constrain such subjects to confess to them is strictly forbidden. (*C. J. C.*, can. 891.)

1240. Chaplains of prisons, hospitals, and other similar institutions hold their faculties from the bishop, who, for a serious reason, may concede to them parochial rights over the houses in which they exercise their functions. The powers of major or minor military chaplains are governed by special regulations issued by the Holy See.

1241. *Delegated jurisdiction in danger of death.* In danger of death, any priest, whether irregular, excommunicated, suspended, interdicted, schismatic, heretical, or apostate, can by law validly and licitly absolve any penitent from all sins and censures, no matter how notorious or reserved they may be, and this even though a duly authorized priest is available. However, absolution given by a priest to his accomplice *in re turpi*, when the accomplice is in imminent danger of death, while valid, is illicit on the part of the confessor except in cases where the penitent cannot or will not confess to another priest.

1242. A penitent who, in danger of death, has been absolved from a censure very specially reserved to the Holy See, when the danger is past, must have recourse to the Sacred Penitentiary, or to the bishop, or to any other person who has faculties in these matters. The same rule applies to a person who, in danger of death, was absolved from a censure *ab homine,* though the confessor had no proper delegation. The penitent must have recourse to the superior who issued the sentence. If in the two foregoing instances, the penitent fails to comply with these regulations when the danger is past, he reverts to his former status. A decision of the Sacred Penitentiary of March 12, 1912, includes soldiers conscripted for war in the category of persons who are in danger of death.

1243. *Delegated jurisdiction at sea.* All priests who make an ocean trip may validly and licitly absolve the faithful who travel with them, even though the boat passes through the diocese of other bishops or puts in at some port, provided they have been approved either by the bishop of their own diocese or by the bishop of the port from which the ship sailed, or by the Ordinary of any of the ports at which it touches. They may even absolve the faithful from cases reserved to the Ordinaries of these different places. Whenever the ship puts in at some port during the trip, they may absolve not only penitents who for any reason come aboard, but if they themselves go ashore, any persons who request them to hear their confession, in which case they may absolve also from sins reserved by the bishop of that place. According to an authentic interpretation of canon 883, issued May 20, 1923, this last faculty cannot be exercised for more than three days if it is convenient to apply to the local ordinary.

1244. *Jurisdiction supplied by the Church.* The Church supplies jurisdiction in common error, *i. e.*, not when one or two persons, but when a whole group erroneously believe the confessor to be approved. Absolution is valid, therefore, even though given without any jurisdiction, including the *titulus coloratus,* provided it is commonly believed that the priest who gives it has jurisdiction. Of course, such an absolution would be gravely illicit, except in cases of extreme necessity.

1245. The Church supplies jurisdiction in positive and probable doubt of fact and law, in which case the absolution is licit if the cause is just. Canon 207 states that jurisdiction granted for the internal forum is still valid, even though the priest, through inadvertency, does not realize that his faculties have expired or has used up the number of reserved cases for which he has faculties.

1246. A priest who hears confessions without jurisdiction incurs suspension *a divinis,* and one who absolves from reserved cases without the proper delegation, incurs a suspension which bars him from hearing any further confessions.

1247. *General principles.* He who delegates jurisdiction or grants permission to exercise jurisdiction, may restrict the same as to persons and places. He is cautioned, however, not to use this right except for grave reasons. The local Ordinary and the religious superior may suspend or repeal such a delegation or permission, but they may not infringe upon the right of the subject to have recourse to the Holy See. For grave reasons, the local Ordinary may prohibit pastors and canons penitentiary from exercising jurisdiction in the sacred tribunal of Penance, but he may not deprive of jurisdiction all the priests of a duly established religious house, without consulting the Holy See.

1248. Priests who have ordinary or delegated jurisdiction may hear the confessions of all persons who present themselves to them, irrespective of what diocese or parish they come from. They may validly and licitly absolve Catholics of another rite, and the faithful are permitted freely to select their confessor from among priests of another Catholic rite, provided the priest be approved by the local Ordinary. But while a confessor who has ordinary jurisdiction may absolve his own subjects throughout the world, a priest who has only delegated jurisdiction may validly make use of the same only within the limits of the territory for which it was granted. If the priest is a stranger, he must, over and above the jurisdiction, have the permission of the pastor of the church.

1249. Delegated jurisdiction ceases in the following ways: (1) when the time limit has expired; (2) when the number of cases for which it was granted has been exhausted; (3) when the delegation is directly recalled; (4) when the priest leaves the diocese, if the diocesan statutes so ordain; (5) when the mandate has been complied with, if the delegation was granted for special cases; (6) when the delegated priest renounces his jurisdiction and his renunciation is accepted by his superior; (7) when the delegating person ceases to hold office, provided the terms of his delegation read, *ad beneplacitum nostrum,* or something similar, or when it was granted to some particular person and the executor had not yet begun to make use of his faculty.

Observe that all pastors and priests engaged in the ministry of souls have a grave obligation in justice, by virtue of their office, to hear the confessions of the faithful entrusted to their care every time they are reasonably asked to do so. In cases of urgent necessity, all confessors, and in danger of death all priests without exception, are bound to hear confessions by the law of charity.

1250. *Reserved jurisdiction.* We shall treat, first, of reservation itself; and, second, of the absolution of reserved cases.

1251. *Reservation itself.* Who may reserve cases or sins? He who has ordinary jurisdiction and delegates it to another may except certain grave sins. In these cases, the lawful superior selects certain grave sins and restricts the jurisdiction of his subordinates in regard to them, in an effort to eradicate some public vice or raise the standard of Christian discipline. Reserved sins are termed *reserved cases* to distinguish them from *reserved censures*.

1252. The following persons may reserve sins, with or without censure: (1) the Sovereign Pontiff; (2) the local Ordinary; (3) the superior general of an exempt clerical Order and the abbot of an independent monastery with the advice of their respective councils. The vicar-capitular may not reserve sins, nor, without a special mandate, the vicar-general.

1253. The Council of Trent declared that the Pope and the bishops can reserve certain cases: "If anyone saith, that bishops have not the right of reserving cases to themselves . . . ; let him be anathema." (Sess. 14, can. 11.)

1254. Bishops should establish reserved cases only in synod, or at least after consultation with the cathedral chapter or the diocesan consultors, and the most prudent pastors (*curatores animarum*) of the diocese. Cases reserved by bishops or superiors of religious Orders should not exceed the number of four, and the reservation should remain in force no longer than its purpose demands. Inferior authorities should abstain from reserving to themselves sins which are already reserved to the Holy See, even if by reason of a non-reserved censure. They should also refrain from reserving sins to which the law has already attached a censure that is not reserved. Finally, local Ordinaries should see to it that the people are apprised of the sins that have been reserved.

1255. *What is required for a sin to be reserved?* Theologians require five conditions for a sin to be reserved: (1) The sin must be formal, as far as the species of malice is concerned for which it is reserved, so that if, by accident, the sin were formal from standpoints other than this special malice, the censure would not be incurred. (2) The sin may be occult, but it must be external. (3) The sin must be either objectively or subjectively grave; an exteriorly slight sin, rendered grave through the intention of the sinner, could not be reserved. (4) The sin must be consummated, *i. e.,* perfect in its species. Attempted sins may not be reserved unless the law expressly reserves imperfect acts. If the guilty cause is withdrawn before the act is consummated, the sin is not reserved. (5) The sin must not be doubtfully grave, doubtfully committed, or doubtfully reserved. A penitent is not obliged to mention in a later confession a sin remitted by an ordinary confessor in doubt of fact or law, if he discovers that the sin he has committed was reserved.

1256. *Does he who sins in ignorance of a reserved sin actually incur the reservation?* We must distinguish between sins reserved without censure and sins reserved with censure. In regard to the former, some writers are of the opinion that, since the reservation is a penalty, it is not incurred by those who are not aware of its existence. The majority of theologians, however, hold that the reservation is nevertheless incurred, and this is the more commonly followed opinion today, especially in regard to sins reserved by the bishop. In some dioceses the bishops expressly state that the reservation is not incurred by persons who are ignorant of its existence, but in others they as emphatically declare that it *is*. The attitude of the latter seems to be more in keeping with canons 895 and 897, which state that the reservation must be necessary or at least useful. This wording would seem to indicate that the outstanding purpose of a reservation is not penal, but purely medicinal. Observe that bishops usually reserve sins without censure, but nevertheless they should be deemed to have in mind principally the censure. The Holy See has reserved to itself only one sin, namely, the false denunciation before an ecclesiastical tribunal of an innocent priest, charging him with the crime of solicitation in confession. Formerly this sin was very specially reserved to the Holy See; now it is only specially reserved, on account of the excommunication which is attached to it. In this instance, the reserved case may be incurred without the censure, as will become apparent from what we shall have to say in regard to sins reserved *with* censure.

1257. When the Sovereign Pontiff—and the same applies to the local Ordinary—reserves sins with censure, then either the text of the reservations contains, or does not contain, such terms as: *praesumpserit, ausus fuerit* or *scienter, studiose, temerarie, consulto egerit,* or others which indicate that the subject must have full knowledge or deliberation of what he is doing. In the former case, any diminution of imputability, either on the part of the intellect or of the will, exonerates the subject from the censure, and consequently all ignorance (except affected ignorance of the law and the penalty) and all fear, even though slight, have the same effect. In the latter case: (1) even crass or supine ignorance of the law or of the penalty does not excuse the subject from any penalty *latae sententiae;* (2) if this ignorance is neither crass nor supine, it excuses from those penalties *latae sententiae* which are medicinal, but not from those which are vindictive; (3) drunkenness, the omission of due diligence, mental weakness and the impulse of passion do not exonerate from penalties *latae sententiae,* as long as the guilt is grave; (4) grave fear does not exonerate from penalties *latae sententiae,* if the sin committed is detrimental to the faith, to duly constituted ecclesiastical authority, or to the spiritual welfare of souls. (See no. 2229, 1, 2, and 3.)

1258. Persons who have not reached the age of puberty do not incur penalties *latae sententiae,* but adults who instigate such persons to crimes which have these penalties attached, do incur them. (*C. J. C.,* can. 2230.)

1259. If several persons co-operate in the perpetration of a crime, all incur the censure, even though the law speaks of only one, if there is question of a sin which by its very nature demands an accomplice, or if those who co-operate are influenced by a command or physical concourse, always supposing that without co-operation the crime could not be committed and that the law does not explicitly provide otherwise.

1260. *Absolution of reserved cases.* We shall treat, first, of this absolution in general; and, second, of the absolution of an accomplice in particular.

1261. *Absolution of reserved cases in general.* Who may absolve from reserved cases? In dealing with this question, we shall treat absolution from reserved sins and from reserved censures together. In this way we shall avoid useless repetitions.

1262. Censures should not be reserved unless such a measure is justified by the grievousness of the crime, the need of enforcing discipline, and the spiritual welfare of the faithful. No censure, not even one that is not reserved, ceases of itself, but all censures persist until the penitent repents and obtains absolution. No priest may deny this absolution to a penitent unless he refuses to amend his evil ways. If a penitent has incurred several censures, he may be absolved from one and not from the others. Consequently, he who seeks absolution must indicate all the censures from which he wishes to be absolved, otherwise the absolution is valid only for those he mentions. If, however, the absolution requested for particular censures were general, it would cover also those cases omitted in good faith, with the exception of censures very specially reserved to the Holy See; but it would not cover those censures omitted in bad faith.

Censures *latae sententiae* may be multiplied in one and the same subject, whether they be of the same or of different species. They are multiplied: (1) if various crimes, to each of which a censure is attached, are committed, either by the same or by distinct actions; (2) if the crime to which the censure is attached has been committed repeatedly, in such wise that there are several distinct crimes; (3) if the same crime is punished with different censures by several superiors, and was committed once or repeatedly.

Censures *ab homine,* or those inflicted by means of a special precept or condemnatory sentence of a judge, are multiplied if there are several precepts or several sentences, or various distinct parts of the same precept or sentence, to each of which a censure is attached. (*C. J. C.*, can. 2244.)

Vindictive penalties, such as suspension or the interdict, which are inflicted for all times or for a definite period, cannot be lifted by absolution. They cease only when the time limit has expired, or when a dispensation is granted, either by the Holy See or the local Ordinary, as the case may be.

1263. Censures *ab homine* are strictly reserved to the

person who imposes them or who issues the sentences, to his competent superiors, or to his successors in office, or his delegates. The superior does not cease to be competent when his subject is removed, even permanently, from his jurisdiction, and the Ordinary whose subject he becomes may not, without special delegation, absolve him from a censure of this kind inflicted by another Ordinary.

1264. Censures *latae sententiae* are reserved only when the law declares them to be such, in which case they are reserved either to the Ordinaries or to the Sovereign Pontiff. Both a censure and a sin may be reserved to the Pope, either simply, specially, or very specially. Bishops may not attach a censure reserved to them to a crime that already has a censure reserved to the Holy See. Censures reserved to Ordinaries by common law are, strictly speaking, papal censures.

1265. The faculty to absolve from episcopal cases, strictly so called, or cases reserved to the local Ordinary, with or without censure, is granted by law to the vicar-capitular, the vicar-general and the canon penitentiary. Canon 899 says that this faculty should also be habitually granted to rural deans, with the power to subdelegate priests of their district for individual cases, especially in towns and places far removed from the episcopal city.

1266. By law, pastors and other administrators of parishes can absolve from episcopal cases, no matter how reserved, during the time in which the faithful can make the Easter duty. The same faculty belongs to missionaries for the time of a mission, but not to the priests who assist them in hearing confessions.

1267. From papal censures reserved by common law to the Ordinary, the bishop and his vicar-general can absolve their subjects and transient strangers, but major superiors of religious Orders can absolve only their subjects. In public cases, local Ordinaries and religious superiors may remit the penalties visited by common law with the exception of (1) cases brought to court for trial; (2) cases reserved to the Holy See; (3) penalties entailing inhability to benefices, offices, dignities, positions in the Church, active and passive vote, and privation of them, perpetual suspension, infamy of law, privation of the right of patronage and of a privilege or favor which has been conceded by the Apostolic See.

1268. In occult cases, the local Ordinaries and major superiors of religious Orders may absolve from the penalties *latae sententiae* of the common law, and delegate this power to others. They may not, however, absolve from a censure very specially reserved to the Holy See. (*C. J. C.*, can. 2237.)

1269. The faculties conceded to bishops by the Sacred Penitentiary have not been repealed by the decree of the Sacred Congregation of the Consistory of April 25, 1918. The majority of bishops, moreover, in virtue of special indults, possess more extensive powers than those indicated in the Code. These faculties extend even to public papal cases. In virtue of a decree of the Sacred Congregation of the Consistory, dated March 7, 1922, the bishops of Europe, with the exception of those of Italy and Russia, can obtain from the Sacred Penitentiary the following faculties for a period of five years: (1) the faculty to absolve all penitents from all censures and penalties incurred for the crime of heresy, with the exception of heretics who deliberately attempt to spread heresy among the faithful; (2) the faculty to absolve, with the proper restrictions, all those who have defended, read or retained in their possession books written by heretics, schismatics or apostates in defense of heresy, schism or apostasy, or any other books forbidden by name in Apostolic letters; (3) the faculty to absolve those who directly or indirectly have impeded the exercise of ecclesiastical jurisdiction in either the internal or external forum; (4) the faculty to absolve from censures and ecclesiastical penalties inflicted on persons who take part in a duel; (5) the faculty to absolve, with the proper restrictions, all who hold membership in Masonic or other similar secret societies; (6) the faculty to absolve from censures and penalties incurred by violating the enclosure of religious.

1270. In the case of absolution from censure incurred by the crimes of heresy, schism or apostasy, the excommunication is reserved to the Holy See only when the absolution is given in the internal forum, in which case the priest should apply for delegated powers to the Sacred Penitentiary or to the bishop, if he has them. Canon 2251 states that if absolution from a censure is given in the external forum, it holds good for both the external and the internal forums. If it were given in the internal forum, the person who obtained absolution in this way may, if no danger of scandal be present, could conduct himself as if he were absolved in actions pertaining to the external forum. Unless the absolution is proved in the external forum or lawfully presumed, the censure may be urged by the superior having jurisdiction in the external forum, until absolution has been granted therein, and the censured person must obey.

What we have said in regard to absolution granted in the internal forum and its consequences in the external forum, applies to all other censures whenever there is no danger of scandal. As soon as the excommunication incurred for the aforesaid crimes is submitted to the external forum of the bishop, it ceases to be reserved to the Holy See. By making use of his ordinary power, the bishop (but not his vicar-general) may, without special mandate, but with the restrictions prescribed by law, absolve a penitent from this censure even in the external forum, after he has abjured his error. The penitent must abjure his error in presence of the bishop or his delegate and two witnesses. Once the censure has been removed, the sin is no longer reserved, and as a general rule, when a censure is removed in the external forum, the absolution is valid also for the *forum internum*.

1271. Confessors other than bishops, who wish to condone penalties *latae sententiae* reserved to the Holy See, need a general delegation if the censures are simply reserved, a special delegation if they are specially reserved, and a very special delegation if they are very specially reserved. According to an opinion that was probable up to our time, religious confessors had the power to absolve from cases or censures reserved by common law to the bishops. The New Code has nothing to say concerning this matter, and Prümmer is of the opinion that the state of this question is the same now as it was before the appearance of the Code.

1272. *When may one absolve from reserved cases without delegation?* In general, any confessor approved by the Ordinary of the diocese or of the convent may absolve from sins to which is attached a censure reserved to no one, or a censure which, like suspension, does not prevent one from receiving the Sacraments, provided the penitent is not obstinate and is otherwise well disposed. If the reserved censure does not prevent one from receiving the Sacraments, it is not removed by the absolution of the sin; it must be removed by the person who has the right to do so. If a superior has removed the censure or the penalty reserved in the external forum, any confessor may absolve the penitent from his sin.

1273. Any confessor approved by the local Ordinary may absolve the following penitents from sins reserved without censure: (1) a sick person who cannot leave the house; (2) a person who wishes to confess on the eve of marriage;

(3) whenever the lawful superior has refused the faculty to absolve, requested for some particular case, and also in cases where the confessor judges that the faculty to absolve cannot be sought from the said superior without grave inconvenience to the penitent or without danger of violating the sacramental seal; (4) any person who has committed a sin that is reserved and who goes outside the diocese for no other purpose than to obtain absolution. If, however, the same sin is reserved also in that other diocese, the priest cannot absolve the penitent. The reservation of which there is question here, is the reservation of the sin reserved to the Ordinary or to the Holy See, and not the reservation of the censure. This is the official interpretation of the Commission for the Interpretation of the Code, dated Nov. 10, 1925. Strangers may be absolved in this same way, even if their cases are reserved with a censure *latae sententiae*, but not if the censure is *ab homine*. They may not be absolved from sins reserved in the diocese where they go to confession, even if these sins are not reserved in their own diocese.

1274. A confessor approved by the local Ordinary may absolve religious, even exempt religious, from cases reserved, even with censure, to their superior; but he may not remove a censure reserved *ab homine* to their superior nor absolve from cases and censures reserved to the local Ordinary.

1275. Reserved sins, when once remitted, are no longer reserved if the penitent subjects them anew to the power of the keys. It is probable, too, that the reservation of sins ceases through an invalid or even sacrilegious absolution, granted by a confessor who has the necessary faculties, provided the penitent confesses his reserved sin or at least does not voluntarily conceal it. Although the absolution in this case would be null and void, the penitent should perform the penance imposed for his reserved sin, after which any approved confessor may probably absolve him. It is certain, notwithstanding the opinion of St. Alphonsus to the contrary, that at the time of a jubilee the reserved sins and censures of a penitent who performs the works prescribed to gain the jubilee, cease to be reserved if he fails through forgetfulness to mention them in confession.

1276. If a confessor, in ignorance of the reservation, absolves a penitent from the censure and the sin, the absolution from the censure is valid, except in the case of censures very specially reserved to the Holy See. The absolution would be invalid if he absolved from a censure reserved *ab homine* to the Sovereign Pontiff. Any confessor who knowingly absolves in this way commits a grievous sin, and the absolution is invalid. He incurs, furthermore, excommunication simply reserved to the Holy See if he absolves from cases and censures specially and very specially reserved to the Holy See. If he ignores the other papal cases, he incurs suspension and is barred from hearing confessions.

1277. The same suspension is incurred by a confessor who absolves from episcopal cases.

Is absolution valid when given without the proper delegation either through ignorance, or inadvertence, or in full knowledge of the facts? The answer depends upon the intention of each bishop. If serious inconvenience would result from disturbing the penitent's mind in this matter, he should be left alone; otherwise he should make a general accusation of his sins and receive absolution in accordance with the regulations. If the Ordinary declares that he supplies in these cases, there is nothing further to do.

1278. In danger of death any priest may absolve from all sins and censures in the internal forum. In two cases, however, namely, those reserved very specially to the Holy See, and those imposed *ab homine,* the penitent is bound, after recovery, to have recourse for the imposition of a penance to the person who imposed the sentence *ab homine* for sins and censures reserved *ab homine,* and to the Sacred Penitentiary, the Bishop or some one else possessing the necessary faculties for sins and censures very specially reserved to the Holy See. If the convalescent neglects this duty, he falls again under the same censure. In danger of death, absolution given to an accomplice *in re turpi* is always valid, and from the penitent's viewpoint licit. It is gravely illicit from the standpoint of the confessor, however, if another confessor is available to whom the penitent may and is willing to confess.

1279. In cases where censures *latae sententiae* cannot be borne without great danger or scandal or loss of reputation, or when it is extremely difficult for the penitent to remain in mortal sin until the faculty to absolve him has been obtained from the superior, any confessor may absolve from any censure in sacramental confession, no matter in what manner the censure is reserved. In such cases, the confessor must impose upon the penitent the obligation, under penalty of reincidence, to have recourse within one month to the Sacred Penitentiary, or to the Bishop, or to another person possessing faculties from the Holy See. Recourse may be had either personally by the penitent, or at least, by letter sent through the confessor.

As a general rule, the confessor should offer the penitent his services in this matter. Observe, however, that a confessor delegated to absolve from reserved censures is not a competent superior to whom recourse may be had after absolution has been granted in urgent cases, but nothing is to prevent the penitent who has received absolution in the manner just described, and even after recourse has been made by letter, to confess to another confessor, who has delegated faculties to absolve. After this absolution, the confessor should impose his penance, and then the penitent is not obliged to the other penances which will be issued by the superior in answer to his recourse.

If in some extraordinary case recourse should prove, morally speaking, impossible, the confessor may absolve without the obligation of recourse and, in addition to the ordinary penance, impose a special satisfaction for the censure, which he shall require to be performed within a specified time. If the penitent neglects to perform the penance and satisfaction imposed for the censure within the specified period, he reverts to his former status. Recourse is held to be morally impossible when the confessor is certain that he will never see the penitent again, when the penitent cannot have recourse by letter or when he cannot prudently present himself to some other confessor.

In cases where a priest absolves his accomplice *in re turpi,* recourse must be made, even though the same be morally impossible.

A confessor who absolves from some censure in an urgent case may absolve also from irregularities secretly incurred as a result of the censure.

1280. We have included among urgent cases the one of a penitent who finds it very difficult to remain in sin until the faculty to absolve has been obtained from the superior. The typical case in point is that of a censured priest who wishes to celebrate Mass. Such a priest should address himself to any confessor, if no delegated confessor is available. We might add that it is quite permissible and even praiseworthy to excite in the penitent a disposition in virtue of which he finds it extremely hard to remain in the state of mortal sin.

1281. The regulations we have just cited are all contained in canon 2254, although this canon speaks of censures, and not of reserved cases. But the only case reserved to the Holy See appears to be comprised within this canon just as the two cases formerly reserved without censure were contained in the decree of the Sacred Penitentiary, dated Nov. 7, 1888. The sins reserved to Ordinaries by law are certainly comprised within this canon, although canonists are not agreed as to whether the cases which the Ordinary reserves to himself are contained therein.

Prümmer and Noldin are of the opinion that canon 2254 has no reference to episcopal cases properly so called, while Ferreres and Arregui hold that it has.

The negative opinion does not result in as many inconveniences, because the confessor may give indirect absolution of episcopal cases which ordinarily are without censure. Noldin believes that a person may obtain indirect absolution in this way, outside the case of necessity, if he desires to receive Communion or celebrate Mass.

1282. The controverted question just mentioned involves another, which is also quite practical. In an urgent case, must a person who has to confess only sins reserved by diocesan law to the bishop, confess to a simple delegated priest? According to the opinion of those who claim that these cases are included in canon 2254, such a person should do this before receiving Communion or celebrating Mass, and have recourse to the bishop within the space of one month. Those who hold the opposite opinion logically reach another conclusion. In any case, a penitent who has mortal sins not yet confessed, other than cases reserved to the Ordinary, must confess them before receiving Communion or celebrating Mass, and those who have none, must at least have perfect contrition. According to some writers, a person who in case of necessity has been indirectly absolved in this way from sins reserved without censure, may receive Communion and celebrate Mass even out of pure devotion.

1283. Absolution from censures in the sacramental forum is included in the usual form prescribed by the Ritual for the absolution of sins. In the non-sacramental forum, absolution from a censure may be given in any form, but for absolution from excommunication it is better to use the formula contained in the Ritual. (*C. J. C.*, can. 2250.)

1284. *The absolution of an accomplice.* The sin of an accomplice of either sex *in materia turpi* is so rigidly reserved from the viewpoint of the priest accomplice that he may never validly absolve from it outside of the danger of death, even though the penitent is reconciled to God by perfect contrition and by the absolution of these same sins indirectly received from a confessor possessing the faculty to absolve, and even though the confessor has the power to absolve from all censures and reserved cases, or the penitent has the right to be absolved by any confessor from all reserved cases. Any confessor who absolves his accomplice, even through crass ignorance, incurs excommunication very specially reserved to the Holy See, in such wise that no priest, not even one delegated to absolve from censures specially reserved to the Holy See, may, even during the time of a jubilee, absolve from this excommunication, unless special mention is made of the sin in the bull or indult. (See nos. 1274 and 3098.)

1285. If a priest who has absolved his accomplice, and was in turn absolved from his sin by special permission of the Holy See, relapses into the same sin, mention should be made of this circumstance in addressing the second petition to Rome.

1286. Bishops of missionary countries ordinarily secure from Propaganda faculties to absolve from this kind of excommunication for a set number of cases, on condition that the person who is thus absolved promises to write, or have some one write through his confessor, to the Sacred Congregation of the Penitentiary, *tacito nomine*, within the space of two months, giving the number of the accomplices whom he has absolved and the number of times he gave them absolution, promising at the same time that he will comply with the requirements of the said Congregation, under pain of relapsing into excommunication.

1287. For the confessor to incur the censure, the sin must be grave on both sides, and external in character. Consequently, a priest would not be guilty of this crime if he committed sins of this kind with a drunken or sleeping person or with one who firmly believed that the actions in which he or she concurred were not sinful.

The sin must be *mutual* in such wise that the consent of both parties is made manifest in some way. These two conditions suffice, so that a mere impure conversation or grave and mutual sins of sensuous aspects suffice to render the sin reserved. And this even though the priest sinned before being ordained and the penitent made several confessions which were invalid or doubtfully valid to another confessor. The case would be different if the penitent had been validly absolved.

1288. According to some authors, a priest may absolve a penitent who was formerly his accomplice, but who has secured absolution from this sin through the proper channels if such a penitent accuses himself of this former sin only; according to other authors, he may not.

1289. *In articulo mortis* and in danger of death, which may prudently be assumed to be real, although in reality it is not, a priest may validly and licitly absolve his accomplice if no other confessor is available, or if the accomplice refuses to confess to another, or if it is impossible to secure another confessor without danger to the person's character and without scandal. He absolves validly only: (1) if another priest, even one not approved, is present and the accomplice does not object to confessing to him; (2) if he does not take the necessary precautions to secure another priest, while seeking at the same time to remove all danger of scandal and defamation of his accomplice's reputation. In both cases he incurs excommunication. He does not incur excommunication if he absolves through inadvertence, in which case his absolution is more probably valid for sins other than those of complicity, which in this instance are remitted indirectly, or if, in imminent danger of death, he begins to hear the penitent's confession in the absence of any other priest, and completes this confession after the other priest arrives; or if he completes a confession begun in danger of death after the danger is past. In the two latter cases his absolution is valid. If the penitent completed his confession in danger of death, at which time he mentioned all his sins of complicity, the confessor could absolve him from sins he forgot to confess, once the danger is past; it would be different, however, if the sins he forgot to confess were sins of complicity.

1290. The confessor probably does not incur excommunication if he indirectly absolves his accomplice at a time when the latter is obliged to conform to the precept of annual confession, if he fears grave defamation of character or scandal might result from a refusal of absolution. According to several writers, he does not incur excommunication if the penitent will run the risk of committing a sacrilege by making his confession to another and cannot remain away from the Sacraments for a long period of time without danger of defamation of character or scandal. Outside the danger of death, the penitent is obliged to confess his sin of complicity to some other confessor.

If the penitent in good faith fails to confess his sin of complicity, but confesses other sins of which the priest accomplice absolves him, the absolution is valid, but the penitent is under obligation to confess his sin of complicity to another. Some writers, whose opinion is probable, believe that the confession is valid if the penitent confesses this sin and others in good faith, and the confessor absolves him in bad faith. The confessor does not incur excommunication, therefore, if the penitent does not confess the sin of complicity committed with him, unless the priest induces him either directly or indirectly to conceal this sin. If the penitent conceals his sin of complicity from the priest with whom it was committed, the confessor is obliged to see to it that his penitent accomplice confesses to another. Finally, the confessor does not incur excommunication if he hears the confession of his accomplice, but does not give absolution; but if he makes a pretense at giving absolution by reciting some prayer in place of the form, he incurs excommunication, even though the penitent concealed his sin, if the priest even indirectly induced the penitent to do so. He does not incur excommunication if he absolves a penitent of whom he doubts whether it is his own accomplice.

Several authoritative writers like Lehmkuhl, Tanquerey, Bucceroni, d'Annibale, Noldin, are of the opinion that *per epikeiam*, the absolution of an accomplice, when given under extraordinary circumstances very much akin to extreme necessity, is both valid and licit. An instance in point would be that of a penitent living in a far distant missionary country, where no other priests lived except the one with whom the sin was committed, and the penitent could not undertake a long and tedious journey in quest of another confessor. The absolution of the confessor in this case would be indirect only, so that the penitent would be obliged to confess the sin anew, should the occasion ever be offered to him. The sin of a penitent who has been a priest's accomplice is not reserved by common law, although it may be reserved by the statutes of the diocese. The reservation exists if the penitent was solicited in confession. (See no. 1296.)

Art. II. Duties of the Minister.

1291. A priest who has the approbation and jurisdiction of the bishop may validly hear confessions in the church of a parish priest without the latter's permission. He may not, however, do so licitly. Outside the church he may hear the confessions of the sick, and in a chapel he needs only the permission of the rector. We shall treat, first, of the duties of the minister in confession; and, second, of his duties after confession.

1292. *Duties of the minister in confession.* We may divide this section into two others: the duties of the minister towards all penitents, and the duties of the minister towards certain classes of penitents.

Towards all penitents the confessor should be a father, a physician, a teacher, and a judge.

He is a *father*, because he begets the penitent until Jesus Christ is formed in him. Let him show himself a father, therefore, either at the beginning or at the end of the penitent's confession, centering his attention on the illiterate, the poor and the sinners, after the example of Jesus Christ who came to save sinners. (See no. 1115 ff.) Let him not rebuke the penitent in the course of his confession, let him be kind in his manner of interrogating him, let him be patient with those who are slow in confessing their sins, and forbearing with those who are rough and unruly. In this way no penitent will leave the sacred tribunal angry and irritated. Let him show no preferences, except for the poor, the sick, and the aged. We may well question the zeal of a confessor who follows the bent of his nature in the confessional, attending more to the dress, sex, and character of his penitents than to the condition and needs of their souls. Zealous priests know enough to give men the preference over women, sinners the preference over the pious, and the sick the preference over those in good health. St. Alphonsus utters words of indignation against a confessor who spends with pious persons an amount of time sufficient to effect the conversion of a large number of sinners.

1293. As a *physician,* the priest should know the cause of the evil and, consequently, (1) seek out the habits, occasions of sin, dangers and temptations of the penitent; (2) cure the ailment by charitably admonishing the penitent and prompting his attrition and contrition by strong and effective motives. (See nos. 1006 and 1313.) He is under grave obligation to incite to contrition and firm purpose of amendment penitents who are illiterate, ignorant, or doubtfully disposed. How many penitents have forgotten the act of contrition, and how many more pronounce it only with their lips! The priest has no obligation of this kind in regard to those who are well instructed in their religion and lead lives of piety. (See no. 1044.) (3) The confessor should guard the penitent against relapse into sin by prescribing medicinal penances. (See no. 1149 ff.)

1294. As a *teacher,* the priest must (1) instruct his penitents by word and example. A priest who gives a bad example to his penitents is guilty of sin; if he solicits one or several to acts of impurity, he incurs perpetual inability to celebrate Mass, and the bishop should prohibit him from hearing confessions for all time. The foregoing penalties are all *ferendae sententiae.*

1295. What is the sin of solicitation in confession? It is the sin of an authorized or unauthorized priest who by words or signs incites a penitent of either sex to commit, not any kind of sin, *sed ut sive secum, sive cum alio turpiter peccet, vel utitur paenitente ad alterum seducendum.* The priest may solicit a penitent (1) in the act of confession, *i. e.,* immediately before or after, or during the penitent's confession. The case would be different if a period of time intervened, as, for instance, if the confessor said to the penitent: "Wait for me a minute," or "Meet me at a certain place," and then solicited the party there. (2) He may solicit on the occasion of a confession, even though the confession never takes place, for instance, if he solicits the penitent and the latter immediately asks in all sincerity to make a confession, or if he gives the penitent a letter of a soliciting nature, even though the letter is to be opened some time later, or if he solicits a penitent whose weakness is known to him through confession, indicating to the penitent that he does so because of the information he has received. According to some writers, the obligation to denounce a confessor does not exist in this case. (3) He may solicit under pretext of hearing the penitent's confession, *i. e.*, if he invites the penitent to confess to him for the purpose of seducing him later, or if requested by a mother to hear the confession of her daughter, he solicits the latter, or if he advises a woman to feign sickness in order to solicit her, or, finally, if the confessor, or both the penitent and the confessor, simulate confession for the purpose of deceiving others. (4) He solicits, finally, if, being in the confessional or in some place set aside for that purpose, he feigns to hear the penitent's confession and merely carries on conversation for the purpose of inciting the penitent to do wrong, even though the penitent asked nothing more in the confessional than to be allowed to go to confession the next day. According to Berardi, the case would be different if the priest's conversation resulted only in inspiring the penitent with a dread and horror for the sin, even though his words were instigated by the vices to which he was addicted. The case would be different, too, if, being in the confessional and not actually hearing any confessions, he solicited a woman who happened to be in the vicinity of the confessional, although with no intention of going to confession, and, according to an opinion which is probable, if he was acting only as an interpreter for the penitent.

1296. *The obligation to denounce a priest who solicits.* In every one of the above cases a penitent is bound to denounce the priest who solicits, even though he be a relative, but not a close relative, under pain of incurring excommunication if the denunciation is deferred longer than one month, even though the crime is a secret one and the penitent is the only one who knows of it. He is bound to denounce the confessor, even though some one has already denounced him, and even though the penitent gave his consent. The penitent is not bound, however, to reveal this last circumstance, and the ecclesiastical judge is not free to raise this question. Some writers would dispense relatives of the confessor up to the third degree, if no serious and public injury results from this omission for the general discipline of the Church and the welfare of souls.

The obligation to denounce a priest who solicits exists also, but not under pain of censure, for all those who possess certain knowledge of his conduct, even though such a person has not yet reached the age of puberty. The only exception to this rule is the case in which the act of the soliciting priest has been made manifest for the purpose of obtaining advice. Moreover, according to a decision of the Sacred Congregation of the Sacraments, a confessor should be denounced who, through fear, consents to solicitation on the part of the penitent, but in this case the penitent is not obliged to betray his own self. Every confessor—the soliciting confessor excepted—is bound *sub gravi* to apprise the penitent of this obligation if he is ignorant of it, even though he foresees that the penitent will not acquiesce, because the private good of the penitent must yield to the general welfare of souls. The penitent must be apprised of this obligation, even though much time has elapsed since the act of solicitation and the soliciting priest has amended his ways or has been sufficiently punished, if the priest has lapsed into the same crime since the time of his punishment, and more probably even if he has never relapsed. Theologians except the case in which it can be foreseen that the penitent, who is *in articulo mortis,* will refuse to denounce such a confessor if he is apprised of his duty in this respect. Berardi adds that in such a case a priest may merely advise denouncing the guilty confessor when it can be foreseen that the penitent will not acquiesce immediately, in which case the priest should oblige him to speak of this matter in some future confession. A confessor is not obliged *sub gravi* by positive law to apprise a person who knows of solicitations, but who has not been solicited, nor a person who comes to him for some other purpose than confession, although in every case he must reply truthfully to all questions put to him on this matter. By positive law he is not obliged to inform the penitent of the censure incurred.

1297. The obligation of denouncing a priest who has solicited is not binding on a person who has been solicited independently of confession, even by a priest who has administered Sacraments other than Penance, or one who was solicited by a layman or a cleric pretending to hear confessions. Laymen and clerics who pretend to hear confessions should be denounced as suspect of heresy within the space of one month. (See nos. 3263, 3725.)

1298. Is there any obligation to denounce a bishop who solicits in the confessional? It is certain that one may lawfully denounce him, but several authors are of the opinion that the penitent is not bound to do so. St. Alphonsus prefers the opinion which obliges to denounce him to the inquisitors or to the Holy See.

1299. The foregoing regulations have been enacted by

positive law, but there is a natural obligation binding upon all those who know for certain that such and such a priest is a wolf in sheep's clothing, and is working for the destruction, not of one soul, but of several, to denounce him and thus put an end to further scandal.

1300. When in doubt concerning the identity of the priest who solicited, the penitent who is certain that solicitation took place, should report the matter to the bishop, if there is some assurance that the latter will be able to discover the guilty party. The greatest caution should be used to safeguard the reputation of an innocent party, and yet, if the act of soliciting appears doubtful, as, for instance, if the priest compliments a woman on her good looks in the confessional, or makes her a present, he should be denounced if it is clear from the circumstances that his intention was evil. The act of soliciting must not be regarded as doubtful if the words of the soliciting priest are of a serious nature, although his intention in making use of them appears doubtful. But, if after all the evidence has been weighed, there is still room for prudent doubt whether or not the priest has solicited, he should not be denounced. Prudence in these matters cannot be too strictly enjoined, because it is a known fact that women sometimes accuse innocent priests out of hatred or jealousy—a very grievous sin that is reserved to the Holy See. (See no. 1257.)

1301. If the penitent refuses to denounce the confessor for slight reasons, or out of shame or fear of slight or grave but improbable inconvenience, his objections should be brushed aside. Grave and well-founded fear may, however, constitute a sufficient reason for deferring the denunciation or applying for a dispensation, in which case the penitent may be absolved, if he is under grave obligation to receive Communion, provided he promises to denounce the priest when the impediments cease, or to accept the decision of the superior if the dispensation cannot be obtained.

1302. If the penitent has no serious reasons for refusing to denounce an offending priest, or if, in view of the circumstances, the act of solicitation has resulted in contempt for the Sacrament or injury to souls, he must not be absolved unless he promises to denounce the guilty party. Moreover, if it is feared that he will not live up to his promise after receiving absolution, he should be refused the same until after he has actually denounced him. An exception to the above rule would be the case of a penitent who promises in all sincerity to denounce the confessor, but is unable to return to the same priest for absolution. If the penitent refuses absolutely to denounce the guilty priest, the confessor should defer absolution, and kindly request him to return at some later date. In the meantime he should consult the Ordinary or the Sacred Penitentiary, clearly exposing the case to them without divulging the penitent's name. The excommunication incurred by delay in denouncing a priest is not reserved, hence any confessor may absolve from it, provided the penitent promises to conform with the law. If the penitent fails to keep his promise, he does not re-incur the same censure.

1303. *How is the denunciation to be conducted?* The penitent must denounce the guilty priest, as we have stated, within the space of one month. If the denunciation is enjoined by natural law, it should be conducted as we have indicated above. No legal form is required, but it is enough to inform the Ordinary of the scandal in the best possible way. The denunciation of a priest who has solicited in the confessional must be conducted according to the form prescribed by the Church. From the standpoint of Canon Law an anonymous denunciation is null and void and does not exempt the penitent from his obligation. As a general rule, the person solicited should go to the inquisitor of the local-

ity where the confession took place, if there is such an official, or to his or her own Ordinary, or to the Ordinary of
the locality where the crime took place, or to the Ordinary
of the guilty party, even though the latter were exempt
from his jurisdiction. Vicars Apostolic may receive the denunciation, but, according to an instruction of the Holy
Office, they must send to the Holy Office, through the intermediary of Propaganda, the name of the soliciting priest in
a sealed letter. Ordinaries must send a duplicate of the
form of denunciation to the Congregation of the Holy Office.
If the person solicited is not able to appear before the
judge except by letter or messenger, he or she should request the Ordinary to delegate some one capable of receiving information pertaining to the ecclesiastical forum. If
the penitent is unable to write, or can write only with difficulty, the confessor may proffer his assistance, although
it is not becoming that he should receive the denunciation.
He should take care not to inquire into the name of the
person who did the soliciting, but if the person solicited
refuses to denounce this name to any other person, the Ordinary or the Sacred Penitentiary may delegate the confessor
canonically to receive the denunciation. Moreover, the Holy
Office is in favor of his taking charge of the matter when, by
doing so, he can be of assistance to the penitent.

1304. In delegating a confessor to receive a denunciation,
the Sacred Penitentiary lays down the following rules for
him to follow: He must (1) note the day when the denunciation was made; (2) place the person who is denouncing
under oath to speak nothing but the truth; (3) ascertain all
the details of the case: in what it consisted, the number of
times, the circumstances of place and time, the witnesses,
if there is any evidence that others too have been solicited,
what is the reputation of the accused, and whether the accuser
is instigated by love or hatred; (4) give the name and sur-

name of the soliciting priest and the person solicited, and if the name of the soliciting priest is unknown, a description of his person, characteristics, etc. (according to an instruction of the Holy Office the same procedure is required when the Ordinary delegates the confessor, in which case the latter assists the person denouncing by a series of questions, carefully noting his or her answers); (5) obtain from the accuser and the witnesses, if there are any, an oath of silence and their signatures to the document. If there are witnesses whose testimony is conflicting, without being contradictory, the bishop should not inflict any penalties, but forward all the details of the case to Rome. *Ex informata conscientia* the bishop may suspend a priest whom he knows to have solicited from several denunciations that have been made to him.

1305. A denunciation by a mere letter addressed to the superior, and not drawn up according to the prescribed formalities, does not suffice. Such a denunciation is permitted and even obligatory if the formalities cannot be complied with, because of danger of imminent death or other reasons which would defer the act for a lengthy period of time. It would be permitted, also, if it were urgent to make the denunciation immediately, even though one were able to conform to the regulations later on. This simple form of denunciation would not dispense the penitent from complying with the prescribed formalities later on, should his superior insist upon this.

1306. According to a decree of the Sacred Congregation of Bishops, a confessor should not hear the confessions of women after sundown or before sunrise, except in cases of necessity. In these latter cases he should never hear their confessions in the dark, or without witnesses, and there should always be a separation between the priest and the penitent. Canon 909 emphatically states that the confessional for women must always be in an open and conspicuous place, as a rule in a church or public or semi-public oratory appointed for women. The same canon states that the confessional must be so constructed that there be an irremovable perforated grate between the penitent and the confessor. Confessions of men may be heard in private houses, but those of women must not be heard outside the confessional, except in cases of illness or other necessity.

If missionary priests are obliged to hear the confessions of women in private houses, outside the cases indicated in the canons, the women should at least cover their head with a veil. The confessor should show no preferences, he should never look penitents directly in the face, neither while they are actually confessing, nor while they are awaiting his instructions, nor while they are in the act of withdrawing.

The confessor should never give grounds for the suspicion of avarice. To a request sent in by an archbishop as to whether or not a priest should be allowed to receive Mass intentions while seated in the confessional, the Sacred Congregation of the Propaganda replied: *"Profecto tolerandum minime videtur."* The same Congregation added that a priest seated in the sacred tribunal of penance should not receive money for any purpose and under any pretext. The same motive underlies the regulation of certain diocesan synods that no priest is to impose as a penance the obligation to offer Mass stipends. In requiring the penitent to make restitution, the confessor should not volunteer his services, but rather advise him to hand the money to some other priest, without indicating to him that he is making restitution.

1307. The confessor must instruct his penitents by words and teachings. Hence he is under obligation to possess knowledge. "It is my firm belief," writes St. Alphonsus, "that a confessor who runs the risk of hearing confessions without possessing sufficient knowledge, is on the road to damnation." A priest should have this knowledge, even though he be approved, except in imminent danger of death, and except also in the case where his superior entrusts this duty to him, assuring him to rest at ease, provided the superior knows him well. A superior sins grievously who approves an ignorant subject, unless he does so out of necessity. Likewise, a penitent sins grievously who knowingly confesses to such a priest, unless it is impossible for him to find another confessor.

1308. The priest is in duty bound to continue his study of moral theology. Experience without science does not suffice; moreover, it may easily lead into error in difficult matters. Eminent knowledge is not a requisite, but competent knowledge is. The latter consists in knowing how to form a prudent judgment in the sacramental forum, when to doubt, and where to seek advice in difficult problems. In cases of doubt, the confessor may give absolution without solving the case, if there are urgent reasons for his doing so, provided the penitent promises to abide by the decision of another confessor, or of the bishop, after his case has been more thoroughly studied.

1309. A confessor possesses competent knowledge when he knows which sins are grave and which slight, also the kinds of sins and the circumstances which affect their malice. He should also know the laws of restitution in case of stolen goods or injured reputation, the more commonly reserved sins, excommunications, censures and irregularities, the impediments to matrimony, the principal duties of the various states of life, the disposition required of the penitent to receive absolution efficaciously, and the various remedies for sin.

1310. The confessor is under obligation to teach. It is certain that he is bound to teach his penitents the things necessary to receive the Sacrament of Penance worthily and to live a Christian life. The pastor is bound by his office to instruct his parishioners in all their religious duties, but the confessor who is not a pastor is not bound strictly and *per se* to teach them all they must and should know. It is enough if he teaches them the things necessary to receive absolution worthily and obtains from them a promise that they will seek instruction. If the penitent finds it extremely difficult to secure said instruction, the confessor is bound in charity to come to his assistance.

1311. In practice it is best not to dismiss ignorant penitents and defer absolution until such time as they secure the necessary knowledge, especially if they are idiots or in their second childhood, because the more this time is deferred, the harder it becomes to instruct them. The best course of action would seem to be to give them the necessary instruction in as succinct a form as possible. The following might serve as an illustration: "My son, there is only one God who governs all things by His Providence. He will reveal Himself to the good in Heaven, but will exclude the wicked from His sight for all eternity, for our soul is immortal. In God there are three distinct and co-equal Persons, but only one God. These Persons are: the Father, the Son, and the Holy Ghost. There are three distinct Persons in God just as there are three distinct faculties in your soul. God has neither body, nor feet, nor hands, as you have. He is present everywhere, although we do not see Him. He is an invisible spirit like the angels, but, of course, infinitely more perfect. One of these three Persons, the Son, descended from Heaven and assumed a body and a soul like ours. He was born on Christmas Day and died for all sinners on Good Friday. Had He not suffered the pains of death, we would have been refused entrance into Heaven. By His death He merited the divine assistance or grace which is absolutely necessary to obtain salvation. To secure this assistance, prayer is indispensable. When God descended upon this earth, He spoke to men, and especially to the Apostles. To the latter he imparted all the information necessary for salvation. Christ explained His doctrine to them openly, emphatically asserting that He was God and that God spoke through Him. The truth of all these things He substantiated by His works and miracles. Miracles are wondrous works which God alone can do and which prove the divine character of some doctrine. Jesus Christ healed the sick and raised the dead. When He Himself died, the sun was darkened and He rose from the grave by His own power, manifesting Himself to more than five hundred disciples. He now reigns gloriously in Heaven, whence He will come to judge us some day. His teachings and His miracles are set forth with the greatest precision in the Gospel by His disciples, who performed even greater miracles than their Master. This Gospel is revered by all Christians and even by heretics. Since Jesus Christ was God, He could neither deceive nor be deceived, for both reason and revelation teach us that He is knowledge and truth. History attests to the fact that God has spoken to man and He has told us Himself that He came to teach all truth. We must, therefore, believe all that He has said, and as the Gospel and history tell us, He has established on earth a Church whose duty it is to instruct all men in these matters. The outstanding figures in the early Church were the Apostles, with St. Peter at their head. Their successors are the bishops and the Pope, the latter being the successor of St. Peter. Christ promised to remain with this Church until the end of time, that she might continue to teach the truth brought from Heaven by Him. A great many miracles have been performed in course of time, which prove that the Catholic Church is divine. She has all the marks of divinity indicated by God in His Gospel. Her doctrine is holy, she has always been able to boast of men who could perform miracles, she has bestowed benefits without number on all peoples, and without arms she has overcome all the attacks of her enemies. All the martyrs, saints, and doctors have believed and continue to believe everything which this Church teaches, because she teaches only that which has been revealed by God, and God can neither deceive nor be deceived. It is this same God who has promised the Church the spirit of truth that it might remain with her unto the end. We find the principal teachings of the Church in the catechism, which is substantially the same in all places, and which is taught by all the bishops and priests of the entire world. Do you believe everything that the Church teaches and God has revealed? If you do, repeat with me: 'O my God, because Thou art truth itself and infinite science, and hast revealed these points of doctrine, I believe Thy words and all that the Church teaches.' (See no. 2201.)

1312. It is with good reason that St. Alphonsus warns us always to place the motive before the act which the motive is to produce. The motive, indeed, is what incites us to perform the act.

It is certain from the Gospel and the teachings of the true Church that Jesus Christ has promised grace to those who pray, forgiveness to those who repent, and Heaven to those who practice virtue. He Himself has said that He has promised us all these things, that He is faithful to His promises, that He is powerful enough to keep them, that He is sovereignly good towards all and capable of affording them supreme happiness, since He is the sovereign Good and possesses all perfections. We may say in all assurance therefore: 'O My God, Thou hast assured me of Thy promise, and Thou art faithful, all-powerful, all-good, and all-merciful;

hence I hope to obtain Thy grace, pardon for my sins, and Heaven, where I will see Thee face to face, through the merits of Jesus Christ.' (See no. 2191 ff.)

1313. If God is to forgive you, you must repent of your sins. What would have become of you if you had died in mortal sin? What possible good can we derive from sinning? We have been as rebellious as the prodigal son, and have lost Heaven as a consequence. What evil has God ever done to us? He has suffered and laid down His life for us; why, therefore, should we offend Him? Therefore repeat with me: 'O my God, I am heartily sorry for having offended Thee,' etc. (See no. 1062.) Courage, my son; henceforth love God, for what is there in Heaven or on earth that can be compared with Him? He Himself has told us that He is goodness, beauty, perfection, and love personified; do you not want to love Him? Repeat, therefore, with me: 'O, my God, I wish to offend Thee no more.' My son, you are certainly well disposed, and I am going to give you absolution, which means the forgiveness of all your sins. I have this power, for God gave it to his Apostles and their successors. Before receiving absolution, you should not fear to tell me anything that is weighing on your mind. This is absolutely necessary, and from now on you should examine yourself seriously, confess all your sins, and have frequent recourse to this Sacrament in order to persevere in your good resolutions. Be mindful, however, that confession without contrition and a firm purpose of amendment can be of no avail to you."

1314. St. Leonard always made it a practice to repeat the act of contrition several times with the penitent. Some people are so easily distracted that a repetition of this kind will prove useful. Other penitents do not even know the act of contrition, in which case, according to Lehmkuhl, the confessor is obliged to teach the penitent the act of contrition and urge him to recite it before each confession. After giving absolution, the priest should caution the penitent against breaking his fast before receiving Holy Communion.

1315. The foregoing method may be used with feeble-minded and illiterate persons and also with little children. If the confessor has to deal with one of our so-called modern intellectuals, who resent being subjected to what they term a childish method, he might proceed as follows: "Before receiving forgiveness for your sins, my dear brother, you should make an act of faith in one God in three Persons." The confessor may then touch upon the essential truths indicated in 1311.

The reader will forgive us for entering into all these details when he learns that Lehmkuhl declares it to be the first duty of the confessor to assure himself of the ability of the penitent to make acts of faith, hope, charity, attrition, and contrition. This learned moralist goes so far as to say that the confessor should have the penitent repeat after him all these different acts before giving him absolution.

1316. The confessor must instruct married people in the duties of their state. (See no. 1580.) If priests were more careful to instruct ignorant penitents—and there are more of these than one might suppose—they would reconcile to God a large number of souls. Do not reason with yourself that others are waiting to go to confession, for you will have to render an account of your actions to God, not for those who are waiting, but for those who are actually confessing their sins.

1317. The priest is under obligation to instruct penitents who are ignorant of the duties of their state in life. Penitents should always be apprised of obligations of which they are ignorant, because vincible ignorance does not excuse from sin. The confessor should be careful, therefore, to answer truthfully all questions of the penitent, for the very fact that he questions him proves that his ignorance is not invincible. A confessor sins grievously who takes it upon himself to give advice and then fails to be sincere, even though he mislead the penitent only in things which are not necessary for salvation. Examples in point would be advice concerning the practice of virginity or entrance into the religious state. (See nos. 1531 ff. and 3342.) The confessor should set all human respect aside and not be afraid to say: "You may not do this," when he knows that a thing is wrong. A confessor is not obliged to go beyond the penitent's question, for instance, if the penitent asks if such or such an act is sinful, it is enough if the confessor replies that it is, without adding: *grievously*.

The confessor should instruct the penitent, even though his ignorance be invincible, every time that his silence could be interpreted as an approval of wrongdoing.

He is obliged to instruct the penitent, also, every time the ignorance of the latter bears on principles of the natural law, their more immediate conclusions, and the things necessary as means of salvation.

Again, he must instruct the penitent every time the latter is apt to remain in a proximate occasion of formal sin as a consequence of not being apprised of the facts. Confessors act very imprudently, therefore, if they neglect to remind their penitents of the obligation to avoid the occasions of sin, on the pretext that penitents are ignorant of this law. Génicot regards as probable the opinion of those who say that a penitent need not be instructed, who, it can easily be foreseen, will not profit by such advice, and might even desist from receiving the Sacraments, when he is in occasions of sin in which he knows he commits sin, although he is ignorant of his duty to avoid these occasions, provided the occasions themselves are not such as will bring about the complete spiritual ruin of the penitent or such as cannot admit of good faith. We leave to the reader to judge whether or not this doctrine differs sufficiently from the condemned proposition indicated in no. 1330.

Finally, the confessor must instruct the penitent if his ignorance is detrimental to the public welfare, unless a greater injury follows from admonishing him. Priests should be told of their obligation to absolve little children, reprimand sinners, encourage frequent Communion, and vocations to the religious state, etc. If a confessor has reasonable grounds for supposing that a fellow-priest is not fulfilling all his obligations, he is bound to question him in regard to them. He should issue a warning to clerics in the habit of committing mortal sin, and aspiring to sacred Orders, as we shall indicate in no. 1341; to persons solicited concerning their obligation to denounce the guilty party, and to students who know of fellow-students who are a bad influence in college, as indicated in no. 1098.

1318. In all the cases mentioned in the foregoing number, the penitent should be admonished, even though there is little or no hope of his profiting by the admonition. Some writers are of the opinion, however, that when no good result can be expected from such an admonition or from the refusal of absolution, and especially when it can be foreseen that the penitent will take great offense at what is told him, the confessor may defer the admonition until after he has given absolution, and then administer it in indefinite language.

1319. The manner of admonishing the penitent should be the more mild and meek as he appears more recalcitrant. Outside of these cases, the penitent is to be admonished, even if he be in invincible ignorance, and if it appears certain or more probable that he will profit by it; but in the case of an equally probable doubt, the penitent should be left in good faith. Formal sin is always more grievous than material sin, unless the latter is injurious to the common good of souls. As a general rule, the confessor should not apprise a penitent who is in good faith of the invalidity of his or her marriage, before obtaining a dispensation; what is more, he may oblige such a party to render the *debitum* in case of refusal. Before a marriage takes place, the confessor is obliged to make known the impediment to the penitent, except probably in the case where the impediment will never be found out later and the confessor has no hope that his admonition will be heeded. Finally, the confessor should always endeavor to dissipate the error of a penitent who regards as sinful an act which is not sinful and as grievous a sin that is only venial.

1320. As *judge,* the confessor must first investigate the case; and, secondly, pronounce sentence.

At times, the confessor is bound to question the penitent on the number and kind of his sins, the circumstances which change their nature, the causes, habits, and occasions of these sins, and above all, the obligations of the penitent towards his neighbor, especially when the latter is one of his subordinates. The confessor is obliged to question the penitent in this way every time he has reason to think that the penitent is not explicit enough, when it is quite possible for him to be so. The confessor need not put forth extraordinary diligence in his examination of the penitent, but must use ordinary care and precaution. Let him be mindful, too, that the ignorant have fewer obligations in these matters than others, and that in their case a few simple questions will suffice. A priest is obliged to question a well-instructed penitent who is gross and vulgar.

Confessors should never show signs of impatience in the confessional, urging penitents to hurry with their confession or bring it to a close, or asking ignorant persons to withdraw and re-examine their conscience. Their manner of questioning penitents should always be discreet and never curious or useless, especially at the beginning of confession and in regard to sex matters. Confessors should conduct themselves with the greatest reserve, and not ask penitents if they have committed sins into which persons similarly situated rarely fall.

When the object of the penitent's act is sinful, it is not necessary that the confessor question him in regard to his consent, unless he has some special reason for doing so. The confessor should not interrupt the penitent while he is making his confession, although he would do well not to defer his questions until the end, if one or two pointed questions sufficed to make an accusation patent and clear. It is better, also, immediately to request of a penitent that he give up some sinful practice, when the latter accuses himself of it, especially if the confessor fears that he might forget to do so later on, although it would be a mistake to rebuke the penitent at this moment. (See no. 1115 ff.)

1321. If, from information received from outside sources, or from some other motive, the confessor fears that the penitent will not answer his questions truthfully, he should nevertheless believe the penitent in all cases. If he knows with certainty that the penitent is lying in regard to some grievous sin, either because he actually saw him commit the sin or because trustworthy witnesses attest to the fact, he should refuse him absolution, if it cannot be presumed that the penitent has forgotten the sin, has already confessed it, or has a good reason for omitting it in his confession. If the confessor knows of the sin of a penitent through the confession of this penitent's accomplice, and unless the accomplice has actually begged him to question him in regard to the matter, he cannot ask the penitent any pointed questions concerning this sin, because of the seal of confession. The most he can do is to exhort him to make a sincere confession, provided that in doing so he does not arouse his suspicions. Theologians are not agreed as to whether the confessor may give absolution in such a case. Some are of the opinion that he may not give absolution, but that he should conceal this fact by reciting some prayer of equal length as the form. The confessor might do this if he felt sure that the penitent would not ask him if he had given him absolution; should he fear that the penitent might ask him such a question, he should give him absolution at least conditionally. To our way of thinking, any other course of action would be detrimental to the sacramental seal.

1322. The confessor, as judge, pronounces the sentence. In virtue of a quasi-contract, absolution must be given *ex justitia* and *sub gravi* to every penitent who is well disposed and confesses his mortal sins. This rule includes children seven years of age and even younger, if they have the use of reason. This much is certain on the authority of all theologians. If the penitent has only venial sins, it would be a grievous sin on the part of the confessor to deprive him of the grace of absolution for a long period of time, if he is sufficiently disposed. If the penitent has not even venial sins, for which he is sorry, or a sin of his past life, the confessor should not absolve him, because of insufficiency of matter, but invite him to withdraw in peace and receive Holy Communion. (See no. 1214.)

If the penitent accuses himself of sins that are only doubtfully grave, and is well disposed, the confessor should give him absolution. In judging whether or not a penitent is well disposed, the confessor need not have certitude, strictly so called, as in the case of the matter for the Holy Eucharist; moral certitude in the broadest sense of the term suffices. As a matter of fact, this is the only kind of certitude the confessor can have, and it consists in a prudent probability that the proper disposition is present. If the penitent accuses himself clearly and sincerely of his sins, and promises to fulfill all his duties as a Christian, the confessor may be certain that he is well disposed, unless indications exist to the contrary. Finally, although the confessor has reasons for fearing that the penitent will not persevere in his good resolutions, he should not allow himself to be influenced by this fear, provided the penitent is not thinking of the dangers which he, the confessor, foresees, and is disposed to serve God. (See no. 1328.)

1323. Canon 886 states that if the confessor has no reason to doubt of the disposition of the penitent, he may neither deny nor defer absolution. If the penitent gives his consent, however, the confessor may defer absolution should he judge this measure useful.

To a penitent who is doubtfully disposed the confessor must refuse absolution until he appears sufficiently disposed, unless he has a grave reason for not deferring absolution. In the latter case he may absolve the penitent conditionally, according to the explanation given in no. 1213 ff. In any case, the confessor should not defer absolution beyond a period of two weeks. Doubtfully disposed penitents should be invited to pray and to return soon to the sacred tribunal. (See no. 1208 ff.)

1324. Absolution must be *refused* to any person who gives no sign of sorrow, has no intention of amending his evil ways, refusing, for instance, to make restitution or amends for serious injury inflicted, forego deep feelings of hatred, become reconciled to his enemies, abstain from unlawful intercourse or give up a proximate occasion of sin. The confessor has the right to impose a salutary penance, but not to impose a penance not prescribed by divine or human law. The confessor may not impose upon a penitent, under threat of refusal to absolve him, a duty to which, according to probable opinion, the penitent is not bound. The reader is referred to no. 2688 for the application of this rule to restitution, to no. 1329 for its application to occasions of sin, and to no. 1301 for its application to solicitation. Every priest would do well to bear in mind the words of St. Alphonsus: "Whenever a penitent appears indisposed, the confessor is bound, as far as he can, to assist in disposing him for absolution." If his efforts prove of no avail, he should at least request the penitent to make an act of perfect contrition. He should ask him to repeat this act as often as possible, to seek to regain the friendship of God through prayer, and to return to the confessional as soon as he feels himself properly disposed.

1325. *Duties of the confessor towards different kinds of penitents.* In no. 1296 we dealt with penitents solicited in confession; in nos. 1572 and 2552 we shall treat of those guilty of onanism, in no. 2447 of those guilty of hatred, in no. 2234 of heretics, and in no. 1341 of clerics who have contracted bad habits. Here we deal with habitual and relapsing sinners.

Habitual sinners in general. Habitual sinners are those who have contracted the habit of sin by repeated acts. A smaller number of external sins is required to constitute a bad habit than in the case of internal sins. Five external sins in one month would constitute a habit if they were not all committed the same day. A sin committed with an accomplice once a month for a whole year constitutes a habit. A far greater number of sins is necessary to constitute a habit when there is a question of sins of the heart or the lips.

1326. A habitual sinner may not be absolved if he gives no hope of amendment. This is certain from the condemnation of the contrary proposition. A penitent gives hope of amendment when he confesses his evil habit for the first time and promises to make use of the means indicated by the confessor. The latter may not deny him absolution if he refuses to go to confession several times in the course of a year, because there are other means of amendment. Let the confessor, however, be mindful of these words of St. Alphonsus: "The habitual sinner, *praesertim pollutionis,* who does not make use of frequent confession, cannot promise to amend his life short of a miracle." Hence, the duty to preach frequent confession.

1327. If the habitual sinner, to whom the confessor has pointed out means of amending his ways, has not made use of these means, but has fallen back into the same or similar sins without resistance immediately after confession, he is called a *recidivus.* St. Alphonsus is of the opinion that a *recidivus* may not be absolved the second time unless he shows extraordinary signs of contrition, but less severe theologians are of the opinion that he may be absolved two or three times. If through lack of solicitude on the part of the confessor, the penitent has not been apprised of the means to amend his ways, he may be absolved. Absolution should, therefore, be refused to a *recidivus* until he shows extraordinary signs of repentance, *i. e.,* signs other than mere confession of his sins with a promise to amend his life; and this is true even though he has only venial sins to confess, if he does not mention some sin of his past life for which he is sincerely sorry. (See no. 1044.) Sinners would not find it so easy to sin if they found it more difficult to obtain absolution.

1328. If the confessor has a grave reason for not refusing or not deferring absolution, he should give it conditionally (see no. 1213), even though the penitent shows no extraordinary signs of contrition. Such extraordinary signs are: special efforts in the use of the means indicated by the confessor, a certain amount of improvement since the last confession, less frequent relapses, and greater resistance offered to temptations, a spontaneous confession, especially if the penitent has had to overcome some internal or external conflict, or if he has been moved by some external grace, such as a sermon, a death, a serious illness, the confession of a sin concealed in a previous confession, a greater degree of contrition manifested by tears or other signs, and, finally, a request for additional means to help him amend his ways. A list of such means is given in no. 1149.

A *recidivus* may be absolved if he shows one of these signs, but absolution may always be deferred, especially if the confessor wishes to remove an occasion of sin. It is always better to give than to defer absolution in the case of secret sins of the flesh, supposing that the penitent shows extraordinary signs of contrition.

1329. *Penitents in the proximate occasion of sin.* An occasion of sin is any person or circumstance that leads one into sin. Remote occasions are those in which a person rarely falls, and there is no obligation to avoid them; proximate occasions are those in which a person frequently falls, and the penitent is bound to shun these at all costs. If a penitent converses with another person once every month and sins six times a year, or if he is placed in circumstances where he experiences such violent temptations that he fears he may fall into mortal sin, even though he never fell before, he would be in a proximate occasion of sin.

Proximate occasions may be absolute or relative. An *absolute* occasion is one which by its very nature is calculated to lead any man into sin; a *relative* occasion is one which, owing to a particular weakness, is apt to lead this or that person into sin, although it may not be an occasion of sin for others. Both kinds of occasions may be either continuous or interrupted. An instance of a *continuous* occasion would be the maintenance of a concubine in the penitent's house; an interrupted occasion would be the periodical visit of a penitent to a house of ill-fame. Again, occasions may be either voluntary or necessary, *necessary* occasions being those which it is either morally or physically impossible to relinquish; *voluntary* those that can easily be abandoned.

The principal occasions of sin are: bad company, frequent social intercourse with persons of the opposite sex, cabarets, theatres, dance halls and immoral books or periodicals.

1330. No one who is in a voluntary occasion of sin which he can but will not relinquish, may receive absolution. It makes no difference whether the occasion is continuous or interrupted. This is *certain* from the condemnation of the contrary proposition. If the occasion is not continuous, and if the person who is in it, is not as yet a habitual sinner, he may be absolved two or three times, provided he promises to avoid the occasion. A promise of this sort must be exacted of him, even though he has not yet fallen into sin, if it can be foreseen that there is imminent danger that he will; if he is a habitual sinner or a *recidivus*, he must be dealt with as such.

1331. If the occasion is voluntary and continuous, the confessor may not give absolution until the penitent has actually forsaken it, the reason being that an occasion of this kind is so conducive to sin that the penitent will forget all his good resolutions. We must, however, except the case of a penitent who shows such signs of contrition that the confessor has no fear of his being unfaithful to his promises, also the case of a penitent whom the confessor will not see again, or will see only after a lengthy period of time. Such penitents have a right to absolution.

1332. *Necessary occasions of sin.* We stress the word *necessary,* because the Church has condemned the following propositions: "Proximate occasions of sin need not be forsaken when one has an honest and useful reason for not doing so. A penitent who keeps a concubine must not be re-

quired to dismiss her when she is so indispensable *ad ob-
lectamentum concubinarii,* that without her his life would
be drab and dreary, also when it would be extremely difficult
for the penitent to secure some other servant." Utility is not
a sufficient motive, therefore, for remaining in a proximate
occasion of sin; necessity is the only excuse, *i. e.,* a very
serious inconvenience suffered in one's possessions, in one's
reputation, or in one's very soul. Thus a penitent would
be warranted in remaining in a proximate occasion of sin if,
by forsaking it, he would expose himself to even graver dangers. In weighing all these inconveniences, account should be
taken of the character and disposition of the penitent. The
same inconvenience may be greater for one than for another,
or it may appear such that the penitent is in good faith when
he affirms that he cannot possibly forsake the occasion. (See
no. 1317.) In doubt as to whether or not the occasion is
necessary, the confessor should presume that it is. In this
way, says St. Leonard, he will always procure the spiritual
welfare of his penitent.

St. Alphonsus does not hesitate to assert that, when there
are several theological opinions, the confessor should follow the one that will remove the penitent farthest from
formal sin, and at the same time more effectively serve the
common good. Scandal is not always a sufficient reason, because it not infrequently happens that the scandal ceases
when the occasion is removed. But if, at Easter time or during a mission, the immediate removal of an occasion would
result in scandal, St. Leonard would permit the confessor to
give absolution, provided the penitent promised to renounce
the occasion within fifteen days and emphatically asserted
that he would not be seen alone with the person who caused
him to sin, and would receive the Sacraments in the interval.
But the holy missionary adds that this means cannot always be employed in practice, especially when the penitent's

lapses into sin have been frequent and his temptations violent.

1333. If the occasion of sin is truly necessary, the confessor should indicate to the penitent the means for rendering it remote. Besides the means suggested by St. Leonard, he may add the Sacraments, prayer, and the medicinal penances we have indicated in no. 1149. If the penitent, in spite of all this, relapses into sin, the confessor should treat him as a habitual sinner or a *recidivus*. And if, later on, the confessor has no hope of correcting the penitent by these means, he should force him to abandon the occasion. "If thy right eye scandalize thee, pluck it out." (Matt. 5, 29.) Other writers are more lenient. We suggest that confessors who have penitents who will not avoid a proximate occasion of sin, put to them the pointed question: "If you had a son or a daughter in such an occasion, what would you advise him or her to do?" Let them answer for themselves.

1334. We have dealt with the question of mutes and deaf-mutes in nos. 1070, 1094, and 1095; we must say a word here in regard to *children*. The confessor, and especially the pastor, has a serious obligation of hearing their confessions when they have reached the age of reason, and even before this time, if they have already fallen into sin. He is obliged, also, to instruct them in the things necessary for salvation, dispose them for absolution, and absolve them like other penitents, especially if they have committed grievous sins. There is no justification for refusing these little ones the grace of Jesus Christ, especially if they are about to receive the Sacrament of Confirmation. Following the example of the Saviour, the confessor should seek to encourage them by kind words, for, according to Lehmkuhl, the priest who discourages them from going to confession by harshness of manners or language is guilty of a mortal sin.

It is not wise, however, to have the children come to confession in large groups, because they quickly become distracted, and the confessor cannot devote sufficient time to each. Before hearing their confessions, the priest should instruct them by means of special catechisms written for that purpose. It is always easier to instruct and dispose little children than adults, especially hardened sinners.

1335. Jesus Christ instituted the Sacrament of Penance for the remission of sins, provided the penitent confesses them all. "You must tell me all your sins," the confessor may say to the child, "otherwise God will not forgive them. Accuse yourself of all the mortal sins you have committed, otherwise neither God nor I will love you." If the priest fears that the child has not been absolved, or has concealed some sin, he will do well to question him in regard to his entire life, during the time of a mission or a retreat. At other times, if the child does not know whether or not he received absolution, the confessor need not have him repeat all his previously confessed sins, unless the priest to whom the child made his last confession informs him that he did not give him absolution. *Quod factum est praesumitur recte factum.*

The confessor should inquire first into the child's age, then ask him if he swears, misses Mass on Sundays, disobeys his parents, quarrels, hates others, etc. He should then ask him if he has seen other people do wicked things. This is the best way to approach the delicate question of sex, because the child is naturally inclined to accuse others and consequently will answer this question in all sincerity. The confessor may then ask: "Were you with them when they did these things; what did they do?" If the child answers that they threw stones, or stole apples, the confessor should ask if they did worse things than these. If the child answers in the negative, the confessor may rest assured that he has

done no wrong; but if he answers in the affirmative, the confessor should continue: "No doubt they made you do bad
things, too, by looks, words, or actions." (See no. 1125.)
Here the confessor must show great prudence and reserve.
St. Alphonsus instructed his priests to ask children with
whom they slept, and if they played during the night. Questions such as these put to children, servants, and sons and
daughters will make known to the confessor the occasions of
sin of the respective parties. He should then urge the children
to reveal this danger to their parents and teachers, and make
them promise him they will sleep in a separate bed. In this
connection, all parents should see to it that each one of their
children and servants sleeps in a separate bed. (See no.
2411.)

Nothing can be of greater advantage to the spiritual welfare of both children and adults than to discover the proximate occasions which lead them into sin, and the confessor
has no more efficacious way of correcting their bad habits
than to persuade them to speak of these matters to their
parents, teachers, or tutors. "Did you commit these sins
with little boys or little girls? Did you commit them alone?
Did you commit them with some grown-up person? Did you
think about these things? Did you wish to do them? How
many times?" The confessor would do well to ask children
if they have spoken ill of others, been insincere in confession, broken the laws of abstinence, been greedy, etc. He
should also instruct them that they do not break the law of
abstinence by eating meat when they have nothing else to
eat. He should end by exciting in them sentiments of charity
and contrition (see no. 1313), indicating to them the means
of saving their souls, and giving absolution while observing
the rules set forth in the following number.

1336. If it is certain that the child has sufficient use of
reason—and this can be easily discerned from the manner in

which he confesses his sins and answers the questions put to him—the confessor may absolve him if he appears sufficiently disposed. But if he is a *recidivus,* the confessor should deal with him as he would with an adult. In missions, when it is difficult for the confessor to hear children's confessions a second time, he may absolve them conditionally the first time, for fear that if he does not absolve them, they will not return.

1337. If the confessor doubts whether a child has the use of reason, as, for instance, when he notices that the child does not remain quiet in the confessional, but looks around and plays with his hands, he should absolve him conditionally if there is danger of death, or if he is obliged to conform to the law of the Church requiring him to make an annual confession, especially if he accuses himself of a sin that is doubtfully mortal. "In a case of this kind," writes St. Alphonsus, "I judge that the confessor should absolve the child, even outside the danger of death and the obligation of annual confession."

Absolution may always be granted conditionally when the confessor has reason for giving it in this way, as when he seeks to withdraw a child from the state of sin into which he has fallen. Such a child must be absolved conditionally, even though he be a *recidivus.* Absolution should be deferred only in the case of those who have the full use of reason, because there is always hope that in deferring forgiveness, the confessor will render these children better disposed, whereas it is difficult to conceive how children who have not the full use of reason, could improve on their dispositions. Some writers, whose opinion is probable, claim that doubtfully disposed children may be absolved *sub conditione* every two or three months, even though they accuse themselves of only venial sins, the reason being that to defer absolution in their case might result in depriving them for a long time of sacramental, and perhaps also of sanctifying, grace, for it is quite possible that they have on their conscience a mortal sin which they forgot to confess.

1338. Confessors should not give lengthy penances to children. If the children have barely reached the age of reason, it is better to impose upon them a short penance, which they may recite while in the confessional. Above all, the confessor should avoid asking them to beg forgiveness of their parents, and he should see to it that they perform their penance in a place where they will not be disturbed by others.

Priests cannot expect children to amend their lives, or to have the proper disposition for Holy Communion, or to persevere in grace, if they are not willing to hear their confessions frequently. Children, indeed, have a greater need of weekly confession than other persons. (See nos. 936, 1328.)

The regulations we have just indicated for the absolution of children should be followed also for feeble-minded adults, who remain children all through life.

1339. Of young people of both sexes St. Alphonsus says: "Confessors should be on their guard against permitting young men to visit their fiancées and young girls, and their parents to admit the young men into their homes. It is morally impossible for young people to engage in conversation without experiencing some temptations. It is my opinion that it is very difficult for young men and young girls who are in love with one another not to be in a proximate occasion of sin. These interviews are grievously sinful if they lead to sin or to the danger of sinning grievously, if they take place between persons differently situated in life, or who are unable to marry, as happens if one of the two is already married or consecrated to God, or if these interviews take place at night, without the parents' permission, under pretense of amusement or recreation, or if one of the two parties concerned knows that the other is tempted." These words are objectively true, but it seems useless to lay down a rule of conduct that will be inevitably disregarded. For the duties of those about to enter the married state the reader is referred to no. 1580.

1340. The confessors should urge young people to practice the virtue of chastity, by stressing the necessity of frequent confession and Communion. He should not take it upon himself—except for special reasons—to select their state of life for them, but should rather urge them to embrace that state to which he prudently judges them to be called. Let him be on his guard especially against dissuading young men from entering the religious life out of human respect, for, according to St. Thomas, this would be grievously sinful.

1341. The confessor must refuse absolution to those who aspire to a sacred order and who are addicted to vicious habits, until they have acquired the positive holiness necessary to receive this order. St. Leonard is of the opinion that a requisite for this positive holiness is one or two years spent in the state of grace. Penitents in this class are to be refused absolution *sub gravi,* even though well disposed, unless they promise not to receive the order until certain of the sincerity of their good resolutions. If *ordinandi* are ignorant of this ruling, the confessor is bound to instruct them, even though he can foresee that his admonition will be of no avail, and even though he is hearing the confession of an *ordinandus* who, once he has received absolution, will not reveal his state of conscience to his ordinary confessor. A pastor or any priest sins grievously in issuing letters of recommendation to an *ordinandus* who is not a positively good subject, or without securing exact information concerning the righteousness of his conduct.

1342. The holy Doctor adds these words, which we will allow to stand in the original: *"Non sit ergo facilis confessarius ad permittendum adolescentulo, ut suscipiat statum presbyteri saecularis sine longa et probata experientia recti finis. Sacerdotes enim saeculares habent eandem, imo majorem obligationem ac religiosi, et contra remanent in iisdem saeculi periculis."*

1343. The confessor should not permit young girls who desire to consecrate their lives to God to vow themselves to a life of perpetual chastity if they are not firmly established in virtue, well instructed in the rules of the spiritual life, and habituated to prayer. He may permit them to make temporal vows of chastity between two feast-days. Berardi is of the opinion that if a young girl, who has not as yet satisfied the above conditions, has set her heart on making a perpetual vow of chastity, and the confessor fears that by refusing his permission he may completely discourage her, the priest may consent to her making a vow of chastity until he judges her action to be no longer expedient.

1344. *Persons tormented by the devil.* The confessor should not put too much faith in obsessions, which are frequently the product of the imagination. He should not, however, reject them all on *a priori* grounds. When persons tormented by the devil are pursued by horrid specters and suffer physical torments, the confessor should advise them to pray, bear these trials patiently, and subject themselves in all things to the will of God. The most difficult subjects for the confessor are those who *turpibus visionibus, motibus ac etiam tactibus vexantur a daemone.* Such souls are in great danger if they do not make use of the most efficacious remedies, and if they relent in works of prayer, mortification, and humility. If the penitent does not consent to diabolic attacks, the confessor should endeavor to lend him encouragement and gently persuade him to confess anything of a troublesome nature. Often enough, these faults are only venial in character. If the penitent consents to these attacks, the confessor will find it harder to effect a cure. He should question the penitent concerning the form which the Evil Spirit assumes and in what place he manifests himself, for these circumstances may often change the nature of the sin. The confessor should be on his guard, for penitents of this type often conceal their sins, and must not be given absolution unless they agree to make use of the prescribed means.

1345. These means are: frequent prayer, repeated protests against any intention of sinning, private exorcism administered either by the confessor or by the penitent himself. The obsessed one should carry on his person the crucifix, a copy of the Holy Gospels, and a relic of some saint. He should make frequent signs of the cross with holy water both on his own person and over his bed.

1346. *Pious persons.* We shall deal with scrupulous penitents in no. 1888 ff. Concerning pious persons, St. Alphonsus says: "One perfect soul is more pleasing to God than a thousand imperfect ones. Consequently, should a confessor meet with a penitent who does not commit mortal sins, he should do all in his power to lead him on the way to perfection and the love of God."

In order to direct souls on the way to perfection, the confessor should have an idea in what perfection consists. The perfection of any being consists in its union with its end. God is the end of man, consequently, the perfection of man consists in his being united to God. The disposition by which man unites himself most perfectly to God, is that of love or charity. Perfection in this world consists in charity; hence, charity consists principally in loving God, and secondarily in loving our neighbor, because the perfection of God or the divine good is reflected like an image in the soul of man, so that the love of one's neighbor is also essential to perfection.

1347. All men are obliged to love God above all things for His own sake, and all the other precepts are calculated to prevent offenses against God and neighbor. And yet, there are different degrees in charity. The first and the highest degree consists in loving God as much as He is capable of being loved, and God alone can do this; the second consists in loving God purely, perfectly, and without interruption. This manner of loving God is the perfection of the elect in Heaven, and, according to St. Thomas, is impossible to man here below. Because of the infirmity of human nature, we cannot, indeed, always think of God, nor be constantly moved by His love.

1348. There is a third degree of charity which is possible in this world, and this is in turn divided into two. The first is the easier and more essential; it consists in this that man loves nothing as much as he loves God, does nothing against the will of God, and consequently avoids mortal sins. The second, which presupposes the first, consists in applying one-self to God and divine things, giving to other things only the barely necessary attention. This it what we understand, and what is generally understood, by perfection.

Not all who have charity and the perfection which is the necessary appendage of charity, attain to these heights, and yet they are just. The question is: Are all men obliged to aim at this second stage of the third degree, in other words, are all obliged to seek the perfection of charity? St. Thomas replies that he who attains to the last degree of charity, does not offend against the precept, even though he does not attain to the second stage, for it is manifest that he who does not commit mortal sin is deserving of Heaven. But it is equally manifest that he who avoids mortal sin is obliged *sub levi* to avoid venial sins and tend towards that perfection to which even slight imperfections, especially when voluntary, are an obstacle. We may, therefore, preach to all the faithful that they should strive after that perfection which consists in avoiding both mortal and venial sins, for this kind of perfection is within reach of all.

1349. Is one obliged to strive after that special and accidental perfection which consists in following the counsels? *Per se* there is no obligation binding any one to follow the counsels, unless one happens to be a religious or has bound himself to these things by a vow, because *per se* the counsels are not binding. To treat them with disrespect, however, would be a serious fault, and to fail to observe some of them would be to expose oneself to venial, if not mortal, sins. For this reason priests should not hesitate to exhort the faithful to keep the counsels and strive for the perfection which they are calculated to give, but they should be careful not to speak of them as *per se* obligatory. Our Lord said: *"Estote et vos perfecti, sicut pater vester caelestis perfectus est,"* and St. Paul: *"Aemulamini charismata meliora."*

1350. With all these things in mind, the spiritual director should seek to impress upon his penitents the important truth that perfection does not consist in the counsels, or the moral virtues, or vocal prayer, but in perfect charity, and he should strive to lead them first by the *purgative,* then by the *illuminative,* and finally by the *unitive* way. For men, according to St. Thomas, begin by loving God, then strengthen themselves in this love, and finally perfect themselves in it.

1351. The *purgative* way is the one followed by those who are beginning to love God, their chief concern being to triumph over their bad habits and passions, which are the cause of severe temptations. The *illuminative* way is followed by those who are fortified in charity and seek to increase it by the practice of the moral virtues. The moral virtues are, indeed, an excellent preparation for the attainment of perfect charity, and penitents are able to give themselves over to the practice of these virtues in proportion to the success they meet with in obtaining control over their passions. (*S. Theol.*, 2a, 2ae, q. 24, art. 9.) The *unitive* way is followed by those who have successfully overcome the obstacles of beginners, are in actual possession of the moral virtues, and united with God by the close bonds of divine charity. They are called *perfect* because, although they are capable of further advancement in the spiritual way, progress is not their principal aim. They strive above all things to become more and more closely united to the Sovereign Good, and in loving this Good, they advance in perfection, for charity is ever capable of increase in this life. (*Ibid.*, q. 24, art. 4.) It is true that those who are in the purgative way are in a position to practice virtue and make acts of love of God. Indeed, they should be incited to do these things. But above all, they should be drilled in fighting their evil inclinations and in the practice of the moral virtues, otherwise, when their first fervor is passed, they will still find themselves the prey to many serious faults, and without the adornment of the greater virtues.

1352. The chief concern of the director of souls should be to remove from the path of his charges every obstacle to perfection and every attraction to sin, to instruct them in the practice of virtue, and to point out to them the means to attain their end. For, although the moral virtues, the counsels, and exercises of piety are not perfection, they are indispensable means thereto, and no one can attain perfection without them. To practice none of them would be to remain an ordinary Christian, although to arrive at perfection it is not necessary to observe them all. (See no. 3325 ff.) For this reason persons living in the world may attain to perfection without practicing the three evangelical counsels, although the latter are the most efficacious means of arriving at perfect charity, being for this reason called counsels of perfection. Exercises of piety and the counsels of perfection should not be treated lightly, therefore, for although books are not to be mistaken for knowledge, knowledge cannot be acquired without books. In like manner perfection cannot be attained without some of the counsels and some of the exercises of piety, and because not all of these means are indispensable, it is the duty of the spiritual director to indicate those which are best suited to the condition of the penitent. The entire spiritual direction of souls may be reduced to four things: meditation, contemplation, mortification, and the reception of the Sacraments, and since we have already dealt with the latter (in no. 936), we shall devote a few paragraphs here to the three other means of advancing in perfection.

1353. *Meditation.* "The confessor should lose no time," writes St. Alphonsus, "in initiating the penitent to a life of prayer, and he should not desist in this, even though the penitent says he has no time." We shall indicate a very simple method in no. 2263. "The penitent," continues St. Alphonsus, "should be made to give an account of this exercise; he should be asked how he made it, or at least whether he made it at all. Confessors must answer to God for negligence on their part in these matters, for they are bound, as far as possible, to secure the spiritual progress of their charges. Mental prayer should be recommended not only to timid souls, but also to sinners, who more often than not return to their vomit because they have not given the matter sufficient reflection." Above all, no confessor should allow a penitent to give up mental prayer simply because he experiences nothing but dryness in this exercise.

1354. *Contemplation.* In meditation, the soul reaches out to God through the faculty of reasoning, and in this way is essentially active; in infused contemplation, God becomes the object of the soul's contemplation, and all activity is on His part. But before arriving at passive contemplation, the soul usually passes through an intermediary stage, known as prayer of recollection, in which the intellect applies itself without effort to the contemplation of some mystery, and, being totally recollected, is concerned only with the fruition of truth. Contemplative rest is practically identical with this kind of prayer, although in this act the intellect does not apply itself to the contemplation of some one truth in particular, but in general to the knowledge of God, towards whom it is gently and irresistibly drawn. Some writers are of the opinion that the soul must remain completely passive in this kind of rest, but St. Alphonsus does not agree with them. True, the soul does not need to make an effort when it is so irresistibly drawn towards God; neither is it obliged to apply itself to meditation, having already found the object of its thoughts and desires; yet, in order to merit, it must act by formulating of its own accord acts of love, desire, contrition, and a firm purpose of amendment. With the help of divine grace all may attain to this kind of contemplation and all may seek it as a great means of sanctification. The same is not true of the extraordinary states of which we shall treat now.

1355. Before making certain souls objects of His extraordinary graces, God is accustomed to purify them by making them pass through periods of extraordinary sensible dryness, or by withholding from them all sensible devotion. These periods are much longer and far more terrifying than those which sometimes afflict the souls of ordinary Christians. After this spell of spiritual aridity, God floods the soul with the gift of joyous contemplation, of which we shall have a word to say later. But before effecting this passive union of the soul with Himself, God causes it to pass through a period of spiritual dryness, which does not affect the senses, but is like a light from above, revealing to the soul its utter unworthiness and insignificance. The soul then turns to God in all sincerity, only to find itself repelled and given over to temptations of blasphemy and others of a similar nature.

This is no time for the confessor to display timidity or hesitancy; he should hasten to strengthen such a soul, recommending it to confide in God without fear and with as much peace of conscience as possible. To offset any possibility of the soul's drifting into a state of torpor, God permits the recurrence of this kind of spiritual dryness before effecting a passive union with it.

1356. After the soul has been purified by spiritual dryness, God firmly establishes it in contemplation. This contemplation is termed *affirmative* when, through the light of grace and without any effort on its part, the soul perceives some created or divine truth; it is termed *negative*—and this is the more perfect of the two—when the soul knows the divine perfections in a confused manner because it is overflooded with light. It is just as if the bodily eye were flooded with the light of the sun, for the soul has a very high conception of God, although this conception is necessarily indistinct.

1357. The first degree of contemplation is *supernatural recollection*. It differs from the recollection of which we spoke in no. 1354, in that the soul produces it by its own special acts, with the ordinary assistance of God, whereas God Himself produces supernatural recollection by means of a light which He infuses into the soul and which stimulates it to acts of sensible love. In this second kind of recollection the full strength of God's love is immediately communicated to the external senses, so that they too become recollected.

1358. In *quietude,* which is the second degree of contemplation, the love of God communicates itself immediately to the soul. It does not always spread to the senses, although this may happen at times. The will seems to lose its freedom and to be able to love nothing else but God, whereas the intellect and the imagination sometimes remain free and operate independently. In these last two degrees, the soul should make no effort to gather together its thoughts, for to attempt this would be to lose its repose. The soul should perform only those acts to which it feels inclined.

1359. The third degree is *negative contemplation,* of which we have already spoken in no. 1356. In this kind of contemplation all the interior, and sometimes all the exterior, powers of the soul are held in check, and the soul is occasionally overcome by a sort of spiritual inebriety. In this state the soul is easily given over to transports of love.

1360. Finally the soul attains to *union* with God. There are two kinds of union. The first is *active* and consists in the union of the human with the divine will. It is in this union that perfection consists and as such it is becoming to all persons. The second union is *passive,* and it is of this union that there is question here. In the other degrees God manifests Himself as really present and the soul feels itself intimately united with Him. The confessor should bend every effort to maintain souls who are thus privileged in a spirit of true humility, for it not infrequently happens that persons who have attained to this third degree later on fall into sin.

1361. Following upon simple passive union, with a period of intervening spiritual dryness, we have the *union of spiritual nuptials*. This latter union comprises three degrees: (1) *ecstasy,* in which all the powers of the soul are held in check as in simple union, and also all the senses; (2) *rapture,* in which the body, under the powerful influence of grace, is sometimes raised above the ground and rendered as light as a feather; (3) *elevation of the spirit,* in which the soul is carried outside of itself, and is greatly terrified thereby.

1362. The most perfect union of all is that which is called *spiritual marriage;* in it the soul is so transformed that it seems to be one with God. The powers of the soul are not held in check, but the will loves God and the intellect is well aware of the union existing between the soul and Him. Such a union is not transient like the foregoing, but stable and lasting. The soul perceives its passions as from afar off, and is seldom molested by them.

1363. Besides these spiritual communications, theologians distinguish *visions* and *locutions*. Visions are of three kinds: (1) *external,* effected through the eyes; (2) *imaginative,* effected through the imagination; (3) *intellectual,* effected through intelligible images infused into the intellect, by means of which a person does not see things themselves, yet knows them better than if he actually saw them.

1364. *Locutions* are of two kinds, successive and formal: *successive* locution, in which the soul hears itself answering itself in meditation as if a second person were present; and *formal* locution, in which it hears words uttered outside of itself. This second kind of locution is called *substantial* when the words heard effect what they signify, as, for instance, when the word *love* is followed by an outburst of affection.

The confessor should permit his penitent to narrate his experiences without manifesting any desire to know them. He should maintain the greatest secrecy in regard to them and see to it that the penitent does the same, for it is absolutely essential that these souls be kept humble. When these kinds of extraordinary grace do not result in a diminution of faith—and the different degrees of contemplation never do—and when the soul which is favored with them maintains itself in humility and the fear of God, and makes progress in the love of God, it may continue to desire them, if it is thoroughly acquainted with their workings. But souls who are not acquainted with their workings would do well to content themselves with *active* union with God. If the confessor deems it apropos, he may reassure souls who are favored with these sorts of graces and who have not suffered a diminution of faith, but he may also leave them in a wholesome kind of fear, which will keep them lowly and humble without causing them any inconvenience. If these extraordinary graces result in a diminution of faith because they happen to give a few distinct perceptions of supernatural truths, such as are had in visions, locutions, and revelations, the penitent should do all in his power to reject them, not by ridiculing them—this is never permitted—but by protesting to God that he wishes to serve Him in the simplicity of faith. This is the advice which the confessor should give in all cases of this kind.

1365. *Visions* are to be looked upon with suspicion if they are too frequent, if they plunge the soul into disorder, if they do not occur suddenly, and if they leave the soul arrogant and proud. When the confessor notices that the visions of his penitent are imaginary or diabolical, he should warn him of this fact, without causing him any consternation. Any failure on the part of the penitent to listen to advice should be regarded as an ill omen, and the confessor would do well to protect him from further illusions by humiliating him, and, if necessary, by forbidding him to receive Holy Communion. Exceptions may be made in the case of weak-minded individuals. If the confessor is at a loss to know whence these visions come, he may consult priests more learned than himself. If he is in doubt, he should not hastily proclaim that they originate from the devil, even though his penitent is still very imperfect, because God sometimes gives these graces to imperfect souls. He should advise his penitent to strengthen himself in the service of God and pray to be delivered from these visions. He should never permit his penitent to reveal anything in these visions that would be contrary to the rules of Christian prudence. The foregoing instructions have all been taken from the *Praxis* of St. Alphonsus, abbreviated to suit our present purpose.

1366. *Mortification.* At the beginning of conversion, the confessor should moderate the exercise of mortifications, and require that his penitent seek permission for any acts he wishes to perform. Exceptions to this rule must be made, of course, in regard to negative mortifications, which are always more useful and less dangerous. Examples of such are mortifications of the eyes, ears, and tongue, and moderation in eating, drinking, and clothing. The confessor should wait for the penitent to ask his permission in regard to other kinds of mortification such as fasting, the use of the discipline, the hair-shirt, etc., and should always grant less than the penitent requests, especially in the matter of privation of sleep. He should never refuse to grant all petitions if the penitent is already well strengthened in virtue, but should aim more especially to train him in the exercise of the mortification of the passions, teaching him to be silent under reproach, ever ready to return good for evil, and to make acts of self-denial. External mortifications induce internal ones, and when they are possible, become indispensable even to keep the senses in subjection. This fact can easily be verified in the lives of the saints.

1367. To the foregoing instructions of St. Alphonsus we may be permitted to add a few of our own. The confessor should lead his penitent along the road of perfection by degrees (see no. 1351), teaching him to bear first with little and later on with greater things. He should see to it that the penitent faithfully fulfills all the duties of his state, says his prayers devoutly, assists at Mass with devotion, occupies his time to the best advantage, converses with his neighbors without offending against charity, and performs his acts of devotion in a pleasing and unassuming way. He should incite the weak to effort, comfort the afflicted, and try the more generous souls. He should gently but firmly correct those who trust too much in their own judgment, take care that those who receive Communion frequently, confess their sins once a week, or at least once a fortnight, and impress upon all the importance of spiritual direction if they do not wish to go astray.

1368. He should prescribe for all a definite rule of life, inclusive of morning and evening prayers, particular and general examen, attendance at Mass, visits to the Blessed Sacrament and the Blessed Virgin, spiritual reading, the recitation of at least five decades of the rosary, the reception of the Sacraments, and occasionally a spiritual retreat in preparation for death.

1369. *In regard to the dying.* The pastor is bound *ex justitia* to assist the sick, especially by recommending their souls to God. This proposition is *certain* by the unanimous consent of theologians. He is particularly obliged, writes St. Alphonsus, to lend special assistance to sick persons who have led a life of sin. The same is true of criminals condemned to death. He should not leave them to their fate once he has administered the Sacraments, but return to them, make inquiries concerning the exact time of their execution, and if possible assist them at the last moment. Lehmkuhl quite correctly observes that even though the priest may suffer grave inconveniences, he must do all he can to render remote the danger of eternal damnation, especially in the case of men who have led a life of crime. The obligation would be less serious in the case of a person concerning whose perseverance one would have moral certitude.

The obligation of assisting at the deathbed of the sick is not so strictly reserved to the pastor that the other priests are exempt from it when the pastor is absent or prevented. When a pastor is obliged to absent himself, he should always obtain a substitute who is both prudent and pious, and if no priest is available, a lay person, who will suggest pious ejaculations and prayers to the one dying after he has received the Sacraments. The pastor should not wait to be called to the house of the sick, but should repair there of his own accord, not once, but frequently.

1370. If the dying person has a horror of confession, the priest at first should not mention the subject, but with prudence and charity gently endeavor to suggest the matter. If there is little time left, he should be more firm, enlisting if possible the services of the dying person's friends and physician. Two extremes must be carefully avoided. The first consists in permitting a sick person to die without absolution because he failed to make a complete confession; integrity is not obligatory at a time like this. The second consists in refusing the Sacraments to a dying person who has lost consciousness, with the expectation that he will regain it, which rarely happens. In the latter case, the priest should immediately give the absolution, and then request the bystanders to inform the penitent of his actions if he regains consciousness, in order that he may set his mind at peace by a more complete confession. In danger of death, any priest may *in foro interno* absolve from all censures and all reserved sins, even those specially reserved, provided he reminds the penitent that he must have recourse to lawful authority if he ever recovers. If the censure is a notorious one, the penitent should be required to make some sort of statement outside the confessional before a trustworthy witness to the effect that he is sorry and promises to satisfy for his faults. As a general rule this statement will suffice. If the penitent is living in public concubinage, he should be made to separate himself from the person with whom he is living. If this measure were deemed impossible, or if the other party refused, the sick person should be required to promise before two witnesses that he will abstain from all carnal intercourse, after which he may be given absolution. If the sin of concubinage is occult, the priest should seek to marry the two guilty parties, if this is possible and no evil effects are to be apprehended. The pastor may secure from the Ordinary the habitual faculty to dispense from ecclesiastical impediments in cases of this kind.

If marriage is out of the question, the priest should secure from the dying person the promise to break with his accomplice as soon as he is able to, and in the meantime to abstain from all carnal intercourse. In both cases it is best to induce the other party to leave the dying person, in order not to expose him to too strong a temptation at the last hour.

Should the dying person consult the confessor concerning his temporal affairs, the latter should be careful not to lay himself open to an accusation of avarice. He should advise the sick man to have his heirs carry out his wishes. (See no. 2691.)

Anything that might prove a source of temptation to the dying man should be removed from the sick-room. The crucifix and other pious images should be placed before his eyes, and he should be instructed in the manner of overcoming temptation. Both he and the persons present should be induced to make short, but frequent acts of faith, hope, charity, and perfect contrition. The sick person should not be annoyed by the constant repetition of these prayers, but at the approach of death, acts of charity and contrition should be suggested to him almost incessantly, and in a loud tone of voice, so that he may hear them as he drifts into unconsciousness.

1371. In no. 1097 ff. we laid down rules for the giving of absolution, and in nos. 920, 925, 928, and 1092 for the administration of the Holy Viaticum. The reader would do well to re-read them at this juncture. In no. 1401 we shall speak of Extreme Unction. (See also no. 2235.)

1372. When the priest is administering the Viaticum and Extreme Unction he may, if he deems it advisable, request the relatives of the sick man to withdraw, so that they may not disturb him by their cries and wailings. He may request the same when the person is entering upon the last agony or is about to give up the ghost. If it is impossible to dismiss the assistants, even when the priest hears the dying man's confession, he should excite the latter to contrition, have him accuse some slight, or preferably some grave sin, for fear that he will not have sufficient contrition for a slight one, and then administer absolution. The priest should be careful not to disturb the patient unnecessarily and thus hasten his death, and he should not require that his lips be completely closed when he is administering Extreme Unction.

Antonelli teaches that, in the opinion of the majority of physicians, the only sure signs of death are rigidity of the body coupled with the beginnings of putrefaction. Putrefaction has set in when the abdomen turns greenish in color. According to this opinion a priest could give absolution and administer Extreme Unction as long as these signs are not present, especially if no physician has as yet pronounced the person dead. If need be, he could explain his actions to those present, to avoid all danger of scandal.

Lehmkuhl, and other theologians before him, have recommended that every newly ordained priest study some good method of preparing the dying. That is why we have listed such a method in this work.

1373.   *Duties of the minister after Confession.* We shall treat, first, of certain mistakes that he should rectify; and, secondly, of the seal.

Mistakes that he should rectify. Mistakes which render the Sacrament invalid because of some grave fault on the part of the confessor, resulting in serious and lasting harm to the penitent, must always be rectified, even at the cost of grave inconvenience. Confessors who are thus at fault are guilty of injustice. If the harm caused the penitent is not lasting, either because the penitent has already confessed to another priest, or because he has received some other Sacrament, the confessor need not apprise him of his mistake. However, Lehmkuhl is of the opinion that, in the case of a dying person who has already received the Viaticum, the confessor must rectify a mistake which has resulted in the penitent's confession being invalid, because it is not certain that the Holy Eucharist has remitted his mortal sins. If the confessor's fault is only slight, there is no obligation for him to rectify his mistake, unless he is the penitent's pastor, or the penitent will run the risk of not receiving another absolution or another Sacrament.

1374. *Mistakes regarding the integrity of sacramental confession or penance.* Unless the confessor has positively coöperated in these mistakes, he is not obliged to rectify them outside the confessional, the reason being that he exercises his functions of physician only in the confessional. But if, through some serious mistake of his, he has positively led the penitent into error regarding this matter, he is bound to rectify his mistake, even outside the confessional, if he can do so without serious inconvenience, and after he has obtained the penitent's permission. This is the teaching of St. Alphonsus, but other writers exempt the confessor from all obligations outside of confession in these cases. At times, too, silence by design on the part of the confessor will have a positive influence on the penitent.

1375. *Mistakes which have a bearing on the obligations of the penitent.* The confessor is bound *sub gravi,* and even at the risk of grave inconvenience, to rectify a mistake which has resulted in serious harm for the penitent or a third party, if his coöperation was positive and his mistake serious. If his coöperation was only negative, or if it was positive, but the mistake slight, he is still obliged to rectify his mistake at the risk of slight (but not of grave) inconvenience. Thus a confessor is bound to make restitution, if through malice, vincible ignorance, or serious negligence, he has dispensed a penitent from so doing and has not rectified his mistake, or has attempted to rectify it only when it was too late or when the penitent was no longer in the mood or in a position to fulfill his obligations. If, under the same conditions, he has positively enjoined restitution upon a penitent, when he should have acted otherwise, and has not informed the penitent of his error in time, he is also bound to restitution.

If a penitent makes his confession to the same priest, the confessor may and must rectify mistakes that have occurred in a preceding confession, but if he wishes to rectify these mistakes outside the confessional, he must first seek and obtain the penitent's permission to speak of these matters with him. If the confessor has not given the penitent absolution, or if he has given it invalidly, he may inform the penitent of his mistake outside the confessional, without first obtaining the penitent's permission.

1376. *The sacramental seal.* By natural, divine, and ecclesiastical law there is the strictest obligation binding the confessor to keep the secret of the confessional with all persons, including the penitent himself, in regard to all sins, even venial, and in regard to anything mentioned by the penitent in confession with a view of receiving absolution. Any one who would teach or think otherwise should be denounced as professing heresy. Violation of the sacramental seal has all the malice of a sacrilege, an injustice against the virtue of fidelity, and an unjust detraction. The obligation admits of no exceptions or levity of matter except perhaps in the case where the violation was indirect, or the danger of rendering confession odious was very remote. The injustice involved in such a violation may also admit of levity of matter. The obligation perseveres even after the death of the penitent, and nothing excuses from it, not even danger of grave harm or death. Furthermore, no one is allowed to follow a probable or a more probable opinion in this matter.

The safest opinion is the only course open, both in doubt of fact and in doubt of law. An instance of a doubt in fact would be whether or not the absolution was really sacramental, and a doubt of law, whether or not there is controversy among theologians concerning the obligation to secrecy in this or that case. The obligation of the seal is binding for every sacramental confession, whether incomplete or sacrilegious, but only for sacramental confession. It does not, therefore, exist in the case of a person who merely seeks advice or whose purpose is to deceive the confessor. In the first case, however, the confessor is bound to secrecy in virtue of the natural law. The obligation does not exist either, if a person confides in a priest outside the confessional, even though under the seal of the confessional, unless the matter confided to him pertains to a confession to be made or already made. In doubt as to whether or not what was told pertains to confession, the safest course must be followed.

1377. If a priest is questioned concerning what he has heard in the confessional, he may always assert under oath that he knows nothing. If he is asked whether or not he gave absolution, he may answer: "I did my duty," or "I am not obliged to answer such questions." If he is asked whether or not his penitent should receive Communion, he may answer: "Ask him." In hearing the confession of a sick person, the priest should first obtain his permission to tell some competent person whether or not he wishes to receive Communion.

1378. Who are bound by the secret? (1) The confessor; (2) the non-approved priest and the layman hearing confessions of penitents who confessed their sins to them in good faith; (3) all persons who obtain confessional knowledge in any way whatsoever, hence interpreters, superiors whose permission has been sought for the absolution of reserved cases, and persons who have involuntarily heard the confession of some sin, because they happened to be in close proximity to the confessional, who have learned of the sin from another, or who write out the confessions of illiterate persons, or persons not acquainted with the language spoken by the confessor; (4) the person reading a letter sent to a superior, requesting permission to absolve from some reserved sin, and even a person who would read such a note found in the confessional after the person had received absolution, or which was given to the priest in view of absolution. Any person who, outside the above-mentioned cases, would read a writing of this nature that had been lost, would not be bound to the sacramental, but merely to a natural, secret.

1379. The penitent is not bound to secrecy in regard to his confessor, because the law of secrecy has been established in favor of the penitent, and not in favor of the confessor. Nevertheless, he is bound by a natural secret not to reveal anything detrimental to the confessor or to the Sacrament. The confessor, on the other hand, is bound to secrecy in regard to his penitent, not in the act of confession itself, nor immediately after giving absolution before the penitent withdraws, nor when the penitent returns to confess his sins, but only outside the confessional. In this latter case he cannot speak to the penitent without his permission of anything that has reference to his confession, unless the penitent himself first broaches the subject. When the penitent does this, the priest may answer the question put to him, but he may not pass on to another. The permission of the penitent must be *formal*, and not *presumed*, *free*, and not *recalled*. When the confessor has obtained this permission, he may inform the accomplice, etc. As a rule, however, it is not expedient to seek this permission. In cases of this kind it is better to advise the penitent to speak of these matters outside the confessional.

1380. *What is to be kept secret?* Everything heard in confession, the revealing of which would render the Sacrament odious, or result in harm to the penitent or to others (accomplices), is to be regarded as matter for secrecy. Hence matters for secrecy are: (1) All sins, even venial ones. To speak of sins known through some other channel is not to break the seal, although such conduct may easily result in scandal. Some persons, indeed, would be only too ready to believe that the priest is telling what he has heard in the sacramental forum, should he converse in this manner. (2) All the circumstances of sin, even those explained after the person has received absolution. (3) The object of sin, as, for instance, when a person states that he hates his father because of his evil conduct, the evil conduct of the father becomes a matter for secrecy. (4) The sins of the accomplice. (5) The penance imposed. (6) Anything that would hold the penitent up to ridicule, or that would deter the faithful from receiving the Sacraments, such as revealing natural defects, ignorance, inability, etc. (7) The virtues of the penitent, and even his confidences, if he has made them known in the confessional to acknowledge his ingratitude towards God. The same would not be true if he had acted in this way to reveal the state of his soul. (8) Scruples, if the knowledge of their existence would result in harm to the penitent, but not if they redounded to his praise. Sins committed in the confessional, such as impatience, etc., do not *per se* fall under the seal, although a confessor would be violating the seal *per accidens* if, by revealing them, he intimated that he had refused absolution, or something of this kind.

1381. Should the confessor notice at the very beginning of a confession that his penitent is deaf, he might tell him in a loud tone of voice to present himself at some other time or in some other place. Should he perceive the penitent's deafness only in the course of the confession, he should not tell him to come at some other time, for fear that those present might think that he had committed some serious fault. The best course to follow in this case would seem to be to absolve the penitent and enjoin a light penance (see no. 1095), or a grave penance by means of some sign.

1382. The act of confessing one's sins does not fall under the seal, unless the penitent makes his confession *incognito,* is desirous that no one know that he has had recourse to the Sacrament of Penance, or is afraid that he will be suspected of some serious crime. Refusal or deferring of absolution is matter for secrecy, but not the absolution itself. It is better, however, not to mention that one has given absolution to one person for fear of the implication that some one else has been refused. In hearing a person's confession before witnesses it is important that the confessor do not allow them to hear whether or not he is giving absolution. (See no. 1385.)

1383. If a penitent requests a note certifying that he has been to confession, the confessor should not state that he has absolved him if he has not. A confessor would not be acting prudently if he declared that he gave absolution to a person who really received it, because if the formula is changed for one who did *not* receive it, the secret would be violated. Nevertheless, if there existed printed certificates to the effect that the bearer had received absolution, the confessor could give one of these to a penitent who had been refused the Sacrament. If a penitent who is ill-disposed requests a certificate outside the confessional, the confessor may not refuse it, unless the confession was manifestly feigned. Should he request the certificate in the act of confession, the confessor may give him the same, provided he has accused himself of one sin and requires the certificate for some one of the usual reasons, as, for instance, before Easter or before marriage, etc. The confessor may also give the same certificate if he fears grave inconvenience from a refusal. In all other circumstances he should refuse to deliver a certificate even in the confessional. The formula that may be used on these occasions is: "I have heard the confession of N," with the signature and date appended.

1384. When is the secret violated? The secret of confession is violated *directly* when a person expressly reveals what is matter for secrecy. (See no. 1380.) The secret is violated indirectly when, through knowledge acquired in the confessional, a person says or does something which may, even unwittingly, give offense to the penitent or to others. In cases of doubt the safest course should always be followed. To violate the secret of the confessional, it is not necessary that the person to whom the confessor is speaking should know the person spoken about, but it is enough if the latter can be suspected.

1385. The seal may also be violated *indirectly*. This is done, for instance, when the confessor praises one of his penitents to the detriment of another; when he states concerning a thief that he confessed his sins of theft with great contrition; when he scolds a penitent or questions him concerning some of the circumstances of sins in such a manner that he can be heard by persons outside the confessional; when he discusses the sins of one of his penitents with another confessor who also knows of this penitent through confession; when, after hearing a few confessions, he states that he has absolved from such or such a sin; when he gives information touching certain sins in such wise that it is easy to suspect who committed them; when he states such or such a vice is rampant in such or such a convent, order, village not having more than 3000 members or inhabitants, respectively; when he looks down upon a penitent after having heard his confession and was not in the habit of doing so before; when he purposely avoids hearing his confession, or refuses him Communion, even occultly, because he knows through confession that he is not well disposed; when he scores special vices which only one or two persons in a community have confessed to him, at the risk of causing the latter serious inconvenience (the case would be different if he preached against certain ordinary vices committed by a number of penitents), and when, in consulting with some other priests, he offered explanations which clearly indicate the author of the crime. In the matter of consultation, it is better to have recourse to books than to individuals, or if this procedure is unsatisfactory, to seek out a priest to whom the penitent is unknown, or to ask the penitent's permission to consult with another, or to make the case a hypothetical one, or to ask the penitent to state his case to some other confessor. (See no. 1308.) A confessor violates the seal also when he hears a sin discussed that has been confessed to him, and leads the persons engaged in the discussion to think, even by his silence, that he is not completely ignorant of the facts, also when he makes use of information received in the confessional to direct those under his charge, as, for instance, when he does so to keep the unworthy out of office. If, however, this knowledge has come to him through other channels, too, the confessor may and must do his duty.

1386. The secret is not violated when the confessor makes nothing known, or causes the penitent no harm. Thus a confessor may make use of knowledge received in the confessional to pray for the penitent, to read certain books, to correct his own faults, or to fulfill the duties of his state of life with greater attention. Finally, it is better never to speak before laymen of sins heard in the confessional, even though there be no risk of the penitent suffering any inconvenience, because these matters can easily become a subject for scandal.

When a confessor speaks with the formal permission of

his penitent concerning sins heard in the confessional, he may and must state that he is speaking of things known through this channel and has his penitent's permission.

An instruction formulated by the Holy Office (1921) requires that Ordinaries and superiors of religious orders forbid their subjects to speak in private conversation, and even in their religious instructions and lectures on theology, of cases that have come to their attention through the confessional, even though it be certain that the persons cannot be identified. The reason for this measure is that the faithful are easily scandalized and do not relish the fact that their difficulties are aired, even though their names are not divulged.

According to the New Code, any confessor who directly violates the seal of confession incurs excommunication *latae sententiae,* very specially reserved to the Holy See.

CHAPTER III

THE SUBJECT OF PENANCE

1387. Any baptized person who has sinned is a subject for the Sacrament of Penance. This Sacrament is necessary for every man who has sinned mortally as a necessary means of forgiveness, in reality or at least in *desire.* This is *certain* and *proxima fidei* (*de fide* according to most theologians), for the Council of Trent says: "This Sacrament of Penance is necessary unto salvation for those who have fallen after baptism; as baptism itself is for those who have not as yet been regenerated." (Sess. 14, ch. 2.) There exists a grave obligation to receive it for those who have committed mortal sin, by divine precept, as we stated in no. 1068, and by ecclesiastical precept, as we shall see in no. 2990. This law is binding upon all adults, the deaf, the dumb, and idiots, as also upon all children who have reached the age of seven years. (See no. 1334 ff.) Hence, there is a counter-obligation binding all pastors to instruct these persons so that they may receive the Sacrament worthily. St. Alphonsus says that if pastors cannot have these persons instructed by others, they are obliged to do it themselves, no matter what the inconvenience (*cum quantocumque suo incommodo.*) "It is a very serious abuse," says Lehmkuhl, "for the pastor to defer hearing the confessions of children until the year in which they are to make their First Communion. He should hear them as soon as they are in danger of offending God and of remaining in sin, something which not infrequently happens before the age of seven, and even six." And he adds: "The pastor should see to it that little children who are seriously ill make all the acts of a Christian before dying, and he should not fail to give them absolution, either conditionally or unconditionally, no matter how he feels about their having sinned or not." (See no. 1093.)

1388. Every penitent must know that there is one God, whose Providence governs all things, who will reward the good in Heaven by the vision of Himself, and punish the wicked in hell. No confessor may give absolution to persons who are ignorant of the mysteries of the Blessed Trinity, the Incarnation, and the Redemption. The question has been asked if such an absolution would be valid. The matter is controverted, and in practice the safest course should be followed. (See no. 2205 ff.) It is not enough to know God through reason, but it is necessary to know Him as the Author of the supernatural order and the supernatural end of man. (See no. 2204.) The penitent should know, also, of the necessity of grace and prayer, and he is bound to have contrition, a firm purpose of amendment and satisfaction, at the risk of rendering the Sacrament null and void. He must have a sufficient knowledge of these dispositions and be resolved to learn what is necessary by necessity of precept.

FIFTH TREATISE

Extreme Unction

1389. Just as Confirmation completes the Sacrament of Baptism, so Extreme Unction completes the Sacrament of Penance. Extreme Unction is defined as a Sacrament of the New Law which, through the ministration of the priest, the anointing with the blessed oil, and the prescribed prayers, restores to the sick health of soul, and not infrequently also health of body. It is *of faith* that Extreme Unction is a Sacrament. (See nos. 756 and 776.) We shall treat, first, of the Sacrament itself; secondly, of the minister; and thirdly, of the subject.

CHAPTER I

THE SACRAMENT ITSELF

Art. I. Matter and Form.

1390. *The Matter.* The remote matter of this Sacrament is olive oil blessed by the bishop. This is *certain* from the words of the famous Decree to the Armenians. "Anointing him with oil in the name of the Lord" (James 5, 14.) The use of any other but olive oil would render the Sacrament invalid. It is necessary, too, that this oil be blessed by the bishop or by some priest delegated for that purpose by the Pope. (*C. J. C.*, can. 945.)

It is probable that the oil must be blessed in view of its

being used for the Sacrament of Extreme Unction, so that any other kind of oil, like Holy Chrism, for instance, which is blessed by the bishop, but not for the purpose of serving in the administration of Extreme Unction, can be used conditionally only in case of necessity when oil for the sick is not available. If, after administering the Sacrament in this way, the minister is able to secure some oil for the sick, he should readminister the Sacrament conditionally.

1391. The bishop blesses several kinds of oils on Holy Thursday: (1) The *Oil of the Sick,* which is the matter of Extreme Unction and serves also for the exterior anointing of bells; (2) the *Oil of Catechumens,* which is used to anoint catechumens on the breast and between the shoulders, the hands of those ordained to the priesthood, and the heads of kings; (3) *Holy Chrism,* which serves as matter of Confirmation, for the anointing which follows the administration of Baptism, for the interior anointing of bells, for the consecration of chalices, patens, altars, etc.

1392. It is probable that a single drop of oil suffices for the matter of this Sacrament; but in practice one should use more. According to general opinion, it suffices to dip the end of one's finger in the oil before each anointing. There is a grave obligation to renew the Holy Oils each year. The old oils, which may not be used except in default of the new, should be burned, and this can be done very conveniently in a lamp before the tabernacle. If there is not enough blessed oil, one may add a small quantity of oil that has not been blessed, and this mixture may be renewed several times a year if necessary.

1393. The *proximate matter* of this Sacrament is the anointing by the priest. According to the Ritual he must anoint: (1) the two eyes or the lids, (2) the two ears on the lobes or lower extremities, (3) the two nostrils, (4) the mouth, with a single unction on the closed lips, (5) the two hands, on the inside for laymen, and on the outside for priests, (6) the feet above or underneath the soles, whichever is most convenient. This last anointing should not be omitted without a reasonable cause. The anointing of the loins must always be omitted.

The anointing is administered in the same way to the dumb and the blind as to others; but, in the case of persons who are mutilated, the unction is applied to those parts nearest the missing organ. The priest must, under pain of venial sin, commence each anointing on the right side and make the sign of the Cross with his right thumb dipped in the Holy Oil. He should prolong the form in such a manner that it is completed only with the second anointing. After the second anointing the priest dries the places that have received the unctions with pellets of cotton, which he should be careful to take away and burn. The ashes should be thrown into the sacrarium. (See no. 1402.)

The Greeks apply the unctions to the forehead, the chin, the two cheeks, the breast, the hands and the feet.

1394. It is *certain* that it is not necessary for the validity of the Sacrament, (1) to administer it by physical contact of the hand; in times of pestilence one may anoint with a little stick dipped in the oil, which must be burnt afterwards; nor (2) to follow the usual order of the unctions. According to common opinion, however, it would be a grave fault to act otherwise without a sufficient reason.

Only one anointing of the lips is necessary, and many authors do not think it a grievous sin to disregard the order in the unctions, or to apply only one unction to each sense.

1395. Only one anointing is necessary for the validity of the Sacrament. Canon 947 declares that in case of necessity, only one unction need be applied to each sense, or, better still, to the forehead, together with the shorter form: *"Per istam sanctam unctionem indulgeat tibi Dominus quidquid deliquisti.*" It is true that a decree of the Sacred Congregation of March 9, 1917, demands that, if the danger has passed, all the unctions should be supplied without condition. (See also *C. J. C.*, can. 947.) This is not to insure the validity of the Sacrament, but to afford the sick person the spiritual benefits of cleansing and strength.

If the sick person happens to die while the unctions are being given, the priest may apply one single unction to the forehead, using the more general formula and with the condition: *"Si vivis."* If the sick person had already received one unction before breathing his last, the priest would not be bound to apply the others, but if he had not received any, it would be more proper for the priest to anoint at least the forehead with the short formula and without the condition: *"Si vivis."* The priest would not be bound to say the other prayers in this case.

1396. *The Form.* According to the Council of Trent and the Ritual, the form to be used is: *"Per istam sanctam unctionem et suam piissimam misericordiam indulgeat tibi Dominus quidquid per visum deliquisti"*; and the priest repeats it for each of the senses, saying (instead of *per visum*) *per auditum, per odoratum, per gustum et locutionem, per tactum, per gressum.* The following words, at least, are essential to the form: *"Per istam unctionem indulgeat tibi Dominus quidquid deliquisti."* The sick person or those attending him answer: *Amen.* The form should be deprecative, for, according to common opinion, the Sacrament would be invalid if it were indicative or imperative. In any case one may omit the prayers which precede the form. If death is imminent, only one form need be used, as we have stated in no. 1395. If the priest has time, he is bound to recite these prayers under pain of mortal sin, but if the sick person should happen to die while the unctions are being applied, the priest should not continue. If the priest should die in the act of applying the unctions, the priest who is called to take his place should not repeat the unctions already made, unless a quarter of an hour has passed. In this latter case he should repeat the unctions conditionally.

Art. II. Institution by Christ.

1397. It is an article of faith that Jesus Christ instituted this Sacrament, as we have stated above in no. 756; and St. James has thus promulgated it: "Is any man sick among you? Let him bring in the priests of the Church; and let them pray over him, anointing him with oil in the name of the Lord. And the prayer of faith shall save the sick man, and the Lord shall raise him up; and if he be in sins, they shall be forgiven him." (James 5, 14–15.) According to the most general opinion, Jesus Christ instituted this Sacrament after the Resurrection.

Art. III. Effects of Extreme Unction.

1398. There are five effects: (1) an increase of sanctifying grace; this is *of faith,* since Extreme Unction is a Sacrament of the living; (2) the remission of sins; this is also *of faith,* according to the text of St. James (see no. 1397.) Extreme Unction remits both venial and mortal sins; it remits venial sins *per se;* but some affirm that it remits mortal sins by its own efficacy; others, that it remits them only *per accidens.* Both opinions are probable.

Those who teach that this Sacrament remits mortal sins, not *per accidens,* but *per se,* affirm that it remits them not directly, but indirectly, because (3) this Sacrament remits part of the punishment due to sin, and the remains of sin, *i. e.,* debility for good, spiritual torpor, attachment to sensible things, distrust, anxiety, etc. But the remains of sin cannot be removed unless the sin itself is taken away. (4) It comforts the soul and gives it courage for the final struggle; this is *certain* and *proxima fidei*. (5) This Sacrament sometimes gives health. This, too, is *certain* and *proxima fidei*. Extreme Unction does not, however, restore health infallibly, but creates a well-founded hope if its administration is not deferred until only a miracle can save the life of the sick person. A person acts neither according to reason nor to faith when he awaits the last agony before receiving this Sacrament.

1399. *Does each anointing produce grace?* Some affirm that it does, others that it does not; and the latter say that grace is produced only at the last anointing. There are many anointings, but there is only one Sacrament, the effects of which, if impeded by some obstacle, are revived after this obstacle has been removed, as stated in no. 779 ff.

CHAPTER II

THE MINISTER

1400. The minister of Extreme Unction is the priest. This is *of faith*, according to the text of St. James, cited in no. 1397, and the Council of Trent: "If anyone says that the priest alone is not the proper minister of Extreme Unction; let him be anathema." (Sess. 14, can. 4.)

If several priests simultaneously applied the unction to the different senses of the same sick person, using the proper form, the Sacrament would be valid, but gravely illicit, except in case of necessity; but it would be invalid if one priest pronounced the words while another applied the oil. Among the Greeks, seven or three priests administer the unctions to the sick. Jurisdiction is not necessary to administer this Sacrament; the power of orders suffices. Every priest, then, even one excommunicated, may give Extreme Unction validly; but only the priest delegated by the pastor may give it licitly; and, except in case of necessity, he who administers the Sacrament without this delegation, at least presumed, sins seriously.

Every priest may administer this Sacrament licitly when the pastor or his delegate is absent or incapacitated; moreover, he is bound to administer it *sub levi*, when the necessity is ordinary, and *sub gravi* in a grave spiritual necessity. In case of necessity, permission may be presumed; but, aside from this case, it should not be presumed too readily.

In all clerical religious communities the superior has the right and the duty, either in person or by another, to administer the Holy Viaticum and Extreme Unction to the professed, the novices, and others who live day and night in the religious house, either as servants or for the purpose of education, or as guests or convalescents.

In the houses of nuns with solemn vows, the ordinary confessor, or the one who takes his place, has the same right.

In other lay congregations and Orders this right and duty belongs to the pastor, or to the chaplain to whom the Ordinary has given full parochial powers. (*C. J. C.*, can. 514.)

1401. What is the obligation of administering this Sacrament? It is grave and *ex justitia* for the pastor. This is *certain*. Moreover, the Roman Catechism says "that they sin *very grievously* who delay in administering Extreme Unction to a sick person, until he has lost hope of recovery and begins to lose the use of his senses and even life itself." They should administer it as soon as there is danger, and not await the moment of death. (See nos. 2435 and 3680.)

It is a salutary practice to administer Extreme Unction after the Holy Viaticum. Lehmkuhl says that a pastor sins grievously who does not put forth a discreet effort to warn the negligent sick in time, and to fortify them by this sacrament. (See no. 1403.)

1402. *How should it be administered?* There is an obligation *sub levi* to administer Extreme Unction after the Viaticum, repeating the *Confiteor*, but if the sick person is unable to receive, the priest must give him Extreme Unction. Except in urgent cases, the priest is required *sub gravi* to wear the surplice and the stole; he should, *sub levi*, have a wax candle and a server. Women should be barred as servers, and if the priest is alone, he should answer the prayers himself. It is a venial fault to omit the sign of the Cross in applying the unctions; but it would be a grave fault to omit the prayers, except in case of necessity. The Holy Oils are not to be carried in solemn procession like the Viaticum, yet not with any undue secrecy, unless prudence demands it. The priest need put on his vestments only in the sickroom. Usually he should not keep the Holy Oils in the rectory, at least when the church is not far away, and yet the pastor should keep the Holy Oils during the night when he foresees that a sick person will be in danger. As a rule the Holy Oils should be kept in the sacristy in a place set aside for that purpose, or in the church in a little case, but never in the tabernacle. The pellets of cotton, the crumbs of bread, and the ablution water, should be thrown into the fire, not by laymen, but by the priest or the server.

CHAPTER III

THE SUBJECT

1403. Every baptized person who has had the use of reason for some time, and who is dangerously ill, is a subject for Extreme Unction. A condemned criminal is not a subject, and neither is a woman in confinement, unless illness follows, nor a soldier before battle. And yet, the Sacrament should be given to those who have been poisoned, to a person who, being ill, must submit to a surgical operation which he will probably not survive, and to old and decrepit persons. All admit that this Sacrament is not necessary as a means of salvation; but it is certainly of precept, and the obligation becomes grave: (1) when a sick person in the state of mortal sin cannot receive the other Sacraments; (2) if, by refusing it, he would give great scandal; (3) if he refuses it contemptuously. Excluding these cases, is there an obligation *sub gravi* to receive Extreme Unction? This is disputed; some reply in the affirmative, others in the negative. At all events, as Lehmkuhl remarks, parents, children, husbands, and wives sin grievously who do not inform the sick person of his true state, so that he may prepare for death, and who will not warn him themselves or allow the doctor or the priest to do so. (See no. 1401.)

1404. Extreme Unction may and must be given to dangerously ill adults immediately after Baptism, to remit the remains of sins committed before Baptism, which remains Baptism does not remit, and also to strengthen the sick. But Extreme Unction should not be given to children who have not the use of reason, nor to those who have always been feeble-minded. One can and ought to give it to children under seven, who have the use of reason, as Pope Benedict XIV teaches. If the priest doubts whether or not they have the use of reason, he may anoint them with this condition: "*Si capax es.*" The duty of administering this Sacrament is very grave, when the priest cannot help by the surer method of absolution, poor children who have sinned. The Sacrament should also be given to the blind, the deaf, the dumb, the insane who have had lucid intervals, unless they are inclined to commit actions that would bring dishonor upon the Sacrament. But if this inconvenience can be avoided by holding or tying the patients, the Sacrament may be administered to them. If the priest doubts whether they have had lucid intervals, he may give them the Sacrament conditionally. In like manner he may administer it to persons in delirium, taking care to remove the risk of irreverence towards the Sacrament. Extreme Unction may be administered unconditionally to those who have lost the use of their senses, if they have led Christian lives, and conditionally, if they have lost the use of their senses in the very act of sin, like drunkards, persons who have been wounded in a quarrel, those who have only doubtful dispositions, or are heretics in good faith. According to Lehmkuhl, this Sacrament is a surer means of salvation than Penance and the Holy Eucharist for those who are deprived of the use of their senses and do not give signs of repentance, provided they have attrition.

Extreme Unction should not be given to the excommunicated unless they have previously received absolution from their excommunication and from their sins, at least conditionally. It is more probable, however, that one may administer this Sacrament to those who have lost the use of their senses in the act of sin, as, for instance, in a duel.

It should not be administered to those who, being impenitent and obstinate, openly persevere in mortal sin; but if in doubt, one may give it to them conditionally. (See *C. J. C.*, can. 942.) Doubt is not utterly impossible when a person has often refused the Sacraments while conscious.

It is often necessary to refrain from administering this Sacrament, especially before witnesses, to those who have refused it up to the time of their agony, if they do not give some sign of repentance, and if to administer it might bring contempt on the Sacrament. We should observe that the priest must never give Extreme Unction under this condition: *"Si tu es dispositus,"* not even mentally. Other conditions which concern validity may be used, for example: *"Si tu es capax."* The sick person must be well prepared; but when the priest can determine nothing more than that the patient is not ill-disposed, he may give him Extreme Unction unconditionally. (See no. 768.) If, by chance, he is ill-disposed at that moment, the effects of the Sacrament will revive when he repents. The Sacrament would be administered invalidly to a person only slightly ill. In a serious illness, but in absence of the danger of death, it would be administered validly but illicitly. In short, it is given validly and licitly, not only at the moment of death, but even in every probable danger of death. Missionaries who, in their long journeys, meet persons sick with fever or some other disease lasting several months, may give them Extreme Unction and the Viaticum when they foresee that the patients will die during the year and they will not be able to be with them at that time.

1405. Extreme Unction may be given several times to the same sick person, in different or in successive maladies; but it may not be re-administered in the same illness, even if the patient seems better during four or five days. In a prolonged illness, if he seems better during one month and is believed to be out of danger, the Sacrament may be re-administered should he have a relapse. If one doubts positively that the state of the sickness has changed, it is likewise necessary to re-administer the Sacrament, but conditionally. Some writers of authority think that this Sacrament may be given anew—not the same day, to be sure, but after a week has passed—if a new sickness is joined to the first, thereby adding a new peril, as, for example, if apoplexy should combine with consumption.

One should avoid assuming too quickly that the soul has departed from the sick person. Only stiffness of the body and the beginnings of putrefaction constitute certain signs of death; consequently, one may apply the unctions conditionally to a sick person who does not show these signs, especially if a physician has not pronounced him dead, unless in doing so the priest would arouse contempt for the Sacrament among the spectators.

1406. *Which are the dispositions required?* (1) Interpretative intention suffices, as we have said in no. 812; (2) the reception of the Sacrament of Penance, or at least contrition, since this is a Sacrament of the living; Extreme Unction produces its fruits, however, when it is received by one who cannot confess, but who has only attrition; (3) the reception of the Holy Eucharist, if possible. The other dispositions, such as firm faith, a desire to live in conformity with the will of God, help this Sacrament to produce greater fruits, but are not absolutely necessary. (See no. 776.)

SIXTH TREATISE

The Sacrament of Holy Orders

1407. The word *Order* is generally used to indicate the rank of clerics who have been consecrated to carry out the different functions of the Church. In this treatise, the word *Order* signifies the sacred rite by which the power to carry out these functions and the grace to do this well are conferred. Understood in this sense, Orders is a Sacrament of the New Law in virtue of which man receives a spiritual power, coupled with the grace to carry out ecclesiastical functions well. It is *of faith* that Holy Orders is a Sacrament. (See no. 756.) We shall treat, first, of the different Orders themselves; secondly, of the minister of this Sacrament; and thirdly, of the subject.

CHAPTER I

THE DIFFERENT ORDERS IN THEMSELVES

1408. We must first observe that *tonsure* is not an Order, notwithstanding the opinion of certain writers to the contrary. It is an ecclesiastical ceremony, and according to some was instituted by St. Peter, according to others, by some ecclesiastic not antedating the third century. The bishop may confer tonsure outside the confines of his diocese, but if he does so, he may not use the insignia of his office.

1409. By the ceremony of tonsure, a man passes from the lay to the ecclesiastical state, in other words, he casts his lot with God, consecrates himself to His service, and, at least probably, assumes *sub levi* the obligation of wearing the tonsure and the ecclesiastical garb. He is certainly obliged *sub gravi* to wear the ecclesiastical garb if, together with the office, he receives a benefice. A tonsured cleric is capable of receiving ecclesiastical jurisdiction and a benefice; he has also the privileges of the forum and the canon (see no. 3576) and is bound to observe all the rules of conduct prescribed by the Church for ecclesiastics. (See no. 3538.) A person who received minor Orders without first receiving tonsure would sin grievously, but he would not need to be tonsured before receiving further promotion.

1410. The bishop confers tonsure by clipping the hair of the candidate to indicate that he must renounce the vanities of this world. He cuts it in the form of a crown, in memory of Christ's crown of thorns, and to remind the recipient of his royal dignity. The cleric is, then, clothed in a new garb symbolical of his renouncement of the world, and in a white surplice to signify the unblemished purity which must be his. The surplice may be worn by laymen, but the latter may never wear the alb, the dalmatic, or the cope, even though they be regulars.

1411. It is *of faith* that there exist several Orders in the Church: "If any one saith, that, besides the priesthood, there are not in the Catholic Church other Orders, both major and minor; let him be anathema." (C. of Trent, Sess. 23, can. 2.)

Nevertheless, there are not several Sacraments of Orders, but only one, since all have reference to the same end, which is power over the real body of Jesus Christ in the Holy Eucharist, and over His mystical body in the administration of the Sacrament of Penance. This power is vested in its entirety in the priesthood and in the other Orders only in part.

1412. The Council of Trent enumerates among the minor

Orders those of Acolyte, Exorcist, Reader, and Porter, called minor because they communicate the power to minister only remotely to the priest; and among the major Orders those of Subdiaconate, Diaconate, and Priesthood. According to common opinion today, the episcopacy is an order distinct from the priesthood. (In the Greek Church the subdiaconate is a minor Order.)

It is controverted whether or not the minor Orders and the major Order of the subdiaconate are sacraments. Theologians who follow St. Thomas affirm that they are, those who follow St. Alphonsus state that they are not.

Art. I. Minor Orders.

1413. *The Order of Porter*. This Order confers the right *ex officio* to open, close, and guard the doors of the church. The Porter has in his keeping the sacred vessels, rings the bells, ejects from the church unworthy persons, infidels, non-tolerated heretics, denounced excommunicated persons and those under the interdict. These persons may listen to the sermon, but they may not assist at the Sacrifice of the Mass.

1414. *The matter*. The remote matter, according to some writers, is any sort of keys, and this is the opinion of the Sacred Congregation of the Penitentiary. According to others, it is the keys of the church, made from any kind of material, provided they open the door. In practice it is better to follow the second opinion. One key alone suffices for validity. The bell is not matter for the Sacrament.

1415. The proximate matter is the tradition of the key or keys by the ordaining minister himself. It is controverted whether or not the keys must be touched by the candidate physically or merely morally. In practice, physical contact with the keys is required as being the safer course.

1416. *The form*. The form is contained in these words: *"Sic age, quasi Deo redditurus rationem pro his rebus, quae his clavibus recluduntur."* In the ceremony of opening and closing the door it is not necessary that the candidate open and close it with the key.

The special virtue to be practiced by the Porter is found in the Scriptural text: *"Zelus domus tuae comedit me."*

1417. *The Order of Reader.* This Order gives the candidate the spiritual power to read the Sacred Scriptures aloud in church. The Reader must read principally the lessons of the First Nocturn and the prophecies at Mass. He is also required to sing in church, instruct children and the ignorant in the rudiments of the Christian faith, and, finally, bless the bread and the new fruits.

1418. The *remote matter* is the Missal, the Breviary, or the Holy Bible, but not any ordinary book. The *proximate matter* is the tradition of this book.

1419. The *form* is contained in these words: *"Accipe et esto verbi Dei relator habiturus, si fideliter et utiliter officium tuum impleveris, partem cum iis, qui verbum Dei bene ministraverunt ab initio."*

1420. The virtues to be particularly emphasized by the Reader are special devotion towards Holy Scripture and the truths of religion, and zeal in the instruction of the ignorant.

1421. *The Order of Exorcist.* This Order gives the spiritual power of expelling devils from the bodies of the possessed. The chief function of the exorcist is to expel devils from bodies by the imposition of hands and special exorcisms. The priest alone is commissioned to expel the devil from the soul through the administration of Baptism. Today no exorcist may conduct solemn exorcisms in public, using the formula set aside for that purpose by the Roman Ritual, without the express permission of the bishop. To act otherwise would be to commit a very grave sin. The exorcist may, however, conduct private exorcisms. (See nos. 460 and 1345.) He must also prepare the water and the salt for the blessing of Holy Water, and invite those who are not to receive Holy Communion to yield their places to those who are.

1422. The *remote matter* is the Book of Exorcisms, the Ritual, the Missal or the Pontifical; the *proximate matter*, the tradition of this book.

The *form* is contained in these words: *"Accipe et commenda memoriae, et habe potestatem manus imponendi, super energumenos, sive baptizatos, sive catechumenos."*

1423. The principal virtues of the exorcist are: hatred of sin, mortification, and a spirit of prayer.

1424. *The Order of Acolyte.* This Order bestows the spiritual power to carry the cruets and the candlesticks, and also to light the candles on the altar. The chief function of the acolyte is to prepare the wine and water for the Holy Sacrifice, to carry the candlesticks, and to assist the subdeacon and the deacon at the altar.

1425. The essential *remote matter* is twofold: (1) the candlestick with an unlighted candle; (2) empty cruets. An ordinary candlestick could not be used as matter for the Sacrament. The *proximate matter* is the tradition of the remote matter. The ordination is completed and the character imprinted—if any character is imprinted at all—by the tradition of the second matter, which is more noble in character because closer to the Blessed Sacrament. The ordination would be valid but illicit, if the cruets were filled and the candle lighted.

The *form* is twofold. The first is contained in these words: *"Accipe ceroferarium cum cereo, ut scias te, ad accendenda ecclesiae luminaria, mancipari, in nomine Domini,"* and the second in these: *"Accipe urceolos ad suggerendum vinum et aquam in Eucharistiam Sanguinis Christi, in nomine Domini."*

1426. The virtues of the acolyte are contained in these words, which the bishop addresses to the recipient: "Walk then as children of light. . . . Be, therefore, solicitous in all justice and goodness and truth, to enlighten yourselves and others and the Church of God."

Art. II. Major Orders.

1427. *The Subdiaconate.* The subdiaconate is not a sacred Order among the Greeks, but has been regarded as such among the Latins from the twelfth century on. In this century the custom was introduced of raising subdeacons to the episcopacy without dispensation, and so the Order was regarded as a sacred one. It is defined as a major Order which gives the spiritual power of carrying the chalice to the altar, of assisting the deacon, and of singing the Epistle at the solemn Mass. The subdeacon also carries the cross in processions and washes the palls and corporals.

1428. The *remote matter* is twofold and both are essential according to common opinion. The first is an empty chalice and paten. If there were wine in the chalice, the ordination would probably be invalid and would have to be repeated. Both the chalice and the paten must be consecrated, according to a few writers, whose opinion should be followed in practice. The second is the Book of the Epistles, the Missal, the Breviary or the Holy Bible.

The *proximate matter* is the tradition of the remote matter, and among the Greeks, the imposition of hands.

1429. The *form* is also twofold. The first is contained in these words: *"Videte cujus ministerium vobis exhibeatis, ut Deo placere possitis,"* and the second in these: *"Accipite librum epistolarum, et habete potestatem legendi eas, in Ecclesia sancta Dei, tam pro vivis, quam pro defunctis, in nomine Patris,"* etc.

1430. The subdiaconate imposes upon the person receiving it the obligation of wearing the ecclesiastical garb, of celibacy and perpetual chastity, and also of reciting the

Divine Office. Very probably also this Order imposes the obligation of wearing the tonsure. In the ceremony of ordination, the candidate is required to take the vow of chastity. (See nos. 3541 and 3563.)

1431. It is controverted whether or not the deacon and the subdeacon sin grievously when exercising their solemn functions in the state of mortal sin. Some affirm, others deny it.

1432. The virtues of the subdeacon are expressed in these words of the Pontifical: "If hitherto you have been remiss in coming to church, be henceforth diligent; if hitherto drowsy, be henceforth wakeful; if hitherto given to drink, be henceforth sober; if hitherto lacking in purity, be henceforth chaste." (B. of O., p. 38.)

They are also indicated by the vestments which he receives —the amice symbolizing the purification of the tongue; the alb, chastity; the maniple, the fruit of good works; and the tunic, holy joy.

1433. *The Diaconate.* The diaconate is a Sacrament of the New Law which gives the spiritual power immediately to assist the priest at Mass, to offer with him the paten and the host, and the chalice and the wine, to read the Gospel, and, with the permission of the Ordinary or the pastor, to preach to the people. In cases of necessity the deacon may also administer solemn Baptism and the Holy Eucharist, but to act in this capacity he must have the special permission of the pastor or the Ordinary. To do so licitly, it is enough if the pastor be prevented, and there be some one to be baptized or to receive Holy Communion. In danger of death, this permission is not required, except for solemn Baptism. (See nos. 839 and 908.) The deacon may also carry the Blessed Sacrament in the ciborium or the ostensorium.

1434. It is *certain* that the diaconate is a Sacrament. Some theologians are of the opinion that this is a truth *proxima fidei.* There is the sensible sign, the institution by Christ, and the production of grace.

The sensible sign is the matter, and although some regard the imposition of hands as the sole essential matter for the diaconate, since it alone is used by the Greeks both for the diaconate and the subdiaconate, according to the safer opinion, the Sacrament consists of two matters: (a) the imposition of the right hand of the bishop, who must physically touch the candidate (a ceremony which must be repeated together with the form if there was no physical contact the first time), and (b) the tradition of the Gospel Book, the Holy Bible or the Missal to the recipient, who must touch it physically (this ceremony must also be repeated if there was no physical contact the first time).

The *form* is also twofold. For the first matter it consists in these words: *"Accipe Spiritum Sanctum ad robur, et ad resistendum diabolo et tentationibus ejus, in nomine Domini;"* and for the second in these: *"Accipe potestatem legendi evangelium in ecclesia Dei, tam pro vivis quam pro defunctis in nomine Domini."* According to a probable opinion, only the second matter imprints the character.

1435. The diaconate was instituted by Jesus Christ, for the Council of Trent explicitly states: "If anyone saith, that in the Catholic Church there is not a hierarchy instituted by divine ordination, consisting of bishops, priests, and ministers; let him be anathema." (Sess. 23, can. 6.) According to some writers, Jesus Christ instituted the diaconate at the Last Supper; according to others, after the Resurrection.

1436. In the diaconate, there is also produced grace. The Council of Trent defines that it is not in vain that the bishop says: "Receive ye the Holy Ghost" (Sess. 23, can. 4.) Moreover, the diaconate imprints a character. (See no. 1444.)

1437. The virtues of the deacon are courage and zeal in preaching the word of God; obedience to the Gospel, symbolized by the stole which signifies the yoke of the Lord; a life without blemish and charity towards the poor, symbolized by the dalmatic. The first office assigned to the deacons, indeed, was ministering to the poor.

1438. Deaconesses, who formerly received some sort of ceremonial but not sacramental consecration through the imposition of hands, stood guard at the doors of the church through which the women entered. They also prepared women for Baptism and assisted the priests in administering it to them.

1439. *The Priesthood.* This Order gives the spiritual power to consecrate the body and blood of Jesus Christ and to absolve the faithful from their sins. It is *of faith* that this Order is a Sacrament; see the Council of Trent (Sess. 23, can. 1–4; cfr. no. 756.)

1440. *The sensible sign.* According to the more probable opinion, the only essential matter is the second imposition of hands by the bishop, for this is the only matter used by the Greeks. But there is a probable opinion maintaining that the first imposition of hands is necessary for the Sacrament, because the bishop must touch the candidate physically. In matter of fact, the Holy Office has decreed that an ordination in which the bishop has failed to touch the candidate physically must be repeated *sub conditione*. It was also decided, in 1900, that an ordination in which the bishop had omitted the first two impositions, but had made them after the Communion, should be repeated. Another probable opinion maintains that the tradition of the chalice with the wine and the paten with the host is the only essential matter. According to some, the sacred vessels must be consecrated. Finally, a fourth opinion maintains that the tradition of instruments is essential, and also the third imposition of hands by the bishop. In practice, the safest opinion should be followed.

Three matters are, therefore, indispensable: the first imposition of hands by physical contact, the second imposition of hands, the tradition of instruments, and the third imposition of hands.

A similar controversy exists in regard to the form. In practice, it is better to use the formula which accompanies the second imposition of hands, *viz.: "Oremus, fratres carissimi, Deum Patrem omnipotentem,"* etc. Lehmkuhl, however, is of the opinion that the form is more probably the prayer *"Exaudi"* with the Preface which follows; the second with the placing of the instruments in the hands of the candidate: *"Accipe potestatem offerre sacrificium Deo, missasque celebrare, tam pro vivis, quam pro defunctis, in nomine Domini";* the third accompanies the third imposition of hands, which must establish physical contact with the candidate (see no. 1434): *"Accipe Spiritum Sanctum, quorum remiseris peccata, remittuntur eis; et quorum retinueris, retenta sunt."*

It is a controverted point whether or not the ordination of a Latin subject according to the Greek rite would be valid, but it is certain that the ordination of Greeks is valid, irrespectively of the rite followed.

1441. For the ordination of a priest to be valid, it is essential that the bishop present to him, together with the chalice and the paten, at one and the same time the species of bread and wine which are the integral parts of the Sacrifice, given that the power to offer the Sacrifice is indivisible. According to the safest opinion, the chalice and the paten must be consecrated, but some writers do not make this a requirement. If there were no host on the paten and no wine in the chalice, the entire ordination ceremony would have to be repeated, and the same would be true if there were any doubt concerning the tradition of instruments in the ordination to the subdiaconate, the diaconate, the priesthood, and the episcopacy. In the case of minor Orders, comprised within the other Orders, it would not be necessary to repeat the ordination ceremony.

For the ordination of a priest to be valid, it is essential, according to a probable opinion, that the candidate should touch both the chalice and the paten, although the Holy Office has declared valid the ordination of a priest who touches only the paten and the host, but not the chalice. Very probably, also, the ordination would be valid if the candidate touched the chalice with the host, but not with the paten; or with the paten, but not with the host, although St. Alphonsus is of the opinion that it would be more prudent to repeat the ordination in this case. In ordinations to the other Orders, several candidates are permitted to touch the instruments at one and the same time, but not in an ordination to the priesthood. (See no. 1414.) Although certain rites are not essential, they oblige *sub gravi*. Such are the anointing of the hands, the tradition of the vestments, the recitation of the Canon together with the bishop. Then again, some rites are so indispensable that, if they have been omitted, they must be supplied after the ordination ceremony. We shall treat of the latter in the next number.

1442. Essential mistakes regarding matter and form must be rectified *sub gravi*. The entire ordination must be repeated if these mistakes affect the power over the real body of Christ, which power is given in the first and second imposition of hands and the tradition of the instruments. If these mistakes affect only the power over the *mystical* body of Christ, which power is given in the third imposition of hands, it is not necessary to repeat the entire ordination, but only this latter part, in which case the ordination need not be completed by the bishop who left it incomplete. According to common opinion, an ordination that is certainly invalid may not be repeated except in the next ordination;

but if it is merely doubtful, it may be repeated within a few days, or at any time.

If the mistakes are accidental and of less importance, as when the newly ordained priest fails to read the Canon, nothing need be supplied; but if they are serious, as when the candidate does not consecrate together with the bishop, or the bishop fails to anoint the recipient's hands, these rites must be supplied, otherwise the newly ordained priest sins grievously both in neglecting to have the ceremonies supplied and later on in exercising the functions of his Order. According to the opinion of St. Alphonsus, the rites may be supplied at any time and on any day. If instead of using the Oil of the Catechumens in the anointing, the bishop used Holy Chrism, this rite need not be repeated.

1443. The priesthood was instituted by Jesus Christ. This is *of faith,* for the Council of Trent says that, at the Last Supper, Christ instituted the priests of the New Testament and commanded them to offer the Holy Sacrifice by these words: "Do this in commemoration of me." He gave these same priests the power to absolve from sin, after His Resurrection, as we saw above (no. 1217).

1444. Holy Orders produces second sanctifying grace because it is a Sacrament of the living. It is *of faith* that the priesthood produces this grace: "I admonish thee, that thou stir up the grace of God which is in thee, by the imposition of hands" (2 Tim. 1, 6.) It is *certain* that this grace is produced by the diaconate, as stated in no. 1434. For the other Orders, the question is controverted.

The priesthood and the diaconate also give sacramental graces. It is *of faith* that the priesthood imprints a character, *certain* that the diaconate does, and *probable* that the other Orders do. All writers are agreed that the latter confer at least an ecclesiastical character, similar to a scholastic degree conferred by some institution of learning. For this reason, no Order is conferred upon the same candidate a second time. Each order gives the recipient the right to exercise the functions proper to it.

1445. The virtues of the priest are those practiced by Our Lord Himself.

1446. *The Episcopacy.* The episcopacy is an Order which gives the spiritual power to confirm the faithful, ordain the ministers of the Sacraments, and consecrate objects destined for divine worship. The bishop consecrates kings, virgins, altars, the Holy Oils, and Holy Chrism; he blesses abbots, pronounces solemn benedictions, and is a judge in matters of faith.

Is the episcopacy a Sacrament distinct from the priesthood? Formerly this question was a controverted one, but the opinion commonly accepted today, and which must be followed, is that it is a Sacrament distinct from the priesthood, and that it imprints a special character. It is a settled matter that the episcopacy produces an increase of grace other than that given by the priesthood, and that it gives more extensive powers than those communicated by the latter. Episcopal consecration is reserved to the Holy Father, and no other bishop may licitly confer it without special delegation from him.

1447. The essential matter is certainly the imposition of hands by the consecrating bishop, and probably also the imposition of the Gospel Book on the head and shoulders of the candidate, the anointing of his head with Holy Chrism, the tradition of the ring and the crozier, and physical contact between the consecrating minister and the recipient of the Order.

The forms are the words which accompany these different matters. It is *certain* that the consecration of a bishop is valid, even though the two assistant consecrating bishops are not present, provided a dispensation has been obtained from the Holy See, without which it would be certainly illicit, but more probably valid. It is controverted whether or not the episcopal consecration of a deacon would be valid. The more probable opinion maintains that it would not be.

1448. The divine institution of the episcopacy is *of faith;* it took place at the Last Supper. The production of grace is proved from the Council of Trent, which defines that the consecrating minister does not say in vain: *"Accipe Spiritum sanctum."*

1449. *The Sovereign Pontiff.* The supreme office of Sovereign Pontiff does not confer any spiritual power superior to that of the bishop, but immediately after his election and before his elevation and solemn consecration (which is not a Sacrament), the Sovereign Pontiff acquires complete jurisdiction over the universal Church, just as the Ordinary acquires his jurisdiction before his consecration.

It is controverted whether or not the Pope may chose his successor. Some writers assert that he may, others that he may not. According to Suarez, the Pope would be acting within the limits of his power in providing a special method of electing his own successor in a case of clear and urgent necessity. According to the common law, the cardinals, at least those who are deacons, elect the Pope. All, even those who may be excommunicated, must be convoked to the secret conclave, and the election must take place by ballot, compromise, or inspiration. (See no. 3488.)

CHAPTER II

THE MINISTER OF THE SACRAMENT OF ORDERS

Art. I. Who is this Minister?

1450. The consecrated bishop is the ordinary minister of the Sacrament of Orders. This is *of faith,* from the words of the Council of Trent: "If anyone saith, that . . . bishops have not the power of ordaining; or that the power which they possess is common to them and to priests; let him be anathema." (Sess. 23, can. 7.) But since this power is one of Orders and not of jurisdiction, it follows that every bishop, even though heretical, may ordain validly. This is why the ordinations of the Greek schismatics and the Jansenists are held to be valid. Leo XIII declared all Anglican orders invalid because of a substantial change in the rite of ordination. The ordinations of the Protestant bishops of Germany, Norway, Sweden, and Denmark are also regarded as invalid. Vicars and prefects Apostolic, abbots and other prelates *nullius* have the same power to ordain as diocesan bishops, if they are vested with the episcopal character.

The extraordinary minister of this Sacrament is the simple priest who, by law or Apostolic indult, has the power to confer certain Orders. Even though they be not bishops, Cardinals may confer tonsure and minor orders throughout the entire world to candidates presenting dimissorial letters from their respective bishops. Ruling abbots who are priests and have lawfully received the abbatial blessing, may give tonsure and minor Orders to those of their religious subjects who are at least simply professed. Vicars and prefects Apostolic who have not the episcopal character, have the same power in regard to their secular subjects, and even in regard to other candidates, provided these present dimissorial letters from their respective Ordinaries. The power of these prelates does not, however, extend beyond the time and place of their mission. A priest who transcends his power in conferring an Order, acts invalidly, whereas a bishop who acts in the same fashion always ordains validly. (*C. J. C.*, can. 951 ff.) If a priest is not vested with the episcopal character, he can never validly ordain another priest, even with Apostolic delegation; although with this same delegation, he may ordain a subdeacon and probably also a deacon.

Art. II. Conditions for the Licit Administration of this Sacrament.

1451. The bishop must have ordinary or delegated jurisdiction over the candidate. Canon Law states that the proper bishop in the case of the ordination of secular priests is he in whose diocese the candidate has a domicile together with his place of birth, or only a domicile without place of birth. In the first case, the candidate must have been born in the diocese, because his father, or—in case he is an illegitimate child—his mother had a domicile there at the time of his birth. In the second case, the candidate must have lived ten years in the diocese, or at least must live there at present, and have the intention of remaining there as far as can reasonably be foreseen. In both cases the candidate must take an oath that he intends to remain attached to the diocese. This oath is not necessary in the case of a cleric who has already been incorporated into the diocese by tonsure, or in that of an alumnus who is destined for another diocese, or in that of a professed religious. (*C. J. C.*, can. 956.)

1452. The bishop acquires delegated jurisdiction over a candidate through dimissorial letters required by law. The person who issues dimissorial letters may himself ordain candidates, if he has the episcopal character, and, as a general rule, the local Ordinary must ordain his own subjects. For a sufficient reason, however, the local Ordinary may examine his own subjects and have them ordained by some other bishop.

Dimissorial letters confer upon the bishop delegated jurisdiction, in virtue of which he may give tonsure and the other Orders, but not dispense from canonical impediments.

The pope may issue dimissorial letters throughout the Church; the bishop may issue them in his own diocese, as soon as he has taken possession, even though he is not yet consecrated. The vicar-general may issue them by special mandate of the bishop; and the vicar-capitular, with the consent of the chapter, after the see has been vacant for one year. Before the end of this year, he may give dimissorial letters only to those who must be ordained on account of some benefice they have received, or are to receive, or on account of an office which the needs of the diocese require to be filled.

Dimissorial letters should not be issued until all the prescribed testimonial letters have been received, in accordance with canons 993–1000. If, after the Ordinary has issued dimissorial letters, a sufficient period of time elapses to contract an impediment, the bishop should not proceed with the ordination until he has received new testimonial letters; but if the candidate has lived in the diocese of the bishop ordaining him, the latter himself should collect the testimonials.

The proper Ordinary may send dimissorial letters to any bishop in communion with the Holy See, with the exception of a bishop of a different rite. To send them to a bishop of a different rite, the Ordinary must have an Apostolic indult. Any bishop may licitly ordain a non-subject who presents dimissorial letters, provided he has no reason to doubt the authenticity of the documents.

No one is allowed, without a special Apostolic indult, to promote to higher Orders a cleric who has received some Orders from the Sovereign Pontiff.

Dimissorial letters may be limited or revoked by the person issuing them, or by his successor in office, but once they have been issued, they do not expire with the loss of office by the grantor. (*C. J. C.*, can. 963.)

Dimissorial letters issued for major orders are valid also for minor ones.

Exempt religious cannot lawfully be ordained by any bishop without dimissorial letters from their own major superiors. The bishop to whom these religious superiors must send the dimissorial letters, is the bishop of the diocese in which is situated the house where the candidate for ordination lives as a member of the community.

Major superiors may send dimissorial letters to another bishop: (1) with the permission of the local Ordinary; (2) if the local ordinary is absent; (3) if he is of a different rite; (4) if he is not holding any ordinations on the next ordination days; (5) if the see is vacant, and the person in charge has not the episcopal consecration.

In each of these cases, the ordaining bishop must have an authentic statement from the episcopal curia giving the reason why the religious are sent outside the diocese for ordination. Religious superiors are strictly forbidden to send their candidates for ordination to another house of the Order, and thus defraud the bishop of the diocese of his right, or to defer ordinations intentionally to a time when the bishop will be absent, or will not hold ordinations. (*C. J. C.*, can. 967.)

Superiors of exempt religious may not issue dimissorial letters for major Orders to those of their subjects who have not taken solemn and perpetual vows. The ordinations of members of other religious organizations are regulated by the laws for seculars and by indults. Canon 964 revokes every privilege by which superiors could formerly give dimissorial letters for major Orders to temporarily professed members. Superiors may give dimissorial letters for tonsure and minor Orders to all temporarily professed religious.

CHAPTER III

1453. Only a baptized man can validly receive Orders; women are barred by divine law. (See nos. 1441 and 1447.)

Art. I. Requisites for Validity.

An adult must have at least the habitual intention. It is better, however, that he have the virtual intention, because some authors look upon the habitual intention as insufficient. Hence, any person who is forced against his will to receive Orders is not validly ordained.

Art. II. Requisites for Liceity.

Some of these requisites regard the candidate, others the ordination itself.

1454. Of the requisites which regard the candidate, some are negative, others positive.

Negative requisites. The candidate must be free from all censures and impediments. Any person who receives Orders while under censure commits a grievous sin. His ordination is valid, however, but he cannot exercise the Orders he has received in this state without incurring an irregularity. This is why the bishop forbids any candidate who has an impediment to make the step under pain of excommunication. Such an act of protest on the part of the bishop does not preclude his intention to ordain persons of this type who may be present, unless it is certain that he positively stipulated otherwise, because the bishop is bound *sub gravi* to have the intention of ordaining all candidates present. In no. 3031 we shall treat of censures; in this place we deal only with irregularities and impediments, since these are cognate topics.

IRREGULARITIES AND OTHER IMPEDIMENTS

1455. We shall treat, first, of irregularities and impediments in general; secondly, of irregularities and impediments in particular.

Irregularities and impediments in general. Irregularities and impediments are canonical obstacles to the reception of tonsure and Orders and the exercise of Orders received. They differ from censures in that, as a general rule, the latter are penalties and not impediments. An irregularity is either *ex defectu* or *ex delicto,* according as it arises from the lack of some quality necessary for the exercise of Orders or from some personal fault. Simple impediments differ from irregularities in that they are by their very nature temporary.

1456. How are irregularities and simple impediments incurred? Ignorance of irregularities and simple impediments does not excuse the candidate. Irregularities and the other impediments are incurred *ipso facto* without it being necessary for an ecclesiastical judge to pass sentence. If the irregularity arises from some personal fault or simple impediment, it is not necessary that the candidate commit a crime or know of the law or the penalty to incur it. If the irregularity arises from a crime (*ex delicto*), this crime must be serious and complete, but need not necessarily be publicly known. The delinquent party must also know of the law forbidding such an act, otherwise his crime would not be formal. He need not, however, know of the irregularity which will arise from such a transgression on his part.

Children who have not yet reached the age of seven cannot incur irregularities *ex delicto,* since the law of the Church presupposes that they have not yet reached the age of reason. Neither do children who are seven years of age, but have not yet reached the age of reason, incur irregularities, since they are not yet capable of committing mortal sin. In doubt of law, no one need regard himself as irregular; in doubt of fact, the Ordinary may dispense, provided there is question of laws from which the Sovereign Pontiff usually dispenses. (*C. J. C.*, can. 15.) Faults committed before Baptism do not give rise to irregularities, but sins committed by persons who, outside the case of extreme necessity, receive Baptism from the hands of a non-Catholic, do.

1457. Which are the effects of irregularities and other impediments?

1. Irregularities and impediments are obstacles to the reception of Orders, including tonsure. In cases of this kind, candidates who are irregular or labor under a simple impediment, receive Orders validly, but commit a grave sin in doing so. The ordaining minister also sins grievously.

2. They are obstacles to the exercise of the sacred Orders received. Irregular candidates, or those laboring under a simple impediment, exercise their functions and administer the Sacraments validly, but their actions are gravely illicit, unless they are excused by fear of some serious harm, or the irregularity is only partial, and hence does not prohibit the exercise of ecclesiastical functions. Persons who exercise their functions in these circumstances do not incur censure or any additional irregularity. The irregular candidate is not deprived of his jurisdiction, consequently he may make free use of the same, and, if he is a pastor, may assist at marriages.

3. Irregularities and simple impediments usually render a candidate unfit to receive a benefice. A candidate who has only a partial irregularity, arising from some form of infirmity which prevents him from becoming a priest, may validly and licitly receive a benefice not attached to the Order of the priesthood. If he is irregular *ex delicto,* he may validly and licitly receive a benefice which does not require the exercise of a sacred Order or the care of souls, but merely the

recitation of the Divine Office or some similar function which a layman can perform. If the benefice requires the exercise of a sacred Order or the care of souls, some writers opine that the act of conferring it is null and void, while others claim that the act must be annulled by the sentence of a judge, and that there is no obligation to make restitution of the fruits of the benefice before that time. The act of conferring the benefice is certainly illicit, even in the latter case, and the irregular candidate should relinquish his rights to the benefice, unless he is in good faith. But even if he be in good faith, he must obtain a dispensation from his irregularity. If, after receiving a benefice, a candidate becomes irregular as the result of some infirmity, he may not be deprived of his benefice, but if he becomes irregular *ex delicto*, he must seek the proper dispensation. Should he fail to apply for or obtain the dispensation, he must immediately forfeit his rights to the benefice, unless he is in dire need of means of support. He must not be deprived of the fruits of his benefice if he had some other person perform the duties of his charge in his stead.

1458. How do irregularities and simple impediments cease? An irregularity is by its nature perpetual, hence it ceases only by dispensation. A simple impediment, on the other hand, is by its nature temporary, and hence ceases not only by dispensation, but also by the cessation of the cause. An irregularity arising from illegitimate birth may also be removed by legitimation and religious profession. In his request for a dispensation from irregularities and other impediments, the applicant should list all his impediments. A general dispensation from irregularities and other impediments is valid also for major orders and for benefices that are not consistorial, *i. e.*, not conferred by the pope in consistory. Any person who has received such a dispensation is henceforth barred from becoming a Cardinal, a bishop, a prelate *nullius,* a major superior of an exempt religious Order, or a dignitary of a cathedral or collegiate chapter. Candidates who received such a dispensation before the promulgation of the New Code do not become fit subjects for benefices by reason of this promulgation, because the canons are not retroactive.

Irregularities and simple impediments are not multiplied by a repetition of the same cause, except for homicide, in which case the number of murders committed must be indicated; but they are multiplied by a repetition of different causes. They are multiplied also if several irregularities or other impediments result from one and the same act, as, for instance, when a person joins some Protestant sect. In this latter case two irregularities are incurred, the first, infamy; the second, defection from the faith.

The general dispensation from irregularities and other impediments includes those omitted in good faith, except irregularities *ex delicto* in the judicial forum, and those arising from homicide and abortion. They are not valid for irregularities omitted in bad faith.

1459. The Sovereign Pontiff can dispense from all irregularities and all impediments arising from purely ecclesiastical law, but he very seldom dispenses from homicide and bigamy. If the irregularity is occult, the petition must be addressed to the Sacred Penitentiary, and the name of the applicant withheld. All other petitions must be addressed to the S. C. of the Sacraments, which is the competent authority for all irregularities properly so called, and all simple impediments. Petitions for such dispensations must indicate the true name of the applicant and be accompanied by a letter of recommendation from the Ordinary. Petitions regarding the suspension incurred by priests who migrate to America or the Philippine Islands without dimissorial letters must be addressed to the S. C. of the Consistory.

1460. Ordinaries are permitted to dispense their subjects, or delegate others to dispense them in the internal forum, whether sacramental or extra-sacramental, from all irregularities incurred by secret crimes, except deliberate homicide and effective procuration of abortion, and other crimes brought to court. They may also dispense from all irregularities and impediments that are doubtful as to the fact. Dispensations granted by the Ordinary are valid for the reception and exercise of Orders. Dispensations from irregularities given in the internal extra-sacramental forum must be in writing, and note must be made of them in the secret records of the episcopal chancery.

Canon 990 states that every confessor has this faculty in urgent occult cases, in which the Ordinary cannot be asked and there is imminent danger of great harm or infamy. The confessor may make use of this faculty only in order that the penitent may licitly exercise the Orders he has already received. Noldin is of the opinion that, in urgent cases, the confessor may dispense in the sacramental and extra-sacramental forum all penitents, both secular and regular, as well as all those who come from some other diocese. According to Prümmer, a cleric who incurs an irregularity arising from effective and sinful abortion, and who cannot refrain from exercising an Order he has received without danger of great infamy, may use *epikeia*, and apply for a dispensation after exercising his Orders, the reason he assigns being that the confessor cannot absolve him from the irregularity, and positive law does not oblige in case of serious inconvenience.

Irregularities and other impediments in particular. We shall treat, first, of irregularities *ex defectu;* secondly, of irregularities *ex delicto;* and thirdly, of simple impediments.

1461. There are seven irregularities *ex defectu*.

1462. *Natales.* All illegitimate children are to be regarded as irregular *ex defectu*. By illegitimate children we are to understand all born of fornication, adultery, incest, a sacrilegious marriage, or a marriage that is null because of some diriment impediment, whether known or unknown to the parents, or a marriage contracted without the publication of the banns and without the necessary dispensation. If the banns were proclaimed in the usual way, or if the marriage was contracted before the pastor and two witnesses after a dispensation from the banns had been secured, the children born of the marriage must not be regarded as illegitimate, even though only one of the two parties was ignorant of the impediment, and even though he entertained some doubt concerning the same.

Children who are born of such a marriage after the good faith of their parents has ceased, are not to be regarded as legitimate, whereas those who were born before that time always remain legitimate.

Children of infidel parents lawfully united in marriage are not to be considered illegitimate, and neither are waifs or infants whose legitimacy is doubtful. Sons of priests, born of lawful wedlock, are not irregular, but they may not directly inherit their fathers' benefice. *Filii nati ex usu conjugii illicito propter votum solemne castitatis in ordine sacro vel in professione emisso,* are illegitimate.

Children born at least six months after the marriage of their parents, and at most ten months after the dissolution of such a marriage, are to be regarded as legitimate. The adulterous child of a married woman is not irregular, unless his illegitimacy can be proved by solid arguments. *Nuptiae demonstrant patrem.* Where legitimacy is in doubt, there is no irregularity, although it is always safer to apply for a dispensation *"ad cautelam."* Petitions for such a dispensation should be made in cases of waifs and children concerning whom there is doubt whether they were born before or after marriage.

This first irregularity ceases with solemn religious profession, subsequent marriage—if at the time of conception or gestation or birth the marriage was not forbidden by some diriment impediment—and finally, by dispensation. The dispensation granted by an ordinary or universally delegated power to permit or legalize a marriage, legitimizes the children, unless they are the outcome of an adulterous or sacrilegious marriage.

Illegitimates may also be legitimized by a formal act of legitimation issued by the Holy Father in the form of a rescript.

1463. *Corpus*. Men with physical defects, who on account of debility cannot safely, or for reason of deformity with due dignity, engage in the sacred ministry of the altar, are to be regarded as irregular.

The following are some of those who cannot safely engage in the sacred ministry of the altar:

1. The blind. Persons who are deprived of the sight of the right or left eye may be ordained if the bishop judges them capable of reading the Canon. Priests who become blind after their ordination may obtain from the Holy See permission to celebrate Mass, provided there is no fear of their making mistakes, and they be assisted by some other priest.

2. Persons who are completely deaf.

3. Mutes and stammerers who cannot speak without great difficulty and without provoking others to laughter.

4. The lame, who cannot celebrate Mass without the use of a staff, or who have a wooden leg, cannot be ordained, unless the physical defect can be concealed. Those who become lame after ordination may celebrate if the inconvenience is not too great. Some writers even hold that a

priest who uses a staff may celebrate Mass by resting his hands on the altar. Persons who can celebrate without the use of a staff may be ordained, even though their legs are out of shape, provided this defect can be concealed and the exercise of their functions does not cause them too much inconvenience.

5. Persons who have only one hand, who lack the three last fingers or the thumb, or whose thumb and index finger are paralyzed, are also irregular. For a just cause, the latter might be permitted to administer Extreme Unction with the remaining fingers. Persons who have no index finger may obtain a dispensation.

6. All those who cannot celebrate Mass without danger of making serious mistakes, as, for instance, those who shake or cough almost continually; those who have a horror for wine and who might spill or vomit the Precious Blood; and finally, those who are constantly running a fever.

1464. The following cannot, for reasons of deformity, engage in the sacred ministry of the altar:

1. Persons who lack an important member of their body, who have no nose, or whose nose is completely deformed, or whose face is hideous by reason of a natural or artificial eye.

2. Lepers and those whose figure is completely marred. The latter may celebrate in private, provided there is no danger of scandal.

3. Monsters, hunchbacks, pygmies, giants, hermaphrodites. Many writers hold that such persons are to be barred from all Orders leading up to the priesthood, while according to others, they may receive those Orders the functions of which they can perform without too serious an inconvenience. If defects of this type appear after ordination, the persons afflicted with them may continue to exercise the functions of their respective Orders. The bishop is the sole judge as to

whether a defect is grave or slight. If he judges it to be slight, he may permit the candidate to advance in Orders or to exercise the functions of the Orders he has already received.

1465. *Animus* refers to defects of the mind. The insane, epileptics, and persons possessed by the devil, are irregular. If insanity is not the result of fever or some accident, it renders the candidate irregular for all time. If, in the opinion of a reputable physician, a complete cure has been effected, the candidate should apply for a dispensation to the Holy See. If persons become thus afflicted after the reception of Holy Orders, but later on completely recover from their sickness, they may be permitted by the Ordinary to exercise the Orders they have received. (*C. J. C.*, can. 984.)

1466. *Non bigamus.* By bigamy the law understands men who have successively contracted two or more valid marriages. (*Ibid.*)

1467. *Mala Fama.* Infamy is defined as the complete or partial loss of a good reputation. Persons who have incurred either of these by law are irregular. Infamy is termed of law (*legalis*) if the law attaches a stain to the perpetration of some crime, or an ecclesiastical judge inflicts it upon a delinquent through a formal sentence. It is termed of fact (*popularis*) if a person is accused of having committed some crime, if the crime is attributed to him, or if an ecclesiastical or civil judge condemns him for a crime which, in the eye of the public, completely or partially deprives him of his good name. To incur infamy of fact, it matters not whether public opinion is true or false, or the sentence of the judge is just or unjust. (See no. 1483.)

Here there is question only of infamy of law. Infamy of fact is only a simple impediment, of which we shall treat in no. 1483. Infamy of law, whether public or occult, renders a candidate irregular. It is also a canonical penalty.

1468. *Defectus lenitatis.* A judge is irregular who has pronounced the sentence of death against some individual brought to trial. If the sentence is an unjust one, the judge is irregular *ex delicto homicidii*. It makes no difference if the judge pronounces such a sentence alone, or in conjunction with his colleagues; it is enough if his influence in the matter is efficacious and the death sentence is carried out. The members of the jury are in all probability not irregular. The prosecutor and the witnesses are certainly not irregular, since they do not pronounce the sentence, and the judge himself does not incur the irregularity if he is unbaptized.

1469. The New Code also regards as irregular persons who have held the office of executioner, and those who, of their own accord, have undertaken the office of immediate assistants in the execution of a death sentence. Officials and soldiers who carry out a death sentence in the army are not considered irregular if they are acting under orders. The New Code makes no mention of the former irregularity incurred by voluntary service in a just war for all who killed or mutilated others. (*C. J. C.*, can. 894.)

1470. Irregularities *ex delicto*. The following persons are irregular because of crime (*ex delicto*): apostates from the faith, heretics, and schismatics.

1471. Persons who, outside the case of extreme necessity, allow themselves in any way to be baptized by non-Catholics are irregular. The New Code makes no mention of rebaptism, although it is probable that persons who are rebaptized by non-Catholics incur an irregularity.

1472. Married men, clerics in major Orders, religious with solemn or simple, perpetual or temporary vows, who attempt marriage or go through the civil formalities of marriage, and men who attempt marriage with a validly married woman, or with a nun bound by either perpetual or temporary vows, are also irregular. It is not necessary that these marriages or so-called marriages be consummated.

1473. Voluntary murderers, and those who procure abortion, if effective, and all who coöperate therein, are also irregular. An indirectly voluntary homicide no longer renders a person irregular. Coöperators are all those who, of their own accord, concur in a homicide or an abortion, issue orders for or advise the same, or furnish the means of committing the crime. Physicians who procure the abortion or practice craniotomy, therefore, incur an irregularity, as do also soldiers who volunteer for service and are instrumental in killing others in an unjust war, and judges, accusers, jurymen and witnesses who coöperate in an unjust death sentence.

1474. Men who mutilate themselves or others, or who attempt suicide, are also irregular. By mutilation we understand the cutting off of an essential limb which has its own particular function. If no grievous sin is committed by the person thus mutilating himself or others, no irregularity is incurred.

1475. The Code forbids the practice of medicine, especially surgery, to clerics with very few exceptions. Clerics who practice medicine or surgery incur irregularity if death ensues. If the cleric has permission to practice medicine or surgery, he does not incur irregularity; neither does the cleric who is not the cause, but only the occasion, of a death.

1476. Men who usurp the exercise of an act of Orders reserved to clerics in sacred Orders, and clerics in sacred Orders who exercise an act of major Orders after they have been forbidden to do so as a canonical penalty, either personal or local, corrective or punitive, also incur irregularity. As may be seen, this irregularity is henceforth restricted to the exercise of acts of major Orders. Moreover, it follows not only from the violation of a censure, but also from suspensions and interdicts of a purely vindictive character, if they are violated by the exercise of a major Order. The common practice of today is to permit the exercise of the functions of a subdeacon at solemn Mass to simple clerics, provided they do not wear the maniple. As a general rule, in order to incur irregularity, the layman or the simple cleric must exercise an act of a major Order in solemn fashion, wearing the sacred vestments and taking part in the ceremonies proper to that Order.

1477. *Simple impediments.* These are also seven in number. The following persons are simply forbidden to be ordained: Sons of non-Catholics, as long as their parents persevere in their error. The Pontifical Commission has interpreted this part of canon 987 to mean that this impediment affects only the children in the paternal line and in the first degree (July 14, 1922.) It is controverted whether or not the impediment ceases at the death of the non-Catholic parent. Some are of the opinion that it does, others, that it does not.

1478. Married men cannot be ordained while bound by the marriage tie. To receive Holy Orders, a married man must obtain a dispensation from the Holy See, even though his wife gives her consent.

1479. Officials and administrators who hold an office forbidden to clerics are also barred from Orders, until they have resigned from office and settled all accounts connected with their office.

1480. Slaves are barred from Orders until they have obtained their freedom.

1481. Men bound to ordinary military service by civil law may not be ordained until they have served their term. The meaning of this law, which is formulated by canon 987, is that in countries where military service is obligatory, young men may not be ordained before or during regular or active military service. The possibility of an extraordinary call for additional service or a general mobilization is no longer an obstacle to the reception of Orders. Men who volunteer for military service are not rendered irregular by this law, although they are by the fact that they engage in a profession barred to clerics.

1482. Neophytes may not be ordained until, in the judgment of the bishop, they have been sufficiently tried in the faith.

1483. Men who are in ill repute on account of some public crime they have committed, are also barred from Orders. This ill repute does not arise from crimes determined by law, but from any crime which the general public considers very serious. Instances of such are: simony, sodomy, adultery, usury, etc. A sentence of condemnation for such a crime, issued by an ecclesiastical judge, will result in the guilty person incurring the impediment of infamy of fact. If the sentence is issued by a civil judge, infamy of fact will result for the guilty person only indirectly. The Ordinary is the sole judge as to whether the reputation of the candidate is good enough or not, condemnation or no condemnation, and persons who are in ill repute on account of some public crime they have committed, are irregular until, in the judgment of the bishop, they have regained their good reputation. (*C. J. C.*, can. 987; see also no. 1467.)

1484. He who ordains an irregular candidate, or one laboring under a simple impediment, commits a grievous sin, as does also he who has himself ordained with an irregularity or some other impediment, and he who exercises an Order for which he is irregular, or from which he is barred by an impediment.

1485. *Positive conditions required in candidates for ordination.* Some of these conditions are intrinsic, others extrinsic.

Intrinsic conditions. The first of these conditions is the state of grace. This is required under pain of sacrilege, at least for the reception of the diaconate and the priesthood. Writers who are of the opinion that all the inferior Orders are Sacraments, logically require this condition of the recipients, and since their opinion is probable, it would be a sacrilege to receive these Orders in the state of mortal sin. Moreover, if the candidate receives Communion at his ordination, the sacrilege is no longer doubtful. The obligation to receive in the ordination ceremony is grave only for candidates who are raised to the priesthood.

The soul of the candidate must be fortified by the grace of the Sacrament of Confirmation even before he receives tonsure, otherwise he may not receive other Orders without a dispensation from the Holy See. The ordinary state of grace is not sufficient for the reception of sacred Orders. The candidate must possess what St. Thomas terms an "extraordinary goodness," i. e., he must lead a holy life and be well established in virtue. It is the duty of the bishop and the confessor to see to it that candidates fulfill these requirements. "It is incumbent upon bishops," says St. Alphonsus, "to see to it that candidates are not only not bad, but positively good, i. e., lead good spiritual lives, are attentive to their religious duties, frequently receive the Sacraments, and are assiduous at prayer and study."

Before conferring any of the sacred Orders, the bishop should request the pastor to make known the candidate's domicile or quasi-domicile. As a general rule, students retain the domicile of their parents. If the ordinations are deferred for more than six months after the proclamation of the domicile, the bishop may request that the statement be repeated. For a just cause, the bishop may dispense entirely with the proclamation, or have it take place in churches other than the parish church. Canon 992 states that candidates must give due notice to the Ordinary of their intention to receive Orders. In May, 1931, new and elaborate rules of investigation, to be followed by bishops in conjunction with rectors of seminaries, were issued; they require an oath from the candidate of his intention and full understanding of the obligations he assumes.

This proclamation is not necessary for minor Orders, although candidates should present credentials from their respective pastors and teachers. These credentials are dispensed with in the ordination of religious, even of those with simple vows.

1486. A divine vocation is also required. All writers are agreed on this point: "Neither doth any man take the honor to himself, but he that is called by God, as Aaron was" (Hebr. 5, 4.) The sure marks of a sacerdotal vocation are: (1) the necessary knowledge, or, in a child, the ability to acquire the same; (2) good conduct, purity of life, and an upright intention of working for the honor and glory of God and the salvation of souls. Any one not possessing these qualifications who contrives to gain admittance to the priesthood commits a grave sin of presumption.

A candidate who possesses the necessary qualifications, but is not certain if he is called to sacred Orders, may present himself to the bishop for examination, and the latter will decide his case.

Canon 971 makes it unlawful for any one to force a man in any way, or for any reason, to embrace the clerical state, or to bar a properly qualified person from that state. Any one who is constrained by grave fear to receive Holy Orders, may be restored to the lay state and relieved of the obligation of celibacy and the recital of the Divine Office, unless he ratifies his previous act after ordination. It is equally unlawful to force any candidate who has received one Order to accept a superior one, or in case of refusal to prevent him from exercising the functions of the Order he has received, if in the judgment of the Ordinary he is sufficiently worthy.

Tonsure and minor Orders should not be conferred upon a man who has no intention of becoming a priest.

For a canonical reason the bishop and major superiors may, with or without a canonical trial, bar their subjects from the reception of Holy Orders. Clerics may have recourse, however, to the Holy See and, in the case of religious, to the superior general in the event of being barred by the provincial.

In the case of a person being ordained for a benefice which requires the exercise of major Orders, the desire to be promoted to higher Orders is required *sub gravi*. A person in minor Orders who reverts to the lay state is not guilty of sin.

1487. *The required knowledge.* Canon 972 states that care should be taken to receive aspirants to sacred Orders into the seminary at an early age. All candidates must stay in the seminary at least for the entire course of theology, unless in particular cases, and for serious reasons, the Ordinary dispenses from this rule. Candidates for Holy Orders who, with the permission of the bishop, live outside the seminary, must be entrusted to the care of some responsible priest, who shall watch over them and instruct them in virtue.

The theological studies should not be made privately, but in proper theological schools, according to the plan of studies prescribed by the canons. Neither seculars nor religious are to receive the tonsure before they begin their course in theology; subdeaconship may not be given until the end of the third year of theology; deaconship, after the commencement of the fourth year, and the priesthood not until the beginning of the second semester of the fourth year.

The Holy See sometimes dispenses religious from this last rule, in which case the Sacred Congregation of Religious, by order of the Pope, must add the following clause to the wording of the dispensation: "Provided they persevere in the serious study of sacred theology and refrain in the meantime from exercising the functions of their ministry." The responsibility of superiors in this matter is very grave. On October 23, 1923, Pope Pius XI declared that all dispensations granted from this rule since the appearance of the New Code must be interpreted in this sense.

The school year must comprise nine complete months of study terminated by a successful examination. Both seculars and religious must take an examination before being promoted to an Order. The examination should be made to bear on the Order which the candidate is to receive, and if it be a question of major Orders, on other treatises of sacred theology.

It is the bishop's duty to determine the method of examination as well as the subject matter in which candidates are to be examined. It is also his duty to select a board of examiners. If the candidates are religious, the bishop may leave the matter of their examination to their superiors. The examination of both secular and religious candidates is to be conducted before the bishop of the diocese, who has by law the right to ordain, or who gives dimissorials to his subjects. He may also, for a just reason, leave this matter to the ordaining bishop, if the latter is willing to attend to it. The bishop who ordains the secular or religious subjects of another bishop, who present to him dimissorial letters from their superiors, certifying that they have successfully passed the examination required by the canons, may accept the statement of such letters if he so chooses. He is not obliged to do so, however, and if he conscientiously believes that a candidate is not qualified, he should not promote him.

Canon 1406 prescribes that all candidates for subdeaconship make a profession of faith before the Ordinary according to the form approved by the Holy See. If the local Ordinary deems it proper, he may require candidates to repeat this profession of faith before the diaconate and the priesthood. The Code makes no mention of the anti-modernist oath, but a decision of the 22nd of March, 1918, declares that, until further notice, it must be taken in all circumstances in which it is required. This oath must be taken before the reception of subdeaconship, until the Holy See rules otherwise.

1488. *Extrinsic conditions. Canonical necessity*. The secular candidate must be useful or necessary to the churches of the diocese. A bishop may, however, ordain a subject who purposes to assist in a church of some other diocese after his excardination and incardination have been effected according to the laws of the Church.

Canonical Age. There is no age prescribed for the reception of tonsure and minor orders, but since canon 976 requires that the candidate have commenced his theology, he should be at least eighteen years old. Subdeaconship is not to be given before the candidate has completed his twenty-first year; deaconship before his twenty-second; the priesthood before his twenty-fourth; and the episcopacy before his thirtieth—all complete years. A candidate who presents himself and receives ordination before reaching the canonical age, commits a grievous sin and is not permitted to exercise the functions of the Order he has received. Bishops who have received the faculty to dispense from the defect of age, may make use of it even in the case of religious.

1489. *The exercise of the Order received*. Authors are not agreed as to whether the exercise of the functions of the Order received is required *sub levi* of a candidate who wishes to advance to a higher Order. The New Code has nothing to say about this point and hence would seem to favor the opinion of those who hold that the exercise of these functions is not of precept.

1490. *Canonical title*. The candidate is required *sub gravi*, to have a title for subdeaconship, and the bishop who ordains one without a title, incurs suspension, which prevents him from conferring Holy Orders for a whole year. This suspension is reserved to the Holy See, and the bishop must assume the obligation for himself and for his successors or, during the vacancy of the see, for his chapter, to supply the needy cleric with proper sustenance until provision can be made for him. The board of examiners who approve a false title are the first ones obligated.

The title by which one is ordained must be certain for the whole life of the cleric, and truly sufficient for his proper maintenance, according to the rules laid down by the local Ordinaries. There are several different titles. For the secular clergy the canonical titles are: that of benefice, that of patrimony, and that of service of the diocese or mission.

1. *The Title of Benefice.* By a benefice we understand an income levied on ecclesiastical goods in the actual possession of the owner and sufficient for his subsistence. Candidates who are ordained by the title of benefice are not free to renounce the same, unless they acquire another sufficient title. If less than one-fifth of the income sufficient for the maintenance of the cleric is lacking, the ordination is nevertheless licit, and if the ordaining minister is the candidate's own bishop, he is permitted to supply what is lacking in the benefice by patrimony.

2. *The Title of Patrimony.* In default of a benefice, secular clerics are ordained by the title of patrimony. Patrimony is a perpetual income possessed by the candidate, which is not levied on ecclesiastical goods, but on goods which are nevertheless stable. This title must be recognized and approved by the local Ordinary. A pension paid by the State or by others in the form of a perpetual legacy may be substituted.

3. *The Title of Service of the Diocese or Mission.* In default of any other title, the diocesan bishop may ordain his

subjects by the title of "service of the diocese," and if his see is under the S. C. of the Propaganda, by the title of "the mission." In either case the candidate must promise under oath to serve the diocese or the mission for all time, subject to the authority of the local Ordinary.

For regulars, the canonical titles are: that of "poverty" or "solemn profession" and that of "the common table." The first of these titles is the one by which religious with solemn vows are ordained; the second is the one by which religious with perpetual simple vows are ordained. Religious who have no perpetual vows are governed by the same laws as seculars. In practice they require indults from the Holy See.

1491. *Dimissorial letters.* The candidate must present dimissorial letters, if he is to be ordained by a bishop other than his own, and in the case of religious, if his religious superior has not the episcopal character.

Certificates. Secular candidates and non-exempt religious must present: (1) a certificate testifying that they have successfully passed their examination for ordination; (2) a certificate of their last ordination, and, if they are to receive first tonsure, the baptismal and Confirmation certificates; (3) a certificate of studies required for the order they are to receive, according to canon 976; (4) testimonials from the rector of the seminary, or from the priest in charge of those who do not board in the seminary, testifying to their good moral standing; (5) testimonials of every Ordinary in whose diocese they have stayed for a sufficient length of time to contract a canonical impediment.

The time sufficient to contract a canonical impediment is to be taken to mean a period of three months for soldiers and six months for others, after the candidates have reached the age of fourteen. The bishop may demand testimonials also for a shorter period and for the time prior to the age of fourteen.

If the bishop in whose diocese a candidate has lived for a period of time, cannot ascertain anything definite concerning the behavior of the young man in question, and hence cannot testify that the candidate has not incurred a canonical impediment, or if the candidate has been living for a short time in so many dioceses that it would be either impossible or at least extremely difficult to obtain all the needed testimonials, the ordaining bishop may demand that the candidate take an oath that he is free from irregularity. If the candidate, after the testimonials have been obtained and before the ordination takes place, spends more time in the diocese of the bishop who first issued them, new testimonials are necessary if his stay extends over three or six months.

The religious superior in his dimissorial letters must attest not only that the candidates for Orders have made profession and are members of the community, but also that they have made the requisite studies and fulfilled the other requirements of law. The bishop who has received these dimissorial letters does not need any others.

1492. *The retreat.* Canon 1001 requires that candidates for first tonsure and minor Orders make at least three full days' retreat, and candidates for major Orders at least six days.

If a candidate receives first tonsure and minor Orders within a short space of time, the same three days' retreat will suffice for both ordinations. If within six months a candidate receives several major Orders, the bishop may reduce the days of retreat for the diaconate to not less than three. If, after the retreat is finished, the ordination is delayed for any reason for more than six months, the retreat must be repeated; if the ordination is delayed for less time, the Ordinary shall decide whether or not the retreat is to be repeated.

Religious must make a retreat in their own house or in

some house belonging to the Order or congregation, according to the judgment of their superior. Seculars must make it in the seminary or in some other place designated by the bishop. The superior of the house of retreats, and in the case of religious their own major superior, must issue a statement to the bishop to the effect that the candidates have duly made the exercises.

1493. *The manner of conferring ordination.* The different Orders must be conferred successively without the omission of any. The omission of an Order does not render the Sacrament invalid, but gravely illicit. The episcopal consecration of a cleric who had not received the Order of the priesthood would, however, probably be invalid. Any candidate who has been ordained *per saltum*, may not exercise the functions of the Order received until the Order omitted has been duly conferred, and if he does, he incurs an irregularity which must be referred to the Holy See. Doubtfully conferred Orders, except for a truly grave reason need not be repeated, except in the cases of the priesthood and the episcopacy. If a cleric has received some Orders in an Oriental rite, and afterwards obtains an indult from the Holy See to receive further Orders in the Latin rite, he must first receive those Orders of the Latin rite which are not given in the Oriental rite. (*C. J. C.*, can. 1005.)

1494. *The proper intervals to be observed.* In ordinations, the intervals of time between Orders are to be observed, during which clerics shall exercise the Orders received according to the regulations of the bishop. Without a special faculty of the Holy See, one is not permitted to confer tonsure and a minor Order, or all the minor Orders on the same day. Only three minor Orders at the most may be conferred the same day, and the bishop should determine the intervals to be observed between first tonsure and the office of porter, and between the different minor Orders.

Without special permission of the Holy See, minor Orders and the subdiaconate or two major Orders may not be given on one and the same day. All customs to the contrary are henceforth condemned. The usual interval to be observed between minor Orders and the subdiaconate is one year, and between the subdiaconate and the diaconate and the priesthood, three months. The Code gives bishops the faculty to reduce this interval according to necessity or utility. The reason for conferring the priesthood sooner after the subdiaconate than is usual, must be more serious than that for reducing the time limit between the other Orders.

1495. *Time of Ordination.* Major Orders must be conferred during Holy Mass on the Ember Saturdays, on the Saturday before Passion Sunday, or on Holy Saturday. For grave reasons, the bishop may give major Orders on any Sunday or holyday of obligation. (*C. J. C.*, can. 1006.)

Customs to ordain at times other than those specified by Canon Law are reprobated and abolished. Bishops who have obtained the faculty to ordain outside these times, may not make use of it on two or more consecutive feast days. According to Noldin, this faculty is personal to the bishop who obtained it. Hence he may make use of it in ordaining candidates who present themselves to him with dimissorial letters, and also have his own candidates ordained outside the specified times by bishops who have not this faculty.

If the faculty carries the words: *"Extra tempora et non servatis interstitiis,"* the meaning would seem to be that sacred Orders may be conferred during three consecutive feast days, unless the indult specifies otherwise.

Whenever an ordination has to be repeated, or ceremonies are to be supplied, whether absolutely or conditionally, the ceremony may take place outside the prescribed ordination days and in secret. (*C. J. C.*, can. 1007.)

Candidates who are promoted to major Orders are bound to receive Communion at the ordination Mass.

The consecration of a bishop must take place on a Sunday or on the feast of an Apostle, during the Holy Sacrifice.

Place of Ordination. Cardinals have the privilege of performing the ordination ceremony in any diocese, and need but notify the local Ordinary if they wish to pontificate in his cathedral. A bishop may not, outside his own diocese, give those Orders which require the use of mitre and crozier without permission of the local Ordinary. (*C. J. C.,* can. 1008.)

In conferring any of the Orders, the bishop must faithfully follow the order of ceremonies laid down in the Roman Pontifical. This book prescribes the use of all the pontifical insignia for the collation of sacred Orders. For the collation of tonsure and minor Orders, the Pontifical prescribes only the mitre. All five may be conferred outside the diocese, but probably without crozier and mitre, just as the bishop is permitted to confirm his own subjects outside the diocese without crozier and mitre, although the Roman Pontifical prescribes these insignia for Confirmation.

1496. General ordinations should be held publicly in the cathedral church and in the presence of the cathedral chapter. If they are held in another place of the diocese, the more prominent church should be selected, and the clergy of the place should be present. For a just reason, the bishop may hold special ordinations in other churches, or in the chapel of the episcopal residence, in the seminary, or in a religious house. First tonsure and minor Orders may be conferred also in private oratories. (*C. J. C.,* can. 1009.)

1497. The obedience promised to the bishop obliges the priest to remain attached to the service of the church to which he is appointed, even though his position is not irremovable, unless he decides to enter religion. (See no. 3353.) Priests who are not attached to the service of any special church, may not leave the diocese without the bishop's permission.

1498. After ordination, the names of those ordained, of the minister of ordination and also the place and date must be recorded in a book specially set apart for that purpose in the episcopal curia. Also a certificate of ordination should be issued to each *ordinatus*. All the documents required in the various ordinations must be carefully preserved. (*C. J. C.*, can. 1010.)

1499. The faithful should be exhorted, especially during the Ember Days, to pray ardently that God may give worthy ministers to His Church. Mothers of families should be urged to pray that God call some one of their children to become a priest, and young men should be taught to live lives of purity, so that God may call several among them to consecrate themselves to His service.

EXAMINATION OF CANDIDATES

1500. Candidates who are preparing themselves for first tonsure should carefully study nos. 750–796; 810–817; 1407, 1408, 1409, 1410; 1450–1500; 3031; and 3082–3173. They should also read attentively nos. 3082–3173, know the ecclesiastical penalties, nos. 3173–3193, the obligations of clerics, 3505–3538, the responsibilities of a benefice, if they are to be promoted to one, nos. 3591 and 3592, and also read attentively nos. 3538–3591.

1501. Candidates who are preparing for the reception of minor Orders should study nos. 1500, 1411–1427, and, finally, the rudiments of faith, as found in nos. 2190–2256.

1502. Candidates who are preparing for the subdiaconate must know all the matter we have indicated in nos. 1500 and 1501; 1427–1433; 3525 and 3509 ff.

1503. Candidates who are preparing for the diaconate must know the matter we have indicated in nos. 1500, 1501 and 1502, and also nos. 1433–1439.

1504. Candidates who are preparing for the priesthood must know the matter we have indicated in nos. 1500–1503, inclusively; also nos. 1439–1446.

In order fully to understand the double power conferred by the priesthood over the real and mystical body of Christ, candidates should know perfectly the two treatises on the Holy Eucharist and the Sacrament of Penance (nos. 879–1389. They should know also the matter and form of Baptism, nos. 830–835, and of Extreme Unction, nos. 1389–1397, and nos. 1401–1407.

1505. They should be mindful of the fact that they cannot validly assist at marriage or give absolution without possessing at least delegated jurisdiction, and that they cannot, outside the case of necessity, licitly administer the other Sacraments without at least the presumed permission of the pastor. No permission is required to hear the confession of a sick person outside the church. For the absolution of the dying we refer to no. 2691.

SEVENTH TREATISE

MATRIMONY

1506. Matrimony may be considered as a contract, in which case it is defined as an agreement in virtue of which a man and a woman lawfully concede to each other the power over their body for the purpose of procreating children, and mutually assume the obligation of living together. Being of both natural and divine right, this contract does not depend upon civil law, like other contracts, and the contracting parties are not free to modify it at their own discretion. It can exist apart from the Sacrament only in the case of infidels, whose marriages are lawful as contracts without being sacramental.

1507. Marriages are divided into *canonical* and *civil,* according as they are celebrated in conformity with the laws of the Church or those of the State. They are *real* or *putative* according as they are objectively valid or invalid; in the latter case, the marriage being entered into in good faith by at least one of the parties, as long as the fact of the invalidity is not known to both. A marriage is said to be *presumed* if, because of certain facts, the law supposes it to have been validly contracted; it is termed *attempted* if it is objectively invalid, because entered into by either party or both with the knowledge of an existing diriment impediment.

Lawful marriage is that validly entered into by unbaptized persons. Christian marriage is said to be *ratified* if it exists merely in the state of a bare contract; *consummated,* if the contract has been followed by the conjugal act. Until proof of the contrary is offered, all marriages are presumed to have been consummated if the couple have lived together. Marriages are *public* if contracted with at least the main formalities prescribed by the canons; *secret* if entered into with the proper permission, but without the proclamation of the banns. In the latter case the regulations laid down by law must be strictly observed. Among these is the regulation forbidding one to enter into the parish register secret marriages or "marriages of conscience," as they are sometimes called; an entry of this kind must be made in a separate book kept in the chancery office. The names of children born of such unions must also be entered into this same book, and both the bishop, the pastor and the witnesses are bound to secrecy in these matters, unless they are constrained to speak to avoid scandal. A *clandestine* marriage is one entered into before an authority other than the Church.

A *morganatic* marriage is one contracted by an aristocrat or plutocrat with a person of inferior rank, with the understanding that the inferior party and the children born of the union shall not inherit the rank or property of the superior. Such a marriage is permitted only on condition that the children are duly provided for.

1508. It is certain that between baptized persons no marriage can exist apart from the Sacrament, notwithstanding any civil laws to the contrary. Pope Leo XIII is very clear on this point: "Let no one then be deceived by the distinction which some court legists have so strongly insisted upon— the distinction, namely, by virtue of which they sever the matrimonial contract from the Sacrament, with the intent to hand over the contract to the power and will of the rulers of the State, while reserving questions concerning the Sacrament to the Church. A distinction, or rather a severance of this kind cannot be approved; for it is certain that in Christian marriage the contract is inseparable from the Sacrament; and that for this reason, the contract cannot be true and legitimate without being a Sacrament as well." (Leo XIII, Encyclical *"Arcanum."*) A marriage is invalid, therefor, if entered into with the predominating intention of excluding the Sacrament.

1509. Purely civil marriages are nothing more than forms of concubinage, and even though persons enter into them with the intention of contracting marriage before the Church, they are not to be regarded as true marriage contracts. Coupled with the sin of adultery, a civil marriage gives rise to the impediment of crime.

1510. The Church does not censure parties who, for a just reason, comply with the law which prescribes the civil act, provided their intention be merely to live up to the requirements of the law and thereby gain civil recognition for their marriage. (*C. J. C.*, can. 1063.)

The official in this case is even permitted to admit the parties in the eyes of the Church. If a grave reason be present, the official is permitted to admit persons whose intention is to remain content with the civil act, provided there is no special Church legislation to the contrary and the union can be put in order later.

An official cannot be a party to a marriage between two persons, when the marriage is a criminal act. An instance of such a marriage would be that intended by two parties, one of whom is divorced and has a husband or wife living. He could not be a party to a contract of this kind even at the expense of losing his position, for this is the express answer given by the Sacred Congregation of the Penitentiary. His reason for being a party to such a union would have to be far more serious. Heretics and others who are not subject to the regulations of the canons may, of course, contract real marriages before civil authority, and the official has always a sufficient reason for assisting at such marriages.

1511. Marriage between Christians is defined as "a Sacrament of the New Law, conferring the grace necessary to sanctify the lawful union between man and woman, as well as the grace to procreate children in all holiness and to educate them in the ways of God." It is *of faith* that Matrimony is a Sacrament (cfr. no. 756.)

1512. All questions concerning the validity or liceity of the marriage contract, therefore, belong to the domain of the Church. This is *of faith,* from the words of the Council of Trent (Sess. 24, can. 12.) It is *certain* that these questions belong to her domain *alone,* because she alone has power over the things of God. Civil law has authority only in the sphere of the purely civil effects of marriage, such as property, wills, etc.

We shall treat, first, of the Sacrament itself; secondly, of the minister; and thirdly, of the subject.

CHAPTER I

THE SACRAMENT ITSELF

Art. I. Matter and the Form.

1513. The *remote* matter of the Sacrament of Matrimony is constituted by the bodies of the two parties; the *proximate* matter and the form of the Sacrament is the matrimonial contract or consent. This is *certain* from the words of the Decree to the Armenians: "As a rule, the efficient cause of Matrimony is the mutual consent of the parties expressed by word of mouth, the parties being present." The Sacrament of Matrimony is the contract itself, and the contract is made by the express consent of the contracting parties. Improbable, therefore, is the opinion of those theologians who placed the form of the Sacrament in the words of the priest or officiating minister: *"Ego vos conjungo."* This will be made clearer in the following number.

1514. *The essential form.* It is commonly held that the expressed consent of the contracting parties constitutes the *matter*, in so far as it indicates the surrender of their bodies, and that this same consent constitutes the form, in so far as it indicates the acceptance of this surrender. Such an acceptance completes the act of surrendering and specifies it very determinately. The consent expressed is the visible sign of the union between Christ and His Church, of the grace which ensues, and that which sanctifies the union of the contracting parties.

1515. The *Sacrament* alone consists in the act whereby the contracting parties give and accept their consent; the *Sacrament and the thing* consists in the permanent state or bond resulting from this act.

1516. For the validity of the marriage contract, it is *certain* that the personal consent of the contracting parties is essential, and that the consent of the parents does not suffice. It is *of faith,* against Protestants, that the consent of children minus that of their parents is valid. But marriage is ordinarily gravely illicit if the parents are justly opposed to it, or if it is known that they will be grievously offended by it. If only one parent is opposed to the marriage, the children are more excusable, but in all cases children should be advised to consult their parents.

Canon 1034 states that the pastor shall earnestly warn young people not to contract marriage against the reasonable objections of their parents, and that if they nevertheless persist against the lawful objections of their parents, he shall not marry them, but refer the matter to the bishop. (*C. J. C.,* can. 1034.) If the children are of age, and have good reasons for entering into the marriage contract without the consent or knowledge of their parents, the pastor may marry them.

1517. To become the valid form of the Sacrament, the matrimonial consent must be vested with certain positive and negative qualities.

Positive qualities. As in every contract, the consent of the two parties entering into the marriage union must be:

1. *Mutual,* and this needs no explanation.

2. *Real* and *interior.* A person simulating consent commits a sacrilege and deceives the other party. Such a person is bound to repair his fault, and by valid consent, if this be necessary, to make up for the injury done. He would not be bound to make reparation if he acted under pressure or unjust fear, or if the other party forfeited his rights. (See no. 809.) He cannot ask for or render the *debitum* before he has given valid consent. He cannot require that the other party believe in his act of deception, even though he affirm it under oath.

3. *Deliberate.* The consent must be given when in the full possession of one's reason and with the reflection necessary for any human act.

4. *Personal.* For the liceity of the marriage contract, Canon Law requires that the persons be in each other's presence and that they express the marriage consent by word of mouth.

Deaf-mutes may contract licitly by means of signs, such as nodding their heads or putting forth their hands, when they are questioned by the priest. Marriage may be contracted by means of an *interpreter* when the parties do not know the language of the officiating minister or that of the witnesses, provided there be no serious reason to doubt the good faith of the interpreter.

Marriage by proxy is always valid, if the mandate is lawful; it is licit only if there is a just cause for marrying in this way. It is not necessary that the proxy be of the same sex as the person issuing the mandate. To be authentic, the mandate must be written by the person who is absent, and expressly indicate his right to contract marriage with the person named. It must be signed by the Ordinary or the pastor of the absent person, or by some priest delegated for this special purpose by either the Ordinary or the pastor. It may be signed by only two witnesses. If the person issuing the mandate does not know how to write, this should be noted in the mandate and an additional witness employed, otherwise the mandate is void. (*C. J. C.*, can. 1089). The pastor must not assist at a marriage contracted by proxy or through an interpreter, unless there is a good reason for contracting in this unusual way, and unless he is certain of the authenticity of the mandate or the truthfulness of the interpreter. If time permits, the pastor should obtain the bishop's permission to assist at such marriages; diocesan statutes may add additional precautions.

1518. *Negative qualities.*

1. By the natural law, the consent of the contracting parties must be free from violence.

2. By ecclesiastical, and very probably by natural, law the consent must be free from all grave fear inspired *ab extrinsico* in an unjust manner. Canon 1087 states that marriage is invalid if entered under *grave fear* or *force*, which an outside agency brings to bear upon a person *unjustly*, and by which the person is forced to choose the marriage as a means to free himself from the force or the threats. No other fear renders a marriage null, even though it is actually the cause of the contract. To annul a marriage, fear must be grave in all its circumstances, *i. e.*, by reason of both the proximity of the danger and the temperament of the person acting under it. It is not necessary that it be inspired by the other contracting party. Reverential fear does not render a

marriage invalid, unless it makes for at least a relatively un-just and grave fear clothed with all the conditions we have mentioned above. (See no. 2820.)

By natural law, the consent must be free from all substantial error. Error is substantial when it bears upon the person or when, concerning a certain quality, it amounts to error of person. Such error renders marriage invalid.

Canon 1083 states that error concerning any quality of the person renders marriage invalid only in two cases: (1) If the error concerning a quality amounts to an error of person; (2) If one contracts marriage with a person who was believed to be free when he or she is in fact a slave properly so-called, in countries where slavery exists.

Error is substantial and renders marriage invalid if it concerns the nature of the contract, *i. e.,* if the contracting party does not know that marriage is a permanent union between man and woman, for the purpose of generating offspring. Ignorance concerning the nature of marriage is not presumed by law in persons who have attained puberty (*C. J. C.,* can. 1082.) Mere error concerning the unity, indissolubility or sacramental dignity of marriage does not annul the consent, even if such error caused the consent. (Can. 1084.) Error or ignorance concerning the means of procreating children is not substantial and does not annul the marriage. The knowledge or opinion of the nullity of marriage does not necessarily exclude matrimonial consent. (Can. 1085.) Error concerning a quality laid down as a *conditio sine qua non* certainly invalidates the marriage, but this point forms part of the question of conditions, of which we are about to speak.

1519. Canon 1092 deals with the *conditions* which the parties have added to the marriage contract and have not retracted. They are governed by the following principles:

1. If the condition is concerning the future and either necessary, or impossible, or sinful, but not against the es-

sence of marriage, it is considered as not added to the contract.

2. If the condition is concerning the future and against the essence of marriage, it renders the marriage invalid.

3. If the condition is concerning the future and licit, it suspends the validity of the marriage.

4. If the condition is concerning the past or the present, the marriage is valid if the condition is realized, but invalid if it is not realized. (Can. 1092.)

A condition concerning the future is contrary to the substance of marriage if it is repugnant to the unity and indissolubility of the contract or to the procreation of children, as, for instance, if the contracting parties reserved to themselves the right to commit adultery, to divorce one another, to practice onanism, or abortion, or infanticide. A condition contrary to the substance of marriage renders the contract invalid only if it takes precedence over the intention to contract a valid marriage. This is what happens when the condition is expressly included by mutual agreement in the marriage contract, or if one or other or both of the contracting parties make known explicitly an intention to enter into the contract only on condition that he or she or both be not obliged to accept all the substantial obligations of the married state. The intention to fulfill these obligations is not, however, necessary for the validity of the contract.

The intention, and even a condition appended by the contracting parties to the effect that they will practice perfect chastity in the married state, probably does not render the contract invalid, provided the parties give and accept the right over one another's body. A right may be given and accepted without there being any intention of making use of it, for the right is one thing, and the use of the right another. In cases of this kind the right is given on condition that the other party will not make use of it, and yet in such a way that, even though the other party has accepted the condition, he may still use the right if he so desires.

We might add that, if a marriage appears doubtful because of a condition that has been appended to the consent, this consent should be renewed absolutely, if at all possible. In all other cases recourse should be had to the Ordinary.

Art. II. Canonical Form of Celebrating Marriage.

1520. Canon 1094 states that those marriages alone are valid which are contracted either before the pastor or the Ordinary of the place or a priest delegated by either, and at least two witnesses. The term Ordinary is to be taken here in the broad sense indicated in canon 198. The competent minister of the Sacrament is the pastor of the place where the marriage takes place. Ordinarily it is the bride's pastor, though, for a just cause, and with the permission of the bride's pastor, the bridegroom's pastor, and for that matter any pastor, may receive the contracting parties into his parish and assist at their marriage. The Ordinary and the pastor can validly assist at marriages only within the limits of their jurisdiction. If they wish to assist at marriages elsewhere, they need a special delegation from the Ordinary of the place or the pastor of the parish. By pastor we are to understand any priest who, by reason of any title whatsoever, has full jurisdiction over a parish, provided he is not excommunicated, interdicted or suspended from office by a condemnatory or declaratory sentence of the ecclesiastical court. (See no. 1524.)

The Ordinary and the pastor can assist validly at marriages from the day they have taken canonical possession of their benefice, according to canons 1409 and 1444, or, if they have no benefice, as soon as they have entered upon their office. The competency of the Ordinary and the pastor to assist as ministers at marriages ceases as soon as they resign their office or are deprived of it, and as soon as they are transferred. A bishop who has been transferred remains a competent minister in the capacity of capitulary vicar of the diocese from which he is transferred, up to the time he takes possession of the diocese to which he is transferred. The pastor who has been suspended from jurisdiction or benefice, can validly assist at a marriage.

Within the limits of their territory the Ordinary of the place and the pastor assist validly at the marriages not only of their subjects, but also of non-subjects. In the latter case, they need the permission of the Ordinary or pastor of these persons, otherwise their act is illicit.

1521. The Ordinary and the pastor who can validly assist at marriages may also give permission to another priest validly to witness marriages within the limits of the diocese or parish respectively. (*C. J. C.*, can. 1095.) This permission must be granted to a specified priest for a specified marriage. General delegation cannot be given except to regularly appointed assistants, for the parish to which they are appointed; otherwise the permission or delegation is invalid. (Can. 1096.) It would not suffice, therefore, to say: "I delegate the priest whom you will send." The latter should be designated by name and office in order to avoid all misunderstanding.

1522. The delegation must be a real positive act; presumption and tolerance do not suffice in this case. It may be given by word of mouth, in writing, or by sign. To be certainly valid, the delegation must be known to the person delegated. It is doubtful if a priest assists validly at a marriage to which he has asked to be delegated, if the delegation has been given, but not as yet received at the moment he assists.

In order validly and licitly to assist at a marriage, the delegated priest must comply with the regulations laid down in his delegation, as well as with those required of pastors. He must not be forced to assist by violence or grave fear, and he must ask for, and receive, the consent of the contracting parties. Neither the priest delegated nor the pastor can remain content with merely passive assistance at marriages; if they do, the marriages are invalid.

As a general rule, the priest delegated may not subdelegate another, unless he has explicit permission to do so. *A fortiori,* the subdelegated priest cannot again subdelegate. Nevertheless, a priest who has been delegated *ad universitatem causarum* by an ordinary power inferior to that of the Pope, as well as a priest who has been delegated by the Pope himself, but not on account of his personal qualities, may subdelegate another priest, if he has not been forbidden to do so. The Ordinary and the pastor should not give permission to assist at a marriage until they have themselves ascertained the free status of the parties concerned.

1523. Delegation ceases when it is revoked by the person giving it, but not at the death of said person or the cessation of his right to delegate. The decree *"Ne temere"* stated that a priest delegated to assist at a marriage while excommunicated, interdicted or suspended from office, assists at that marriage invalidly. The New Code has nothing to say on this point, but it is our opinion that the regulation has not been changed. Moreover, canon 2264 states that acts of jurisdiction exercised by an excommunicated priest are unlawful, unless, not being a *vitandus,* he is called upon to perform these acts by the faithful. If he has been excommunicated by sentence, these acts are invalid.

1524. To assist licitly at a marriage, the Ordinary and the pastor must lawfully ascertain the free status of the contracting parties. They must ascertain also that at least one of the parties has a domicile or quasi-domicile in the place of marriage, or has lived there for at least a month. In the case of *vagi*, it suffices that they be actually staying in the place. All investigations of this kind should be conducted by the pastor of the bride, who also grants to another the permission to assist at the marriage. For just reasons, however, the pastor of the bridegroom may conduct them, and also assist at the marriage, according to canon 1097. *Positis ponendis*, every pastor assists validly and licitly at the marriage of persons who have no ecclesiastical domicile or quasi-domicile. If time permits, however, the pastor should refer the matter to the Ordinary and obtain his permission. The same rule applies if only one of the parties is a *vagus*. (*C. J. C.*, can. 1032.)

Marriages of parties belonging to different rites must be contracted in the presence of the pastor of the bridegroom, unless a particular law rules otherwise. (Can., 1097.)

1525. The pastor who assists at marriages without the permission required by canon 1097 may not keep the stole fee, but must forward it to the proper pastor of the contracting parties. The churches of religious, even those exempt, are, from the standpoint of marriages celebrated therein, under the jurisdiction of the Ordinary of the place and the pastor. (S. C. S., March 12, 1910.) The jurisdiction of military chaplains and others of this kind is determined by special regulations of the Holy See.

The form prescribed by the canons for the celebration of marriages is obligatory, even if a Catholic is marrying a non-Catholic, except in regard to the ceremonies, which the Holy See has decided should be suppressed in this case.

The assistance of the competent priest must be active, otherwise the Sacrament is null and void. By stating that it must be active, we mean that he must, *positis ponendis*, ask and receive the consent of the contracting parties, even though one of them be a non-Catholic. The concessions formerly made by the Holy See on this point have all been revoked. This is the authentic interpretation of canon 1102, given March 10, 1928.

1526. The two witnesses must be possessed of the qualities generally required of witnesses. It suffices that they have the use of reason, that they be trustworthy, that they be capable of doing what is demanded of them, and that they be willing to act as witnesses. Their presence must be physical and simultaneous, and for liceity, they must be Catholics, unless for a grave reason the bishop permits non-Catholics to assist in this capacity.

1527. Those held to the canonical form of marriage are: All persons baptized in the Catholic Church, and all converts to the Church from heresy or schism, even though both the first mentioned and the converts should afterwards have fallen away, if they contract marriage among themselves. Canon 1099 and the authentic interpretation of the Pontifical Commission dated October 16, 1919, appear to include under this same law persons who, born of Catholic parents, have received a non-Catholic education from the earliest years of discretion.

1528. The following are not held to the canonical form of marriage: (1) Non-Catholics, whether baptized or unbaptized, when they contract marriage among themselves; (2) non-Catholics, whether baptized or unbaptized, when they contract marriage with a Catholic of the Oriental rite; (3) Catholics of an Oriental rite, when they contract marriage among themselves.

By non-Catholics we understand also persons who, born of non-Catholic parents (can. 1099) or of parents of mixed religion (authentic interpretation of Oct. 16, 1919), have been baptized in the Catholic Church, but reared before the age of discretion in heresy, schism, infidelity, or irreligion.

1529. Since the form of marriage is governed only by ecclesiastical legislation, it can be dispensed with in certain instances. Canon 1098 states: (1) that if the Ordinary or the pastor, or a priest delegated by either, cannot be had, or the parties cannot go to him without great inconvenience, marriage may be contracted in danger of death validly and licitly in the presence of two witnesses; and (2) that, even apart from the danger of death, marriage may be contracted without the presence of an authorized minister, if it can be prudently foreseen that such a state of affairs will continue for a month.

1530. In either case, if there is another priest not delegated who can be present, he should be called to assist at the marriage together with the witnesses, but only the two witnesses are necessary for the validity of the contract. (*C. J. C.*, can. 1098.) In such a case the priest is possessed of all the powers mentioned in canons 1095 and 1096.

Whenever marriage is contracted in this way, the priest, if there be one present, and otherwise the witnesses, must see to it that the marriage is entered in both the baptismal and matrimonial records. (Can. 1103.)

The contracting parties are never bound to call in a priest who is excommunicated, interdicted or suspended from office, although they may do so if they wish. It is not necessary that the danger of death be imminent, nor that the contracting parties have an urgent reason for marrying.

1531. It has been asked if the regulations laid down by canon 1098 apply to the entire population of a country. Before the promulgation of the Code, the common opinion among theologians was that they did, because the decree *"Ne temere"* expressly mentioned the words *"in the region."* Since the appearance of the Code, however, many ecclesiastical writers have taken the opposite view, justifying their stand by the fact that canon 1098 does not contain these words. Nevertheless, even today prominent writers are not lacking who still hold to the former opinion. These writers base their view on a decision issued by the S. C. S. on January 31, 1916, regarding the case of a priest who, by reason of legal conflict, was prevented from assisting at a marriage. The decision read that in each case recourse should be had to the Holy See. An authentic interpretation of the canon in point, issued March 10, 1928, put an end to the controversy regarding the impossibility of having the Ordinary, the pastor or a delegated priest assist at the marriage. The mooted question was whether the impossibility had to result from physical absence or moral difficulty, for instance, that which would arise from legal conflict. The answer given was that it had to result from physical absence. In practice, therefore, marriages contracted without the presence of a competent minister, and without recourse to Rome, should be looked upon as both illicit and invalid if, in a particular case, the impossibility of obtaining a priest resulted only from a conflict with the civil law. The only exception is the danger of death, in which any priest may dispense with the canonical form.

Civil marriages are obligatory in France, Switzerland, Belgium, Germany (outside the danger of death), Holland, Hungary, Luxemburg, Roumania, and several republics of Latin America, etc.

The impossibility of contracting marriage before a competent minister does not exist if, without too great inconvenience, the contracting parties can journey to the territory of another Ordinary or pastor and celebrate their marriage in his presence.

1532. We herewith append a summary of ecclesiastical discipline relative to the canonical form of marriage before the appearance of the Code.

In the very beginning, the Church does not appear to have insisted on any special canonical form in the celebration of marriage. Little by little, the custom of contracting marriage

in the presence of the Church assumed a character of obligation, as regards liceity, but not validity. The present form
was prescribed by the Council of Trent, under pain of nullity
in all countries where its decrees were promulgated. It is impossible for us to give a complete list of these countries.
Nevertheless, since the effects of the new legislation are not
retroactive, cases may occur in which it would be necessary
to know whether or not the decrees of the Council were
promulgated or not. It might prove useful, therefore, to
know that they were promulgated in France, Algeria, Italy,
and the adjacent islands, Belgium, Spain, and Portugal. In
Canada and in certain other countries like Holland, except
the province of Limburg, and Russian Poland, the decrees
of the Council were promulgated, but the Holy See has declared that heretical and mixed marriages contracted in
these countries were valid. For the rest of Poland, Russia,
Ireland, Westphalia, etc., the Holy See has declared valid
mixed marriages in places where the decrees of the Council
were promulgated, and valid, but gravely illicit, all clandestine marriages. Strangers who repaired to these countries for
the sole purpose of marrying could not contract a valid
clandestine marriage, but *vagi* could do so. In Strasbourg the
decrees of the Council were not published until after the
Protestants of that city had become organized; it is probable, therefore, that the marriages of heretics contracted
there were valid.

1533. On January 18, 1906, Pope Pius X issued the Constitution *"Provida"* which promulgated the decree *"Tametsi"* in the then existing German Empire. In virtue of this
Constitution all clandestine marriages contracted by two
Catholics from the 15th of April, 1907, on are null, whereas
the clandestine marriages of heretics and persons of mixed
religion are valid. The Constitution *"Provida"* does not affect the validity of clandestine marriages contracted up to

that time by two Catholics, but the clandestine marriages contracted between two heretics or between a heretic and a Catholic were revalidated April 15, 1906, provided there existed no diriment impediment, that the marriages had not been dissolved by an ecclesiastical sentence, and that the consent of the contracting parties still persisted. Later on, the decree was extended to include Hungary.

1534. On April 19, 1908, the decree *"Ne temere"* came into force. Purely Catholic marriages made throughout the world were declared valid only on condition that they were contracted according to the prescribed canonical form. The same rule was made to apply to mixed marriages, but an exception was made in favor of Germany and Hungary, where mixed marriages contracted clandestinely were declared valid, provided that both parties were Germans or Hungarians, or rather born in one or other of these countries, that the marriage was contracted within the confines of these countries, and that the non-Catholic party had never been a Catholic after reaching the age of discretion.

1535. The Code states that even mixed clandestine marriages are no longer valid in any country and that the Constitution *"Provida"* has been abrogated. Today clandestine marriages, whether Catholic or mixed, are everywhere invalid and illicit, whereas those of heretics and schismatics who have never been Catholics after reaching the age of discretion are everywhere valid.

Art. III. Divine Institution.

1536. It is *of faith,* from the words of the Council of Trent, that Christ instituted this Sacrament. (See no. 756.) St. Paul intimates as much when he says: "This is a great sacrament, but I speak in Christ and in the Church." (See also C. of Trent, Sess. 24.)

When did Christ institute this Sacrament? Some aver that

it was when he attended the marriage feast at Cana; others, when He said: "What therefore God hath joined together, let no man put asunder;" and still others, that it was after His Resurrection. It is clear that marriage as a contract was instituted by God, since it is the natural and indispensable means of multiplying the human race, and God is the Author of nature. This truth is taught in Sacred Scripture, but before the time of Our Lord marriage was not a Sacrament.

Art. IV. The Effects of Matrimony.

1537. In discussing the effects of Matrimony some authors consider the parties taken separately, others the parties taken together, and others, finally, the children. Concerning the latter we have only to say that Matrimony renders them: (1) legitimate (see no. 1462) and (2) subject to parental authority, thus giving them the right to food and sustenance and also to a Christian education. We shall offer a brief discussion of the other effects immediately.

1538. *The effects of Matrimony in the parties taken separately.* Matrimony confers grace. This is *of faith,* from the words of the Council of Trent: "If anyone saith that matrimony does not confer grace; let him be anathema." (Sess. 24, can. 1.) Since Matrimony is a Sacrament of the living, the grace which it confers is second grace. Matrimony confers also sacramental grace, which perfects natural love, confirms the indissolubility of the marriage bond, and sanctifies the married. The Sacrament aids the contracting parties in bearing with the infirmities of the flesh, in generating their children in Christian piety, and in imparting a Christian education to them.

1539. Manifestly, then, marriage is good, honest, and holy. This truth belongs to the domain of faith against the Manichaeans. "If thou take a wife, thou hast not sinned" (1 Cor. 7, 28.) "He that giveth his virgin in marriage, doth well." (1 Cor. 7, 38.) According to the Catechism of the Council of Trent, there are three advantages which arise from marriage: offspring, faith, and the Sacrament. *Offspring* is not to be understood as referring solely to the procreation of children, but also to the discipline and education by which children are reared to piety; *faith* is not the habitual faith infused in Baptism, but the fidelity which the husband plights to the wife and the wife to the husband; and the *Sacrament* is the indissoluble tie.

1540. From all this we are permitted to conclude that any Christian who does not feel himself called to a more perfect state of life, may contract marriage provided he conforms to all the regulations prescribed. Parents and princes sin grievously, therefore, when they unjustly withhold this right from those under their charge. "The holy Synod," says the Council of Trent, "enjoins on all, of whatsoever grade, dignity, and condition they may be, under pain of anathema to be *ipso facto* incurred, that they put no constraint in any way whatever, either directly or indirectly, on those subject to them, or on any others whomsoever, so as to hinder them from freely contracting marriage." (Sess. 24, ch. 9.)

1541. *The inferiority of this state.* It would be wrong to conclude that the obligation to marry is binding upon all. The obligation to propagate the human species would be binding only in the event of there being danger of this species dying out. To use a comparison of Suarez, the precept of almsgiving does not bind when all are rich (*De voto castitatis*, ch. 1, 6); he adds: "It is hard for me to believe that after the death of our first parents there was a time when this precept was binding upon all men, or even upon some person in particular, because when the need ceases, the obligation ceases also. . . . With this in mind, I have endeavored to show from the words of Scripture and the writings of the Fathers that no precept existed under the Old

Law, obliging men to marry, . . . and that if this obligation did not exist under the law of Moses, *a fortiori* it does not exist under the law of grace." As to the positive divine precept, it is doubtful whether it existed before the Christian era, and it is *certain* that it does not exist under the New Law. "The words 'Increase and multiply,'" says the Catechism of the Council of Trent, "do not impose on every individual an obligation to marry; and now that the human race is widely diffused, not only is there no law rendering marriage obligatory, but, on the contrary, virginity is highly exalted and strongly recommended in Scripture as superior to marriage, as a state of greater perfection and holiness."

1542. There are, however, a few cases in which a person is obliged *per accidens* to enter into the marriage contract, to wit: (1) if the marriage would promote, not a private good, but the common good of a country; (2) if a man had deceived a young girl by promising to marry her. In this last instance, according to an opinion which we must follow in practice, the man must marry the girl, except in the cases which we shall refer to in no. 2527; (3) if a person is given to lust and does not wish to take any other means of curbing his passion. Some writers are of the opinion that he is also obliged to marry when he cannot take any other means, but this last view is rejected by St. Alphonsus. "Who among us," he asks, "cannot pray, and through prayer triumph over all evil inclinations?" Anyone who wishes to take other means, is not, therefore, obliged to marry, and may not be constrained to do so by his confessor, especially in countries where the Church laws in regard to marriage are held in disrepute. "Who would be foolish enough to hold," again asks St. Alphonsus, "that marriage is the only possible means of curbing our lower appetites?" A number of authors are of the opinion that it is harder to remain pure in the married state than in that of celibacy.

1543. Therefore, children are not obliged to obey their parents when the latter command them to marry; this is the common opinion of theologians. A father may request his son to marry for a just reason, for instance, to perpetuate the family, but he may never force a child to marry who is bent on following a higher state of life. *A fortiori,* a person should not feel himself called to the marriage state by a special divine vocation if he feels a natural propensity for that state, no more than a person who is always hungry should feel that he is not called upon to fast.

1544. Neither is marriage one of the counsels. All theologians, according to Suarez, agree on this point. There are cases in which marriage should be advised, but in order that a work be one of the counsels, it is necessary that it be better than the one which is opposed to, and cannot be performed simultaneously with, it.

1545. Celibacy is a better and more blessed state. This is *of faith,* from the words of the Council of Trent: "If anyone saith that the marriage state is to be placed above the state of virginity, or of celibacy, and that it is not better and more blessed to remain in virginity, or in celibacy, than to be united in matrimony; let him be anathema." (Sess. 24, can. 10.) This point is made clear by the Scriptures: "He that giveth not his virgin, doth better." (1 Cor. 7, 38.) The Fathers of the Church are unstinted in their praise of virginity.

The vow, then, to marry is null and void, since it is not concerned with a better thing. The Catechism of the Council of Trent expresses itself as follows on this point: "As it is the duty of the pastor to propose to himself the holiness and perfection of the faithful, his earnest desires must be in full accordance with those of the Apostle, who, writing to the Corinthians, says: 'I would that all men were even as myself,' that is, all embraced the virtue of continence. If there be any one blessing superior to every other, it surely falls to the lot of him who, unfettered by the distracting cares of the world, the turbulence of passion tranquillized, the unruly desires of the flesh extinguished, reposes in the practice of piety and the contemplation of heavenly things." (*On Matrimony;* see no. 2082.)

1546. Celibacy is permissible. This truth *belongs to the domain of faith.* It is *certain* that celibacy is possible, because nothing is counselled or commanded that is not within the power of man, assisted by divine grace, and God gives the grace to any one who requests it of Him. And although Calvin taught that it was Christ's intention to deter Christians from practicing celibacy when he said: "Let him who can understand, understand," St. Jerome, St. Thomas, (*Opusc.* 18, ch. 8), Suarez (*De Voto Cast.,* ch. 1, 21) and others contend that it was the opposite idea He was trying to convey. That virginity and celibacy are possible can be proved from experience and from the injunction placed by the Church even upon those of her priests who live in the world, that they might exercise their sacred functions with greater purity, free themselves from earthly cares, and give themselves up more unreservedly to the work of saving souls.

1547. Celibacy is not of precept *in se.* This is certain, otherwise marriage would be sinful. *Per accidens,* however, celibacy is of precept for those who are impotent as well as for those who have taken the vow of chastity.

1548. Celibacy is one of the counsels. This is *certain,* from the words of the Council of Trent. The Catechism of the Council says: "The earnest desires of the pastor must be in full accordance with those of the Apostle, who, writing to the Corinthians, says: 'I would that all men were even as myself'; that is, that all embraced the virtue of continence." In times such as these, when men are more given over to the pursuit of worldly pleasures and loves, than to that of the things of God, the priest must preach this truth in public and in private, at the risk of its disappearing from our midst. It is a truth expatiated upon by St. Paul, and after him by all the holy Doctors: St. John Chrysostom, St. Basil, St. Ambrose, St. Augustine, and St. Jerome. Certainly it is an act of virtue to preach a good that is possible, superior, counselled, and more blessed, even if advice of this kind results only in deterring young persons from entering into hasty marriages, keeping their minds free from impure thoughts, and placing them on their guard against the sin of onanism after they have embraced the marriage state.

1549. If it be a virtuous act to exhort young people to that which is "better," it is most certainly a sin to deter them from it. This truth applies to every one, but especially to confessors and pastors, who by virtue of *their office* must procure the welfare of souls. Speaking upon this subject, St. Thomas remarks that to stifle desires such as these before they have even seen the day, is to exhibit a cruelty paralleled only in Babylon, and a spirit of malice reminiscent of King Herod. (*De Eruditione Princip.*, V, 30; see also no. 1317.)

To practice virginity or celibacy without the vow is a counsel, and to bind oneself by vow, is, in the words of Suarez, another counsel. (*De Statu Perf.*, I, 8, 3.) He adds that the vow of chastity is a good thing, nay a very good thing, and that if this vow be considered apart from circumstances, this proposition is *of faith.* (*De Voto Castit.*, I, 16.) It is better, indeed, to surrender both the tree and its fruits than to surrender the fruits alone. In suggesting the vow of chastity, however, the confessor should abide by the rules laid down in no. 1343.

1550. *The effects of Matrimony in the parties taken together.* Marriage *in fieri,* or the contract raised to the dignity of a Sacrament, gives to each one of the contracting parties the right over the body of the other. This right is called the *bond*. We shall speak, first, of the bond itself, and, second, of its properties.

1551. *The bond itself.* This right is of the essence of the Sacrament, so that any one who purposely excludes it, contracts invalidly. By reason of this right, all acts which are useful and suited to the process of procreation, and which, outside of wedlock, constitute the sin of fornication, are made licit, but all sins of lust which are contrary to the natural end of marriage, and which the parties may commit either among themselves or with others, are of a graver nature than those committed by single persons, and take on the special character of adultery. (See no. 2544 ff.)

1552. If the right is of the essence of the Sacrament, the same is not true of the use of the right, and so if two contracting parties, having the intention of bestowing this right, promise to God or to one another that they will not make use of the right, their marriage must be considered valid. Such parties should take care, however, not to posit the act of consummation as the *conditio sine qua non* of the contract. Moreover, conditional marriages are illicit, from what we have said in no. 1519. It would be both dangerous and imprudent to vow to practice chastity in marriage before entering into a marriage contract, because it is much safer and much easier to practice chastity outside the married state than within. Nevertheless, it is not forbidden *in se* for two persons who have taken the vow of chastity to marry with the resolution of keeping this vow, if there is no danger of breaking it. On the other hand, if the two contracting parties practice restraint by mutual agreement after marriage, they are the worthy rivals of our first parents in the state of innocence, even though the primary end of marriage is not attained, and they are following in the footsteps of St. Joseph and the Virgin Mother. *"Sine carnali commixtione,"* says St.

Thomas, "marriage is rendered more holy." (*Suppl.*, q. 42, art. 4.)

1553. One of the contracting parties sins gravely if he refuses the *debitum* to the other. Canon 1111 does away with the right to refuse the *debitum* during the first two months of married life.

1554. *The properties of the bond.* There are two such properties: unity and indissolubility.

Unity. Plurality is opposed to unity. Plurality is simultaneous when a woman has several husbands at one and the same time. This is called simultaneous *polyandry.* If the husband has several wives at one and the same time, this is called simultaneous *polygamy.* Plurality is successive when one of the spouses contracts marriage with several parties throughout the course of his life, not simultaneously, but after the death of his former consort.

Simultaneous polyandry is opposed not only to the divine, but also to the natural law, written in the very conscience of man. This is the opinion of all writers, who treat such a practice as equal to prostitution. It is held in horror even among pagans.

1555. *Simultaneous polygamy* is not so opposed to the essence of marriage, and for this reason, God permitted it to the patriarchs, and according to a few writers, even to the gentiles before the advent of Christ. It is, however, opposed to the secondary and natural end of marriage, or the peace of the family and absolute equity of the contract, since the woman surrenders her body to one man, but he surrenders his to many women.

By divine law, simultaneous polygamy is forbidden to both Christians and infidels, because Jesus Christ is the universal legislator. Consequently, an infidel who is converted to the Catholic faith, must dismiss all his wives except the first, whom, in law, he must retain, unless he contracted no truly valid marriage with any. For a just cause, the Sovereign Pontiff may dissolve this marriage and several theologians are of the opinion that he has this right, provided the marriage was not consummated after the pagan's conversion. Ballerini substantiates this view by several facts.

Pius V permitted the Indians to retain the wife with whom they received Baptism; Gregory XIII allowed slaves sold in lands far removed from their original dwelling places and separated from their first wives, whom they could no longer summon, to contract marriage with Christian women; and the S. C. of P. in 1807 issued an answer to the bishop of Cochin China to the effect that, if an infidel converted to Catholicism has several wives and his first wife refused to embrace her husband's religion, he might retain any one of them who joined the Catholic faith, provided he and she renewed their consent in the presence of their lawful pastor and two witnesses.

1556. Among Christians, it is *of faith* that polygamy is forbidden by divine law: "If anyone saith, that it is lawful for Christians to have several wives at the same time, and that this is not prohibited by any divine law; let him be anathema." (C. of Trent, Sess. 24, can. 1.) In the beginning God instituted marriage between one man and one woman, and Jesus Christ restored marriage to its primitive purity when He said: "Therefore they are now not two, but one flesh." (Mark 10, 8.)

1557. Successive polyandry and polygamy, *i. e.*, second marriages, are not forbidden. This is *certain* from the words of the Council of Florence: "We affirm that it is lawful to contract not only second marriages, but even ulterior ones," and from canon 1142 of the New Code.

1558. It is *certain* that, *in se*, second marriages are neither commanded nor counselled. (See no. 1542.) *Per accidens,* they may become a precept, as in the cases enumerated above.

1559. Widowhood is not only permissible, but also possible, even when the party is still in the prime of life. It is a better and more blessed state than marriage, and consequently is counselled like virginity and for the same reasons. This is *certain.* "But I say to the unmarried, and to the widows: It is good for them if they so continue, even as I." (1 Cor. 7, 8.) "More blessed shall she [the widow] be, if she so remain, according to my counsel." (*Ibid.,* 7, 40.) It follows that it is good to counsel widowhood, and evil to deter one from it, unless the motive be to avoid the danger of incontinence: "For it is better to marry than to be burnt." (*Ibid.,* 7, 9.) And let it be observed that in this text St. Paul refers not to the temptation, but to the fall into temptation.

1560. *Indissolubility.* This term may apply either to the bond, or to separation from bed and board.

The *indissolubility* of the bond. Indissolubility does not mean unity, for a marriage might not be one and yet be indissoluble, and *vice versa.* Indissolubility is essential to the marriage contract, in such wise that if two persons, even heretics, entered into it with the agreement that they would dissolve it some day, their marriage would be invalid. The case would be different if they entered into the contract thinking that it could be dissolved. (See no. 1557.)

1561. Consummated marriage (*per effusionem seminis intra vas debitum*) is by divine law indissoluble as to the bond among Christians. It is *certain* from the words of the Council of Trent (Sess. 24) in cases of adultery, heresy, absence of one of the parties, or when cohabitation has been rendered too difficult. Jesus Christ confirmed the indissolubility of this bond when he said: "What therefore God hath joined together, let no man put asunder" (Matt.

19, 6.) "If anyone saith that the Church errs, in that she declares that, for many causes, a separation may take place between husband and wife, in regard of bed, or in regard of cohabitation, for a determinate or for an indeterminate period; let him be anathema." (C. of Trent, Sess. 24, can. 7.) The wife is bound by this law as long as her husband lives.

Although the Greeks recognize the indissolubility of the marriage bond, they tolerate divorce in cases of adultery, but the Roman Church forbids such a practice to the Greek uniates even in extreme cases.

According to a decision of the Holy Office, issued to the bishops of France May 27, 1886, judges may not pronounce civil divorces in favor of parties validly married in the eyes of the Church. Lawyers are not allowed to plead such cases, and magistrates are not permitted to unite in civil marriage parties civilly divorced. Several writers are of the opinion, however, that the concurrence given in these cases is only material, and that it may be licit for a just reason, provided the intention of the official be to break not the religious contract which the civil law cannot reach, but only the civil effects of marriage. (See no. 2470.) Christians may not have recourse to the civil courts for the purpose of obtaining a divorce, without committing serious sin, unless permitted to do so by duly constituted ecclesiastical authority. This is the opinion of the eminent theologian Lehmkuhl. Others include the case of a woman who has knowledge that her husband is about to seek a divorce and who starts proceedings against him first in order to obtain the right to keep and educate her children. The same writers add that the judge is bound to do all in his power to bring about a reconciliation, or if not, at least a separation of body and goods. If the parties should persist in their first intention, he may lend his assistance, if he fears very grave inconvenience, and in particular the loss of his position, even though he knows that the parties have the intention of contracting another marriage.

1562. Marriage not consummated *per effusionem seminis intra vas* (*nam coitus sine seminatione non sufficit ad consummationem*) is called *ratum* by theologians, when such a marriage is contracted by the faithful, and it may be dissolved, even though the parties have indulged in the marriage act before the marriage ceremony. This is *of faith* from the words of the Council of Trent (Sess. 24, can. 6), that such marriages may be dissolved by solemn religious profession. Some are of the opinion that solemn religious profession produces this effect by divine privilege; others say that it is the Church who affixes to the religious profession this right, of which we shall have more to say later.

Marriage that has not been consummated may also be dissolved by a dispensation of the Sovereign Pontiff. This is *certain* from the practice sanctioned by the Church in canon 1119. The Holy Father will grant such a dispensation for a good reason at the request of either or both parties, or one of them, even though the other objects.

Outside these cases the marriage bond is indissoluble by divine law; it is not even dissolved by the reception of Holy Orders.

1563. The question as to whether or not consummated marriage is indissoluble by the natural law is a controverted one among theologians. Some are of the opinion that it is; others that it is not, but the Syllabus has condemned the following proposition: "Marriage is not indissoluble by the natural law." It is certain, indeed, that divorce is not favorable to the education of the offspring, nor to the mutual fidelity of the parties. And yet divorce is not absolutely opposed to the essential end of marriage, for Moses permitted it to the Jews, and according to several authors the marriage bond among the Jews was broken by divorce. In the presence of these conflicting views, we should not condemn, says Hurter, the practice of the gentiles permitting divorce in case of adultery or chronic sickness. It would seem, however, that the Syllabus should settle the question definitively; but if not, it is at least certain that infidels who are in these circumstances, and who are converted to the Catholic faith, may request and obtain from the Sovereign Pontiff that he dissolve the first bond. (See no. 1542.)

1564. By a divine law, promulgated by St. Paul, marriage contracted by two infidels may be dissolved as to the bond, if one of the parties is converted to the Catholic faith and the other will not consent to live in peace, or will not live in marriage without giving insult and offense to the Creator. This is *certain* from the practice sanctioned by the Church in canons 1120–1127 and from the words of St. Paul: "But if the unbeliever depart, let him depart" (1 Cor. 7, 15), and it holds true even in cases where the infidel party does not seduce the converted party to sin for a lengthy period of time, but does so subsequently.

An answer issued by the S. C. of P. gives the right to a Catholic woman converted from infidelity to leave her husband in cases where he causes her to sin mortally against the virtue of chastity, and marry another. If the occasion of sin arises not from the husband, but from persons living in the same house, she may leave her husband, but not remarry, when such a measure is the only way out of the difficulty.

1565. Before the converted and baptized party may validly contract a new marriage, he or she must first summon or interpellate the unbaptized party and ask if the other party wishes to be converted and baptized, and if not, whether he or she is willing to live in marriage without offense to God. Interpellations must always be made, unless the Holy See has decreed otherwise, something which it always does when the interpellations are useless or dangerous. In all cases, the Catholic party may never dispense himself from such interpellations and remarry. As soon as the interpellations have been made, or dispensation from them has been granted, the converted party is free to remarry. The interpellations need never be renewed, but the dispensation from them must be renewed in cases where the second marriage is postponed. If the infidel party agrees to live in peace with the converted one, without offense to God, after being interpellated, the marriage bond is not dissolved. An exception to this rule is the case where the law forbids one to cohabit with certain infidels, because of a special danger of perversion or possible scandal. As a general rule, cohabitation is permissible in all infidel lands, except with Jews, in whose case the Church will not allow cohabitation, no matter where they have their domicile.

There are certain Christian countries where the Church, generally speaking, forbids cohabitation of the newly converted party with the infidel. According to Noldin, the Catholic party in these countries may remarry as soon as the infidel party has refused to become converted. Since this opinion is not certain, however, it is best to have recourse to the Holy See, who may remedy the situation by granting a dispensation. If the newly converted party contracts a second marriage after Baptism without interpellating his or her former consort, or without seeking a dispensation from the interpellations, recourse must be had to the Holy Father, and the facts of the case clearly laid before him. If the infidel party, who has been interpellated, answers that he or she is willing to come and live in peace with his or her former consort, but that he or she is prevented from doing so, the Catholic party may remarry, if he or she is not the cause of the existing impediment. (D. H. O., 1880.) Another decision makes it clear that the motive for which the infidel refuses to live in peace with the other party need not always be faith; any other motive non-imputable to the Catholic party after Baptism, has the same effect. If the converted party furnishes the ground for separation to his or her consort after Baptism, and wants to remarry, he or she must have recourse to the Holy See. A converted party who has been dispensed from the interpellations may regard a second marriage as valid, even though he learns later on that at the time when the second marriage was contracted, the other party had also joined the Catholic Church. The reason for this is that they have not consummated a Christian marriage and, therefore, the Holy See can grant a dispensation.

1566. The interpellations should be made as a rule in summary and extrajudicial form by the Ordinary of the converted party. Such an Ordinary must grant the unbaptized party, at his or her request, a certain length of time to reflect before giving an answer. Failure to answer within the specified time must be regarded as a negative reply, and an extension of the time limit must be granted only at the request of the unbaptized party. Interpellations made privately by the converted party are always valid. They are also licit, if the above mentioned form cannot be observed, in which case there must be proof of the interpellations by at least two witnesses or by some other means provided for and acknowledged by law. (*C. J. C.*, can. 1123.)

1567. The unbaptized party is to be considered as not wanting to live in peace with the baptized party and without offense to the Creator, if he or she offends gravely with such a party against conjugal purity, lives in concubinage, refuses to have the children educated in the Catholic religion, or refuses to allow his or her consort to practice the Catholic faith. Canon 1124 states emphatically that the convert who, after Baptism, lives again in marriage with the unbaptized party does not thereby forfeit the right to enter upon a new marriage with a Catholic. He can make use of such a right, if the unbaptized party happens to change his or her mind, and, without the fault of the other party, separates, or does not live peacefully and without injury to the religious obligations of the converted party. (Can. 1124.)

1568. In all the above mentioned cases, the marriage is dissolved only when the converted and baptized party enters into a second marriage with a catechumen or a baptized person. Whence we must conclude that if the converted party does not remarry, and the unbaptized party does, and later on turns Catholic, the unbaptized party is bound to return to his or her former consort.

If the husband in such a marriage is converted first, and receives Holy Orders or pronounces solemn vows, his marriage is not dissolved, although he may not return to his wife because of his vow, and she may not contract a second marriage. Several theologians are of the opinion, however, that the marriage is dissolved when the converted husband embraces the religious state, provided the marriage is not consummated after he receives Baptism, even though it were consummated beforehand. In both of these cases, and even in a case where the converted husband vows to live a life of celibacy, and then finds it difficult to obtain a dispensation from his vow in order to rejoin his wife, who has also become converted, the Holy See may be petitioned to dissolve the marriage bond.

1569. If both parties become converted, receive Baptism, and then consummate their marriage, the Holy See cannot dissolve the bond. If the marriage has never been consummated, the Holy See can dissolve the bond as in the case of non-consummated marriages between the faithful. If the marriage was consummated before Baptism, but not afterwards, the Holy See can still dissolve the bond.

1570. The Pauline privilege is not intended for persons who contract marriage with infidels with the proper dispensation of the Holy See, although a marriage contracted by the converted party with an infidel with the proper dispensation dissolves the first marriage bond.

Theologians are not agreed as to whether or not converts from infidelity to heresy may make use of the Pauline privilege. The opinion of those who hold that they may is more probable.

1571. *The indissolubility of the bond as to bed and board.* As a general rule, husband and wife are bound to live together under pain of mortal sin. This conclusion follows quite naturally from the terms of the marriage contract. The Council of Trent states explicitly that: "If anyone saith that the Church errs, in that she declares that, for many causes, a separation may take place between husband and wife, in regard of bed, or in regard of cohabitation, for a determinate or for an indeterminate period; let him be anathema." (Sess. 24, can. 8; see also nos. 2414 and 2415.)

1572. The following are some of the legitimate reasons for separation from bed and board: *The consent of the two parties,* provided there be no danger of incontinence. With this mutual consent, the two parties may separate for a specified period of time, in order to engage in some special occupation, or perpetually, out of love for the virtue of chastity, or to enter into religion, and receive Holy Orders with the proper dispensation. *Bodily or spiritual danger* to either party such as might arise from living with a consort who is a heretic, an apostate, or a sodomite. Persons who find themselves in danger of this kind are to be regarded as being in a necessary occasion of sin. (See no. 1332 ff.) In connection with this reason, the Code states that a separation may be granted also if, through cruelties inflicted, one of the parties makes life too difficult (can. 1131), and we hold this to be true even in the case where the suffering party has brought on such cruelties through his or her own fault.

Separation may also be granted if one party joins a non-Catholic sect, educates the offspring as non-Catholic, or leads a criminal or despicable life. In all these cases, common life must be resumed when the reason for the separation ceases. If, however, the separation was pronounced by the bishop, either for a time or indefinitely, the innocent party is not obliged to return, except when the time specified has elapsed or the bishop gives orders to return. (Can. 1131.)

1573. A third reason is *adultery* or *sodomy*. The Code states that for this reason, the other party has the right to stop for all time the community of life, though the marriage bond remains, unless the other party consented to the crime, or was the cause of it, or expressly or tacitly condoned it, or finally, committed the same crime himself or herself. We hold this to be true even in the case where the party who commits the crime is an infidel. In the external forum, the innocent party is reputed to have condoned the crime if, after the adultery, he or she exchanges kisses or embraces with the other party, has marital relations with the guilty partner, or continues to live with said partner for a period of six months. If the innocent party had no intention of condoning the crime by such marks of affection, the crime could not be reputed to have been forgiven in the internal forum.

1574. Suspicions of adultery do not suffice, any more than do kisses, embraces, or impure touches. It is enough, however, to find the adulterers *in eodem lecto,* or to come upon a letter in which the guilty party confesses having committed adultery. The innocent wife or husband is not obliged to dismiss the guilty partner, except perhaps to administer a correction or avoid scandal; but he or she always may.

1575. Two parties may *themselves* apply for separation

quoad torum for all the reasons enumerated above. More probably they may do likewise in a case of separation *quoad habitationem,* when adultery has been committed, as long as the crime is certain, even though occult, and provided there be no danger for either the soul or the body.

In all other cases, petition for *separatio quoad habitationem* must be addressed to ecclesiastical authority, *i. e.,* the local Ordinary. (*C. J. C.,* can. 1131.)

1576. Canon 1130 states that, in cases of adultery, the innocent party who, either through the sentence of a judge or by his or her own authority, lawfully leaves the guilty party, has no longer any obligation to admit the adulterer back to conjugal life. The innocent party, however, has the right to admit the guilty partner, and oblige him or her to return, unless, in the mean time, such a partner has embraced a state of life contrary to that of marriage with the consent of the innocent party. (Can. 1130.) It goes without saying that the innocent party always has the right to embrace such a state of life.

After the separation, the children are to be placed in the care of the innocent party, and if one of the parties is a non-Catholic, the Catholic party is to have charge of them, unless the Ordinary decides otherwise for the sake of the children's welfare. (Can. 1132.)

CHAPTER II

PREPARATIONS FOR MARRIAGE

The preparatory acts for the reception of the Sacrament of Matrimony are divided into optional and obligatory. The only optional act consists in the engagement or promise of marriage.

Art. I. Engagement or Promise of Marriage.

1577. A promise of marriage may be either unilateral or bilateral, according as it is binding on one of the contracting parties or both. A bilateral promise of marriage constitutes what is generally known as an engagement. The engagement, therefore, is the reciprocal promise of a future marriage, made between persons who are able to enter into such a marriage, whereas a unilateral promise is purely gratuitous, affecting the other person only to the extent in which such a person has the intention of obligating himself. The acceptance of a unilateral promise, which is necessary for validity, does not itself constitute a promise. The explanations which follow apply to both promises of marriage.

1578. *The essential form of the engagement.* To be valid, the promise of marriage must be made and accepted according to the form prescribed by the Church. The rule is that the promise be in writing, and that it be signed by the two parties. If the promise be unilateral, one party signs the promise, the other the acceptance. The Church requires also that the document be signed by the pastor or the local Ordinary or two witnesses. In cases where one or both of the contracting parties does not know how to write, or is unable to write, this fact must be noted in the document under pain of rendering it null and void, and then the document must be signed by an extra witness.

The witness need not necessarily be the pastor or the Ordinary of the parties concerned; any other pastor or Ordinary may serve in the same capacity within the limits of his own territory. The pastor or the Ordinary may not delegate other persons, and the two witnesses must have reached the age of reason and know how to read and write.

1579. The parties may contract and sign promises of marriage through an attorney specially empowered to receive their promise of engagement. The time and place must be appended to the terms of the contract under pain of rendering it null and void.

1580. The engagement to marry does not in law admit of action in the ecclesiastical court to force the other party into marriage, even though it be valid, and there be no just cause to shirk its fulfillment. (*C. J. C.*, can. 1017.) There are some theologians who hold that this law of the Church does not do away with the moral obligation of the promise of marriage thus "rescinded." This opinion does not seem to be in conformity with the text of the law, for since the object of the promise is a Sacrament or a sacred thing, we fail to see how the Church would not have the power to suppress its natural effects. Even a valid promise of marriage does not give the right to force its fulfillment in court, although action for possible injury done by the unjust breaking of the engagement is admitted thereto. Such action may be brought in any civil court.

All Catholics of the Latin rite must observe these essential formalities when making these promises among themselves or with others. It is controverted if Christians belonging to any other rite are subject to the same legislation.

1581. *The qualities of an engagement.* The contracting parties must posit a valid act, *i. e.*, make a real and sincere promise, and have the intention of binding themselves in justice and *sub gravi*. They must act in this way because their contract is bilateral and onerous, so that a party who would act otherwise would be guilty of fraud and bound to restitution, if any injury were done.

1582. *The promise must be deliberate, i. e.*, made with complete understanding of the obligations assumed, as well as a free and perfect will to accept such obligations. Persons are held to be capable of the deliberation required in this case when they have reached the age of seven.

Must error and fear be accounted obstacles in the way of the freedom required validly to enter into a promise of marriage? Error certainly annuls any promise of marriage if it bears (1) on the object of the contract; (2) on the person; (3) on a quality which determines the person; (4) on a quality appended as an indispensable condition. Any error bearing on a purely accidental quality does not annul a promise of marriage, but if such an error is the real cause of the contract, it renders the contract rescindable in favor of the party deceived. This holds true also in the cases of deception or fraud.

Promises of marriage are regarded by several theologians as invalid if contracted through grave fear unjustly inspired *ab extrinseco*. Others regard these same promises as valid but rescindable in favor of the innocent party. It is certain that unjust fear, when it is slight, does not render promises of marriage invalid, although it may render them susceptible of annulment if the fear was the sole cause of the contract. Finally, it is controverted whether or not a ravisher may contract valid promises of marriage with the woman whom he has ravished, as long as she is detained by him.

1583. In order to constitute an engagement, the promise must be *mutual*. The obligation begins only when the two promises have been made and mutually accepted. It is required that the parties be capable of contracting marriage some day. All diriment and impedient impediments, for which the Church is not accustomed to grant a dispensation, render promises of marriage null and void. On the other hand, promises of marriage are certainly valid if the impediments are such as cease to exist with the lapse of time, or depend, like mixed religion, on the will of the contracting party. If the impediment is *in se* perpetual, but the Holy See is accustomed to dispense from it, promises of marriage made with the condition: "if we obtain the dispensation," are looked upon as valid by the majority of writers. Noldin is of the opinion that persons who make a promise of marriage while laboring under some such dispensable impediment are supposed to include this condition, and he cites in favor of his view such eminent authorities as Ballerini, Palmieri, Gasparri, de Angelis, etc. A person who is married cannot make any valid promise of marriage, not even on the condition: "If I survive my consort."

A verified condition pertaining to the past or the present, and appended to promises of marriage, never renders them invalid. If the condition refers to the future, and is both honest and possible, the parties bind themselves to wait for its fulfillment. The obligation to wait for the fulfillment of a condition thus appended would render subsequent promises of marriage illicit and more probably invalid. Once the condition is fulfilled, the promise of marriage is valid.

If the condition which refers to the future is possible, but dishonest, there is no obligation to wait for its fulfillment. After its fulfillment the promises of marriage are valid, although several writers would be slow in granting that they are.

If the condition which refers to the future is impossible or contrary to the essence of marriage, the promises are most certainly null and void. In cases where a future lawful condition is appended to the terms of a promise of marriage, this promise is probably null and void after the fulfillment of the condition, if one of the parties withdrew his or her consent before the fulfillment. Withdrawal of one's consent in cases of this kind is *in se* illicit.

1584. *A promise of marriage made without the knowledge or against the will of parents.* A promise of marriage made without the knowledge or against the will of parents is *in se* valid. *Per accidens* it is invalid if the opposition of parents is right and just, because in this case the object of the promise is an illicit one, and hence the promise itself is necessarily null and void. According to all writers, the opposition of parents is right and just if there be solid reasons for fearing family dishonor, scandal or serious breaches and dissensions, or if the contracting parties come from widely different stations of life, unless other qualities exist which compensate somewhat for differences in wealth or social status. There are some writers, however, who deny that this last objection suffices of itself to constitute a valid reason for parents annulling a promise of marriage of their children.

1585. To render a promise of marriage licit, some authors require the consent of the parents; others claim that it suffices if the children seek the parents' advice in an effort to comply with the terms of the fourth commandment.

1586. *Annullment of promises of marriage.* Two kinds of causes may bring about the annullment of a promise of marriage. The first dissolve the promise in the full sense of the term, and restore to each one of the contracting parties equal rights to liberty; the second dissolve the promises by the will of one of the contracting parties alone, who has a just cause for breaking the contract. In the first case, the promises are annulled, in the second, they are rescinded.

1587. The following are the causes which give to both contracting parties the full right to make promises of marriage, or to enter into marriage contracts with other persons.

Mutual consent, by which the contracting parties excuse one another from the obligation arising out of promises they have made, even under oath. A resolutive condition appended to the contract and fulfilled at a later date has the same effect as mutual consent, and the same is true of the case where the two contracting parties freely allow the time to lapse beyond which they have agreed that the obligation is no longer binding.

1588. *A perpetual impediment,* from which no dispensation can be obtained, and which unexpectedly thrusts itself upon one or both of the contracting parties. Authors are not agreed as to whether or not a subsequent marriage entered into by one of the parties in a case of this kind dissolves the promise of marriage. The affirmative opinion is the more probable. It is certain, however, that such a marriage renders a promise of marriage rescindable. There are no longer any such dispensable perpetual impediments; formerly there were those of spiritual affinity and affinity *ex copula illicita*.

1589. *The choice of a more perfect state of life*. Examples of a choice of a more perfect state of life are the reception of Holy Orders, the vow to enter religion or Holy Orders, and the vow of virginity or chastity. According to several authors, the promises of marriage are dissolved also by the reception of minor orders, entrance into a religious institute or into an ecclesiastical seminary with the intention of studying for the priesthood.

It would be more true to say that the reception of minor orders, or entrance into religion or an ecclesiastical seminary or house of religious formation, merely suspends a promise of marriage, so that, if the party returns to the world, he or she is still bound to keep his or her engagement with the other contracting party. The latter is not, however, bound to wait for developments, because in repairing to one of the above mentioned places, the other party gives up his or her rights. It seems almost superfluous to add that if one of the contracting parties makes a vow of chastity or a vow to enter a more perfect state, merely in order to make a fool of the other party, he or she is not freed from the promise of marriage.

1590. *Rescission* is the annullment of a promise of marriage with sufficient reason by one of the contracting parties. When such a reason exists, the party in whose favor the promise is being rescinded, may break the engagement, although, in a general way, he or she is not bound to do so. If such a party does not make use of his or her right, the other party, who is the cause of the rupture, may not take measures to rescind the contract, unless he or she has a reason for doing so. Three reasons warrant one in petitioning for a rescission of a promise of marriage; they are: infidelity, error, and change.

1591. *Infidelity.* One of the parties is guilty of infidelity if, without the knowledge or consent of the other party, he or she sets up a domicile elsewhere. However, the change in domicile must be notable, otherwise it does not warrant one in petitioning for a rescission; and the same is true if one of the parties moves away at a considerable distance, but hopes to return very soon, or if the other party gave his or her consent and then withdrew the same. The party who remains may set a time limit for the other party's return and the contracting of marriage, and once this time limit is passed, may rescind the promise. An involuntary departure may also at times constitute a just cause for rescinding a promise of marriage.

There is infidelity if one of the parties becomes engaged to a person whose faith differs from that of his or her former partner. Such subsequent promises of marriage, being invalid, cannot annul the former promise; but they do give the innocent party the right to have the latter promise rescinded.

There is infidelity if one of the parties commits a sin of fornication. Such a sin justifies rescission of the marriage promise, unless the other party is guilty of the same sin.

Finally, there is infidelity if one of the parties persists in deferring the marriage ceremony. Generally speaking, a period of three years is regarded as too protracted a delay, if no time limit has been set by the parties to bring the obligation to an end, or to urge that it be terminated. If the time limit set by the parties to end the obligation is passed, the promise of marriage is *ipso facto* dissolved, and if the time limit to urge that the same obligation be terminated is passed, even though this happens through no fault of the one party, the other party may rescind the marriage promise.

1592. *Error.* If, at the time the engagement was entered into, certain things were unknown to one of the contracting parties, which, had he or she known them, would have deterred him or her from making such an engagement, the said party may rescind the marriage promise. The contracting parties are bound *sub gravi* to reveal to each other vices which are harmful or prejudicial to marriage, or else refrain from making a promise of marriage. They are always obliged to reveal sins that render a marriage invalid, even to their own detriment, as also the lack of any quality which the other party would require as a *conditio sine qua non* of future marriage. Sins of this kind must be made known, whether they occur before or after the engagement. Other sins must be revealed out of charity only in case it could be feared that the marriage would be an unhappy one, once these sins became known.

1593. *Change.* Here there is question only of a notable change, and if one of the parties suffers such a change in his body, soul, or fortune, which, had it taken place at the time the engagement was made, would have deterred the other party from entering into the contract, the said other party has the right to rescind the marriage promise. Generally speaking, the fear that the marriage will be an unhappy one is always a sufficient reason for rescinding the contract.

1594. If the cause for rescinding a promise of marriage is evident, the party who has the right to rescind may do so by his own authority, unless there is danger of scandal, or the diocesan statutes decree otherwise. The bishop may require that the annullment of a promise of marriage by consent of the two contracting parties be referred to him. The parties should always have recourse to the bishop if the cause for rescission is only doubtfully sufficient.

For a sufficient reason the Sovereign Pontiff may dissolve promises of marriage by way of dispensation.

1595. A person who conceals a just cause for the annullment of a promise of marriage, or who unjustly withdraws from a marriage engagement, is bound to make restitution for both the positive and negative injury that may result from this action.

If, in spite of a former valid engagement, and the absence of sufficient reasons for rescission, a party presents himself with the intention of marrying another, the pastor must do all in his power to induce said party to respect his former engagement, or else obtain a friendly annullment of the contract and a fair settlement of the injury done. If he finds that his efforts are in vain, he should resign himself to assist at the marriage. The innocent party may have recourse to competent civil authority to obtain an adjustment, and this is what is usually done. Since, however, this is a matter of mixed forum, he may also have recourse to ecclesiastical authority. (*C. J. C.*, can. 1553.) Judiciary acts of this kind are no obstacles to the marriage ceremony.

1596. Once the engagement has been broken, the contracting parties are bound to return one to the other any earnest money that may have been deposited. The party who breaks the engagement without just cause loses such earnest money, and must return any that he or she may have received. If one of the contracting parties dies, the earnest money which he or she has received, must be returned to the other party, unless the amount is insignificant. Contracting parties are not permitted to impose upon one another a serious penalty in cases of rescission, but a slight penalty is probably permissible in cases of unjust rescission.

1597. Engagements no longer constitute impediments to the marriage contract, nor do they give rise to the impediment of public honesty. They are not of precept, although they serve as an excellent preparation for the reception of the Sacrament, and are of some value in the matter of discovering possible impediments.

It remains for us now to speak of the preparations for marriage which are of precept, *viz.*, the canonical examinations. The latter comprise the preliminary investigations and the publication of the banns.

Art. II. The Canonical Examinations.

1598. Before marriage is entered into, it must be certain that no obstacles exist to its valid and licit celebration. In danger of death, if no other proofs are available and no indications exist to the contrary, the sworn affirmation of the parties that they are baptized and that there is no impediment to their marriage, is sufficient. (*C. J. C.*, can. 1019.) If the contracting parties are not in danger of death, they should be examined and the banns of their marriage published.

1599. *The examination of the contracting parties.* The pastor, usually the pastor of the bride, has the exclusive right to assist at the marriage ceremony. In good time before it is to take place, and in keeping with the rulings of the Ordinary of the diocese, he should ask separately both the man and the woman whether they are laboring under any impediment; whether he, and especially she, freely consent to the marriage, and whether they are sufficiently instructed in Christian doctrine. Unless the parties were baptized in his own parish, he should secure their baptismal certificates; he should also see to it that Catholics who have not yet received Confirmation, receive that Sacrament, if they can do so without grave inconvenience. He should instruct the parties in regard to the sacredness of the marriage state, the obligations they assume toward one another, and the obligations of parents towards their children. Finally, he should exhort them to make confession of their sins and receive Holy Communion.

1600. *The publication of the banns.* In order to avoid assisting at marriages that are null and void or illicit, canon 1022 enjoins upon the pastor to announce publicly that the parties are to be married. The obligation thus imposed by the Church upon the parish priest is grave, although it does not affect the validity of the Sacrament. It exists even in a case where there is no possible chance of an impediment existing, because it goes on the assumption that the danger is a general one. The publication of the banns is neither prescribed nor permitted in cases of mixed marriages. The bishop may allow such banns to be published, provided there be no danger of scandal, that the proper dispensations have been obtained beforehand, and that no mention be made of the religion of the non-Catholic party.

1601. The publication of the banns is to be made in church on three successive Sundays or holydays of obligation. If the pastor failed to make one publication, he would be guilty of mortal sin, and if he omitted two publications, he would probably be guilty of venial sin, provided he had taken the necessary precautions to discover any possibly existing impediments. His sin would be certainly venial if he omitted only one publication, or if he made two publications the same day.

1602. The banns must be published during Mass or at other services that are largely attended by the people. If a Sunday and two holydays of obligation succeeded one another within the space of three days, it would be advisable to allow one day to elapse without making any publication.

1603. The banns must be published by the pastor of each

one of the contracting parties or a priest delegated for that purpose, in the parishes of both the man and the woman, or in the parishes where they have a quasi-domicile.

If the parties have their domicile or quasi-domicile in different parishes, the pastors of these respective parishes are their pastors and must publish the banns. If the contracting parties have no parochial domicile, but only a diocesan one, the pastor of the place where they reside is their pastor. The same holds true of those who have no domicile or only a quasi-domicile. The pastor of minors is the pastor of the place where the parents or guardians of these minors have their domicile or quasi-domicile, and also the pastor of the place where the young people have acquired a quasi-domicile. The Church regards all persons who have not yet completed their twenty-first year as minors.

1604. If one party or both have lived in some other place for six months after the age of puberty, the pastor should refer the matter to the bishop, who may either have the banns announced in that place, or otherwise order investigations made concerning the free state of the party or parties concerned. (*C. J. C.*, can. 1023.)

The pastor should also refer the matter to the bishop, if he has any reason for suspecting the existence of some impediment, even though the parties have been living less than six months in another place. The Ordinary should not allow the marriage to take place until all suspicion is removed by a thorough investigation. (*Ibid.*)

1605. All pastors whose duty it is to publish the banns and conduct the canonical investigations, must immediately notify the priest who is to assist at the marriage that the investigations have been made, and inform him by an official document of the results obtained.

1606. The banns must be published clearly and in the vernacular. They must indicate unequivocally the parties concerned, their names, surnames, and place of residence. All this must be done in accordance with the form sanctioned by the customs of the diocese or prescribed by the bishop.

The local Ordinary may substitute another form of publishing the banns in his diocese, by posting the names of the parties at the doors of the church and leaving them there for at least eight days, inclusive of at least two Sundays or holydays of obligation. (Can. 1025.)

All the faithful are obliged, at their earliest convenience, to make known to the pastor or the bishop any impediment of which they may have knowledge.

1607. *Dispensation from the banns*. The bishop, the capitulary vicar, and (unless the bishop has reserved this right to himself) the vicar-general may, for legitimate reasons, of which they are the judges, dispense from the publication of the banns. In urgent cases they *must* dispense from them. In cases where recourse to the bishop is absolutely impossible, the pastor may declare the law non-obligatory, provided he is certain that no impediments exist. (Can. 1028.)

1608. The Ordinary spoken of in canon 1028 is the Ordinary of the place where the parties have their domiciles or quasi-domiciles. The Ordinary may dispense from the publication of the banns not only in his own diocese, but also in the diocese where the parties formerly lived. If the parties belong to two different dioceses, the bishop in whose diocese the marriage is to take place has the right to grant the dispensation. If the marriage is to be celebrated outside either of the two dioceses, either bishop is competent to dispense from the publication of the banns. (*Ibid.*)

1609. It is not necessary that the reason for dispensing from the publication of the banns be a serious one, provided the ends are attained. At times there are reasons why the bishop must dispense, as, for instance, when there is danger that the marriage will be prevented through malice, or the man will forsake the girl he has violated, or the parties will be exposed to infamy or ridicule. He should also dispense from the publication of the banns when the parties concerned are obliged to undertake a hurried journey, or the husband, already married in the eyes of the State, refuses to be married in the eyes of the Church if dispensation from the banns is not granted.

1610. If the marriage ceremony is delayed over a period of six months after the publication of the banns, they must be repeated, unless the Ordinary decides otherwise. In cases where the parties change their place of residence after the parish priest has begun the publication of the banns, the latter must continue to announce the banns, although he is no longer their pastor and cannot assist at their marriage. The pastor of the place where the parties have their new residence is not obliged to announce the banns, although he is their parish priest and alone has the right to assist at their marriage.

1611. *The obligation to make known existing impediments.* The obligation to make known any existing impediments to marriage, even occult, is grave, provided the party has probable knowledge of its existence. This obligation arises from the precept of charity and also from the ecclesiastical law formulated in canon 1027. If the impediment is the result of some secret sin, the contracting parties should be made to renounce their intention to marry or apply for the proper dispensations, provided there is some hope that they will profit by such an admonition. If it can be foreseen that one's personal efforts in this respect will be futile, it is best to make known the impediment to the pastor. The obligation to make known impediments obliges all Christians, even though they may not be able to prove the existence of such impediments in law.

1612. The faithful are dispensed from this obligation if

they should fear grave injury for themselves or for others, if they judge their act of declaration to be useless, or if they know that a dispensation has been obtained for the internal forum.

1613. A person who has obtained knowledge of some existing impediment under oath of secrecy or promise, is not dispensed from revealing the impediment to the proper authorities. According to some authors such a person is dispensed if the secret is of a confidential nature, but the majority of theologians oppose this view. Even the latter, however, exempt professional secrets, such as those of a pastor, a physician, a midwife, or a lawyer, dispensing also a party from making known the impediments when his action will result in the defamation of the character of the person from whom he received the secret. The contracting parties are bound to make known any impediments, even at the risk of defamation of their own characters, unless they prefer to renounce the intention to marry.

1614. A confessor who comes upon the knowledge of a public impediment in the confessional must send the penitent to the pastor; one who comes upon the knowledge of an occult impediment, should do his best to obtain a dispensation for the same.

1615. After the parties have been examined and the banns published, the pastor should not assist at the marriage unless he is in receipt of whatever papers may be necessary. He must wait three days after announcing the banns for the last time, unless there is good reason to dispense with this rule. If there are no impediments, the contracting parties have the right to celebrate their marriage after the three days. When doubt arises as to some impediment, the pastor should investigate the matter, and obtain from at least two trustworthy witnesses a statement under oath. He must always do this, unless such a procedure would bring disgrace upon the parties, and, if necessary, he must place the contracting parties themselves under oath to make a statement concerning the doubtful impediment. As long as the doubt persists, he must not assist at the marriage without consulting the bishop. (See can. 1031.)

CHAPTER III

THE MINISTER

1616. The contracting parties themselves are the ministers of the Sacrament. This is *certain;* it follows from what we have said regarding the matter and form of the Sacraments in no. 1513. And since Matrimony is nothing more than the original contract, raised to the dignity of a Sacrament, the contracting parties are the efficient cause of both the contract and the Sacrament. The view of Melchior Cano, who held that the priest is the minister of the Sacrament, is, therefore, not probable. This fact does not excuse a duly authorized priest from assisting at the marriage ceremony, but before the Council of Trent marriages were regarded as valid even though they were not contracted in the presence of a priest. The words *"Ego vos conjungo"* are not, therefore, an essential part of the Sacrament. Moreover, the Council permitted the use of other formulas according to custom and tradition. An accepted custom which has all the force of law obliges a priest *sub levi* (according to some writers *sub gravi*) to pronounce these words over the parties who are contracting marriage, except in the case of those who are marrying with a dispensation from the impediment of mixed religion. (See no. 1641.) If the priest is performing several marriage ceremonies, he should pronounce the formula over each couple separately, although he is permitted to bless the rings *in globo.*

1617. The solemn nuptial blessing is not of strict precept, although the Church wishes that the parties should receive it. The S. C. R. forbids any priest to give such a blessing outside the Mass, except with a dispensation. There are other cases also in which the blessing may not be given, to wit: when the woman has already received it in a preceding marriage, when one of the parties is a non-Catholic, when a marriage is being revalidated, during an interdict, and, unless the bishop rules otherwise for a just reason, when the solemn blessing of marriages is forbidden. The solemn blessing of marriages is forbidden from the first Sunday in Advent to Christmas, inclusively, and from Ash Wednesday to Easter Sunday, inclusively. Parties who contract marriage in such forbidden times should be admonished to refrain from too much pomp. (Can. 1108.) Canon 1101 states that the pastor should see to it that the couple receive the nuptial blessing, which may be given them also when they have lived in the married state for a long time. It is to be given only during Holy Mass, with the observance of the special rubric, and on all except forbidden days. The parties have a right to the nuptial blessing even if the woman is pregnant or has already given birth to illegitimate children. For information regarding the Mass or the oration *Pro Sponsis,* the reader is referred to no. 1015.

If the bishop has given his permission for the conferring of the nuptial blessing in prohibited times, the Mass *Pro Sponsis* may be read, except on Sundays, holydays of obligation of the first and second class, privileged octaves of the first or second rank, privileged ferias, and the vigil of Christmas. On these days it is permitted to add the oration *Pro Sponsis* under one conclusion, if that day excludes any other commemoration, as, for instance, Easter and Christmas, and under a separate conclusion on all other days.

1618. Marriage between Catholics must be contracted in

the parish church; it cannot take place in any other church, or in a public or semi-public oratory, without the permission of either the bishop or the pastor. The bishop may not permit the celebration of marriage in private houses except in extraordinary cases and for good reasons. He should not allow the celebration of marriage in the churches or chapels of seminaries or of religious women, except in urgent necessity and with due precautions. Marriages between a Catholic and a non-Catholic must be contracted outside the church. If, in the bishop's judgment, this rule cannot be insisted upon without greater evils arising, he may allow such marriages to take place in the church, but never during Holy Mass.

1619. Since the parties themselves are the ministers of the Sacrament, they sin in administering the Sacrament to one another when not in the state of grace. Their sin in this case is grave, although there are some writers who hold the probable view that it is only slight. This sin is quite distinct from the sin of receiving the Sacrament unworthily. We shall deal with the latter in no. 1624.

CHAPTER IV

THE SUBJECT

We shall treat, first, of the subject; and, secondly, of the impediments of the subject.

Art. I. The Subject of Marriage.

1620. Who is the subject? Only a baptized Christian, who has the use of reason, is capable of receiving the Sacrament of Matrimony. Infidels who marry certainly contract validly, but they do not receive the Sacrament. If two such parties are converted to the Catholic faith, their marriage certainly becomes indissoluble; but do they then receive the Sacrament? Some theologians answer this question in the negative, others, more probably, in the affirmative, averring that to obtain this effect it is not even necessary that the converted parties renew their consent. It is also controverted whether or not there is a Sacrament when one of the faithful marries an infidel with papal dispensation. If one of the infidel parties is converted to the Catholic faith, his marriage does not become a Sacrament.

1621. Heretics who observe all the laws which the Church prescribes under pain of nullity receive the Sacrament, provided their Baptism is valid. If a Catholic whose Baptism is doubtful wishes to marry, he must first receive conditional Baptism. When the doubt concerning his Baptism arises after his marriage, the marriage is regarded as valid if, after investigation, the doubt persists. If it becomes known that the Baptism was certainly invalid, the party in doubt must be baptized and then made to renew his or her consent.

1622. Perpetually insane persons are incapable of entering into the marriage contract. Persons who have lucid moments and who know what constitutes a mortal sin and what obligations they assume, may validly marry.

1623. *Dispositions of the subject.* Some of these dispositions are required for validity, others for liceity.

For validity it is required: (1) That the subject have at least the virtual intention of marrying. A habitual intention does not suffice because true and interior consent is the matter of the Sacrament. Moreover, the contracting parties are the ministers, and the minister of the Sacrament must have a virtual intention. (2) The contracting parties must not be laboring under any diriment impediment. (3) They must not exclude the essential ends of marriage.

1624. *For liceity,* the parties must be in the state of grace. Any person receiving this Sacrament in the state of mortal

sin certainly offends grievously; he also sins (either grievously or venially, as we have stated in no. 1619) in administering the Sacrament to the other party. When one of the
parties is not aware that marriage contracted in the state of
mortal sin is a sacrilege, he should not be informed in this
regard, if it be feared that the admonition will be of no avail.
In a case of this kind, the best course is to excite him to perfect contrition. One is not allowed to contract marriage with
an excommunicated person who has been denounced as such.
One commits a sacrilege also in marrying a sinner, but co-
operation of this kind may be condoned for a serious reason,
unless the marriage gives rise to proximate danger of perversion. In practice, the faithful should be advised not to
enter into marriages of this kind under pretense "that the
unbelieving husband is sanctified by the believing wife, and
the unbelieving wife is sanctified by the believing husband,"
because in the very same chapter of his Epistle to the Corinthians, St. Paul asks the pertinent question: "For how know-
est thou, O wife, whether thou shalt save thy husband?"
(1 Cor. 7, 16.) A person living among plague-stricken people
will more easily contract their disease than cure it. (See no.
1545.)

1625. Sacramental confession before marriage is not an
absolute requisite; perfect contrition suffices. In several
dioceses the statutes require that the parties bring a note
testifying to the fact that they have been to confession. If it
is difficult for them to bring such a note, and if it is feared
that in requiring it, the parties will live in concubinage, the
pastor or another priest delegated for that purpose may dispense with the law and assist at the marriage.

1626. The parties must not be laboring under any impediment. (See no. 1629 ff.)

The parties must know the truths of their faith. We shall
have occasion to deal with this point again in no. 2205; suf-

fice it to say here that the parties may not be in ignorance concerning them, for they have need of them both for themselves and for the education of their children. (See no. 2409.) They must know also whatever is necessary to receive the fruits of the Sacrament and sanctify themselves in that state. If they show ignorance in these matters, the confessor must do his best to instruct them without giving offense (see no. 1310 ff.)

The confessor must exercise the greatest prudence in speaking of the marriage act. With no risk of scandalizing any person, the following rules may be given to all: (1) Anything useful and necessary to attain the end of marriage, which is to give children to God and the Church and future citizens to Heaven, is permitted; (2) anything which is absolutely opposed to this end is forbidden *sub gravi;* (3) anything which is neither contrary nor useful to this end is forbidden *sub levi* if done without reason; (4) by mutual consent married people are always allowed to live as brother and sister, and their conduct will be very pleasing to God; (5) married people are permitted to refrain from the marriage act at times when conception is possible, and make use of it only when conception is unlikely. The confessor may add these words of advice: "If any doubts arise in your mind, you had better speak of them in confession, and the priest will enlighten you."

1627. The parties must have in view an honest goal. They would sin grievously if they did not have the intention of performing the duties of their state. (See nos. 2414 and 2544.) Any person does well who marries with the intention of having children or of finding in marriage a remedy against incontinence, for these are the intrinsic, though not the essential, ends of marriage. One may also have chiefly in view ends that are extrinsic to marriage, provided they be honest. An end of this kind would be the maintenance of peace between two families. A person who would have in view an end which is not honest, such as the satisfaction of his passion, avarice, etc., would sin, although his offense would not be serious, if what he had in view was not something grievously criminal.

1628. Ordinarily an effort should be made to deter from marrying parties whose ages, fortunes and characters are widely divergent in order to forestall the many inconveniences which more often than not arise from situations of this kind. In the choice of a partner for life, the highest consideration should be given to what will be an aid, not an obstacle, in the practice of Christian virtue.

Art. II. Impediments.

1629. An impediment is any obstacle to the marriage contract. "If anyone saith, that the Church could not establish impediments dissolving marriage; or that she has erred in establishing them; let him be anathema." (C. of Trent, Sess. 24, can. 4.) It is *of faith*, therefore, that the Church may establish marriage impediments, as she has received from Jesus Christ the power to govern herself and to provide for the salutary administration of the Sacraments.

1630. The Church alone has the right to establish impediments either through the person of her sovereign head or through her general councils. The bishop cannot establish impediments, and neither can the secular power, except in what pertains to the purely civil effects of Matrimony. This proposition is *certain,* because Jesus Christ did not entrust the care of the Sacraments to civil authority. (See no. 1512.) It is controverted among theologians whether or not the princes and rulers of this world have the power to establish impediments which dissolve the marriages of infidels. The more common opinion has it that they may. This opinion is also more in keeping with the practice of the Holy See.

1631. If the princes and rulers of this world take it upon themselves to establish civil impediments for the marriages of Christians, the latter will do well to comply with them at the risk of having their children declared illegitimate by the State. Confessors should not allow parties to contract marriage when they are involved in such impediments, without first referring the matter to the bishop.

The civil law does not recognize the indissolubility of the marriage contract, admitting as causes for divorce, adultery, cruelty, incompatibility, etc. Pastors and confessors should take note of all these facts and refer more difficult cases to the bishop.

1632. For a proportionate reason, the bishop may forbid parties residing within the confines of his diocese to contract marriage for the time that the reason lasts. (Can. 1039.)

1633. The impediments established by the Church are of two kinds: the first prohibit marriage and render it illicit, but not invalid; the second dissolve marriage and render it both illicit and invalid.

1634. *Impedient impediments.* The New Code recognizes three impedient impediments: the simple vow, legal adoption in countries where it constitutes a civil impedient impediment, and mixed religion.

1635. *The vow.* Here there is question of the simple vow, because the solemn vow constitutes a diriment impedient. (See no. 1656.) Four vows render a marriage gravely illicit: the vow of chastity, the vow not to marry but to remain a celibate, the vow to enter religion, and the vow to receive sacred Orders.

The vow of chastity. This vow renders marriage illicit because the person involved ordinarily runs the risk of breaking it in marriage or of doing violence to the right of his consort. (See nos. 1552 and 1636.) When a party who has made such a simple vow contracts marriage without first obtaining a dispensation, he may not, without mortal sin, ask for the *debitum*, although he is bound to render the same.

He is obliged to abstain from all intercourse if the other party be willing, and sins against his vow if he commits adultery or any other sin against chastity outside the lawful use of marriage. In practice, therefore, it is best to apply for a dispensation from the vow, unless the other party indirectly dissolves the same. (See no. 2358.) When the consort of such a partner dies, the latter has no right to enter into a new marriage, even though he obtained a dispensation from his vow during the time of his first marriage; but one who had obtained an absolute dispensation from his vow before entering upon his first marriage, may contract a new marriage. The case would be different, however, if such a person had obtained the dispensation in order to meet a special emergency, such as that of marrying a girl whom he had seduced.

1636. *The vow not to marry, but to remain a celibate.* This vow is regarded as one of virginity, but not of absolute celibacy, and he or she who makes such a vow ordinarily sins grievously in contracting marriage, and must abstain from asking for the *debitum* up to the time when he or she loses his or her virginity. Virginity once lost, the vow is no longer possible, and one does not sin in making use of the marriage act, nor in asking for the *debitum*. Probably also, he does not sin in contracting a new marriage, after his first marriage is dissolved by death. In theory, such a person may be excused from grievous sin against his vow, if, after having pronounced it, he entered into a marriage contract, agreeing with his wife to practice perpetual chastity. (See nos. 1552 and 1562.) He would sin grievously against his vow, however, if, before his marriage, he was guilty of a consummated shameful act; at the same time, he would be free from that time on to marry, unless he had made a vow of perfect chastity.

A girl who marries in complete ignorance of the carnal duties of the married state, and who holds them in extreme horror, may request the Holy See to dissolve her marriage if the same has not been consummated. Were the Holy See to grant such a dispensation, the girl could not marry another without first obtaining permission from Rome. In doubt as to whether the party made a vow of perfect chastity or merely of celibacy, he should be questioned as to the intention which motivated the vow at the time. If he answers that he was moved by the love of purity, it should be concluded that his vow was one of perfect chastity, but if he states that he made the vow to rid himself of the inconveniences of the married state or out of love for virginal integrity, it should be concluded that his vow was merely one of celibacy or simple virginity.

1637. *The vow to enter religion.* A person who pronounces a vow of this kind sins grievously in contracting marriage. He is bound *sub gravi* to keep his promise, if the other party consents, if the other party loses forever the right to ask for the *debitum,* or if the other party dies. The same is true if he made a vow merely to enter a religious congregation. In all other cases he is free to make use of the marriage rights.

1638. *The vow to receive sacred Orders.* A person who pronounces a vow of this kind also sins grievously in contracting marriage. He is bound to fulfill his promise with the consent of the other party, if his wife dies, or if she loses forever her right to ask for the *debitum.* A woman whose husband dies after being admitted to sacred Orders must have recourse to the bishop before contracting another marriage. (See no. 1656.)

1639. *Legal adoption.* This impediment rests not on affinity or blood relationship, but on a conventionality approved of by the state. Those whom the civil law declares incapable of marrying on account of legal adoption, cannot contract marriage validly under the Canon Law. In this particular instance, therefore, the Church adopts the civil law and makes it her own. (Can. 1080.) On these grounds, Leitner avers that the canonical impediment ceases in a particular case when the civil law grants a dispensation.

1640. In Germany, legal adoption constitutes a civil impedient impediment, and failure to regard it as such nullifies the act of adoption. In Switzerland, the civil impediment has only a prohibitive character; legal affinity is no longer recognized. For the treatment of legal adoption in so far as it constitutes a diriment impediment, the reader is referred to no. 1672.

1641. *Mixed religion.* The Church forbids most severely and in all countries marriage between a Catholic and a heretic or schismatic. If there is danger of perversion for the Catholic party and the offspring, such a marriage is forbidden also by divine law. (Can. 1080.) The danger referred to in this canon must be taken to mean not only a heretical, but also a bad Catholic education.

1642. The Church has always looked with disfavor upon marriages of this kind, and bishops and priests should do all in their power to deter the faithful from entering into them. If their efforts prove of no avail, they should see to it that these marriages are not contracted against the laws of God and the Church. Finally, whenever such marriages have been contracted, bishops and priests should take care that the parties are faithful to their promises.

Those who assist at such marriages should observe what canon 1102 has to say on this point: All sacred rites are forbidden, but if greater evils are sure to follow from this prohibition, the bishop may allow some of the usual ceremonies, with the exception of Holy Mass. (Can. 1102.)

1643. The Church does not dispense from the impediment of mixed religion unless the heretical or schismatic party promises to remove all danger of perversion for the Catholic party and allow him the free exercise of his religious duties. Both parties must promise that all their children will be baptized and reared as Catholics. Their promises must ordinarily be in writing, and there must be moral certitude that they will be kept. (Can. 1061.) Some diocesan statutes require that the promise be sealed with an oath, and in all cases the Catholic party has the obligation prudently to work for the conversion of the non-Catholic party. (Can. 1062.)

Once the promises have been made and the reasons for requesting the dispensation ascertained, the pastor may address a letter to the bishop requesting a dispensation. The Catholic party may sin, even though he promise sincerely to fulfill all the conditions required of him, if the Church grants the dispensation for no other reason than out of fear that he will marry before a minister or have his children reared in heresy. He sins against the natural law if, before the Church grants the dispensation, he contracts a mixed marriage in which there is proximate danger of perversion for himself and his children, which he cannot remove. Under pain of excommunication, reserved to the Ordinary, the parties are not allowed, either before or after the Catholic wedding, to approach either in person or through proxies a non-Catholic minister as such, or to give or renew their consent in the Protestant rite, even when the Church has granted a dispensation from the impediment of mixed religion. The Church does not censure parties who are forced by civil law to appear before a non-Catholic minister who acts as an official of the government, but their intention must be merely to comply with the requirements of the law and to gain civil recognition of their marriage. (See can. 1063.) If the pastor knows that the parties will certainly violate, or have already violated, this law, he shall not assist at their marriage, except for very serious reasons and only after he has consulted the Ordinary.

1644. The impediment of mixed religion does not extend to the marriage of a Catholic with an apostate, even though he be a notorious one, provided he does not belong to a religious sect. The marriage of a Catholic with a person belonging to a society condemned by the Church is not to be regarded as one of mixed religion. All diriment impediments render marriage not only illicit, but also invalid. For this reason, one would not even be permitted to marry with an impediment of this kind, even under threat of death, though some theologians do not subscribe to this view when there is question of purely ecclesiastical impediments and serious injury is to be feared. In any case consult the Ordinary.

1645. *Diriment impediments.* Diriment impediments are incurred by all; ignorance of the law does not excuse. (See can. 16.) Impediments of the natural and divine laws affect even infidels, and impediments originating from ecclesiastical law are binding upon heretics. An exception to this last rule is the impediment of disparity of worship and, at least in some cases, clandestinity, but impediments originating from ecclesiastical law are never binding upon infidels. Canon 1065 states, however, that the faithful should be discouraged from contracting marriage with those who have publicly given up their faith, even though they have not joined a non-Catholic sect, and with those who belong to societies condemned by the Church.

The pastor must not assist at such marriages without first consulting the bishop, who, after he has considered all the circumstances, may permit him to assist, provided there are serious reasons, and he has good grounds for believing that the Catholic education of the children will be sufficiently cared for and the danger of perversion for the Catholic party removed. (Can. 1065.) Canon 1066 states that if a public sinner or a person known to be under censure does not first agree to go to confession and be reconciled with the Church, the pastor may not assist at his marriage, unless there is a grave and urgent reason for doing so, concerning which, he should, if possible, consult the Ordinary. (Can. 1066.) A person who knowingly contracts marriage with an impediment of this kind under threat of death, is not permitted to ask for, or to render, the *debitum,* although it is probable that the woman in this case may offer passive coöperation, if there is no danger of her giving her consent. (See nos. 1647 and 1686.)

1646. One is allowed to contract marriage with a doubtful diriment impediment, *i. e.,* when theologians are not agreed as to the actual existence of the impediment. In cases of this kind the Church supplies any deficiency. An exception must be made of cases where the impediment is of natural or divine right, unless the Holy See has declared that the marriage may take place in these conditions, because in cases of this kind the Church cannot supply. In cases when the doubt is one of fact but not of law, one is not allowed to contract marriage, because the opinion which avers that one may, is not probable. *Post factum* a marriage of this kind is deemed valid in certain cases. If John marries Bertha, who is his sister, although he does not know this for sure, or if he marries Anna, who is his cousin by reason of a sin of incest committed by his lawfully married mother, whose husband is regarded as Anna's father, the marriage is deemed valid, because, in cases of this kind the doubt is insoluble and is legally presumed to become a doubt not of fact, but of law.

If a person contracts marriage while in doubt whether or not there is an impediment, when in reality there is none, the marriage is valid. If a person is certain that there is an impediment, when in reality there is none, and is little concerned about the matter, being resolved to live in concubinage, the marriage is invalid. If, in the same case, the person is sorry that the impediment exists, but, not daring to make it known for fear of having his character defamed, carelessly enters into the marriage contract, the marriage is valid, although he should be made to renew his consent *ad cautelam*.

1647. If after their marriage, two parties begin to entertain doubts regarding the validity of the contract, they should refrain from the use of the marriage right, as well as of all acts against chastity allowed in marriage, and bend all their efforts to discover the truth. If only one of the parties is in doubt, he should not ask for the *debitum*, yet he should render it to the other party who is not in doubt, provided the latter has not lost the right to ask for or exact it. He should seek also to clear up his doubt, but if he fails, what he has done must be presumed to have been well done, unless his reasons for doubting engender in his mind moral certitude to the contrary. According to St. Alphonsus, an exception must be made of the impediment of a previous bond, if the second marriage was entered into in bad faith, or in doubtfully good faith, because the right of the first consort is in possession. Other theologians, however, are of the opinion that the party who, after diligent investigation, believes with probability that his second marriage is valid, may lawfully ask for the *debitum*.

The diriment impediments are thirteen in number: (1)

Age; (2) Impotency; (3) Previous bond; (4) Disparity of worship; (5) Sacred Orders; (6) Solemn vow; (7) Rape; (8) Crime; (9) Consanguinity; (10) Affinity; (11) Public honesty; (12) Spiritual relationship; (13) Legal adoption. These impediments are either absolute or relative, according as they render marriage invalid with all persons or only with this or that individual.

We shall treat of each one of these impediments in particular, remarking once again that they do not affect the marriages of infidels, and do not render them null and void, even though these infidels become converted to the Catholic faith after their marriage.

1648. *Age.* According to the natural law, no one can contract marriage who has not the use of reason. One who has reached the age of reason is capable of marrying, even though actually and physically he is incapable. According to ecclesiastical law, the boy must be sixteen years of age and the girl fourteen. Although marriage is valid when these years have been completed, pastors should seek to dissuade young people from marriage at an earlier age than is commonly the custom in the respective countries. The Holy See is not in the habit of dispensing from this impediment, and the bishop may not dispense from it, when in doubt whether or not the prescribed age has been reached. In computing the age of parties account must be taken not only of the year, but even of the exact day.

1649. *Impotentia. Impos non est sterilis qui actum infecunde consummat; sed conjux qui consummare nequit actum ex se aptum ad generationem, ut mulieres et viri carentes organis ad hoc necessariis vel aptis. Impotentia antecedens matrimonium ratum et perpetua, quamvis sit relativa ad talem conjugem et non existeret relative ad alios, dirimit matrimonium ex jure naturali, si sanari nequit mediis ordinariis et licitis, sine periculo mortis et gravi incisione.*

Operatione factâ et impotentiâ sublatâ, non est validum matrimonium, si tempore contractûs requirebatur operatio periculosa, renovandus ergo consensus; si operatio erat levis, valet contractus; si dubie periculosa, ad cautelam consensus est renovandus. An vero teneatur mulier hanc operationem pati? Affirmat S. Liguorius, si agatur de solo gravi dolore tolerando; secus si pudor obstet ne per medicum virum fiat operatio. In dubio an matrimonium sit consummatum præsume consummatum. Impotentia consequens matrimonium non illud dirimit, siquidem invenit matrimonium validum, nec impotentia antecedens quæ non est perpetua, sufficit enim ut corpus quod traditur, aliquando fiat aptum ad finem conjugii. Quando impotentia, quæcumque sit, est certa, reddit illicitam attentationem actus conjugii, unde conjuges separentur quoad torum saltem, vivant sicut soror et frater, et quoad habitationem, si periculum sit proximum lapsus. Si impotentia sit certa et perpetua possunt et debent separari in perpetuum, si periculum adsit incontinentiæ, imo etiamsi possint continentiam servare, nisi senes sint, vel lex civilis obstet et si impotentia est antecedens, pars quæ potens est recurrat ad judicem ecclesiasticum, ut possit ad alteras nuptias convolare.

1650. Si impedimentum impotentiæ dubium sit, sive dubio juris, sive dubio facti, matrimonium non est impediendum (can. 1068.)

Certo impotens est vir, qui nullum habet testiculum, qui non habet penem vel eum tam deformem ut copulam perficere nequeat, qui tali frigiditate laborat ut ad ritam copulam sit ineptus, qui vasectomiam subiit quae nulla arte chirurgica reparari queat.

Mulier certo impotens est, si non habeat vaginam vel eam tam arctam aut occlusam ut nullo modo penetrari possit. Dubia est potentia mulieris cui ovaria, vel uterus, vel uterus et ovaria abscissa sunt. In praxi ergo licite matrimonium init eoque utitur. Quoad ceteras impotentiæ species, conjuges licite quoque utuntur matrimonio usque dum de eorum impotentia certi sint. Ex quo tempore impotentia certa fit, separatio requiritur, si fieri potest, etiam quoad habitationem, nec in posterum experimentum triennale conceditur. Pars quæ ante matrimonium de sua potentia dubitat, compartem monere sub gravi tenetur.

1651. Quid faciendum si impotentia certa sit?

Matrimonium contrahendum inter eos qui perpetua impotentia laborant absolute impediri debet. Matrimonio jam contracto, conjuges relinquantur in bona fide, si putent se in matrimonio valido versari et propter legem civilem vel alia adjuncta non sit spes probabilis eos separandi. Si conjuges in bona fide non sint, et separatio quoad habitationem sit moraliter impossibilis propter legem civilem vel alia adjuncta, separatione facta quoad torum et quidem propria auctoritate conjugum, pastor animarum ne urgeat separationem quoad habitationem, dummodo absit scandalum et proximum periculum incontinentiæ. Si separatio quoad habitationem sit moraliter possibilis, vel si scandalum aut proximum periculum adsit, separandi sunt. In regionibus ubi et lex civilis hoc impedimentum statuit, a judice sæculari nullitatis matrimonii quoad effectus mere civiles declaratio peti potest. In aliis regionibus judex saecularis sæpe matrimonium inter impotentes ex capite doli vel erroris nullum declarare poterit. Conjugum est suum matrimonium nullum propter impotentiæ impedimentum apud Ordinarium loci accusare. Quod si recusent, pastor animarum sicut et ceteri, illud promotori justitiæ vel ipsi Ordinario loci denuntiare potest, qui illius nullitatem declarabit et conjuges separabit. Antea Ordinarius conjuges vel conjugem visitationi subjicit. Virum visitent duo medici periti et graves non simul sed singulatim nec sint ex eis qui a viro jam antea adhibiti sunt. Mulier pudice inspiciatur a duobus obstetricibus singillatim aut, si mulier malit, duobus gravibus medicis singulis, assistente gravi muliere custode honestatis. Nec obstetrices, nec medici ex eis esse possunt, qui curam mulieris antea habuerunt. Conjuges qui suam impotentiam accusant, testes qui septimæ manus nomen audiunt, inducere debent ex consanguinibus vel affinibus vel saltem vicinis, qui de ipsorum probitate et veracitate jurare possint. Nec inspectio conjugum, nec testimonium septimæ manus semper vim plenæ probationis obtinet. Ideo in praxi, sæpius Ecclesia his in adjunctis utitur potestate dispensandi super matrimonio rato.

Impotentia consequens matrimonium non dirimit, cum sit indissolubile. Actus imperfecti inter conjuges impotentes, valido matrimonio contracto, non prohibentur, si fiant sine pollutionis periculo. In periculo pollutionis, requiritur causa cohonestans, ut sint licite. Nec inter eos prohibenda videtur copula vulvaris, quamdiu vaginalis fieri nequit. Copula cum uxore, cui uterus et ovaria excisa sunt, non est illicita. De copula habenda cum viro qui post matrimonium valide contractum vasectomiam subiit Ecclesia nihil definivit. Injectio artificialis seminis virilis in vaginam uxoris certo est illicita.

1652. Quam ad rem spectat quoque hermaphrodismus. Hermaphroditi censentur utriusque sexus participes. Si vere utriusque sexus organis polleant, hermaphroditi veri, perfecti et proprie dicti sunt; hi non existunt nec unquam extiterunt. Hermaphroditi veri quidem sed imperfecti seu improprie dicti ii sunt qui præter organa suo sexui propria aliquo ex organi alterius sexus donati sunt. Ordinarie non sunt impotentes. Hermaphroditi falsi sunt ii quorum organa sexualia ita formata sunt ut non clare distingui possit utrum virilia sint; revera tamen ad unum tantum sexum pertinent. Hi existunt et impotentes esse solent in utroque sexu. Pastor animarum in praxi semper consulat Ordinarium de sponsis hermaphroditis. Hermaphroditi falsi a statu religioso et præsertim sacerdotali arcendi sunt.

1653. *Previous bond*. By a previous bond we are to understand a former marriage which has not been dissolved because the first consort is not dead. The impediment is of divine right. In doubt as to whether or not the first partner is dead, one is never allowed to contract a second marriage. Neither a prolonged absence, nor public rumor, nor the testimony of one witness constitutes a legal proof for the death of the first consort; positive and certain testimony is indispensable. In doubt, recourse must be had to the bishop, and if he also is in doubt, to the Holy See.

An authentic statement to the effect that the first consort is dead, issued by an ecclesiastic, or the oaths of two trustworthy witnesses ordinarily suffice. A statement issued by civil authority does not suffice, although it may assist the ecclesiastical judges in their quest for the truth.

As a general rule, a Catholic marries invalidly for the second time if he believes his first marriage to be valid or his first consort living, although in reality his first marriage is invalid or his first consort dead, because he has principally in mind not marriage, but concubinage. The opposite can easily be true in the case of non-Catholic marriages. If marriage is entered into under these circumstances, with the intention of contracting a real marriage, the contract is certainly valid.

When marriage has been entered into in good faith with a second consort, and the first consort is still living, the marriage is null and void, and the party concerned must return to his or her first consort. If the first consort dies after the second marriage has been entered into, this marriage must be revalidated in public, if the impediment is public, and in secret, if the impediment is secret.

1654. *Disparity of worship*. In no. 1641 we spoke of the impediment of mixed religion between baptized persons; in this place we must deal with the impediment between a person baptized in the Catholic Church, or received into the Church from heresy or schism, and a non-baptized person. The marriage between two such persons is null and void, and the impediment is of purely ecclesiastical origin. If, at the time of the marriage, a certain party was commonly held to have been baptized, or if his Baptism was doubtful, the marriage must be regarded as valid until it is proved that one party was, and the other party was not, baptized (can. 1070.)

The marriage of a heretic or schismatic with a non-baptized person is valid if it was contracted after the promulgation of the Code. In reference to marriage, a doubtful Baptism is considered valid, until proof is established to the contrary.

The marriage of a baptized person who, without dispensation, contracts marriage with a heretic whose Baptism is valid or even doubtful, is to be regarded as valid; but if he marries a heretic whose Baptism is certainly invalid, his marriage is null and void.

One is not permitted to rebaptize a heretic whose Baptism is doubtful, if he is not willing to embrace the Catholic faith; investigations must be conducted, and if they prove fruitless, the marriage is to be regarded as valid. Heretics who belong to a sect, the ritual of which prescribes the essential matter and form of the Sacrament, are regarded in particular cases as validly baptized. Their Baptism is to be regarded as invalid if their ritual does not prescribe the essential matter and form.

The Church has no direct jurisdiction over infidels; she exercises indirect jurisdiction over them, however, when they contract marriage with her subjects.

The Pope alone can dispense from this impediment, and he requires the same conditions to be present as for a dispensation from mixed religion. (See no. 1645.) Over and above these conditions, he will insist that no offense be given to the Creator, that the number of infidels in the locality where the dispensation is applied for, be greater than that of the faithful, that there be a serious reason for wanting to contract such a marriage. At times he may also require that there be some hope of converting the infidel party. A dispensation from disparity of worship is harder to obtain than one from consanguinity.

1655. *Sacred Orders.* Clerics in major Orders cannot validly marry. (Can. 1072.) If they attempt marriage, they *ipso facto* incur excommunication reserved simply to the Holy See, irregularity, loss of their benefices, and degradation from office.

Clerics in major Orders are bishops, priests, deacons, and subdeacons. The valid marriage of a man who later on receives sacred Orders remains intact, irrespective of whether the marriage was consummated or not.

Is the marriage of clerics invalidated by an implicit solemn vow or by a law of the Church? This question is controverted by theologians. Some are of the opinion that the impediment is an effect of the vow which all ordinandi must implicitly make, others make it a matter of divine law. The more probable opinion is that it is the effect of a purely ecclesiastical law. Bishops are never dispensed from this impediment, priests rarely, deacons and subdeacons sometimes, but with great difficulty. A cleric who has received a major Order out of grave fear may, by the sentence of an ecclesiastical judge, be reduced to the lay state, provided he can prove that he was ordained in fear, and did not ratify the ordination afterwards. He is then free from the obligation of celibacy and from the duty of reciting the breviary. (Can. 214.) In the Latin Church a married man who becomes a priest cannot continue to live as a married man after his ordination. In the Greek Church, a subdeacon may marry and, after he is ordained a priest, continue to live as a married man; a deacon and a priest cannot marry, and a bishop is bound to celibacy.

1656. *Solemn vow*. In no. 1635 we spoke of the simple vow; here there is question of solemn religious profession. As a general rule, voluntary solemn religious profession alone invalidates subsequent marriage. The Church could decree the same effect for any other vow of perfect chastity, but as far as we know, she has not done so save for the simple vows pronounced by the scholastics and coadjutors (brothers) of the Society of Jesus. The solemn profession made by certain orders of knighthood, the sole object of which is conjugal chastity, does not invalidate subsequent marriage. The solemnity of religious vows depends entirely upon the judgment of the Church. Marriage is forbidden in particular religious states by purely ecclesiastical law, in *the* religious state it is forbidden by divine law. Except in the case mentioned by canon 1043, dispensation from this impediment is reserved to the Holy See, which grants it only in rare cases. Persons attempting marriage with this impediment incur excommunication reserved simply to the Holy See. A marriage contracted before solemn religious profession is not dissolved by such a profession, if it has been consummated.

1657. *Rape*. If a woman is carried away by violence or fraud and detained as a prisoner by her abductor or his emissaries for the purpose of marriage, this act of rape constitutes a diriment impediment between the abductor and the woman abducted, as long as she remains in his power, even though she consents to marry him. It makes no difference whether the girl is an adult or a minor, the fiancée of the abductor or a total stranger to him; the impediment is the same. Canon 1074 observes that the forcible detention of a woman is held equal to rape, namely, when the man detains the woman by force, in the place where she lives, or to which she came of her own free will, as long as her abductor refuses to give her back her liberty, and always supposing that he detains her for the purpose of marrying her.

If, after being separated from the man and placed at full liberty, the abducted woman consents to marry him, the impediment ceases. If the girl consents to being carried away in spite of her parents, before the rape takes place, the rape is called seduction and does not constitute a diriment impediment. The same is true when a woman is carried away and made to contract marriage with a man who has no concern with her abductors.

1658. *Crime.* This diriment impediment is of purely ecclesiastical legislation. The Church dispenses from it only in rare cases, and never when the crime of homicide is public. The impediment is of three kinds: adultery alone, homicide alone, and adultery plus homicide. To incur the impediment, it is not necessary to know of its existence.

1659. *Adultery alone.* The adultery must be formal, *i. e.*, both parties must know that one is validly married; and it must be completely consummated. Moreover, the crime must be committed with a promise of marriage to be contracted after the death of the party's present consort, or with an attempted civil marriage. The promise must be mutual, accepted, sincere, and absolute. It is absolute, if any condition introduced is fulfilled before the death of the present consort.

It matters little whether or not the promise or the attempted marriage precedes, accompanies, or follows the act of adultery; but if the promise is recalled before the adultery, there is no impediment. The case would be different if the promise were recalled after the act of adultery. It is no longer necessary that the promise of marriage partake of the nature of an engagement. The promise must be made and the act of adultery committed at the time when the party concerned is lawfully married. The impediment would no longer exist if, after the death of the lawful consort, the adulterer married a person other than his accomplice.

According to canon 1053 the dispensation given by the

Holy See from *matrimonium ratum non consummatum,* or the permission to marry again on account of the presumed death of the first partner, always includes the dispensation from the impediment of crime committed by adultery, and the promise of, or attempt at, marriage if there be need of such a dispensation. The impediment of crime incurred by adultery and the killing of the partner by one of the adulterers, or by mutual coöperation, is not, however, included in this dispensation. If an ecclesiastical judge declares that the first partner is dead, his sentence has not the same effect as the dispensation or permission obtained from the Holy See.

In practice this impediment exists when divorcees contract and consummate a civil marriage during the lifetime of their former consort.

1660. *Homicide alone.* This impediment exists when the death of the person follows and is the result of the deed or resolution of each of the accomplices. It is necessary that both parties conspire in the death of the third person, although it suffices that one has the intention and the other gives his consent.

If all the conditions necessary either for adultery or for homicide were fulfilled, the parties would be laboring under two impediments instead of one, and mention of both should be made in applying for the dispensation. If some of the conditions are lacking, either in the case of adultery or in that of homicide, the impediment is known as both homicide and adultery. It is of this latter that we must now treat.

1661. *Homicide and adultery.* This impediment consists in the complete act of adultery without promise of marriage committed before the homicide, but not necessarily before the conspiracy to kill; and in homicide, without conspiracy, even though only one of the adulterers committed the crime in person or through a proxy and even though the other adulterer was ignorant of the fact that he was guilty. It is probable that the author of the homicide must have the intention of contracting marriage with his accomplice either himself or in conjunction with the adulterer, and it is certain that, in the case of homicide coupled with adultery, the latter must precede the former.

Impediments of this kind can become very complex, especially if the crimes involve an injustice towards several marriages. This is what takes place in adultery, when the two parties who commit the crime are married, and in homicide, when the two parties are married and inflict death on the respective consorts.

These impediments are of purely ecclesiastical legislation and are not binding upon infidels. Nevertheless, a Catholic who contracts them communicates their effects to an infidel accomplice. In endeavoring to discover whether or not such impediments exist, the confessor should prudently question persons who, shortly after the death of their consorts, seek to contract marriage with persons of their immediate entourage. They should try to ascertain whether they ever indulged in any familiarities with these persons before the death of their first partner, whether they desired their death, etc.

1662. *Consanguinity.* Consanguinity is the bond uniting persons who are descended from the same stock, and who are bound together by the same blood relationships. It is not necessary that such persons be born of the same mother, *but* not of the same father, or *vice versa,* nor that they be born of the same father *and* the same mother, nor finally that they be legitimate. The *direct* line is the series of parents, one of whom is descended from the other, as, for instance, the grandfather, the father, the son, and the grandson. The series of persons born of one common stock, but not descended the ones from the others, is called the *collateral* line, as, for instance, brothers, sisters, cousins, etc. If the latter are located at exactly the same distance from the common stock, the line is said to be equal, otherwise the line is said to be unequal. The degree is the measure of the distance between one person and another.

1663. In the direct line of consanguinity, marriage is invalid between persons of all degrees. Theologians are not unanimous whether or not it is invalid in virtue of the natural law. They are agreed that it is for the first degree, but they are not agreed for all the others. In the direct line of consanguinity there are as many degrees as there are persons without counting the stock.

In the collateral or branch lines, marriage is invalid to the third degree, inclusively, in such a manner, however, that the impediment is multiplied only as often as the common progenitors are multiplied. The third degree brings the line down to the sons and daughters of first cousins, so that these sons and daughters cannot contract marriage among themselves, nor, *a fortiori*, with those above them in the scale. (Can. 1076.)

Does blood relationship in the collateral line render marriage invalid by natural law? This question is controverted for the first degree, but in practice the Church never grants the dispensation, obliging an infidel who is married to his sister to leave her before being admitted into the fold. The Church does dispense from the second and third degrees.

In counting the degrees in the collateral line, the following rule must be observed. If the line is equal, there are as many degrees as there are persons in the direct line, from the common stock exclusively to one of the collaterals inclusively. If the line is unequal, there are as many degrees as there are persons in the direct line between the common stock exclusively and the collateral the farthest removed from it. If one of the partners is in the third degree and the other in the fourth, there is no impediment.

The rules we have just enunciated indicate the manner of counting the degrees from a purely ecclesiastical point of view; the manner of counting them adopted by civil law is quite different. If the line is equal, civil law doubles the degrees, and if it is unequal, it doubles the degrees of the shorter of the two lines, adding those in excess in the longer line minus the stock.

1664. Before the promulgation of the New Code, the impediment of consanguinity was multiplied in two ways: by the multiplication of the common progenitors, and by the multiplication of the branches ascending to the common progenitors. At present, the impediment is multiplied only as often as the common progenitors are multiplied. In virtue of the new legislation, impediments of consanguinity cannot be multiplied beyond the number four.

Several impediments of consanguinity in a marriage may be of different degrees. In petitioning for a dispensation, therefore, both the number and the degrees of the impediment must be indicated.

1665. It is not difficult to ascertain the degree in the direct line; one has only to ascend to, or descend from, the common progenitor. There is no difficulty in the collateral line either, if the stock or head of the line is known. If the head of the line is unknown, it is best to write the names of the man and the woman at the bottom of the page, and then ascend from the man's name to those of his father and mother, those of his ancestors on both the paternal and maternal side, and those of his great-grandparents in both lines. When this is done, one should repeat the operation for the woman's side, and if no common progenitor is found beyond the third degree, not counting the stock, the partners are not relatives in a prohibited degree. If the stock is found, the degrees must be computed according to the rules formulated in no. 1663.

1666. *Affinity*. This impediment is of purely ecclesiastical legislation. It consists in a bond of quasi-relationship arising from a valid consummated or non-consummated marriage. Affinity exists only between the husband and the blood relations of his wife, living or dead, and the wife and the blood relations of her husband, living or dead. The impediment of affinity invalidates marriage in any degree of the direct line, —in which cases the Church is not in the habit of granting a dispensation,—and in the collateral line to the second degree inclusively. It is easy enough to compute the degrees, because, since affinity arises from the relationship of each consort with that of his own family, it is necessary only to ascertain the degree in which the deceased consort is parent to the future partner. The degree of affinity is the same as the relationship from which it arises.

If a widow wishes to marry the father of her first husband, she will not be able to obtain a dispensation, because the impediment is of the first degree in direct line. If she wishes to marry the brother of her first husband, the impediment is of the first degree in the collateral line, because the brothers are relatives in the first degree in this line. The impediment of affinity is multiplied as often as the impediment of consanguinity, from which the affinity proceeds, is multiplied, so that if a man has successively contracted marriage with two persons who were cousins, and now wishes to marry a third cousin, he is doubly prevented from doing so by the impediment of affinity of the second degree in the collateral line. And if this cousin is doubly related to one of the first two cousins, because they have a double common stock—a situation which arises when their grandparents both on the paternal and the maternal side are common—the impediment is a triple one. It would be quadruple, if the third cousin were doubly related to the first two. The impediment is doubled also if two brothers marry two sisters of another family. In the event of the death of one of the brothers and of the wife of the surviving brother, the latter could not marry the surviving widow, because she had been the wife of his brother and also the sister of his deceased wife. This is a case of double inverse affinity and requires a double dispensation.

1667. Until Pentecost of the year 1919 affinity arising *ex copula licita, i. e.*, from a valid or putative marriage, invalidated the contract to the fourth degree in both lines; and affinity arising *ex copula illicita, i. e.*, from carnal intercourse outside of wedlock, or from a putative marriage publicly regarded as invalid, invalidated the contract to the second degree in both lines. There was also a sort of affinity contracted through incest, if one of the consorts committed adultery with a person related to his partner in the first or second degree. This impediment deprived the incestuous party of the right to ask for the *debitum*. All these impediments have been abolished by the Code.

1668. *Public honesty*. This impediment is a sort of affinity established by purely ecclesiastical law. The essential difference between affinity and public honesty is that the former arises from a valid marriage, and the latter from an invalid one or notorious concubinage. It matters not whether the invalid marriage has been consummated or not, nor what is the reason for its being invalid; and even non-consummated civil marriage is to be regarded as involving this impediment. Concubinage is notorious if, because of an avowal or the sentence of a judge, it is impossible to keep the crime a secret. The impediment of public honesty invalidates marriage in the first and second degree of the direct line between the man and blood relations of the woman, and *vice versa*. (Can. 1077.) The impediment is multiplied by invalid marriages or public and notorious concubinages during which one has lived with persons related to one's future partner in the first and second degree of the direct line.

1669. Before the appearance of the New Code, the impediment of public honesty arose also from a valid engagement—even from one that had been broken—and invalidated marriage in the first degree of both direct and collateral lines. It arose too from a valid or invalid consummated marriage, and invalidated the contract to the fourth degree of both lines. After the promulgation of the decree *"Ne temere,"* the engagement had to be entered into in writing in order to be valid, and the invalid marriage had to be invalid for a reason other than lack of consent, to give rise to the impediment.

1670. *Spiritual relationship.* This impediment is of purely ecclesiastical origin and arises from the administration or reception of the Sacrament of Baptism. It invalidates marriage only between the baptized person on the one hand, and the minister and the sponsors on the other, provided the Sacrament was administered validly and the godparents formally accepted their responsibility.

The minister contracts the impediment of spiritual relationship in every solemn or private Baptism administered unconditionally. If he administers the Sacrament two or more times conditionally, and one of these conditional administrations is certainly valid, he also contracts the impediment. The same holds true of the godparents, provided the same ones stand up for the child at each one of the Baptisms. If different godparents stand up for the child at these Baptisms, none of them contracts the impediment, and neither do they who act in this capacity when the priest supplies the ceremonies. Godparents who have not been designated, and who do not physically touch the one to be baptized, do not contract the impediment, because their act is invalid; but if more than two godparents are designated and touch the child physically, they would seem to contract the impediment, since canon 764, which restricts the number of godparents to two, does not appear to be of an irritant character. Persons who act as proxies do not contract the impediment.

1671. Before May 19th, 1918, godparents who served in that capacity in the administration of Confirmation, also contracted the impediment of spiritual relationship. In Baptism and Confirmation the impediment invalidated marriage between the ministers and the subject of the Sacrament, and also between the godfather and the godmother and the godchild and the father and mother of the godchild. The godfather of the one confirmed did not contract the impediment if he himself was not confirmed. The impediment of spiritual relationship could be further multiplied by the fact that it was contracted also between the godparents and the parents of the subject. Today this impediment can no longer be multiplied.

1672. *Legal adoption.* This is also one of the impedient impediments, as we have seen in no. 1639. According to canon 1080, those whom the civil law declares incapable of marrying on account of legal adoption cannot contract valid marriage under the Canon Law. In this particular instance, therefore, the Church adopts the stand of the civil law and makes the impediment her own. In order to ascertain whether or not there is a diriment impediment of relationship by adoption, and just how far this impediment extends, one must consult the statutes of the individual States.

1673. Before May 19th, 1918, the diriment impediment of legal adoption was, in substance, that of Roman law. Under this law there were two kinds of adoption: perfect and imperfect. By a decree of the supreme authority of the State, perfect adoption, which alone entailed the impediment, consisted in taking the adopted person into the family and giving him all the rights of a child. In due time, the Church began to regard as substantially the same as adoptions recognized by Roman law, adoptions solemnly pronounced by a civil judge, if the adopted one was taken into the family of the persons adopting him.

The former impediment invalidated marriage between the person adopting, the person adopted, and all his descendants; between the adopted person and the lawful children of the person adopting, who at the time of the adoption were subject to paternal authority; between the person adopting and the wife of the person adopted, and even between the adopted person and the wife of the person adopting. This impediment was perpetual. The only exception to this last rule was the impediment of legal adoption existing between the person adopted and the lawful children of the person adopting; this latter impediment ceased as soon as the adoption was dissolved or the legitimate children obtained their freedom.

1674. *The cessation of impediments*. The State can abolish or modify impediments of a purely civil character.

1675. *The cessation of canonical impediments*. Some impediments are perpetual, and, therefore, can never cease. An instance in point is perpetual impotency, and no dispensation can ever be obtained from it, because it pertains to the natural law. Other impediments cease by themselves, and an instance in point is age. Others, finally, can be abolished or modified by the Church, and it is of these that we must now treat. We shall speak, first, of the power of dispensing; secondly, of the causes for dispensation; thirdly, of the manner of obtaining dispensations; and fourthly, of the manner of executing them.

1676. *The power of dispensing*. The Roman Pontiff alone can abolish or modify the impedient or diriment impediments of marriage in the legislation of the Church. True, the Pope cannot dispense from impediments arising from the natural or from the divine positive law. He can, however, dispense from a divine positive law when such a law is founded upon an act of the human will, as happens in the case of vows. He may also declare that, under certain circumstances, impediments of divine positive law are not binding, and he may always validly, and, if there is a sufficient reason, also licitly, dispense from any impediment of the ecclesiastical law.

1677. The Church has never issued any official classification of divine and ecclesiastical impediments. It is certain, however, that lack of consent, impotency, bond of a previous and actually existent marriage that has been consummated, and consanguinity in the direct line, and probably to the first degree in the collateral line, are impediments arising from divine law from which no dispensation may be obtained. Another impediment originating from divine law is the vow, although it admits of dispensation. Very probably also, the episcopacy is an impediment of the divine positive law, from which no dispensation may be obtained. The other impediments originate in ecclesiastical legislation, and dispensations may be obtained from them.

The Church does not dispense from all the impediments with the same readiness. She does not dispense from the impediment of affinity to the first degree in direct line, for instance, when it arises from a valid and consummated marriage, and she does not dispense from the impediment of rape. Ordinarily she does not dispense priests, and very seldom clerics in major Orders or religious with solemn vows, and it is still more difficult to obtain from her a dispensation from the impediment of public homicide. The Pope never dispenses from the impediment of relationship in the first degree in the collateral line, and it is probable that he cannot do so. He seldom dispenses from the second degree touching the first, and in Christian countries he rarely dispenses from the impediment of disparity of worship.

1678. The Code makes a distinction between impediments

of *major* and *minor* degree. The following are the impediments of minor degree:

1. Consanguinity in the third degree of the collateral line;

2. Affinity in the second degree of the collateral line, if it does not touch the first degree;

3. Public honesty in the second degree;

4. Spiritual relationship;

5. The impediment of crime arising from adultery with promise of marriage, or attempted civil marriage.

All the other impediments are of major degree. (See can. 1042.)

1679. The Pope exercises his power of dispensing in an *ordinary manner* through:

1. The Holy Office, which has exclusive jurisdiction over cases involving the Pauline privilege, disparity of worship, and mixed religion;

2. The Sacred Penitentiary, which has jurisdiction for all occult cases of the internal forum;

3. The Sacred Congregation of the Sacraments, which has jurisdiction for all other impediments.

He exercises his power in an *extraordinary manner* through:

1. The Sacred Congregation of Religious, which has the necessary jurisdiction to dismiss or secularize members of religious Orders, and thus make marriage possible for them;

2. The Congregation for the Oriental Church, which has for all the churches of the Oriental rite all the powers of the other Congregations combined, save that of the Holy Office in the matter of the Pauline privilege;

3. The Secretary of State, if the dispensation is issued in the form of a brief.

Dispensations granted to rulers of States may also be issued by the Secretary of State, who, in these cases, must have an understanding with the chancery office of extraordinary ecclesiastical affairs. The Apostolic Chancery Office issues dispensations in the form of a bull. During a vacancy of the Holy See the ordinary organs retain their jurisdiction in the matter of granting dispensations.

1680. *Powers of the local Ordinary.* Without general or special faculties accorded by the Holy See, the local Ordinary has no power to dispense from marriage impediments. (See can. 1040.) The powers conceded by law are ordinary powers and may usually be delegated to others; those issuing directly from the Holy See are delegated powers, and may be subdelegated to the extent permitted by the indult. The Ordinary who has jurisdiction to dispense from matrimonial impediments is the Ordinary of the place where the contracting parties have their domicile or quasi-domicile, or, if they be *vagi,* where they are actually residing. When issuing the dispensation, it is not necessary that the bishop be in his diocese, nor that the parties be within its confines. If the two parties belong to different dioceses, it is enough if one of the Ordinaries issues the dispensation, but it is preferable that it be the one in whose diocese the marriage is to take place.

1681. *Ordinary powers of the bishop.* In doubt of fact, the Ordinary may dispense from a dispensable impediment for ecclesiastical laws only, and only in cases where the Pope ordinarily dispenses (can. 15); but the doubt of fact mentioned in this canon may not be one regarding the death of a former partner. The bishop may not dispense from vows reserved to the Holy See, *i. e.,* solemn religious vows and simple vows pronounced in a religious institute under the jurisdiction of the Pope; from the private vow of perpetual and perfect chastity; and from the vow to enter an order of solemn vows, when these latter vows were made unconditionally after the subject had reached the age of eighteen.

The local Ordinary may dispense his own subjects and

also strangers from vows that would be an obstacle in the
way of their marriage, provided his action is not injurious to
a third innocent party.

The Ordinary may also dispense from the time and from
the publication of the banns.

In imminent danger of death on the part of either party,
and when there is no time to have recourse to the Holy See,
the local Ordinary may, to ease the conscience of one or
both parties or to legitimatize the offspring, dispense, not
only from the canonical form, but also from all the impediments of ecclesiastical origin, public, occult, and multiple,
except the impediment of the priesthood and affinity in direct line arising from a consummated marriage.

He may exercise this power in favor of his subjects, even
though they be absent from his diocese at the time, and in
favor of *vagi* or other strangers who happen to be within its
confines. In doing so, he must avoid all danger of scandal,
and in the matter of the impediment of mixed religion or disparity of worship require and obtain the ordinarily prescribed
guarantees, at the risk of rendering the marriage null and
void. To exercise this power, it is sufficient for him to know
that the marriage will obviate a sin, a proximate occasion of
sin, an enmity, etc. And since scandal may easily arise in the
case of a dispensation granted in favor of a cleric, a religious,
or relative in the second degree of the collateral line touching the first, the bishop will do well to explain his reasons
for granting the dispensation, and also advise the cleric or
the religious to take up his residence in some other part of
the country where he is not known.

When dispensations of this kind are granted, they legitimatize the children born or conceived of such marriages, provided these children are not the issues of an adultery or a
sacrilege. Dispensations granted in virtue of ordinary powers
or in virtue of a delegation given by general indult, always

produce this effect. The same is not true if the delegation is given by way of a private rescript. In this latter case the children are legitimatized by a special rescript of the Holy See. By a subsequent marriage contracted validly or in good faith, or by the validation of a marriage, though not consummated by carnal intercourse, the offspring is also legitimatized, if the parents were capable of contracting marriage with each other at the time of conception, or pregnancy, or birth. (Can. 1116.) Prümmer interprets this canon to mean that all the children conceived or born are legitimatized by the subsequent marriage of the parents, provided they are not the issues of adultery, sacrilege, or incest.

It is certain that if the birth of sacrilegious, adulterine or incestuous children precedes the cessation of the impediment, the subsequent marriage of the parents cannot legitimatize the children; but if they are born after the parents have been dispensed from the impediment, the subsequent marriage of the latter will legitimatize them, since at the time of their birth, the parents were capable of contracting marriage with each other. Children legitimatized by subsequent marriage are to be held equal in all things to legitimate offspring, as far as canonical effects are concerned, unless the canons rule otherwise. The fact that the children have been legitimatized must be entered in the baptismal register.

The local Ordinary has, moreover, the power to dispense in the case which theologians have termed *casus perplexus, i. e.,* when an impediment is discovered on the eve of the marriage ceremony, and the delay caused by referring the matter to the Holy See will result in a serious evil. Under the same conditions, the bishop has the same power in revalidating a marriage. Examples of a serious evil would be defamation of a person's character, scandal, incontinence, serious loss of property, etc.

In the *casus perplexus* the Ordinary may dispense from

the same impediments and under the same conditions as in cases of imminent danger of death. He may not, however, dispense from the canonical form. In dispensing his subjects, the bishop need not be in his diocese, and they need not be within its confines. He may also dispense strangers who actually reside within his territory, and this power, being ordinary, may usually be delegated to another. In very grave danger of death and in the *casus perplexus* the bishop may dispense both in the internal (sacramental and extra-sacramental) and in the external forum. If he dispenses in the sacramental forum, no note is to be made of the matter, but the rescript must be torn up after three days; if he dispenses in the internal extra-sacramental forum, the rescript must be drawn up as usual and the dispensation entered in the secret archives of the chancery office; finally, if he dispenses in the external forum, the dispensation must be entered in the public archives of the parish and the bishop's palace.

1682. *The delegated powers of the bishop.* All the decennial, quinquennial, triennial and annual faculties granted by the Holy See to bishops for the external forum were abolished by the decree *"Proxima sacra"* of the Sacred Congregation of the Consistory, April 25th, 1918. The Sacred Congregation of the Penitentiary has never withdrawn from the bishops the faculty of dispensing their own subjects from the occult impediment of crime in the internal forum, provided there was no conspiracy to kill and the marriage has already been contracted. As a rule, this faculty may be subdelegated to rural deans, missionaries who give retreats and missions, and in some special cases to an approved confessor. The Ordinary who has received this delegation may make use of it even though neither he nor his subjects are actually in the diocese. In granting the dispensation, the bishop should enjoin upon the parties some serious and salutary penance.

According to a decree of the Sacred Congregation of the Consistory of March 17th, 1922, the Ordinaries of Europe, except those of Russia and Italy, may obtain from the Sacred Penitentiary the faculty to dispense from the impediment of occult crime under the same conditions as mentioned above.

Except in countries like France, Spain and Portugal, where Catholics are not obliged to mingle with non-Catholics, Ordinaries may obtain from the Holy Office the faculty to dispense from the impediment of mixed religion and disparity of worship, provided they comply with the conditions, instructions, and limitations prescribed for different cases and different localities.

The bishops have also the power to revalidate *in radice* marriages that are null because of an impediment of minor degree. They may revalidate such marriages if there is too grave an inconvenience in asking the parties to renew their consent, provided the first consent still persists and there is no danger of the parties obtaining a divorce. The party who knows of the impediment must be apprised of the favor that has been accorded him.

Finally, through a *motu proprio* issued April 20th, 1923, Pope Pius XI granted to the Sacred Congregation of the Consistory permission to renew the quinquennial faculties of all the bishops independent of the Propaganda or the Sacred Congregation for the Oriental Church.

When granting a dispensation in virtue of an Apostolic indult, mention should always be made of this fact. Dignitaries inferior to the Holy See must not make use of either their ordinary or delegated powers, once the Holy See has been petitioned for a dispensation, and if, for grave reasons, they do so, they must apprise the Holy See of their action. Bishops who have a general indult to dispense from some one impediment, may make use of their faculty even if the impediment is multiple, and whether the marriage has already been contracted or not, unless the indult specifies otherwise. Likewise, bishops who have a general indult to dispense from several impediments of different kinds, whether diriment or impedient, may dispense even from public impediments if several are discovered in the same person.

If he who has a general indult to dispense from several public impediments meets with a case where there is another impediment from which he cannot dispense, he must ask the Holy See for a dispensation from all impediments in the case. If, however, the impediment or impediments from which he can dispense are found out only after the dispensation has been obtained from the Holy See, he may make use of the faculties. (Can. 1050.)

1683. *The powers of the pastor.* In imminent danger of death and in the *casus perplexus* the pastor has the same power to dispense as the local Ordinary whenever it is not possible to have recourse to the latter. In the *casus perplexus,* however, the pastor's faculties are limited to occult cases.

When must cases be regarded as occult? Older authors are accustomed to term "occult" cases known to only a few persons and which probably will never be divulged; and "public" those which are known to several persons and can no longer be concealed. The public character of a case, therefore, must not be measured by the definition of a public impediment given in canon 1037. An impediment is public when it can be proved in the external forum. In this canon there is no question of the nature of the impediment, but rather of a particular instance of an impediment. The particular instance may well be occult while the impediment is by nature public, as in the case of consanguinity. An authentic interpretation issued December 28, 1927, has declared that the words *"pro casibus occultis"* cited in canon 1045 refer also to occult cases of an impediment which of its nature is public.

Canon 1045 states furthermore that, in the same circumstances, all priests mentioned in can. 1044 have the same faculties when there is no time to have recourse to the bishop or when there is danger of violating the seal of confession. Some writers would have this canon apply not only to the seal of confession, but also to any professional secret. After the pastor has granted a dispensation for the external forum (a dispensation which he may grant only in imminent danger of death) or for the internal extra-sacramental forum, he must at once inform the Ordinary of his action, in order that the dispensation may be entered in the public or secret archives, according as to whether it was given in the external or internal forum. A dispensation granted for the sacramental forum must not be communicated to the Ordinary nor entered in the archives. If the pastor believes that he may and must grant the dispensation, he should select an appropriate formula, inform the parties and witnesses of the dispensation, and require the parties to signify their consent, in his presence and that of the witnesses, unless he has reason to dispense with the canonical form in which case he should enjoin a suitable penance upon the parties.

The Pontifical Commission appointed to interpret the Code declared on the first of March, 1921, that the *casus perplexus* exists if the impediment is discovered by the pastor and the Ordinary only after everything has been prepared for the marriage ceremony, even though other persons knew of it before. If no one knew of the impediment, the pastor may dispense from it; if other persons know or knew of it, the bishop alone may grant the dispensation.

The faculty granted by the Code to the pastor in this case is also granted to any priest who assists at a marriage when there is no time to have recourse to the pastor or the local Ordinary. He may make use of this faculty, however, only in danger of death, or when it can be foreseen that the same condition will continue for months.

1684. *The powers of the confessor.* The confessor has the same faculties in danger of death and in urgent necessity, but only for the sacramental forum.

1685. *Causes for dispensation.* For the dispensation to be *licit*, it is *certain* that there must be a cause for granting it; this cause is even required for validity if the bishop grants the dispensation. The principal causes for granting a canonical dispensation are: (1) a scantily populated territory, (2) the advanced age of the girl (25 years), (3) carnal intercourse or too great a familiarity between the future partners, (4) the need to legitimatize the marriage or the children, (5) the cessation of serious enmities, (6) danger of concubinage, a civil or mixed marriage, a lawsuit, a scandal, (7) the Christian virtues of the man, (8) the excellence of his merits, (9) an important alms given to some charitable cause, (10) the poverty of the widow.

1686. For the dispensation to be *valid*, there must be neither *subreption* nor *obreption* in explaining the cause to rightful authority, the cause being the determining motive for the authority granting the dispensation. A person is guilty of subreption when he conceals what the law obliges him to tell; and of obreption when he states a fact that is false. Subreption and obreption do not render the dispensation invalid when they bear only on causes which induce authority to grant the dispensation more readily.

In doubt as to whether or not the reason for obtaining the dispensation was true or false, if it determined the mind of the one who granted the dispensation, or only made him more inclined to grant it, and in all similar cases, the benefit should be given to the party petitioning for the dispensation. If the principal or final cause for granting the dispensation ceases before the dispensation is communicated to those in whose favor it is granted, the dispensation is of no value. It would be different if the cause ceased after the dispensation was communicated, but before the marriage ceremony. The dispensation from an impediment of minor degree is not invalidated by subreption or obreption, even though the only reason advanced in the petition for the dispensation be false. (See can. 1054.) Dispensation from a major impediment is not invalidated by a slight exaggeration of the motive reason.

1687. *Manner of obtaining dispensations.* As far as possible, one should have recourse to the local Ordinary, who, by reason of quinquennial or other faculties, may have the power to dispense from the different impediments. If the bishop has not the power to dispense from them, he will have recourse to Rome.

Moreover, when there is question of a public major impediment, the Holy See is not in the habit of giving any answer without testimonial letters from the bishop petitioning for the dispensation. For occult impediments of the internal forum, the confessor may make use of his powers without informing the parties, and if he judges it necessary, he should have recourse to the Sacred Penitentiary, either directly, or better still indirectly through his Ordinary, by means of letters, which, if need be, may be sealed. If the confessor fears that in writing to the bishop he would violate the seal of confession, he should address his petition directly to the Sacred Penitentiary, unless he has received permission from the penitent to send the case in to the episcopal chancery. If he has no such permission, he should, in writing to the bishop or the Sacred Penitentiary for the internal forum withhold the true names of the parties concerned and give fictitious ones. If there are two impediments, one public and the other occult, the confessor

should have recourse to the Sacred Penitentiary for the occult impediment, and to the Sacred Congregation of the
Sacraments, or to one of the other Congregations, as the case
may be, for the public impediment. Mention must be made
to the Sacred Penitentiary of the public impediment for
which a dispensation has been requested or obtained from
another Congregation, but the occult impediment must be
withheld from the other Congregation. If the impediment
is public, the pastor must petition for the dispensation; if
secret, the confessor. He should write in the name of the
parties concerned, and, therefore, should speak in the third
person. If the impediment is public, he should indicate clearly
and without abbreviation of the names of the parties, their
diocese of origin and their actual place of residence; if the
impediments are secret, he should withhold the names, the
diocese and actual place of residence, mentioning only the
address to which the answer is to be sent. The greatest care
should be exercised in safeguarding the seal; at the same
time the kind of impediment and the reason for the dispensation should be indicated with the utmost precision.

In all petitions addressed to the Roman Congregation and
to the bishop, the lowest species of the impediment should
be indicated, and in consanguinity and affinity, both the line
and the degree. A dispensation granted for an impediment
of consanguinity or affinity is valid, however, even though
an error regarding the degree is committed either in the petition for, or concession of, the said dispensation, provided
the degree which is objectively true is further removed than
the one indicated. The same is true if the one petitioning
for the dispensation fails to mention an impediment of the
same species in the same or in an inferior degree.

In speaking of the degree, one should indicate whether
it is simple or multiple. Mention must also be made of the
number of impediments, irrespective of whether they are

of the same or different species, or whether the bishop can dispense or already has dispensed from them. Circumstances that render the obtaining of the dispensation more easy or more difficult, must also be mentioned. Thus, one must be careful to state whether the marriage is to be contracted or has already been contracted, whether or not it has been contracted according to the canonical form, whether the impediment is known or unknown, whether the marriage has been consummated, and if so, whether it has been done in good or bad faith. Those who write in for the dispensation are bound also *sub gravi* to indicate the financial standing of those who seek it. An error in a matter of this kind would not invalidate the dispensation unless the indult of the bishop carried this clause: "Granted in favor of poor persons." Dispensations from the Sacred Penitentiary are always gratuitous.

If the Ordinary dispenses from an impediment in virtue of faculties granted him by the New Canon Law, he must impose only a small chancery tax, which he may not exact from the poor. If he is unscrupulous in these matters, he is bound to restitution. If the Ordinary dispenses in virtue of a papal indult, he must protect the rights of the Holy See to the tax levied, just as if the dispensation had been granted by the Holy See itself. This last ruling has reference especially to the quinquennial faculties, which the Holy See has deigned to renew.

Petitions addressed to the Sacred Penitentiary must be written in Latin, even though they pass through the hands of the local Ordinary; the only thing to be written in the vernacular is the address of the party to whom the dispensation is to be sent.

1688. At the end of the petition the pastor, if he is applying to the Ordinary, and the Ordinary if he is applying to the Holy See, must swear to the truth of the statements, recommend the parties to the good graces of the authorities, and ask for forgiveness in cases where this is necessary. In applying for dispensations from the impediment of mixed religion and disparity of worship, they must guarantee to the same authorities that all requirements of the divine law will be complied with and that there will be no danger of a marriage ceremony performed by a non-Catholic minister.

1689. *The manner of executing dispensations*. The Holy See usually entrusts the duty of executing dispensations to the local Ordinary for the external forum and to an approved confessor for the internal forum. The form used by the Holy See in granting the dispensation is termed "commissarial."

Ordinaries are in the habit of granting matrimonial dispensations in commissarial form in occult cases and in a form which is termed *gracious* for public cases. In making use of this latter form it suffices to notify the parties concerned.

1690. The Holy See usually designates the Ordinary of the parties concerned to execute a rescript in the external forum, and more often than not it is the one who issues their testimonial letters or who sends the petition to Rome. The term "Ordinary" is to be taken here in the broad sense indicated in canon 198. The Ordinary who gave letters of recommendation may execute the rescript, even though by the time the dispensation arrives, the persons who petitioned for it have left the former diocese in which they had a domicile or quasi-domicile with the intention of not returning. He is under obligation, however, to advise the Ordinary of the place where the marriage is to be contracted, that the dispensation was granted by the Holy See.

The person executing the rescript would act invalidly if he had not first received the letters of recommendation and assured himself of their authenticity and integrity, unless this information has been furnished him by the person issuing the rescript. The person to whom the Apostolic rescript is addressed must first ascertain if the rescript is issued in commissarial or gracious form, and consequently, whether or not, it needs to be "fulminated." If the favor has already been accorded, he need not examine into the integrity and authenticity of the letters, but only notify the parties that the dispensation has been granted. If the dispensation is issued in commissarial form, the one to whom it is addressed must execute the same, unless it is evident that the rescript is null and void on account of subreption or obreption, or because there are conditions demanded by the rescript which the executor knows have not been complied with by the recipient of the document, or the latter is in the judgment of the executor so unworthy of the favor that its concession would be a scandal to others. In the last mentioned circumstance, the executor must at once inform the ecclesiastical authority granting the rescript, and in the meantime suspend its execution.

The executor of the rescript must either himself or through another ascertain whether or not the statements made in connection with impediments of major degree are true. He should not doubt the word of those who are petitioning for the favor, unless he knows through channels other than the confessional that their intention is to deceive. The validity of the dispensation depends, however, on the truthful representation of the facts, and not on the ability of the authorities to verify them.

Ordinarily the examination of the causes does not offer any serious difficulty, because more often they are not specified in the rescript, and the truthfulness of their character cannot easily be ascertained. When the dispensation is granted in gracious form, the cause must be true at the moment of the concession; but if it is given in commissarial form, the cause must be true at the moment of execution. The dispensation does not cease to be valid when the final cause ceases, even though this cause be the only cause. For the dispensation to be valid, it is enough if only one final cause is true, and for minor impediments, even this is not absolutely necessary.

If the rescript contains an error concerning the degree of consanguinity or affinity, this error does not invalidate the dispensation, provided the degree which is objectively true is further removed than the one indicated. The omission in the rescript of an impediment of the same species, but in equal or inferior degree, does not invalidate the dispensation; but it would be different if, through some mistake, the rescript mentioned a degree of relationship or affinity inferior to the one which actually exists, or if it did not mention an impediment of another species or one of the species, but in a superior degree.

Rescripts are no longer considered invalid on account of an error in the name of the person to whom or by whom the favor is granted, or a mistake in the place of residence, or a mistake concerning the object of the concession, provided, in the prudent judgment of the bishop, there is no doubt concerning the identity of the person and the object of the favor. (Can. 47.)

1691. Strict attention must be paid to any conditions demanded in the rescript, and failure to take note of essential rulings in regard to the method of procedure invalidates the execution of the dispensation. In the case where an essential clause has been disregarded, letters are required which have been termed *"Perinde valere."* Essential conditions are generally expressed by the particles *"si," "dummodo,"* or others of the same meaning. Non-essential clauses do not invalidate the rescript, although they are binding in conscience, *sub levi* or *sub gravi,* according to the case.

When a salutary penance has been prescribed, the same must be imposed. This kind of a penance is always imposed for the impediment of crime. A penance is salutary if it inspires the parties with a horror for their sin, and yet does not induce discouragement. (S. Penitentiary, April 8, 1890.) The "fulmination" of the rescript in the external forum must be done in writing and mention must be made of the authority from whom the rescript proceeds. If the executor has to legitimatize the children, the authority issuing the rescript may note this in the same or in a separate document.

The execution of the dispensation from an impediment is a personal matter which may not be delegated to another, although it is permissible to entrust to some one else the execution of certain preliminary actions. (Can. 57.) The successor in some ecclesiastical office or dignity may execute a dispensation, application for which was made to his predecessor, unless such an application was addressed to the predecessor on account of his personal competency. (Can. 58.) Rescripts issued by the Holy See for forums other than the sacramental should be carefully preserved, or at least mention should be made of them in the episcopal archives. The local Ordinary sends the rescript to the pastor for execution, and he in turn informs the parties concerned. Acceptance of the dispensation is no longer required, unless it be prescribed by special clauses appended to the rescript.

As a general rule, censures are no impediment to the valid reception of favors and dispensations from the Holy See. Exceptions to this rule are excommunications by condemnatory or declaratory sentence, personal interdicts, and suspensions by sentence in the ecclesiastical court. (Can. 36; see also canons 2265, 2275 and 2283.) If the rescript makes mention of the censure, it can always be executed validly and licitly. Moreover, the Holy See usually appends to the faculty to dispense, the power to absolve from censures in so far as this is necessary to insure the effects of the dispensation.

The confessor, whose duty it is to execute a dispensation for the internal forum, must comply with all the regulations we have enumerated for the external forum in connection with the verification of the impediments and their degrees, the causes, the conditions and the penance. If the rescript is issued for the extra-sacramental forum, it must be sent to the bishop, who preserves it or makes mention of it in his secret archives, in order to refer to it if the impediment ever becomes public. Rescripts issued for the sacramental forum must be torn up immediately, *i. e.*, at the most three days after they have been executed, under pain of excommunication *latae sententiae*. If later on the impediment becomes public, a new dispensation is required for the external forum. An impediment is public if it can be proved before a judge. The Holy See and the bishop require that dispensations issued for the internal forum be applied in the act of confession. For this reason, the rescript is usually addressed to a confessor approved by the local Ordinary and designated by those who are petitioning for the dispensation. Some rescripts carry a clause requiring that the confessor hold a university degree. In this case, the confessor must hold the degree specified, else the dispensation is null and void.

The penance imposed by the rescript must be separate from that imposed by confession, but, according to Noldin, the dispensation may be executed outside the Sacrament of Penance, if, in an exceptional case, confession is not expressly required. In no case is the validity of the dispensation contingent upon sacramental absolution or acceptance of the canonical penance. If the impediment (for instance, the vow of chastity) affects only one of the parties, it suffices to dispense this party; if it affects both parties, both must be dispensed by the confessor. It is not necessary, however, that the same confessor should dispense both parties. If the parties have recourse to different confessors, the rescript must be given to one of them, so that he in turn may give it to the other, thus enabling both to obtain the dispensation. This second dispensation is not necessary to remove an impediment which is indivisible; but it is prescribed in order that the confessor may impose a penance on both. In imposing a penance, the confessor should take into account the age and sex of his penitent. Instances of heavy penances are the rosary, the Way of the Cross, assistance at Holy Mass, the reception of the Sacraments. Penances are to be regarded as long if they must be said every week from three to twelve months, or if the Sacraments are to be received once a month for a whole year; they are to be regarded as very long if they last for three years, and very grave and perpetual, if they last until death.

If at the time the dispensation is executed, the case ceases to be occult, the dispensation is invalid even for the internal forum.

The "fulmination" of the dispensation for the internal forum must be done orally. There is no set form, but it must follow sacramental absolution if the latter is given.

Even though the Holy See delegates full faculties to dispense from an impediment and to execute the dispensation for both forums, the person delegated is not obliged *in se* to make use of these faculties, but must prudently consult his conscience.

1692. Dispensation from matrimonial impediments must be entered in the parish or episcopal archives, if they are granted for the external forum, and in the secret archives of the bishop's palace, if they are given for the internal, extra-sacramental forum. In cases where the impediment becomes public, the testimony of the secret archives in the bishop's chancery suffices to prove the existence of the dispensation even for the external forum. Dispensations granted for the sacramental forum must not be entered in the archives, nor cited as evidence for the external forum. If need be, a new dispensation should be requested for the external forum.

CHAPTER V

VALIDATION OF MARRIAGE

1693. One of the most difficult problems the pastor has to contend with is the validation of marriages. In matters of this kind he should proceed with the greatest prudence and reserve. Above all, he should be mindful of the fact stated in canon 1014, that marriage is favored in law, and that, therefore, in case of doubt the law insists on the validity of a marriage until the contrary is proved. In doubt of both fact or law the law insists on the validity of a marriage, and the same principle may be resorted to even when the celebration of a marriage is doubtful, provided the marriage is commonly regarded as valid and the parties themselves believe their union to be a lawful one. A marriage that is doubtful and also detrimental to the faith must be regarded as null and void, because in doubt, faith is favored in law. This is why all doubtful marriages of infidels converted to the Catholic faith are declared to be null and void in cases of the Pauline privilege.

When the marriage is certainly invalid, it must be validated if possible. If it is impossible to validate the marriage because of an insurmountable impediment, the Church offers three ways out of the difficulty.

1. The first consists in requiring that the parties separate, *quoad habitationem*. This is the easiest of the three alternatives, but also the most dangerous. Nevertheless, it must be

insisted upon when the marriage is notoriously null, especially when the parties are in bad faith and cannot remain continent if left together. A marriage is declared null in the external forum by sentence of the local Ordinary, and his declaration must ordinarily precede the separation *quoad habitationem.*

2. If the parties are in bad faith, but their marriage is not notoriously null, they may be permitted to live as brother and sister and separate merely *quoad torum,* if there is assurance that they will remain continent.

3. If the marriage is null, but not notoriously so, the putative husband and wife may be left in good faith if there is an urgent reason for allowing them to do so. It should be remarked, however, that the party who is in bad faith has no right to ask for or to render the *debitum.*

1694. An invalid marriage may be validated by the mere renewal of consent, by renewal coupled with a dispensation, or, finally, by a dispensation alone (*sanatio in radice*).

Parties may validate their marriage by renewing their consent, when the marriage is null exclusively on account of substantial lack of consent. They may also validate their marriage if the impediment ceases, as in the case of age or previous bond, or if it is in their power to abolish it, as in the case of disparity of worship, rape, or impotency. Thus the impediment of disparity of worship is abolished by the conversion of the non-Catholic party, that of rape by the release of the woman detained by her abductor, and that of impotency by a surgical operation. In all cases the renewal of the consent must be a new act of the will for the marriage that is known to have been invalid from the beginning. (Can. 1134.)

1695. If a marriage is null by reason of an impediment for which the Church is in the habit of granting a dispensation, the parties should, as a rule, be left in good faith until a dispensation has been obtained. In case one of the parties is in bad faith, he should seek to withdraw from conjugal duty until his marriage is put in order. If this is impossible, or if both parties are in bad faith or in proximate danger of incontinence—something which may be presumed if the husband is neither away from home nor seriously ill—and especially if the nullity of the marriage is notorious, and separation *quoad habitationem* is morally impossible, the Ordinary should be petitioned to grant the dispensation. This is the famous *casus perplexus*. If recourse to the bishop would require too much time and the case is occult, the pastor may dispense from the impediment, or even the confessor, if the occult impediment is only known through the Sacrament of Penance. According to canon 1045, the pastor and the confessor have the same faculties when there is danger of the seal of confession being violated. (See no. 1683.) In revalidating marriages under such trying circumstances, the bishop, and in the instances mentioned the pastor and the confessor, may dispense from all ecclesiastical impediments, except the priesthood and affinity of the first degree in the direct line, if such affinity arises from a valid and consummated marriage. In imminent danger of death, when recourse to the Holy See is out of the question, the bishop, and, in the cases mentioned, the pastor and the confessor, have the same faculties for the *casus perplexus*, and they may even dispense from the canonical form. Outside the case of imminent danger of death and the *casus perplexus,* the priest should petition for the dispensation from the impediments, just as he does when the marriage is contracted for the first time. He should mention the fact, however, that the marriage has already been contracted.

1696. When the impediment ceases or is dispensed from, the parties must renew their consent. (See can. 1134 and no. 1694.) The parties receive the Sacrament the moment they renew their consent; at that time, therefore, they must be in the state of grace. If they are not in the state of grace, however, their marriage should not be allowed to continue as invalid.

How must the parties renew their consent when the impediment ceases? If the impediment is public, the consent must be renewed by both parties in the form prescribed by law. If it is occult, but known to both parties, it suffices that the consent be renewed privately and secretly by both parties. If it is occult and known only to one party, it suffices that the party who knows of the impediment, privately or secretly renews his or her consent, provided the other party continues in his or her consent (can. 1135.) Marriage which is null and void on account of lack of the prescribed form, must be validated by contracting in the form required by law. (Can. 1137.) There would be lack of the prescribed form if the marriage were celebrated without witnesses or if the minister was not competent to perform the marriage.

If it is too difficult to obtain that the parties whose marriage is null and void renew their consent, there is one final means of validating it; namely, the *sanatio in radice*.

Recourse is had to this extraordinary means of validating marriage whenever there is a grave reason for not revealing the nullity of a marriage to one of the parties concerned, or when the other party refuses to renew his or her consent. Besides the dispensation from, or the cessation of, an impediment, the *sanatio in radice* imparts a dispensation from the law of renewing the consent, and, by fiction of law, a retro-action reaching back to the beginning of the invalid marriage in reference to the canonical effects resulting from the diriment impediment. The *sanatio in radice*, therefore, not only validates the marriage, but also legitimatizes the children. This must not be taken to mean that the dispensation renders the marriage valid from the beginning, for this is impossible, but only that all the canonical effects of the invalid consent are corrected. Canon 1139 is careful to state that marriage contracted with an impediment of the natural or the divine law is not validated by the Church by means of a *sanatio in radice,* even though the impediment has ceased afterwards. The Church is competent to correct canonical effects resulting from ecclesiastical impediments because by her laws she produces these effects.

The Church is accustomed to grant these dispensations, provided the union bears the external appearance of a marriage and is not overtly a mere concubinage. It follows that if two parties were in bad faith when they wittingly contracted with an impediment the effects of which they could easily foresee, the dispensation would not be granted. The case would be different if the parties did not have perfect knowledge of the impediment or if they did not know that the marriage was null and void. This is what takes place when persons contract a civil marriage. Secondly, the Church is accustomed to grant these dispensations provided the consent of both parties persists. It suffices, however, that it be doubtful whether or not one of them has recalled his consent. Without these two conditions the marriage would be without foundation, since the consent constitutes the essential matter and form of the Sacrament. If consent was lacking in the beginning, but was given later on, the *sanatio in radice* can be applied and its effects are produced from the time the consent was given. (Can. 1140.)

If only one of the parties knew that the marriage was null and void from the beginning, or discovered this fact before the dispensation was granted, the dispensation could be of benefit to the ignorant party, provided the other party gave his consent. The *sanatio in radice* can be granted only by the Holy See. (Can. 1141.)

1697. The ordinary faculties which the Holy See grants

to bishops do not include the *sanatio in radice*. To do this a special mandate is needed. If it is possible to execute this dispensation, it should be done in the same way as the others, with the addition of the words *"in radice."* The principal advantage of this dispensation is that, as soon as it is obtained, it is no longer necessary that the party who does not know of the impediment be informed thereof or required to renew his consent. What is more, a *sanatio in radice* may revalidate a marriage without either one of the parties being informed concerning its former invalidity.

The parties should be in a state of grace when their marriage is validated because it is at this time that they receive the Sacrament. This dispensation is usually granted for the internal forum only, but it may be granted also for the external forum, provided that in doing so the authorities act prudently and discreetly.

If the *sanatio in radice* is granted for the internal, extra-sacramental forum, it must be entered in the secret archives of the diocese; if it is granted for the external forum, it must be entered in the public archives of the parish and the diocese.

BRIEF SYNOPSIS OF CLANDESTINITY AND DISPARITY OF WORSHIP

(By the Translator)

A clandestine marriage, according to the *"Tametsi"* of Trent, is any marriage of a baptised person save before one's proper pastor by domicile, quasi-domicile or a month's residence, or a priest delegated by him, and two or three witnesses.

Before April 19, 1908, where the *"Tametsi"* was not promulgated. (For places see text.)

- Two Catholics, valid but illicit.
- Catholic and baptised non-Catholic, valid but illicit.
- Catholic and nonbaptised non-Catholic, invalid.
- Baptised non-Catholic and infidel, invalid.
- Two baptised non-Catholics, valid but illicit.
- Two infidels, valid and licit.

Before April 19, 1908, where the *"Tametsi"* alone was promulgated. (Province of Santa Fe.)

- Two Catholics, invalid.
- Catholic and infidel, invalid.
- Catholic and baptised non-Catholic, invalid.
- Baptised non-Catholic and infidel, invalid.
- Two baptised non-Catholics, invalid.
- Two infidels, valid and licit.

Where the *"Tametsi"* was promulgated with the Benedictine Declaration. (For places see text.)

- Two Catholics, invalid.
- Catholic and infidel, invalid.
- Catholic and baptised non-Catholic, valid but illicit.
- Baptised non-Catholic and infidel, invalid.
- Two baptised non-Catholics, valid but illicit.
- Two infidels, valid and licit.

N. B. The *"Tametsi"* applied to marriages of all baptised persons; locally, it ruled all marriages celebrated in any place where it had been promulgated as a papal decree, regardless of domicile of the contracting parties; personally, it applied to the marriages of all persons domiciled in the territory where it had been so promulgated, regardless of where their marriage was celebrated, unless they had acquired a *domicile for marriage* in an exempted place by at least a month's residence there. But the exempted party, *i. e.,* one not domiciled in territory subject to the *"Tametsi,"* communicated his exemption to the other party, *provided* the marriage was celebrated in exempted territory.

The Benedictine Declaration was to the effect that marriages of baptised non-Catholics with each other or with Catholics were valid even in territory subject to the *"Tametsi."*

After April 19, 1908 (*"Ne Temere"* of Pius X), a clandestine marriage is any marriage not contracted before the pastor of the place of marriage (or Ordinary) or a priest delegated by him, and two witnesses. It applies to the marriages of all baptised Catholics of the Latin rite contracting with any one.

After April 19, 1908, the *"Ne Temere"* holds everywhere, to May 19, 1918.
- Two Catholics, invalid.
- Catholic and infidel, invalid.
- Catholic and baptised non-Catholic, invalid.
- Baptised non-Catholic and infidel, invalid.
- Two baptised non-Catholics, valid and licit.
- Two infidels, valid and licit.

After May 19, 1918, the New Code holds everywhere.
- Two Catholics, invalid.
- Catholic and infidel, invalid.
- Catholic and baptised non-Catholic, invalid.
- Baptised non-Catholic and infidel, valid and licit.
- Two baptised non-Catholics, valid and licit.
- Two infidels, valid and licit.

The *"Tametsi"* in the United States together with the Benedictine Declaration

The *"Tametsi" was never promulgated* in the following Provinces (1885): I. Baltimore; Philadelphia; New York;

Boston; Oregon City; Milwaukee, Cincinnati (except the Diocese of Vincennes); St. Louis (except the city of St. Louis and a few other places mentioned in the next paragraph); Chicago (except some places in the Diocese of Alton, to be mentioned immediately).

The *"Tametsi" was promulgated* in the entire Province of New Orleans; in the Province of San Francisco, with the territory of Utah, except that part of this territory which lies east of the Colorado River; in the Province of Santa Fe, except the northern part of the territory of Colorado; in the Diocese of Vincennes; in the city of St. Louis, and the places called Ste. Genevieve, St. Ferdinand, and St. Charles, of the Archdiocese of St. Louis; in the places called Kaskaskia, Cahokia, French Village, and Prairie du Rocher in the then Diocese of Alton.

The Benedictine Declaration was extended in course of time (by 1885) to all these places, except the Province of Santa Fe.

FOURTH DISSERTATION

GOD THE PERFECTER

1698. We have treated of God the Creator; we have dealt with Him as the natural Ruler of all creation by His natural Providence and the supernatural Ruler of men; and, finally, we have considered Him as the Redeemer and Sanctifier of the human race. It remains for us to study Him as the Perfecter of His creatures. In a first treatise we shall speak of the last ends of man; in a second, we shall deal with the end of the world.

FIRST TREATISE

The Ends of Man

In this present treatise we shall deal, first, with the departure of man from this life and his entrance into the next; and, secondly, with the different states of the soul after death.

CHAPTER I

DEPARTURE OF MAN FROM THIS LIFE AND HIS ENTRANCE INTO THE NEXT

Art. I. Departure of Man from This Life.

1699. *Spiritual* death is the result of sin. It occurs in this life and also after death. There is another kind of spiritual death, which is the death to sin and the life of the soul according to these words of St. Paul, "We are buried together . . . by Baptism into death" (Rom. 6, 4.) There is also a physical death, which is the separation of soul and body. It is of this latter that we must now treat.

1700. "As by one man sin entered into this world, and by sin death; and so death passed upon all men, in whom all have sinned" (Rom. 5, 6.) Experience teaches that all men die. Some authors claim that there will be exceptions to this rule. St. Thomas refutes them by saying that we have all been condemned to death because of sin; we must all arise again; and, therefore, we must all die.

1701. The same Saint adds that the bodies of all men,

even of those who shall be still living at the end of the world, will be reduced to ashes. The meaning of the word "ashes" is derived here either from the *fomes peccati,* which is the cause of corruption, or from the ancient custom of incinerating bodies. Neither Christ nor the Blessed Virgin Mary had this *fomes peccati,* and, therefore, they were exempt from the law of death.

1702. Death, then, is the penalty due to sin, even though it be the natural end of the body, the parts of which are doomed to disintegration. Had man remained in the state of innocence, he would have been assumed into Heaven, body and soul, without having to pass through the doors of death. Either this immortality would have been connatural to the state of grace, or, as some authors maintain, it would have been produced in us by the fruit of the tree of life. "As by one man sin entered into the world, and by sin death." Death is a penalty for baptized persons and a pain for the unbaptized. (See no. 836.) Death, however, is the beginning of a new life, and for this reason it was desired by the saints. "I have desired to be dissolved and to be with Christ" (Philip. 1, 23.) St. Thomas teaches that the body belongs to the human nature of man even after it has been separated from his soul, because in virtue of the order established by God it still tends towards resurrection. (See no. 1719.)

1703. It is certain that men will die only once and that, as a general rule, men do not know the hour of their death. "Watch ye therefore, because you know not the day nor the hour." (Matt. 25, 13.) After death, man can neither merit nor demerit. "The dead know nothing more, neither have they a reward anymore" (Eccl. 9, 5.) The thought of death should incite us, therefore, to spend the short span of our earthly existence in doing good.

Art. II. Entrance of the Soul into the Next Life.

1704. *The particular judgment.* God pronounces judgment upon the soul immediately after its separation from the body. This truth is *certain,* John Calvin to the contrary notwithstanding. "It is appointed unto man once to die, and after this, the judgment" (Hebr. 9, 27.) Immediately after death, man receives his reward or punishment; it follows that he is judged at this time. Moreover, man is both an individual person and a part of the universe. As an individual person he will be judged at the particular judgment; as a part of the universe he will be judged at the general judgment.

1705. Authors are not agreed as to the time, place, and circumstances of the particular judgment. Some claim that it will take place before death, but this does not seem to be likely, because before death man is still a wayfarer. Others are of the opinion that it will take place sometime after death, but their view is not probable. Others finally teach that it will take place immediately after death, and their opinion is more probable. According to the common teaching of theologians this judgment is not necessarily a formal sentence pronounced by God, but consists in an internal illumination of the soul, whereby it clearly perceives of its own accord that it is justly absolved or condemned by its Judge. The sinner does not see God either at the particular or at the general judgment; but he recognizes Him by the clear manifestation of His divinity in the sentence pronounced.

1706. *Who is the judge at the particular judgment?* It is controverted among theologians whether this judge is God or Jesus Christ as man. Holy Scripture asserts very explicitly that "the Father hath given all judgment to the

Son" (John 5, 22.) It is fitting that those who are judged should see their Judge, but to see Him in His divine nature is the reward of the just. Sinners must see Him, therefore, in the nature which He assumed for their sake.

The place of the particular judgment is unknown, although several authors opine that it will occur at the exact spot where the soul leaves the body.

We must not, however, believe, that Jesus Christ descends from Heaven to sit in judgment upon each individual soul. According to a great number of writers, He will appear in the heavens as He appeared to St. Stephen, who exclaimed: *"Ecce video cœlos apertos."* After this, the sentence will be passed.

1707. *Predestination. Its existence.* Predestination is the preparation of grace in the present life and of glory in the next; it is tantamount, therefore, to the will of God destining some souls to grace and glory from all eternity.

1708. *There is such a thing as predestination.* This is *of faith* against the Pelagians. "He chose us in him before the foundation of the world" (Eph. 1, 4.) "Come, ye blessed of my Father, possess you the kingdom prepared for you from the foundation of the world" (Matt. 25, 39.) Nothing takes place in time which is not fore-ordained by God from all eternity, otherwise science and God would be in open contradiction, and some created things would exist independently of God. Finally, St. Augustine teaches the doctrine of predestination, and his views have been approved by the Church.

1709. *Predestination is certain and unchanging.* This is *of faith* against the Pelagians and the semi-Pelagians. "No man shall pluck them out of my hand" (John 10, 28.) The intellect of God is infallible, and no one can resist His will. We must observe with St. Thomas that God has predestined not only the number of the elect, but also each one of them

in particular (1a, q. 23, art. 7); although He wills ante-
cedently that all men be saved and that Christ die for all, as
stated in no. 649.

1710. Without revelation, no one can be certain that he
is numbered among the elect. This is *of faith,* from what we
have said in regard to purification in nos. 719 and 720. We
may form some estimate as to whether or not we are predestined by referring to the numbers we have just indicated.
It is *of faith* that predestination does not deprive man of
his liberty. (See no. 325 ff.)

1711. *The cause of predestination.* It is certain that the
efficient cause of predestination is God, because predestination is an act of God. Its *meritorious* cause is the passion of
Christ. Moreover, it is *of faith* that predestination to grace
is purely gratuitous and that predestination to final perseverance cannot be merited *de condigno.* If we make predestination inclusive of grace, final perseverance and glory,
in so far as God has the intention of bestowing them when
He issues His decree of predestination, it is certain that
this decree is also gratuitous. If we separate the gift of glory
from the other gifts of grace and final perseverance in
adults, and consider only the gift of glory conferred upon
the soul by God, it is *certain* that this gift is bestowed solely
in view of the merits of man; but if we consider the glory
prepared by God for man from all eternity, theologians are
not agreed. Some contend that the intention of God, or the
decree whereby He confers eternal glory, is absolute and
independent of all merit. It would be as if God said: "I
predestine John, hence I shall give him eternal glory and all
the efficacious graces and merits necessary to arrive at that
state." Those who side with this opinion are chiefly Tho-
mistic and Augustinian theologians. The Molinists, on the
other hand, hold that the decree of God is hypothetical.
According to them, it is as if God said: "In view of the

merits which John has acquired by means of grace, I will give him eternal glory." The Congruists are of the opinion that God, according to His knowledge of appropriate circumstances, decrees to confer upon the predestined graces that are infallibly efficacious *ab extrinseco*. There remains the opinion of Catharinus, which has but few followers today, that the divine decree is absolute for some souls like the Blessed Virgin Mary, and hypothetical for others.

1712. *The effects of predestination.* These effects are contained in the text of St. Paul: "Whom he predestined, them he also called" (Rom. 8, 30.) They are: vocation, the assistance of grace in the acquisition of faith and justification, sanctifying grace, eternal glory, and all the natural gifts conducive to it.

1713. Some are called to grace and not to glory, because they lose grace. They also are called elect, although their election is not complete. Their names will be effaced from the Book of Life, which contains the number of the predestined. They were inscribed in this book conditionally, in as much as they had grace, but not absolutely, because they were never to merit eternal life. The names of those who are inscribed in this book absolutely will never be effaced.

1714. *The number of the elect.* The greater part of the angels were predestined; the others have been condemned. Some are of the opinion that there will be as many men saved as there were angels who fell; others, that there will be as many men saved as there were angels who did not fall; others, finally, that there will be as many men saved as there were angels created. It is best to admit that we do not know the number of the elect and leave the matter with God.

1715. Will the majority of men be saved? If account be

taken of all men, it is *certain* that the majority will not be saved. The Scripture tells us: "Many are called, but few are chosen." In May, 1772, a book was condemned by the Sacred Congregation of the Index, because it indicated that the elect will far outnumber the damned. If account be taken only of Catholics, and children be included in this count, according to Suarez, the majority of them will be saved. If account be taken only of adult Catholics, theologians again disagree. Some hold that the majority of these will be saved, but Suarez limits this opinion to those adults who attend the divine offices and receive the Sacraments; others contend with more extrinsic and perhaps intrinsic probability that only a minority of adult Catholics are saved. (See no. 291.)

1716. *Eternal reprobation.* Eternal reprobation is the fore-knowledge and will of God condemning certain souls to damnation. Theologians distinguish between *negative* reprobation, which is nothing more than the privation of eternal life, without any act condemning to endless damnation; and *positive* reprobation, which is the decree of eternal damnation itself. Theologians who hold that predestination to eternal glory is effected by reason of God's foreknowledge of man's merits, refuse to admit this distinction. According to them, positive and negative reprobation alike are the result of sin and take place after sins foreseen. Those who hold that predestination to eternal glory is not the result of merits foreseen, claim positive reprobation takes place after and because of the sins foreseen, but that negative probation takes place before.

Whatever the solution to this question, it is *of faith*, against the predestinationists, Wyclif, Calvin, etc., that positive reprobation is effected on account of sin. "Depart from me, you cursed, into everlasting fire, which was prepared for the devil and his angels" (Matt. 25, 42.) It would be unreasonable and even impious to suppose that God will condemn innocent men to eternal damnation. Finally, the Second Council of Orange has pronounced anathema against all those who hold that some persons are predestined to evil by the omnipotence of God.

1717. The sentence of the Judge and the decree of predestination or reprobation will be executed immediately, in such wise that the just will be forthwith admitted to the vision of the Blessed Trinity, provided they have atoned for all their sins, and the damned will be plunged into the depths of hell. This is of faith against the Millenarians, the Greeks, and a few Protestants. "It is easy before God in the day of death to reward everyone according to his ways" (Eccles. 11, 28.) Moreover, the Council of Florence has proclaimed the same doctrine in the following terms: "We hereby define that the souls of those who have incurred no stain of sin after Baptism, as well as the souls of those who after being stained by sin have been purified, are received into Heaven, where they contemplate one God in three Persons as He is, some more perfectly than others, according to their respective merits; and that those who have departed from this life with the stain of actual mortal sin or that of original sin, will be plunged immediately into hell, there to undergo diverse punishments."

CHAPTER II

THE DIFFERENT STATES OF SOULS AFTER DEATH

1718. St. Thomas enumerates five different states of souls after death: the Limbo of the Fathers (*limbus patrum*), the Limbo of infants, Purgatory, Heaven and hell, and he avers that the Limbo of infants is different from that of the

Fathers, and that both differ from hell and Purgatory. According to the teaching of the same Saint, the souls of the departed do not, as a rule, leave the places where they are located.

1719. St. Thomas also treats of the knowledge of these departed souls. In this world, he says, the intellect of man is unable to know *in se* substances that are divorced from all matter, such as God, the angels, and the discarnate souls of men. Our intellect is concerned with the images furnished by the senses, and the senses being unable to furnish images of spiritual things, the intellect is unable to perceive them as they are. The human soul knows itself through its operations and its powers. By means of this knowledge, it places itself in a position to know spiritual things, which it does not, however, succeed in knowing perfectly by knowing itself, still less by knowing the material things, the nature of which so widely differs from that of spiritual things. And yet, logically speaking, the word "substance" applies to both material and spiritual things.

1720. The souls of the departed can make no further use of sense images, although the *intellectus possibilis* still exists for them and continues to act. Liberated from the body, this intellect experiences greater facility to know immaterial things, although this manner of existing and knowing is less in conformity with its nature. Because it is the lowest of all created intelligences, it cannot easily grasp the nature of the angels and other such superior things, but has to fall back upon data supplied by the senses. We have an analogue in the mind of the illiterate who is unable to fathom the theories of science without the assistance of practical experiment.

1721. The souls of the departed do not derive their knowledge from innate ideas, which they have never had, nor from images supplied by the senses, of which they are now devoid. They do not retain their sense memory, although they still possess all the knowledge acquired on earth through the possible intellect and the intellectual memory. These same souls receive images infused into them under the influence of a natural divine light, which is neither the light of glory nor the light of grace. It was in this way that the angels received the images of all created things at the time of their creation and thus knew of them in a natural way. The angels know themselves in their own substance, which, being immaterial, is the object of their intellect; but they know God through the image they have of Him in their essence, which they see, and they know other angels and other creatures by means of images infused into them by the divine light. The souls of the departed also know themselves immediately, and in knowing themselves, know other departed souls, who are of the same nature as themselves. They know the angels and other creatures by means of images infused by God, but their knowledge is imperfect and not as clear as that whereby the angels know, unless they have been illumined by the light of glory. Finally, they know only those individuals towards whom they are inclined either by means of images infused into them by God, or by the former knowledge they had of them, or by some divine disposition.

Distance is no obstacle to the knowledge of the departed souls, for the Scriptures tell us that the rich man saw Abraham who was dead. As a rule, however, the souls of the departed have no knowledge of the events that take place in this world, unless they are already beatified. The souls of the beatified are at liberty to be where they please, but when the souls of those who are not beatified appear on earth, it is either because they have obtained permission from God, or good or bad angels appear in their place unbeknown to them. The angels can move bodies, but the departed souls can move no bodies other than their own, and the latter only in as much as they animate them, and they animate them only in as much as they are united to them.

1722. The phrase "Abraham's bosom" signifies, strictly speaking, the Limbo of the Fathers, in which the souls of the just men of the Old Law were detained, awaiting the time when Christ would open the gates of Heaven to them. By their faith in a future Redeemer, and by their charity and good works, these holy men were justified both in regard to the guilt of original and actual sin and in regard to the pain due to actual sin. They were detained in Limbo because of the punishments due to original sin, which deprived them of the beatific vision until the price of their redemption was paid. Under the New Law, the faithful who are cleansed of original and actual sin through Baptism, are not excluded from Heaven, although they must still satisfy for the penalties due to original sin by physical death.

1723. The souls of the ancient patriarchs suffered no pain in Limbo, although they were for the time being deprived of eternal glory. This state of privation constituted a sort of punishment, although it was greatly tempered by the well-founded hope that they would some day obtain their release. After the descent of Christ into Limbo this place was completely evacuated.

1724. We have already treated of Limbo in No. 546, and we shall discuss the fate of the children detained there in No. 2100. It remains for us to say a word about Purgatory, hell, and Heaven. In the discussion of these three topics we shall bear in mind the teaching of St. Thomas concerning the status of departed souls. These souls, it will be remembered, no longer have their sense faculties, but recover the ability to exercise these when they become reunited with their bodies.

Art. I. Purgatory.

1725. Purgatory is a place of suffering for the souls of the just who have not yet fully atoned for their sins. We have purposely used the word "suffering"; the souls detained in this place can no longer, strictly speaking, satisfy, because, being no longer wayfarers, they can only suffer in order to hasten their deliverance. According to common opinion, Purgatory is located on this earth and is somehow connected with hell. Some authors are of the opinion that the souls of the departed satisfy for their transgressions in the place where they sinned, and St. Thomas agrees that this may sometimes happen. Others aver with St. Alphonsus that they are purified in hell. We shall treat, first, of the existence of Purgatory; second, of the pains of Purgatory; and, third, of the relation between the souls in Purgatory and those living on earth.

1726. *The existence of Purgatory.* It is *of faith,* against the Protestants, that Purgatory exists. "And making a gathering Judas sent twelve thousand drachmas of silver to Jerusalem for sacrifice to be offered for the sins of the dead" (2 Mach. 12, 43.) "He that shall speak against the Holy Ghost, it shall not be forgiven him, neither in this world, nor in the world to come" (Matt. 12, 32.) If there were no Purgatory, where would the souls of those go who die in the state of venial sin or who have not atoned completely for the temporal pain due to sin? St. Thomas has observed that, in virtue of grace and acts of charity, the souls of the departed can atone for the guilt involved in venial sin by the sufferings which they undergo. These sufferings are voluntary to the extent that they are patiently borne by the souls in Purgatory. Some writers, however, maintain that

the guilt of venial sin is remitted by contrition, which the
soul of the just gives expression to upon its departure from
this world, and not by the pains which it undergoes in the
next.

The existence of Purgatory is proved also by the tradition of all nations and by the statement of the Council of
Florence: "We define that the souls of truly penitent Christians, who die in charity before being purified of their sins
of commission and omission by worthy fruits of penance,
are purified after death by the sufferings of Purgatory."

1727. *The pains of Purgatory.* It is *certain* that the pains
of Purgatory are less severe than those of hell, for the souls
of the just are the friends of God. It is also *certain* that the
souls in Purgatory do not see God intuitively, and as a consequence are temporarily deprived of the beatific vision. It
is doubtful whether these souls suffer any pains of sense.
Some deny that they do, and the Greeks, while believing in
the pains of sense, *i. e.,* physical suffering, deny that this
additional punishment is caused by material fire. They have
not been condemned. The current opinion in the Latin
Church is that the souls in Purgatory are punished by a
material fire similar in nature to that of hell. This is why
the Church prays that they may find a place of refresh-
ment, light, and peace. Whatever their sufferings, it is certain, from the common teaching of theologians, that they
are extremely severe, for justice will take the place of mercy
in the next world.

In opposition to other theologians, St. Thomas teaches
that the slightest pain of sense and privation of the beatific
vision in Purgatory is greater than any suffering in this
world. Cardinal Bellarmine is of the opinion that there
exists in Purgatory a *distinctive sort of prison,* where some
souls are deprived of the beatific vision, but do not suffer
the pain of sense. They are detained in this way, not be-

cause of any sins they have committed, but because they did not sufficiently long for Heaven while on this earth.

1728. It is the common teaching of theologians that the souls of the faithful in Purgatory are comforted in their sufferings by faith, since they do not yet see God; by hope, since they do not yet possess Him; and by charity, since they know they are in the state of grace and are sure of their eternal happiness. According to the teaching of St. Thomas, the opposite doctrine is false, and the Church has condemned it in the thirty-eighth proposition of Martin Luther. The departed can no longer acquire merit, because they have ceased to be wayfarers and are no longer capable of sinning. According to a generally accepted opinion, they can pray and obtain favors for themselves from the hand of God. It is not known, however, if their sufferings admit of decrease, although Cardinal Bellarmine and other theologians hold that they do.

1729. The duration of Purgatory is likewise a matter of conjecture. St. Thomas teaches that some souls are delivered sooner than others, and according to common opinion many are detained for a lengthy period of time. As a matter of fact, the Church permits perpetual foundations of Masses. One thing is certain, and that is, that there will be no Purgatory after the General Judgment. Those who survive at the end of the world will undergo tribulations and sufferings that will make up for their deficiencies.

1730. *The relation between the souls in Purgatory and those living on earth.* According to St. Alphonsus, it is more probable that the souls of the departed pray for those who assist them by their suffrages. St. Thomas and other theologians deny this. According to St. Augustine, with whom a few other theologians do not agree, they may appear on earth by special permission of God. According to Cardinal Bellarmine, they may be recalled to life, although the same doctor affirms that neither the blessed nor the damned can live again, but only those whose eternal fate has not yet been definitively sealed.

1731. *How can the living assist the dead?* According to a probable opinion, they may pray for them, and they are bound by *charity, filial piety,* and *gratitude* to pray for the souls of their parents, and sometimes by *justice* if a contract exists to this effect.

1732. *Suffrages for the dead.* It is *of faith* that the living can assist the souls of the departed. "It is therefore a holy and wholesome thought to pray for the dead, that they may be loosed from sin" (2 Mach. 12, 46.) The Council of Florence defined that the souls of the departed are cleansed by purgatorial pains after death, and in order that they may be rescued from these pains, are benefited by the suffrages of the living faithful, *i. e.,* the Sacrifice of the Mass, prayers, alms, and other works of piety.

1733. *What are Suffrages?* Suffrages are the fruits of supernatural works which, applied to the rest of the faithful, benefit them either like the Mass *ex opere operato,* or like prayer and good works *ex opere operantis.* In order to grasp the full significance of this, we must know that every supernatural work has a double fruit, the one *meritorious* and the other *satisfactory.* The *meritorious* fruit accrues to the one who performs the act and results in his being worthy, either *de congruo* or *de condigno,* of some supernatural reward in this world or the next. The *satisfactory* fruit satisfies for the pain due to sins that have been forgiven. Prayer has a third kind of effect distinct from these two. It is termed impetratory, because he who prays obtains from the mercy of God what he requests either for himself or for others. (See nos. 744, 1144, and 1159.)

1734. *Common Suffrages.* In virtue of the Communion of Saints, the impetratory fruit of prayer and the satisfactory fruit of prayer and of good works can profit all the faithful who are united by the bonds of charity. The Communion of Saints is a dogma of our faith from the words of the Creed. "So we being many, are one body in Christ, and everyone members one of another" (Rom. 12, 5.) Just as the acts of one member of the body benefit the whole body, so one act of one of the faithful benefits the whole Church. But the Church comprises not only the members of the militant Church of Christ here on earth, but also the members of the triumphant Church in Heaven and the suffering Church in Purgatory. The damned are excluded from membership in the Church because they have severed the bond of charity which united them to her. (See no. 1749.)

1735. The same bond of charity is severed also by sinners, and for this reason they do not receive the satisfactory fruit like the just, for punishment is remitted only when guilt is condoned. Nevertheless, as the Catechism of the Council of Trent observes, they are still in the Church to regain the life of grace which they have lost, and they are assisted by those who have spiritual life. Consequently, they derive a benefit from the works of the just which cannot accrue to those who have been cut off from the Church. They share, too, in the prayers of the faithful, who may even be able to merit for them *de congruo*. (See no. 3056.) The just on earth, moreover, share in all the Sacraments and all the satisfactory fruits attached to the good works of the rest of the faithful. The Blessed in Heaven do not share in these prayers or satisfactions because they are no longer in need of them. We reverence them, however, and invoke their aid; and they in turn, come to our assistance, as we shall see later.

1736. The souls in Purgatory have need of the satisfaction and prayers of the faithful and, therefore, share in them. Manifestly they are not assisted by the satisfaction

of the Blessed in Heaven, since the latter can no longer
satisfy. It is controverted, however, whether or not they
can be aided by the prayers of the elect. One opinion states
that they can, and those who advance it rest their proof on
the following prayer recited by the Church in her Office:
"God of forgiveness, we pray Thee, through the intercession
of the Blessed Virgin Mary and all the Saints, grant to
the souls of our departed brethren . . . to be united with
Thee." A second opinion, which is also probable, denies that
they can. A third opinion holds that the souls in Purgatory
are aided by the Saints, not directly, but indirectly, in as
much as the elect in Heaven obtain from God favors for
the living, in order that the latter may apply these suffrages
to the souls of the departed. In this third opinion there is
question only of the general Communion or common suffrages of the members of the Church.

1737. *Special Suffrages*. There are also special suffrages
that can be applied by any private individual, either to the
just on earth or to the souls in Purgatory. It is *certain* that
these special suffrages, in so far as they are satisfactory, can
benefit a person more than the common suffrages. The contrary opinion has been condemned in the nineteenth article
of John Wyclif. St. Thomas teaches that the joy of the
souls in Purgatory in having suffrages applied to some one
among them is in proportion to the amount of charity they
possess. The Catechism of the Council of Trent states explicitly that one may satisfy for another, and it is commonly
held that a satisfactory work applied to another by one of
the faithful remits the debt of the latter in proportion to the
value of the payment made. St. Thomas teaches that he
who merits for another does not merit any less for himself,
but that he who satisfies for another cannot pay two debts
at the same time. He who satisfies for another, however,
merits more than the payment of a debt: he merits life

everlasting. (*Suppl.*, q. 13, art. 2, ad 3.) The impetratory fruit of prayer is not produced *ex justitia,* but through the mercy of God (71, art. 1.)

1738. It is *certain* that special suffrages infallibly benefit the souls in Purgatory, and very probably too, satisfactory works remit their debt *ex justitia.* Some writers are of the opinion that we can assist the souls in Purgatory only by way of impetration and that we can merit for them only *de congruo.* As we have no idea of the debts which these souls have to pay, and as we have still less knowledge of the value of our own works of satisfaction, we should never cease to offer up our suffrages in their behalf.

1739. The Catechism of the Council of Trent requires two conditions for satisfaction. The first is that he who satisfies must be in the state of grace, or a friend of God, because works done without faith and charity cannot be acceptable to God; the second is that the works performed be of their nature painful or laborious. An exception to the first condition is suffrages which benefit the souls in Purgatory *ex opere operato,* like the Sacrifice of the Mass, which is a very efficacious means of lending assistance, and the prayers of the Church recited by an unworthy minister. According to St. Thomas, such prayers are efficacious at least from the standpoint of impetration and probably also from that of satisfaction. Some authors go so far as to say that for these prayers to have impetratory and satisfactory value it suffices that they be instituted by the Church; others require, over and above this condition, that they be recited in the name of the Church and by a minister delegated for that purpose.

According to some authors, the supernatural works of a sinner who has no further attachment to sin can produce satisfactory fruits, not *de condigno,* but *de congruo.* These writers base their conclusion on the early practice of the Church to impose a penance before giving absolution, and upon the authority of St. Thomas, who says that the confessor may enjoin a smaller penance upon a sinner who has already done penance before confessing his sins, because he is probably deserving of less punishment.

1740. St. Thomas adds that the suffrages of sinners can be of no benefit to the souls in Purgatory, unless they be commanded by some one who has charity, as, for instance, the Church or some private individual. Although the prayer of the sinner may not be meritorious, it may be impetratory, because merit is the result of justice, but impetration is the result of grace. For this reason the priest should never tire of asking the faithful to pray for their dead. Mass intentions and alms will incite the ministers of the Church and the poor to offer up prayers for their hasty deliverance.

We cannot apply to others all the impetratory fruit of merit *de congruo* which accrues to our good works, for we are in constant need of the grace of God and are dependent upon Him continually for our own selves. The same is not true of the satisfactory fruit of our good works, several authors to the contrary notwithstanding. Pope Pius IX has attached a number of indulgences to what is known as the Heroic Act of Charity, a sort of vow by which a person renounces all his satisfactions, as well as all indulgences and suffrages, in order to apply the same to the souls in Purgatory. By this same vow a person renounces also all benefits to be derived from the souls in Purgatory and all indulgences, whether they be applicable to the deceased or not. A person satisfies for this vow even though he does not place all this merit in the hands of the Blessed Virgin or makes application of his good works to some individual departed soul. A priest who has the right of a privileged altar must apply this indulgence to the soul for which he celebrates Mass. (See no. 1730.)

We must add that, in all probability, the souls in Purgatory pray for those who come to their assistance. Certainly they will pray for them when they are finally admitted to Heaven.

1741. The application of special suffrages to the souls of the departed must be made by a person who is still a wayfarer, and this application must precede the act of satisfaction. This act must be voluntary and also good, and the Catechism of the Council of Trent further enjoins that the works performed be such as are of their own nature painful or laborious. Besides the Sacrifice of the Mass, of which the Council of Florence makes special mention, every species of satisfaction may be included under the three heads of prayer, fasting, and almsdeeds, which correspond to three kinds of goods, those of the soul, those of the body, and external goods, and which are the three most effective ways of eradicating the three species of concupiscence, the lust of the flesh, the lust of the eyes, and the pride of life.

1742. It is required that he who receives the suffrages be in need of them at the time when they are applied to him, and not afterwards. It is furthermore required that he be in the state of grace, and that the venial sins for which he must satisfy have already been forgiven. According to a great number of theologians it is not necessary that he should be aware of these suffrages or that he should accept them. Suffrages that go unclaimed revert to the one who offers them or to the spiritual treasury of the Church.

Art. II. Hell.

1743. Hell is a place to which the souls of the damned are condemned immediately after the particular judgment to suffer eternal punishment there. The exact location of hell is not known, but it is generally believed that it is somewhere under the earth or near its center. We shall treat, first, of the existence of hell; and, secondly, of the pains of the damned.

1744. *The existence of hell*. Hell exists and its pains are eternal. Both parts of this proposition are *of faith*, the first against the rationalists and the Socinians from the words of the Second Council of Florence, cited in no. 1717; and the second against the Origenists, condemned by the Fifth General Council of the Church. The existence of hell is proved: (1) from Sacred Scripture, "Depart from me you cursed into everlasting fire" (Matt. 25, 41); (2) from the writings of the Fathers, who faithfully echo the teaching of the Bible; (3) from the words of the Athanasian Creed: "Those who have done good will enter into eternal life, those who have done evil will be condemned to everlasting fire"; and (4) from reason. God is just and the wicked very often escape punishment in this life; it is the firm conviction of men that God will punish them in the next. Because it is an offense against God, sin is in a sense infinite; the pains due to sin, therefore, must be proportionate and consequently eternal. Again the pain due to sin is not remitted unless the guilt is effaced by penance; being no longer wayfarers, the damned are in no position to do penance; therefore, their punishment will last as long as their guilt, *i. e.*, for all eternity. Finally, were hell not eternal, the sanction of the divine law would be insufficient, and the sinner could continue offending against the will of God with the full assurance that he would be happy some day. The goodness of God is nothing if not a sovereign hatred of evil, and the mercy of God cannot infringe upon the rights of His justice. All nations have persisted in their belief in hell despite its terrors and its odious connotations.

1745. *The pains of hell*. The different kinds of pain. The twofold punishment of the wicked corresponds, according to St. Thomas, to the twofold nature of sin, which is both a turning away from God and an inordinate turning towards creatures, "In so far as sin consists in a turning away from God," he says, "its corresponding punishment is the pain of loss, which is also infinite; but in so far as sin is an inordinate turning towards creatures, its corresponding punishment is the pain of sense, which is also finite." (1a, 2ae, q. 87, art. 4.)

1746. *The pain of loss*. The existence of this pain is certain: "Depart from me you cursed." The sinner is estranged from God by sin; sin has not been destroyed; therefore, his estrangement will continue forever. This pain is infinite, as St. Thomas is careful to point out. It is the greatest of all pains, and as great as God is great. The damned are perfectly informed concerning their loss, and it is this very knowledge which causes them to suffer so acutely.

1747. According to St. Thomas, children who die without Baptism do not suffer from the privation of the sight of God. They have no knowledge of eternal glory and do not blaspheme God. The opinion of Baius that these children blaspheme God has been condemned. (See no. 546.) "Hatred of divine justice in the damned is tantamount to interior blasphemy; we may well believe that after the resurrection the lips of the damned will blaspheme God just as those of the saints will sing His everlasting praises" (q. 13, art. 4).

1748. In losing God, the damned lose all supernatural gifts. Natural gifts such as intellect and will they retain, as we have had occasion to prove when speaking of the devil in no. 541. But having irretrievably missed their final end, they are estranged from everything good, are saddened by the happiness of the elect, which they perceive in an imperfect manner, desire that all others be damned, and are more grieved when persons who are total strangers to them are lost than when their own parents are condemned. They have a perfect knowledge of the evil they have done and the happiness they have lost, and it is these thoughts that torment them. They think of God only in terms of a chastiser, and they hate the effect of His justice with all the powers of their mind. Their thoughts are only of evil, although they cannot demerit, and this, too, is one of the chief causes of their suffering.

In regard to their last end, they are no longer free of a freedom of necessity, although they are free from coaction and to a certain extent from necessity, being in a position to do or not to do certain things and to will different acts. (See no. 426.)

1749. Since the bond of charity is severed between the damned and God, it is severed also between them and the Church, triumphant, militant, and suffering. They cannot, therefore, appear to men without the permission of God, the elect in Heaven have no compassion on their sufferings, and the faithful on earth can be of no assistance to them by their prayers.

1750. *The pain of sense*. This pain is the just punishment for the sinner's inordinate attachment to creatures. The creature that has been loved in an inordinate way will rise up against the damned, whose pains will increase in proportion to his inordinate love. (St. Thom., *Suppl.*, q. 97, art. 1.) The principal pain of sense suffered by the damned will be that of fire. This is not *of faith,* although it is *certain* from the arguments we have advanced in no. 1744.

1751. Is the fire of hell a material fire? St. Thomas is of the opinion that it is, and Suarez affirms that this opinion is certain and Catholic, since no pain could affect the body were it not material. He adds that the fire of hell is of the same species as ordinary, material fire, although it is possessed of different properties, for it does not need to be kindled nor maintained in existence by combustion. (St. Thom., *Suppl.*, q. 97, art. 5 and 6.)

The same fire tortures the demons and the souls of the departed, even though the latter are now devoid of sense faculties. After the General Judgment this fire will torture also their bodies. The difference in nature between the soul and the body does not prevent the latter from being informed by the former and, therefore, this difference will be no obstacle to a corporeal substance like fire tormenting a spiritual substance like the soul.

How can the soul, which is devoid of sense faculties, be affected by material fire? St. Thomas answers this question by pointing out that fire is by its nature united to a spirit in the same way as a place is united to that which is located in it. In so far as this fire is the instrument of divine justice, it has the power to hold the soul captive, and this fact adds to its torment. Some authors maintain that the fire of the damned is intrinsic to them, but it would seem that we should reject this opinion. According to a decision issued by the Sacred Congregation of the Penitentiary, April 30, 1890, a priest may not absolve a penitent, who, after being instructed, temerariously (*temere*) insists on maintaining that the fire of hell is not real, but figurative.

1752. There are other pains in hell besides that of fire. St. Thomas avers that, after the General Judgment, God will cast into hell all vile and beastly things to torture the souls and bodies of the damned. "The whole world shall fight with him against the unwise" (Wis. 5, 21.) According to the Angelic Doctor, "the worm that dies not" (Mark 9, 43) is undoubtedly a figure of speech, signifying the pangs of conscience; other writers, however, interpret these words literally.

There will be weeping in hell, resulting from pains in the

head and eyes of the damned, but they will shed no tears, because their bodies are incorruptible and also because, if their weeping found an outlet in tears, their bodies would soon suffer destruction.

1753. There will be physical darkness in hell, although by a disposition of Divine Providence there will be enough light for the damned to see the things that torment them.

1754. *Characteristics of the pains of hell.* All the pains of hell will be equal in duration, because they are all eternal, but justice demands that sins be punished in proportion to their grievousness, and so the intensity of these pains will not be the same. This is *certain*, because God rewards each according to his due.

1755. The pains of the damned will not be alleviated in the least, as far as duration is concerned. This is *of faith*. Some of the Fathers, however, have contended that on certain days God grants the damned a respite. This opinion, although not heretical, is presumptuous and vain. In hell there is no redemption, and never will a drop of water fall upon the parched lips of the evil rich man. St. Thomas teaches, however, that the divine mercy reveals itself even toward the damned—in as much as they are not punished as rigorously as they deserve.

Art. III. Heaven.

1756. Heaven is the place where God reveals His essence to the minds of the saints in all its glory. Holy Scripture explicitly states that Heaven is a *place*, although it does not indicate its exact location. In several passages of Holy Writ Heaven is described as existing above the earth. If by Heaven we understand perfect happiness, Heaven is wherever the blessed are, for just as the damned carry within themselves their tortures on this earth, so the angels always see the face of God, no matter where they may be.

We shall treat, first, of the happiness of the elect; and, secondly, of their relations with men.

1757. *The happiness of the elect.* Happiness or beatiude is a state made perfect by the accumulation of all good things. In man, this state includes both the goods of the body and those of the soul. In no. 1805 we shall treat of the beatitude of man's body; here we limit ourselves to the beatitude of his soul. The beatitude of man's soul could be *natural,* and then it would consist in a possession of the sovereign good proportionate to man's natural abilities. As such, it would comprise a knowledge of God abstracted from creatures, and yet more perfect than any knowledge of Him in this world; and in a love of God above all things coupled with the cessation of pain. The beatitude of man's soul may also be *supernatural,* and then it will consist in the intuitive vision not of God's works, but of His very essence, and in the love and enjoyment that result from this vision.

1758. *Objective* beatitude is nothing more than that which renders man happy, and it is philosophically *certain* that God is the objective beatitude of man. God alone, indeed, is the sovereign Good, the alpha and omega of man's existence. This is a truth of experience, for man has never been able to find complete happiness in any created being, whether riches, sensuous pleasures, or worldly honors. *A fortiori,* God alone is the supernatural beatitude of man.

1759. *Subjective* beatitude is the complete happiness enjoyed by the soul in the possession of objective beatitude. It is of this latter that we must treat here.

The principal beatitude of man is in his intellect, because it is principally by his intellect that man is man. The Thomists claim that man's beatitude is entirely in his knowledge; but others are of the opinion that it is not only in his vision, but also in his love of God and the enjoyment which he derives from this love. It is *of faith* against the Palamites, a school of Greek mystics who flourished about the fourteenth century, that man's supernatural beatitude consists in an abstract knowledge of God. That it consists in the intuitive vision of God or in the vision of the essence of God as He is in Himself, will be made clear in the following number.

1760. The vision of God is possible in Heaven, since it is *of faith* that the blessed behold Him there and that Jesus Christ enjoyed the beatific vision while in the wayfaring state. It is even probable that the B. V. Mary had an intuitive vision of God at various times during her life. Some writers are of the opinion that the same privilege was granted to Moses and St. Paul, but other writers dissent from this view. It is *of faith* that man cannot attain final beatitude in this life to the same degree that he can in Heaven. The contrary view maintained by the Beghards was condemned by the Council of Vienne, and it is certain that no man can see the divine essence in this life except by a special divine privilege.

1761. The created intellect cannot see God intuitively without the aid of a special light called the "light of glory." This is *of faith*, from the words of the Council of Vienne against the Beghards, who claimed that the soul does not need to be raised and fortified by the light of glory in order to see and enjoy God. Since, therefore, the natural powers of created intelligence do not suffice to see the essence of God, an increase of power is required. This increase is called an illumination and it is this which renders the blessed godlike, according to the words of Scripture: "When he shall appear, we shall be made like unto him."

1762. We must observe with St. Thomas that the light of glory is not an image or a representation of God, because no image can represent Him. Neither does this light render God more intelligible, because He is already sovereignly intelligible. It is not something intermediary between God and the soul, because the vision is immediate; and yet, it is a means which assists the soul in seeing God, disposing, raising and fortifying the intellect for this purpose. It is not something uncreated, as some have maintained, because everything that exists is either created or is God, and since this light is not God, but a gratuitous gift of God, it is manifestly something created. Neither is it something actual, as some writers have claimed, but something habitual. Whence it follows that glory is the complement of grace and of the same species as grace. Like grace, glory raises the soul to supernatural knowledge and love; but it differs from grace in that it is more perfect, for it is the consummation of grace. "We see now through a glass in a dark manner; but then face to face" (1 Cor. 13, 12.)

1763. Immediately after the particular judgment, or after a sojourn in Purgatory, those who depart this life in the state of sanctifying grace clearly and immediately behold God Himself, one and triune, as He is. All the parts of this proposition are *of faith*. "We shall see him as he is" (1 John 3, 2.) The truth of the above proposition is confirmed also by the following definition of Pope Benedict XII: "The blessed see the divine essence, without there being any need of a creature intervening between them and the object seen. The divine essence manifests itself to them overtly, clearly, and immediately. The vision of the divine essence culminates in rapturous love, and this vision and love render their souls truly happy, relegating faith and hope to the background. This vision and love continue without interruption and without respite until the General Judgment, and after the General Judgment for all eternity."

1764. *Consequences of the beatific vision.* The vision of God not only excludes all ignorance and error, but also enables the blessed to see in God whatever is necessary in Him, *i. e.,* the Trinity, unity, and all the divine attributes.

These form the principal object of the beatific vision. The elect do not understand the divine essence completely, because it is *of faith* that God is incomprehensible, but in and with God they see all existing things, as well as everything pertaining to their own state. They do not know all possible creatures, because this would be tantamount to knowing God completely; and according to common opinion they do not know the secrets of hearts, unless God chooses to reveal these to them. The elect see the things that they know in the Word, *i. e.*, in the divine essence, in which the prototypes of all things pre-exist.

1765. The souls of the elect will know God perfectly, hence they will love Him necessarily and supernaturally. For this reason they will be impeccable. According to some writers the impeccability of the elect will result from the beatific vision itself; according to others from a special privilege of God. In loving God, the elect will love their fellowmen and rejoice in their beatitude. In Heaven there will be neither physical nor moral evil: "And God shall wipe away every tear from their eyes, and death shall be no more, neither shall mourning or wailing or pain be any more, because the first things are past away" (Apoc. 21, 4.)

1766. *Properties of the beatific vision and beatitude.* The beatific vision is eternal and continuous. This is *of faith.* "I believe in life everlasting" (see no. 1763.) "Make to yourselves . . . a treasure in heaven which faileth not; where no thief approacheth, nor moth corrupteth" (Luke 12, 33.) Perfect beatitude is the end of man, towards which he tends of necessity, and God, who is an infinitely wise Creator, would not have given him such an inclination, were he not destined some day to reach his end. Moreover, beatitude would not be perfect if it could be lost or interrupted; therefore, it is eternal and continuous.

1767. *The dowry of the blessed.* By the dowry of the

blessed St. Thomas understands those supernatural endow-
ments that Christ bestows upon His mystic spouses before
admitting them to the beatific vision. This dowry renders
the vision of God more enjoyable, and consists of the three
gifts of contemplation, possession and fruition. Contemplation corresponds to faith, possession to hope, fruition to
charity. These gifts of the soul redound upon the body, communicating to it all its glorious qualities.

1768. *Degrees of happiness among the blessed.* It is *of
faith* against Jovinian and Martin Luther that glory as well
as grace admit of degrees. "In my Father's house there are
many mansions" (John 12, 2.) According to St. Thomas,
these mansions symbolize the various degrees of happiness
that exist among the blessed. The same truth is stressed by
the Council of Florence, which defines that some of the
blessed see God more perfectly than others, according to the
measure of their merits. A final reason for this inequality is
that the Lord is just.

From what does this inequality result? According to the
Thomists, it results from the inequality of light; according
to the Scotists, from the inequality of light and glory and
the greater or less powers of perspicacity. It is improbable
that it results from the inequality of man's natural intelligence, for, as St. Thomas has well observed: "That intellect which has more of the light of glory will see God the
more perfectly; and he will have a fuller participation of
the light of glory who has more charity, because where
there is greater charity, there is a more ardent desire. . . .
Hence, he who possesses the greater charity will see God
more perfectly." (*S. Theol.,* 1a, q. 12, art. 6.)

1769. Besides the *essential* glory common to all the
elect, although possessed by them in various degrees, some
of them will possess an *accidental* glory, which is the joy
caused by a created good. (*Ibid.,* q. 96, art. 4.) One of these

accidental glories is the *aureola,* a word signifying a small crown of gold. It is the special mark of success attached to those who have won outstanding victories over the three archenemies of man. According to St. Thomas there are three such *aureolae.* The aureola of the virgin marks a heroic victory over the flesh; that of the martyr, over the world; and that of the doctor, over the devil, the father of lies.

1770. *The relations of the blessed with the living.* What do the blessed do for the living? It is *of faith* that they pray for them. "This is a lover of his brethren, and of the people of Israel: this is he that prayeth much for the people, and for all the holy cities, Jeremias, the prophet of God" (2 Mach. 15, 14.) "Brethren, pray for us." (1 Thess. 5, 25.) If the saints pray for us while on earth, why would they not continue to pray for us in Heaven? The Council of Trent states: "It is good and useful suppliantly to invoke the saints, and to have recourse to their prayer, aid, and help for obtaining benefits from God, . . . but they think erroneously who deny that the saints who enjoy eternal happiness in Heaven, are to be invoked; or who assert that they do not pray for men." (Sess. 25.)

1771. The saints can pray for us either in an interpretative way, in as much as their merits are always present to the mind of God, or by prayer properly so called, as we have had occasion to state in no. 634. Their prayer is always efficacious, for they only ask what God desires, and God desires that all should receive sufficient grace. If, therefore, the prayers of the saints are inefficacious, the fault lies with the wills of men. In this same article St. Thomas proves that the saints know when we pray. (*Suppl.,* q. 72, art. 3.)

1772. What do we owe the saints in Heaven? By saints we understand the Blessed Virgin Mary, the angels, and all the elect in Heaven. We shall state: (1) what we owe to the saints in general; and (2) what we owe in particular to St. Joseph and the Blessed Virgin Mary because of their singular excellence.

1773. We are permitted to render to the saints a form of worship called *dulia*. (See no. 607.) This is *of faith* against the Manichaeans and the Protestants, from the words of the Second Council of Nicaea: "If anyone saith, that we must not honor the saints before God and seek their intercession; let him be anathema." "Glory, and honor, and peace to everyone that worketh good." (Rom. 2, 10.) The truth of this doctrine is substantiated by the tradition of the Church, which has established feasts in honor of the saints and raised churches near their places of burial. "Manifestly the saints have a right to our veneration, being members of Christ, sons and friends of God, and our intercessors." (*S. Theol.*, 3a, q. 25, art. 6; see also no. 2256 ff.)

1774. Relative worship of *dulia* may be rendered to the images and relics of the saints. This is *of faith* against the Iconoclasts, Vigilantius, and the Protestants, from the words of the Council of Trent: "The bodies of holy martyrs, and of others now living with Christ—which bodies were the living members of Christ, and temples of the Holy Ghost, and which are by Him to be raised unto eternal life, and to be glorified—are to be venerated by the faithful . . . ; so that they who affirm that veneration and honor are not due to the relics of the saints, or that these and other sacred monuments are uselessly honored by the faithful, and that the places dedicated to the memories of the saints, are visited in vain with a view of obtaining their aid, are wholly to be condemned, as the Church has already long since condemned, and now also condemns them. Moreover, that the images of Christ, and of the Virgin Mother of God, and of the other saints, are to be had and retained particularly in temples, and that due honor and veneration are to be given them; not that any divinity or virtue is believed to reside in them, on account of which they are to be worshipped, or that anything is to be asked of them . . . ; but because the honor which is shown them is referred to the prototypes which those images represent, . . . as, by the decrees of the councils, and especially of the Second of Nicaea, has been defined against the opponents of images." (See nos. 611 ff. and 2270.)

1775. The same Council ordains that no one shall be allowed to place, or cause to be placed, any unusual image in any place or church, howsoever exempt, except that image has been approved of by the bishop: also, that no new miracles are to be acknowledged, or new relics recognized, unless the bishop has taken cognizance and approved of them."

1776. It is good and useful to invoke the aid of the saints. This is *of faith*, from the words of the Council of Trent: "They think impetuously who deny that the saints, who enjoy eternal happiness in Heaven, are to be invoked; or who assert . . . that the invocation of them is opposed to the honor of the one mediator of God and men, Christ Jesus." (See nos. 643 and 1773.) The honor paid to the saints redounds upon Jesus Christ, from whom the saints derive all their excellence. The invocation of the saints is of precept for the faithful in general, since the Church prescribes it in the Mass and in her offices, but there is no positive law binding each individual Catholic to invoke their aid.

1777. It is far better to imitate the examples of the saints than merely to honor them. "If we follow the example of the saints in this life," says St. Bernard, "we shall reign with them in the next."

What we have said of the saints in general may be said *a fortiori* of St. Joseph and the Blessed Virgin Mary, of whom we must say a special word.

1778. *St. Joseph.* A mistake commonly made by the so-called wise of this world is to regard St. Joseph as an ordinary workman. He was an eminent man, who practiced virtue in a heroic degree, and in Heaven his power and rank are exceedingly great. (See Cornelius à Lapide on Matt., 1, 16.)

1779. *The dignity of St. Joseph.* St. Joseph was born of the royal house of David, and it is through him, and not through the Blessed Virgin Mary, that Jesus Christ was heir to the sceptre of Judah. He was the spouse of the Virgin Mary, and both she and the Sovereign Lord of the world did not hesitate to call him their master. By the fact of his marriage to the Virgin Mother, he was the foster-father of Jesus Christ, and he is the Father of the Son of God in the same degree that he would have been the owner of the fruits of his field, had God miraculously sowed seed therein. For these reasons Christ was subject to him, and St. Joseph was the guardian and foster-father of his God. It follows that his mission was a noble one. There are missions, says Suarez, which belong to the order of *gratia gratum faciens,* and here the Apostles take first place; there are other missions which belong to the order of the hypostatic union, which is far more perfect, and in which the Virgin Mother ranks first. The mission of St. Joseph was in this order; it, therefore, surpasses all the others.

1780. *The virtues of St. Joseph.* When God selects a person for some mission, He always prepares him for it. God conferred upon St. Joseph the gifts of wisdom and sanctity, in order to fit him for his mission. According to the Gospel narrative, Joseph was just from the time of his marriage; he was adorned with all the virtues and received a notable increase of grace by reason of his association with the Blessed Virgin Mary and her Son. The Fathers of the

Church are of the opinion that he was a virgin, and some of them go so far as to say that he had taken the vow of virginity. Gerson claims that he was sanctified in the womb of his mother, confirmed in grace, and exempt from the laws of concupiscence. "I am firmly convinced," writes St. Bernard, "that the virginity of St. Joseph was most pure, his humility most profound, his charity most ardent, his powers of contemplation most sublime."

1781. *The glories and powers of St. Joseph.* Suarez is of the opinion that St. Joseph died before Christ suffered His passion, that he was raised from the dead by the Son of God, and that he surpasses in glory all the Apostles and St. John the Baptist. St. Francis de Sales is also of the opinion that he is now in Heaven, with both body and soul. He is deserving, therefore, of the worship of *dulia* to the highest degree.

The powers of St. Joseph are in proportion to his glory. "It is not improbable that, in Heaven, Jesus Christ pays more respect and more love to St. Joseph than he did while on earth." (St. Bernardine of Siena.) According to St. Bernard it is given to some saints to act as patrons in certain circumstances, but to St. Joseph has been given the power to assist us in every necessity and defend all those who have recourse to his aid. Pope Pius IX, of happy memory, climaxed all these encomiums by declaring St. Joseph patron of the universal Church.

1782. According to St. Alphonsus, the patronage of St. Joseph can obtain for us three things: the remission of our sins, the love of his Son, for whom he had so much love, and the grace of a happy death.

1783. *The worship of the Blessed Virgin Mary.* The Blessed Virgin Mary is not entitled to the worship termed *latria,* as some heretics have maintained, but she is deserving of the worship termed *hyperdulia,* because of her incomparable dignity, the plenitude of her grace and glory, and her quasi-omnipotence. (See no. 607.)

1784. *The dignity of Mary is incomparable.* It is *of faith* that Mary is the mother of God, and for this reason her dignity is quasi-infinite, because God Himself is infinite. All the saints have sung her praises; about 1600 titles have been bestowed upon her by the doctors and the saints.

1785. *The grace of the Blessed Virgin Mary.* It is *of faith* that the Virgin Mary was conceived without sin. (See no. 534.)

What was the grace of the Blessed Virgin Mary? St. Alphonsus teaches that the grace of the Blessed Virgin Mary was greater than all the graces of all the angels and all men combined, and it is very probable that she possessed this amount of grace at the very first moment of her conception. Theologians commonly teach that she was adorned with all the gifts becoming a creature of God. It is not credible, indeed, that God, who is so lavish in His gifts to ordinary men, should have been sparing in giving graces to His mother, whom He raised to such a high plane. All theologians are of the opinion that the Virgin Mary had use of her free will from the very moment she was sanctified in the womb of her mother; and since it is *of faith* that she was sanctified in her conception, we must conclude that from the time of her conception she was exempted, not only from sin, but also from all its consequences. It is *of faith* that the Virgin Mary never sinned, not even venially, and it *is certain* that in her case the *fomes peccati* was either held in leash, as some maintain, or completely extinguished, as others hold with greater probability. According to some writers, she never experienced any temptation on the part of the devil, but St. Thomas does not subscribe to this view. St. Alphonsus reports that, according to some of the foremost Catholic divines, a meritorious act doubles the amount of habitual grace in a person who accomplishes this act with all the fervor of which he is capable. According to this doctrine, the Blessed Virgin doubled the amount of her grace at every moment of her life, from the first instant of her Immaculate Conception. According to Suarez, she spent almost her entire life in contemplation, and according to St. Alphonsus, by a special privilege of God she never desisted from making acts of charity and love even during her sleep, according to these words of Holy Scripture: "I sleep, but my heart lieth awake."

1786. Whence we may conclude that the Blessed Virgin Mary merited *de congruo*, but not *de condigno*, her divine motherhood and the Incarnation. The mystery of the Incarnation was accomplished in her only when, in obedience to the voice of the angel, she uttered her *"fiat."* Her assent was at once voluntary, free, and meritorious. She is the mediatrix of grace, but not of justice or merit, for all men. Thanks to her the only Mediator of justice between man and God made His appearance on earth. According to some writers, the angels received their grace in view of the merits of Jesus Christ, but even in this instance grace was given in virtue of her mediation. According to all writers, she merited *de congruo* for the angels the accidental glory which accrued to them from the Incarnation and the fruits of the Incarnation, *i. e.*, the salvation of the saints. The grace of the Blessed Virgin Mary was increased still more by the Sacraments which she received. According to Lehmkuhl, she received Baptism, Confirmation, and the Holy Eucharist; according to Suarez, she received also the Sacrament of Extreme Unction.

1787. In view of all this, it is easy for us to understand the words of the Archangel Gabriel: "Hail Mary, full of grace." These words must not be taken to mean that she received the supreme degree of grace or that she was able to produce all the effects of grace, for Christ alone was the meritorious cause of grace for His mother and for all men. However, by reason of her state of life and the mission which God intrusted to her, she received the plenitude of grace; therefore, she received all the graces required for her office as mother of the Son of God. According to St. Alphonsus, who echoes the teaching of St. Thomas, the Blessed Virgin Mary is called "full of grace" because she is able to bestow grace upon all men. It is a wondrous thing for a saint to have a sufficient amount of grace for the salvation of several men, but it is a supreme distinction, enjoyed only by Jesus Christ and the Virgin Mary, to have enough grace for the salvation of all mankind.

1788. After the Incarnation the Blessed Virgin was in a position to bestow all the necessary graces upon the sons of men, not because she was the head of the human race, but because she was the support upon which this head rested. We were careful to state that this was the case *after* the Incarnation, because if Jesus Christ as man was not the physical instrument through which grace was bestowed upon the saints of the Old Testament—and all writers hold this opinion—*a fortiori* neither was the Blessed Virgin Mary.

Hence, we see that the Blessed Virgin possessed in an eminent degree all the virtues which result from charity, and which exist in the soul in proportion to its charity, and the charity of the Mother of God was most perfect and continuous. By her virginity she was most pleasing to God, having made her vow either after her marriage, as St. Thomas contends, or before, because she knew that St. Joseph would not exercise his marriage rights or because she knew through private revelation that he would be the guardian of her virtue. (See nos. 1635 and 1636.) Hence, the humility in which she conceived, hence also, all the virtues which she practiced in a heroic degree. She was presented in the Temple when only three years of age and continued to live there up to the time of her marriage, which she contracted in her fourteenth year. It was during this same year that she conceived the Son of God.

1789. In conceiving the Son of God, the Blessed Virgin Mary witnessed a marvelous increase in graces and virtues. "The nearer an object approaches its source," says St. Thomas, "the more it shares in the effects of this source. The Blessed Virgin Mary came very near to God, since it was from her flesh and blood that He derived His human nature. For this reason she must have received from Jesus Christ an incalculable amount of grace." (*S. Theol.*, 3a, q. 27, art. 5.) Add to all this the examples and words of Christ, His words of solace and comfort, His blood shed especially for her sake; add also the merits accumulated by Mary herself to the end of her life, during which time she was the consolation of the Apostles up to her seventy-second year, and we shall more readily understand how supreme was her grace, and that her death was the result rather of love than of bodily infirmities.

1790. So far we have discoursed on the amount of sanctifying grace granted to the Blessed Virgin Mary; concerning her grace *gratis data* we have only to cite the words of St. Thomas: "There is no doubt that the Blessed Virgin Mary received the gifts of wisdom, the grace of miracles and the gift of prophecy in a super-eminent degree." (*Ibid.*, q. 27, art. 5, ad 3.)

1791. *The glory and power of the Blessed Virgin Mary.* The glory of the Blessed Virgin Mary is in proportion to her grace and merits; therefore, she surpasses in glory all the angels and saints. This is *of faith,* from the words of the Sixth General Council: "If anyone will not confess that Mary is the highest of all visible and invisible creatures;

let him be anathema." According to the common opinion of the faithful, which sound Catholic divines regard as being so certain that no one could deny it without grave temerity, although the doctrine it embodies has not been formally defined by the Church, the body of the Blessed Virgin was raised from the dead and assumed into Heaven. It was not fitting, indeed, that her virginal body, which had been made the temple of the Living God, should be subjected to the corruption of the tomb. The more common opinion has it that Mary was raised from the dead by her Divine Son three days after her demise; others claim that she was raised on the fifteenth, and others, finally, on the fortieth day. Suarez is of the opinion that her body is encircled by a most extraordinary kind of splendor because of the miraculous, chaste, and unprecedented way in which she conceived and gave birth to her Divine Son. This splendor is the distinctive mark of her royal dignity, divine maternity, and unquestioned superiority over the rest of the saints.

The power of the Blessed Virgin is very great. Because she is the Mother of God, she is superior to all created beings. She is Queen of the Angels, Queen of the Saints, Queen of this world, and Queen even of the lower regions, because she it was who crushed the serpent's head. It is no wonder, then, that the majority of theologians agree with St. Alphonsus in saying that the prayers of the Blessed Virgin Mary are more powerful than those of all the angels and saints taken together.

1792. *The Blessed Virgin Mary is the Mother of all men.* In giving birth to Jesus Christ, our Head, Mary became by adoption the mother of all the members of the body of Christ, which is the Church, and, as St. Augustine observes, she coöperates with her Divine Son by her charity in the spiritual regeneration of all the faithful. According to St.

Alphonsus, she united all her merits with those of her Divine Son, in order that we might be saved. She consented to the Incarnation, which is the cause of our spiritual life, and on Mount Calvary she coöperated with Christ in the work of our redemption, not in the sense that she paid our debt, but in the sense that she obtained that the satisfactions and merits of Jesus Christ were made applicable to our souls. She heard from His lips the words, "Mother, behold thy Son," and according to the common teaching of the Fathers and the saints, these words signify all the faithful and even all those for whom Jesus Christ died. For this reason a great number of theologians claim that Mary dispenses all the graces that communicate life to the soul. "This is the will of Him," says St. Bernard, "who has decreed that we should receive everything from the hands of Mary." Is it any wonder, then, that the Church has given her the title, "Gate of Heaven"? Devotion to the Blessed Virgin Mary, according to the unanimous teaching of the doctors of the Church, is an infallible sign of predestination. "Blessed is the man that heareth me, and that watcheth daily at my gates, and waiteth at the posts of my doors." (Prov. 834.) Blessed are they who preach the worship and love of Mary. "They that explain me shall have life everlasting." (Eccles. 24, 31.) St. Bernardine of Siena sanctified the whole of Italy by preaching devotion to the Blessed Virgin Mary, and St. Dominic converted several provinces by the same means.

SECOND TREATISE

The Consummation of the World

1793. The consummation of nature took place on the seventh day; that of grace in the Incarnation of Jesus Christ; the consummation of glory will take place at the end of the world.

We shall treat: (1) the signs that are to precede the general judgment; (2) the resurrection of the flesh; (3) the General Judgment; (4) the state of the world after the Judgment.

CHAPTER I

THE SIGNS THAT ARE TO PRECEDE THE GENERAL JUDGMENT

1794. On one occasion Jesus Christ said to His Apostles: "It is not given to you to know either the time or the hour." *A fortiori* is the time of the General Judgment withheld from the rest of mankind. This is the conclusion arrived at by St. Thomas (3a, q. 73, art. 2), and he adds: "By this answer, Christ numbed the fingers of all those who would seek to calculate the day of the Last Judgment, enjoining upon them to concern themselves with other things. All attempts at calculation have resulted in error, and the same will be true of all attempts in the future." The holy Doctor is careful to add, however, that a great number of events will precede the final coming of Christ in order that men may prepare their hearts and get ready. The events usually enumerated by theologians are: the general preaching of the Christian religion in all parts of the earth, the reign of Antichrist, the return of Henoch and Elias, a universal conflagration, and extraordinary disturbances of nature.

1795. *The appearance of Antichrist.* Some are of the opinion that Antichrist will not be an individual, but a whole sect of persons, who will rise up against God. The more common opinion, however, is that he will be a man of lawlessness, for as such is he designated by St. Paul. (2 Thess. 2, 3.) According to St. Thomas, he will be a man filled with malice, because the devil will infuse more evil into him than into all others combined. (*Ibid.*, q. 8, art. 8.) What is certain is that he will seduce a great number of people.

1796. After this, according to an opinion which some term certain and *proxima fidei*, Henoch and Elias, who are neither dead nor glorified, but live in some unknown place, to which they have been translated, will return to earth to preach against Antichrist, convert the Jews and, as common opinion has it, crown their efforts by martyrdom. "And immediately after the tribulation of those days, the sun shall be darkened, and the moon shall not give her light, and the stars shall fall from heaven, and the powers of heaven shall be moved." (Matt. 24, 29; see also *S. Theol.*, 3a, q. 8, art. 2 and 3.) According to St. Thomas and the majority of theologians, the world will come to an end before the general resurrection by a universal conflagration. This conflagration will destroy our planet and its atmosphere, although it is commonly held that it will not affect the rest of the cosmic system. It will purify the world, destroy all plants and animals, and reduce all men to dust and ashes.

CHAPTER II

THE RESURRECTION

1797. We shall treat, first, of the resurrection itself, and, secondly, of the properties of risen bodies.

1798. *The resurrection itself.* Resurrection is possible, because God can do anything which is not repugnant to the nature of things, and resurrection is not repugnant to the nature of the body. Moreover, it is eminently fitting that the body, which shared the sufferings and pleasures of the soul in this life, should rise to share in its reward or chastisement. Again, the perfection and beatitude of the soul demand that the body which it once informed be reunited with it. Finally, resurrection is an easier work than creation.

1799. *All men will rise again.* This is *of faith* against the Sadducees and the Rationalists, from the words of all the Creeds: "I believe in the resurrection of the body." All that are in the graves shall hear the voice of the Son of God. And they that have done good, shall come forth unto the resurrection of life; but they that have done evil, unto the resurrection of judgment" (John 5, 28 f.) It is certain, therefore, that all men will rise again, and that in rising, each will remain the same as he was during life and at the time of his death. Each will retain the same body and sex, but the state of the wicked will be different from that of the good. All theologians are agreed on these points.

1800. *What will be the cause of the resurrection?* The principal efficient cause of the resurrection will be God and the instrumental meritorious and exemplary cause will be Jesus Christ. "They will hear the voice of the Son of God and those who hear it will live." According to St. Thomas, this voice will be the sound of the trumpet. The ministerial cause will be St. Michael, the Archangel, who, with the assistance of the other angels, will gather together the ashes of the dead. God alone, however, will quicken these ashes.

1801. *When will the resurrection take place?* It is fitting, as St. Thomas has observed, that the resurrection should take place at the end of the world; it is not known, however, when this will be. Moreover, there is nothing to prevent God from raising some souls from the dead before that time, as He has already done in the case of the Blessed Virgin Mary and those who were raised from their graves after Christ's death on the cross and who probably are now united with Him in Heaven. (St. Thomas, *Suppl.*, q. 77.)

1802. *The qualities of the risen bodies.* Characteristics common to all risen bodies are: natural identity and integrity. "If something pertaining to the integrity of human nature is subtracted from the body of man, this body will not be perfect. All imperfection in man will disappear at the time of the resurrection, especially in the case of the elect, hence anything appertaining to the unity of nature will be restored to him." (*Ibid.*, q. 80, art. 4.) Thus reasons St. Thomas, and he goes on to show that risen bodies will possess their integral members, including even their hair, their nails and bodily humors. These bodies will not, however, possess all material parts, otherwise they would be completely out of proportion. (*Ibid.*, art. 5.) The body will be raised, he continues, as it appeared in the prime of life, with all its members, including those which it may have lost through some misfortune. All will not be of the same height, but each will have the height he had or should have had in the prime of life. Any defects will be repaired by the omnipotence of God. (*Ibid.*, q. 81, art. 1, 2.)

1803. *Bodily functions.* All bodily functions that pertain to the vegetative life will cease in the next world, since they are no longer necessary to the body that has reached its full development and is now incorruptible. (*Ibid.*) The senses will continue to exercise their functions, being rewarded in the just and punished in the wicked. (*Ibid.*, q. 82, art. 3.)

1804. *Special transcendent qualities of the risen bodies.* The bodies of the damned will be incorruptible because their punishment is eternal. "In those days men shall seek death and shall not find it" (Apoc. 9, 6); but they will be neither impassible nor endowed with agility. "We shall all indeed rise again: but we shall not all be changed" (1 Cor. 15, 51.) Their bodies will be punished together with their souls, although they will never be consumed by the flames.

1805. *The bodies of the Blessed.* The bodies of the elect will possess four supernatural qualities: (1) impassibility, (2) subtility, (3) agility, and (4) brightness (1 Cor. 15.) The bodies of the elect will be impassible, *i. e.*, beyond the reach of pain and discomfort. St. Thomas ascribes this supernatural impassibility to the complete and perfect dominion of reason over the lower appetites. (*Suppl.*, q. 82, art. 1.) "It is sown in corruption, it shall rise in incorruption" (1 Cor. 15, 42.)

1806. *The bodies of the elect will be subtile.* By subtility we are to understand that quality which subjects the body to the absolute dominion of the soul, and an entire obedience to her control; as we infer from these words of the Apostle: "It is sown a natural body, it shall rise a spiritual body." This quality does not imply that the bodies of the elect are rarefied to the extent of being imperceptible, or that they do not occupy a definite place, or, again, that they are able to occupy the same place as another risen body without the aid of a miracle. (*Suppl.*, q. 83, art. 1, 2.) Neither must we believe that risen bodies are completely spiritualized, as was taught by the heretic Eutyches. Most authors are agreed that they are endowed with the capacity of mutual penetration and can occupy the same space as other risen bodies, but St. Thomas ascribes this prerogative to a special act of the divine omnipotence.

1807. *The bodies of the elect will be endowed with agility.* Under the influence of the spirit, now no longer restrained, the bodies of the elect will be freed from their natural clumsiness and will move with the greatest facility and rapidity in whatever direction they are drawn by the soul. Hence, these words of the Apostle, "It is sown in weakness, it shall rise in power." (1 Cor. 15, 43.)

1808. *The bodies of the elect will be bright.* By this brightness the bodies of the saints shall shine like the sun. "He will reform the body of our lowness, made like to the body of His glory." (Philip. 3, 21.) This brightness is a sort of refulgence, which emanates from the supreme happiness of the soul upon the body. St. Thomas teaches that the brightness of the soul is perceptible in a glorified body as the color of the body enclosed in a glass receptacle is visible through the glass. It will be in the power of the elect to show forth this brightness or to conceal it. This quality is not common to all the elect in the same degree, for, according to the Apostle, "one is the glory of the sun, another the glory of the moon, and another the glory of the stars: for star differeth from star in glory: so, also, is the resurrection of the dead." (1 Cor. 15, 41 f.)

CHAPTER III

THE GENERAL JUDGMENT

1809. The works of men that have been rewarded or punished at the particular judgment will continue to live on after death in the minds of those who survive them. At the end of the world, therefore, when all the works of men have borne their fruit by their good or bad influence on others, they will be judged anew for the accidental glory of the just and the public confusion of the wicked. At this time the enormity of the sins of men will be made manifest, and the justice of God's punishments will become evident.

Who will be the judge? The principal judge will be Jesus Christ. This is *of faith* against Protestants: "From thence He shall come to judge the living and the dead." According to St. Thomas, Christ will appear in all the splendor of His sacred humanity, carrying His cross and bearing the marks of His sacred wounds. Holy men will sit in judgment with Him, showing forth in their hearts the divine decree and manifesting to others the sentence which Jesus Christ will pronounce in His own name. (St. Thomas, *Suppl.*, q. 87, art. 1 and q. 90, art. 2.)

1810. *Who are the holy men who will sit in judgment with Christ?* St. Thomas answers this question and proves that it will be the religious, *i. e.,* those who voluntarily embrace poverty and follow Jesus Christ in the way of perfection. All the angels and saints will approve the sentence. (*Suppl.*, q. 89, art. 2.)

1811. *Who will be judged?* "We shall all be manifested before the judgment seat of Christ." (2 Cor. 5, 10.) Consequently, the good, the bad, and even the angels and the demons, will participate in the General Judgment. The pure spirits will not be judged directly according to their merits or demerits, but only indirectly, in so far as they have influenced the course of human events. "The good angels will derive great joy and satisfaction from the salvation of those whom they excited to do good, and the bad angels will see their torments increased because of the multitude of men upon whom they have brought eternal ruin. (*Suppl.*, q. 89, art. 8.)

1812. *Circumstances of the general judgment.* The site of

the last judgment is unknown, although it is commonly thought that it will be the valley of Josaphat, near the Mountain of Olives. "This Jesus who is taken up from you into heaven, shall so come, as you have seen him going into heaven." (Acts 1, 11. See also St. Thomas, *Suppl.*, q. 88, art. 4.)

How will the general judgment take place? It is more than likely that by a special illumination every man will instantly realize the state of his own soul. Conscience is to God what witnesses are to other men. (See no. 1705.)

The more common and more probable opinion is that each person will comprehend the state of his own soul and that of his fellow-creatures. For the sentence to appear just, it will be necessary that all know the merits and demerits which have caused it. The whole procedure will take but a few minutes, and the more probable opinion is that it will take place mentally and not orally, both for the just and for the wicked. (St. Thomas, *Suppl.*, q. 88, art. 2.)

1813. After the words of the sentence have been uttered by Christ, the universal conflagration will be drawn into the vortex of hell with the souls of the damned. (*Ibid.*, q. 74, art. 9.) The just, with Jesus Christ at their head, will enter Heaven with their glorified bodies. The pains of the damned and the happiness of the elect will be increased after the sentence has been passd.

CHAPTER IV

THE CONDITION OF THE WORLD AFTER THE GENERAL JUDGMENT

1814. The substance of things will not be annihilated, "All the works which God hath made, continue for ever." (Eccl. 3, 14.) Moreover, it is quite fitting that the places which witnessed the victory of Jesus Christ and his saints over the devil, be not destroyed.

1815. *All things shall be renewed.* "We look for new heavens and a new earth." (2 Pet. 3, 13.) The elect will see God in His essence, but not with their bodily eyes. These organs will receive their reward, however, since they will see the divinity in its bodily effects, first in the body of Jesus Christ, then in the body of His saints, and finally in all other bodies. The whole world will be renewed, and man will be glorified. (St. Thomas, *Suppl.*, q. 101, art. 1.) The same learned Doctor adds: "Time will cease, as well as the movements of the heavens, and the stars will shine with greater splendor." (*Ibid.*, art. 2 f.) The elements of the earth will become as resplendent as the heavenly bodies. (Art. 4.) When the end ceases, the means must also cease, and so animal and plant life, which were made to preserve the animal life of man, will cease with his life on earth.

If we wish to attain to this blessed place, where hunger and thirst are no more, we must hunger and thirst after *justice,* of which we shall treat in the moral part of this Compendium.

INDEX

(The numbers refer to the paragraphs and not to the pages)